Caromel · Henrio
A Theory of Distributed Objects

Denis Caromel · Ludovic Henrio

A Theory of Distributed Objects

Asynchrony – Mobility – Groups – Components

Preface by Luca Cardelli

With 114 Figures and 48 Tables

 Springer

Denis Caromel

University of Nice Sophia Antipolis
I3S CNRS – INRIA
Institut universitaire de France
2004 Rt. des Lucioles, BP 93
06902 Sophia Antipolis Cedex, France
e-mail: Denis.Caromel@inria.fr

Ludovic Henrio

University of Westminster
Harrow School of Computer Science
Watford Rd, Northwick Park
Harrow HA1 3TP, UK
e-mail: Ludovic.Henrio@m4x.org

Library of Congress Control Number: 2005923024

ISBN-10 3-540-20866-6 Springer Berlin Heidelberg New York
ISBN-13 978-3-540-20866-2 Springer Berlin Heidelberg New York

Springer is a part of Springer Science+Business Media
springeronline.com

© Springer-Verlag Berlin Heidelberg 2005
Printed in Germany

Typeset by the authors using a Springer TeX macro package
Production: LE-TeX Jelonek, Schmidt & Vöckler GbR, Leipzig
Cover design: KünkelLopka, Heidelberg

Printed on acid-free paper   45/3142/YL - 5 4 3 2 1 0

To Isa, Ugo, Tom,
Taken from us by the Tsunami, Sri Lanka, December 26, 2004

Isabelle, my wife, my lover, my fellow intellect, I miss you so badly.
My soul, my body, my brain, all hurt for you, all cry out for you.
Your smile, your spirit would bring joy and light to all around you.
Your plans were to do voluntary work to help humanity,
I know you would have given courage and cheer to so many.

Ugo, my 8 year old boy, you could not wait to understand the world.
You even found your own definition of infinity: God!
I will remember forever when you would call me "Papaa ? ..."
with that special tone, to announce a tough question.

Tom, my 5 year old boy, you could fight so hard and yet be so sweet.
You were so strong, and you could be so gentle.
Your determination was impressive, but clearly becoming thoughtful.
I will remember forever when after a fight,
you would jump up on my lap and give me a sweet, loving hug.

So many years of happiness and joy,
May your spirits be with us and in me forever

Denis,
Nice hospital,
January 6, 2005

To Françoise, Marc, Laurianne and Sébastien,
and my precious friends

Ludovic,
December 10, 2004

Preface

With the advent of wide-area networks such as the Internet, distributed computing has to expand from its origins in shared-memory computing and local-area networks to a wider context. A large part of the additional complexity is due to the need to manage asynchrony, which is an unavoidable aspect of high-latency networks. Harnessing asynchronous communications is still an open area of research.

This monograph studies a natural programming model for distributed object-oriented programming. In this model, objects make asynchronous method invocations to other objects, and then concurrently carry on until the results of the requests are needed. Only at that point may they have to wait for the results to be completely computed; this delayed wait is called wait-by-necessity. Aspects of such a model have been proposed and formalized in the past: futures have been built into early concurrent languages, and various distributed object calculi have been investigated. However, this is the first time the two features, futures and distributed objects, have been studied formally together.

The result is a natural and disciplined programming model for asynchronous computing, one worthy of study. For example, it is important to understand under which conditions asynchronous execution produces predictable outcomes, without the usual combinatorial explosion of concurrent execution. Even the simplest sequential program becomes highly concurrent under wait-by-necessity execution, and yet such concurrency does not always imply that multiple outcomes are possible. One of the main technical contributions of the monograph, beyond the formalization of the programming model, is a sufficient condition for deterministic evaluation (confluence) of programs.

This monograph addresses problems that have been long identified as fundamental stumbling blocks in writing correct distributed programs. It constitutes a significant step forward, particularly in the area of formalizing and generalizing some of the best ideas proposed so far, coming up with new techniques, and providing a solid foundation for further study. The techniques studied here also have a very practical potential.

Cambridge, 2004-11-15
Luca Cardelli

Contents

Part I Review

Part II ASP Calculus

Appendices

List of Figures

List of Tables

List of Definitions and Properties

Prologue

Distributed objects are becoming ubiquitous. *Communicating objects* interact at various levels (application objects, Web and middleware services), and in a wide range of environments (mobile devices, local area networks, Grid, and P2P). These objects send messages, call methods on each other's interfaces, and receive requests and replies.

Why would we employ objects to act as interacting entities? An answer with a religious twist would be that *object orientation* has, so far, won the language crusade. However, a technical answer has more substance: objects are stateful abstractions. Any globally-distributed computation must rely on various levels of state, somehow acting as a cache for improved locality, leading to greater scalability and performance. In a multi-tier application server, for instance, objects representing persistent data (e.g., Entity Beans) act as a cache for data within the *n*-tier database.

Thus, stateful objects interact with each other. Why should they communicate with *method calls* rather than with messages traveling over channels? One answer is that this is exactly what objects are all about: distributed systems should not abandon such a critical feature for software structuring. *Remote method invocation* in industrial platforms, following 15 years of research in academia, has taken off, and appears to be a practical and effective solution. Moreover, method calls are also about safety and verification, a highly desirable feature for distributed, multi-principal, multi-domain applications. Because method calls and the interface imply the emergence of *types*, remote method invocations fall within the scope of type theories and practical verifications – including static analyses, which rely heavily on inter-procedural analysis.

With distribution spanning the world ever more widely, an intrinsic characteristic of communication is high latency, with an unbreakable barrier of 70 milliseconds for a signal to go half-way around the world at the speed of light. Large systems, with potentially thousands of interacting entities, cannot accommodate the high coupling induced by synchronous calls, because such coupling can lead to a blocked chain of remote method calls spanning a large number of entities. An extreme case that requires non-synchronous invocation is the handling of the disconnected mode in wireless settings. In sum, high latency and low coupling call for asynchronous interactions, as in the case of distributed objects: *asynchronous method calls*. But if we want method calls to retain their full capacity, one-way calls on their own are insufficient. Asynchronous method calls with returns are needed, leading to an emerging abstraction: namely, *futures*, the expected result of a given asynchronous method call. Futures turn out to be a very effective abstraction for large distributed systems, preserving both low coupling and high structuring.

To summarize the argument, scalable distributed object systems cannot be effective without interactions based on asynchronous method calls, with respect to mastering both complexity and efficiency. While acknowledged theories have been proposed for both asynchronous message passing (e.g., π-calculus) and objects (e.g., ς-calculus), no formal framework has been proposed for objects communicating solely with non-blocking method calls. This is exactly the ambition of the current book: to define a theory for distributed objects interacting with asynchronous method calls.

Starting from widely adopted object theory, the ς-calculus [3], a syntactically lightweight extension is proposed to take distribution into account. Two simple primitives are proposed: *Active* and *Serve*. The former turns an object into an independent and potentially remote activity; the latter allows such an active object to execute (serve) a pending remote call. On activation, an object becomes a remotely accessible entity with its own thread of control: *an active object*. In accordance with the above reasoning, we have chosen to make method calls to active objects systematically asynchronous. Synchronization is ensured with a natural dataflow principle: *wait-by-necessity*. An active object is blocked on the invocation of a not yet available result, i.e., a strict operation on an unknown future. A further level of asynchrony and low coupling is reached with the first-class nature of futures within wait-by-necessity; they can be passed between active objects as method parameters and returned as results.

The proposed calculus is named *Asynchronous Sequential Processes* (ASP), reflecting an important property: the sequentiality of active objects. Processes denote the potentially coarse-grain nature of active objects. Such processes are usually formed with a set of standard objects under the exclusive control of a root object. The proposed theory allows us to express a fundamental condition for *confluence*, alleviating for the programmer of the unscalable need to consider the interleaving of all instructions and communications. Furthermore, a property ensures *determinism*, stating that, whatever the order of communications, whatever the order of future updates, even in the presence of cycles, some systems converge towards a determinate global state. Apart from Process Networks [99, 100, 159], now close to 40 years old, few calculi and languages ensure determinism, and even fewer in the context of stateful distributed objects interacting with asynchronous method calls. The potential of the proposed theory is further demonstrated by the capacity to cope with more advanced issues such as mobility, groups, and components.

One objective of the proposed theory is to be a *practical* one. Implementation strategies are covered. Several chapters explore a number of solutions, adapted to various settings (high-speed local area networks with buffer saving in mind, wide area networks with latency hiding as a primary goal, etc.), but each one still preserving semantics and properties. An illustration of such practicability is available under an open source Java API and environment, ProActive [134], which implements the proposed theory using a strategy designed to hide latency in the setting of wide area networks.

The first part of this book analyzes the issues at hand, reviewing existing languages and calculi.

Parts II and III formally introduce the proposed framework, defining the main properties of confluence and determinism.

Part IV reaches a new frontier and discusses issues at the cutting edge of software engineering, namely migration, reconfiguration, and component-based systems. From the proposed framework, we suggest a path that can lead to reconfigurable components. It demonstrates how we can go from asynchronous distributed objects to asynchronous distributed components, including collective remote method invocations (group communications), while retaining determinism.

With practicality in mind, Part V analyzes implementation issues, and suggests a number of strategies. We are aware that large-scale distributed systems encounter large variations in conditions, due to both localization in space and dynamic changes over time. Thus, potentially adaptive strategies for buffering and pipelining are proposed.

Finally, after a comparative evaluation of related formalisms, Part VI concludes and suggests directions for the future.

Acknowledgments

We are pleased to acknowledge discussions, collaboration, and joint work with many people as a crucial inspiration and contribution to the pages herein.

Without Isabelle Attali – Isa, Project Leader of the OASIS team until December 26th 2004, this book would not be in your hands.

Bernard Serpette significantly contributed to the development of the ASP calculus and related proofs.

All the other senior OASIS team members, Françoise Baude and Eric Madelaine, were very supportive and contributed in many aspects.

This book is also the result of many fruitful interactions between theory and practice. Many inspiring ideas came from the practical development of the ProActive library, and from contributors.

Special thanks go to Fabrice Huet and Julien Vayssière, the first two ProActive contributors, implementors, and testers. Many others recently had key contributions, especially the younger researchers and engineers in our team: Laurent Baduel, Tomás Barros, Rabéa Ameur-Boulifa, Javier Bustos, Arnaud Contes, Alexandre Di Costanzo, Christian Delbé, Felipe Luna Del Aguila, Matthieu Morel, and last, but not least, Romain Quilici.

Former Master's, Ph.D. students, engineers, were also a key source of maturation and inspiration: Alexandre Bergel, Roland Bertuli, Florian Doyon, Sidi Ould Ehmety, Alexandre Fau, Wilfried Klauser, Emmanuel Léty, Lionel Mestre, Olivier Nano, Arnaud Poizat, Yves Roudier, Marjorie Russo, David Sagnol.

Finally, colleagues from around the world, Martín Abadi, Gul Agha, Gérard Boudol, Luca Cardelli, David Crookall, Davide Sangiorgi, Akinori Yonezawa, and Andrew Wendelborn, made very useful comments on early drafts of the book or related research papers.

Nice - Sophia Antipolis
London
February 2005

Denis Caromel
Ludovic Henrio

Reading Paths and Teaching

Extra Material and Dependencies

You will find at the end of this book a list of notations and a summary of ASP syntax and semantics that should provide a convenient quick reference (Index of Notations, Syntax, Operational Semantics). This is followed by a graphical view of ASP properties (page 331), and the syntax of ASP extensions (Synchronizations, Migration, Groups, Components).

The Appendices detail formal definitions and proofs of the main theorems and properties introduced in Part III.

Figure 1 exhibits the dependencies between chapters and sections. Each chapter is best read after the preceding chapters. For example, in order to fully understand the group communication in ASP (Chap. 13), one should read Chaps 3, 4, Part III (Chaps. 6, 7, 8, 9), and Chap.10. Going down the lines (Fig. 1), one can follow the outcomes of chapters. For instance, still for group communication in Chap. 13, immediate benefits are parallel components (Sect. 14.5), and a practical implementation of typed group communication within ProActive (Chap. 16).

Text Book

Besides researchers and middleware designers, the material here can also be used as a text book for courses related to *models, calculi, languages for concurrency, parallelism, and distribution*. The focus is clearly on recent advances, especially object-orientation and asynchronous communications. Such courses can provide theoretical foundations, together with a perspective on practical programming and software engineering issues, such as distributed components.

The courses cover classical calculi such as CSP [88] and π-calculus [119, 120, 144], object-orientation using ς-calculus [3, 1, 2], and ASP [52], and advanced issues such as mobility, groups, and components. Overall, the objectives are threefold:

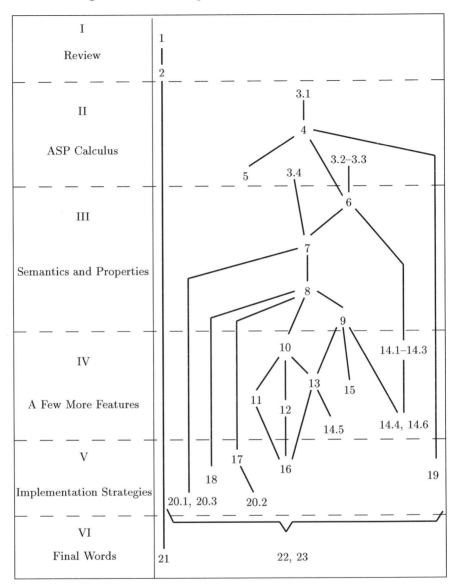

Fig. 1. Suggested reading paths

(1) study and analyze existing models of concurrency and distribution,
(2) survey their formal definitions within a few calculi,
(3) understand the implications on programming issues.

Depending on the objectives, the courses can be aimed at more theoretical aspects, up to proofs of convergence and determinacy within π-calculus and ASP, or targeted at more pragmatic grounds, up to practical programming sessions using software such as PICT [132, 131] or *ProActive* [134].

Below is a suggested outline for a semester course, with references to online material, and chapters or sections of this book:

Models, Calculi, Languages for
Concurrency, Parallelism, and Distribution

1.	Introduction to Distribution, Parallelism, Concurrency	1
	General Overview of Basic formalisms	[39]
2.	CCS, and/or Pi-Calculus	2.1.3
		[73]
3.	Other Concurrent Calculi and Languages	2.1.4, 2.2
	(Process Network, Multilist, Ambient, Join, ...)	[125]
4.	Object-Oriented calculus: ς-calculus	2.1.5
		[4]
5.	Overview of Concurrent Object Calculi (Actors,	2.1.2, 2.3
	ABCL, Obliq and Øjeblik, $\pi o\beta\lambda$, **conc**ς-calculus, ...)	[39]
6.	Asynchronous Method Calls and Wait-by-necessity	3, 4, 5
	ASP: Asynchronous Sequential Processes	
7.	Semantics, Confluence, Determinacy	6, 7, 8, 9
8.	Advanced issues I:	10, 11, 12
	Confluent and non-confluent features, mobility	[125]
9.	Advanced issues II:	13, 14
	Groups, Components	
10.	Open issue: reconfiguration	15, 21, 22, 23
	Conclusion, Perspective, Wrap-up	

The Web page [39] gathers a broad range of information aimed at concurrent systems, also featuring parallel and distributed aspects. Valuable material for teaching models of concurrent computation, including CCS and π-calculus can be found at [73]. The Web page [4] is dedicated to the book *A Theory of Objects* [3]; it references pointers to courses using ς-calculus, some with teaching material available online. Finally, a comprehensive set of resources related to calculi for mobile processes is available at [125].

Assignments can include proofs of the confluence or non-confluence natures of a few features (e.g., delegation, explicit wait, method update, testing future or request reception, non-blocking services, join constructs, etc.). More practical assignments can involve designing and evaluating new future-update strategies, new request delivery protocols, or new schemes for pipelining control. Practicality can reach as far as implementing examples or prototypes, using PICT [132, 131], *ProActive* [134], or other programming frameworks.

A Theory of Distributed Objects online

We intend to maintain a Web page for general information, typos, etc. Extra material is also expected to be added (slides, exercises and assignments, contributions, reference to new related papers, etc.). This page is located at:

http://www.inria.fr/oasis/caromel/TDO

Do not hesitate to contact us to comment or to exchange information!

Part I

Review

1

Analysis

Parallel and distributed languages – including calculi – all fall within the scope of a few important *aspects*. This chapter identifies those aspects and attempts an informal analysis of existing frameworks.

A few basic definitions are first proposed. Then, we explore the fundamental language aspects related to *distribution*, *parallelism*, and *concurrency*. In a second phase, we consider the shift of paradigm, if any, brought in by *objects*.

We finally propose a synthetic table of the aspects and their potential values, and conclude with the overall orientation of the proposal developed within this book.

1.1 A Few Definitions

Let us first introduce a few basic definitions. The first one deals with the very nature of the world we are living in:

Definition 1.1 (Parallelism)
> *Execution of several activities or processes at the same time*

Simultaneously, several activities achieve some actions, be they visible or invisible. In general, we will prefer and use the term "*activity*" rather than process, the latter being both too precise (operating system process) and too overloaded (e.g., design process). Basic examples of parallelism include two multiplications going on at the same time in two different processes, simultaneously printing two different files on two printers, saving the same file redundantly on several disks, etc.

When parallel activities take place in a world with states and objects, trouble begins:

Definition 1.2 (Concurrency)
> *Simultaneous access to a resource, physical or logical*

When at least two activities try to access a single entity, concurrent actions are being carried out, or at least attempted. In many cases, concurrency leads to interleaving, as frequently that concurrent actions actually take place one after the other, or at least appear to do so – our world is in appearance at least rather discrete. Two files printing concurrently on the same printer will produce an unpredictable output; but further analysis can probably separate the interleaving that occurred, be it at the level of a page, line, character, byte, etc. Access to the same memory location is the outmost example of concurrent access, potentially leading to race conditions.

The third definition is more computer specific:

Definition 1.3 (Distribution)
  Several address spaces

With respect to activities, distribution implies that the same state cannot be viewed and shared. Distributed environments assume such a fundamental constraint: namely no single address space. Besides being a reality of modern global computing – spanning the world, shared memory does not allow scalability, even at the smaller scale of a few tens of CPUs. Shared Memory Parallelism (SMP)[1] is by architecture limited to a few processors. This also accounts for Distributed Shared Memory (DSM), where the system manages for and hides to the user the distributed nature of computations. Examples of distribution include PCs on a Local Area Network (LAN), clusters of machines increasingly used for intensive computation, and of course grid computing over a World Area Network (WAN).

While the definitions above attempt to strongly differentiate three physical realities, it is often the case that they are slightly tangled, intentionally or just by mistake. The strong implications that do exist between them are in all likelihood one reason for the confusion. One can achieve parallelism for the sake of speed up or a bigger data set, in which case parallelism is a design choice and a solution – sometimes quoted as *solution domain parallelism*. In such a case, scalability calls for distribution and Message Passing Parallelism (MPP)[2]: distribution proceeds from parallelism. On the contrary, parallelism can proceed from distribution; for instance, the parallel actions of users in a collaborative environment distributed over several locations. Such parallelism is called *problem domain parallelism*.

Finally, there is an hypothesis and a reality that we believe cannot be bypassed:

Definition 1.4 (Asynchronous systems)
  No global clock, and unbounded communication time

---

[1] SMP sometimes refers to Symmetric Multi-Processing.

[2] MPP sometimes refers to Massively Parallel Processing.

Each process runs at its own speed, and communications take a non-predictable time – not to be confused with synchronous or asynchronous communications. Again, this hypothesis proceeds from the need to scale up to large and global systems. On the contrary, *synchronous systems* accept a few strong hypotheses: instantaneous communications (including broadcasting), and instantaneous process reaction to inputs. Such a computational model leads to a total ordering of the events in a system, and to deterministic behaviors. Of course, the synchronous hypothesis does not scale up; no global clock can be assumed all over the world, and communications do take time, especially if they go half-way around the globe. Therefore, there are clearly two correlated challenges still to be tackled for distributed systems:

- asynchronous systems that behave deterministically,
- synchronous systems that can scale up.

This book is an attempt to contribute solutions towards tackling the first challenge.[3]

1.2 Distribution, Parallelism, Concurrency

With the main concepts defined, let us now study how calculi and languages deal with them: what are the concepts and constructs used by languages to handle distribution, parallelism, and concurrency?

1.2.1 Parallel Activities

Provided we are beyond the frame of purely sequential execution or fully implicit parallelism, the very first aspect a language deals with is the definition of *activities*. Whether statically or dynamically defined, a language always features concepts and constructs permitting the definition of parallel executions. Processes (tasks), threads, actors, active objects, or just the parallel evaluation of expressions or functions, exemplify the main abstractions.

For instance, Process Networks [99] use a notion of sequential processes with a statically defined interface. Formalisms like CCS [117] or π-calculus [120] employ activities that are rather the parallel evaluation of an expression. Somehow in between, Actors [9, 11] are based on the parallel execution of a function with a stateful behavior. During the course of this book, we will develop activities based on the notion of an *active object*: a main object + a single thread + a queue of pending requests.

Many other dimensions of activities could be discussed (static or dynamic, flat or imbricated, sequential, quasi-sequential or parallel, etc.). The review of some languages in the next chapter will concentrate on the following:

---

[3] If successful, the second challenge might actually fade away as there will be an asynchronous way to safely and securely program large-scale critical applications.

> Aspect **Activity** taking value in
>
> - Process
> - Expression evaluation
> - Actor
> - Active object

The nature of activities has a strong impact on the nature of *activity identifiers*, which in turn influences the language capacity to deal with them in a uniform and flexible manner. For instance, if activities are just expressions being evaluated in parallel, they usually have no identity that can be communicated, hence the notion of channels (see below).

1.2.2 Sharing

A second and strongly differentiating aspect is *sharing* of state between activities. The fact that several activities can or cannot reach the same state, leading to interleaving and potential race conditions, has a dramatic influence on both programming style and intrinsic properties.

We consider that sharing is fully absent when no passive state can be reached from several activities. Of course, a language without sharing can simulate it with an activity encapsulating some state, further accessed and modified through communications.

> Aspect **Sharing** taking value in
>
> - Yes
> - Some
> - No

For instance, CSP [89] and π-calculus [120] fully disallow sharing, and they are purely communication based; indeed, the absence of state and memory guarantees the absence of shared memory. On the contrary, MultiLisp [83] is fully based on shared memory. Languages with threads (e.g., pThreads [133, 126], Java threads [82, 108]) are typical examples of sharing. Note that the Java platform offers a mixed approach with some sharing in the case of Java RMI communications: two remote objects in the same JVM can freely share state.

1.2.3 Communication

As soon as sharing and interleaving are not the unique option for interactions between activities, *communication* comes into play as a crucial aspect.

Channels are a first option for enabling communications between activities. In that case, communication takes the form of messages being sent and received over channels. Message is a very basic, and somehow primitive, abstraction for interactions. The advent of procedural languages has led to the practical use of a higher level communication pattern: *remote procedure call (RPC)*. The information being communicated is no longer raw data, but a request for a procedure execution, together with its parameters. The piece of code to execute upon reception is encoded into the message itself, to be compared with socket-based systems where the receiver usually first decodes the message to find out what to do with it, i.e., what piece of code to execute. It is striking to observe that most of the formal work on parallel calculus is still within the paradigm of channel-based communications, while programming languages have been for a long time now in the era of procedure and method calls: Turing machine and automata-based formalism has been widely replaced with the λ-calculus that captures functional abstractions and applications. Section 1.3.1 will detail an important object enhancement of RPC-based communications, namely Remote Method Invocation (RMI).

Aspect **Communication Base** taking value in
• Channel
• RPC

Besides the basic form of communication, the nature of information being exchanged is also influential. The capacity to send and receive either activity identifiers or channel names induces an important characteristic: dynamic topology, a feature both theoretically and practically systematically used nowadays.

With respect to exchanging data, the choice between *copy* or *reference* semantics arises, pass-by-value vs. pass-by-reference.[4] Maintaining reference semantics across physically disjoint address spaces leads to generalized references: a kind of Distributed Shared Memory (DSM). Leading to complexity and poor scalability,[5] this option is rather marginal, at least in general purpose systems. The second solution, (deep) copying to manage distribution, is rather popular and quite effective. From RPC to Java RMI, including Network Objects [32], the automatic copying of data being referenced within a communication can occur. While validated by practice, it must be clear that this solution imposes a semantic shift when going from PC (Procedure Call) to RPC: the user ends up with the task of maintaining coherency of copies when needed.

An interesting solution has been proposed to diminish this semantic change: *copy–restore semantics*, which puts back the parameter's value after the call. The principle is clearly related to a call-by-name semantics. One can refer to [155] for a presentation and a discussion on calls by copy–restore, and the differences with a pure call-by-reference. Somehow, copy–restore semantics bridges the gap between DSM and deep copy. However, if the framework

---

[4] Reference semantics for parameter passing is given various names in the literature, e.g., *call-by-sharing* [109, 34], *call-by-object-reference* [98] .

[5] *Call-by-visit* and *call-by-move* were proposed in Emerald [98] to optimize access to object parameters, maintaining a reference semantics.

is to be scalable, copies have to be made somewhere. So, since no automatic system has proved to be able to decide by itself, it boils down to where and how the user can specify the copies to take place, and of course the action needed to reconcile a global semantics. Moreover, copy–restore does not work properly for multiple (asynchronous) calls between two activities. We will return to the crucial aspect of (deep) copying several times in the course of this book.

Recently, *lazy pass-by-value* or *lazy parameter passing* was proposed in [63]. The idea is quite simple: by default a pass-by-reference semantics is used, and a deep copy of a parameter is triggered only upon some specific operations on the caller side. It comes in two flavors: explicit (the caller explicitly triggers a parameter copy), or implicit (a parameter copy is automatically triggered by some indirect operation, e.g., a strict use of the parameter). For the sake of homogeneity, lazy parameter passing will be identified in the communication passing aspect below as *lazy copy*.

Not only can passive data be copied along communications, but also, instead of passing references to activities, activities themselves can be deep copied. A feature we believe captures at its best a practical facet is *mobility of activity*.[6] Such computational or process mobility is present in calculi (e.g., higher order π-calculus, Ambient, Obliq), but only in a few languages, probably reflecting the difficulty of implementing process mobility in operational frameworks.

The table below summarizes the issue of passing semantics under the embracing name of *communication passing*; of course, in the particular case of RPC and RMI, it is usually referred to as *parameter passing*.

Aspect **Communication Passing** taking value in
• Generalized reference
• Copy, and deep copy
• copy–restore
• Lazy copy
• Copy of activities (mobility)

With respect to the communication semantics per se, there is of course the dichotomy of synchronous vs. asynchronous communication. The reality is much more complex with large variations, and to some extent a continuum: purely synchronous, asynchronous with rendezvous, asynchronous FIFO preserving, asynchronous out of order, asynchronous without any guaranty including delivery, etc. We will refer to that aspect of communication semantics as *communication timing*.

This continuum reflects the wide range of possible effects of a communication and possible acknowledgments returned to the source activity. A syn-

---

[6] Not to be confused with *code mobility*, where only stateless and continuation-less code is transmitted.

chronous communication timing blocks the communication sender until the message is treated. For asynchronous with rendezvous communivcation, the sender waits for an acknowledgment ensuring that the message has been received but not necessarily treated (e.g., it has been stored in the context of the callee by a dedicated thread). Asynchronous FIFO preserving communication ensures that all messages sent from a given sender will arrive in the sending order, whereas for pure asynchronous communication without guarantee, messages can arrive out of sending order. In some contexts where there is no possibility of storing a message (e.g., no queue of received messages), as in the π-calculus [120], asynchronous communication with rendezvous cannot exist.

Aspect **Communication Timing** taking value in

- Synchronous
- Asynchronous with rendezvous
- Asynchronous FIFO preserving
- Asynchronous without guarantee

We cannot resist an anthropomorphic analogy to those communication semantics. From top to bottom, they correspond to the following everyday communications:

- Phone
- Fax
- Express mail
- Standard surface mail, email

Phone is truly representative of the long, unbounded, handshake phase occurring in a synchronous communication: some action can take place at the receiving side when the two activities are in rendezvous. Asynchronous with rendezvous is incredibly close to fax transmission where the sender is usually blocked until completion of sending, followed by a guarantee of delivery. Moreover, it also reflects that the receiver is usually not directly involved in reception: the target fax machine plays the role of an independent receiving thread of the transport layer. FIFO preserving is close to an express mail delivery where, usually, messages do not pass each other. Finally, without any guarantee, communications can arrive out of sending order, much like our surface mails and emails. See [55] for an effective formal study of the consequences arising from different communication semantics in the case of messages (send and receive vs. RPC here). Charron-Bost, Mattern, and Tel characterize computations which are possible depending on the communication type. Among other things, they demonstrate the hierarchy:

Synchronous $\subset$ *Causally Ordered* $\subset$ *Asynchronous FIFO.*

Client–server interaction has generalized *one-sided communications* with anonymity of client upon service on the server side. However, *two-sided communications* are still very strong in the calculus arena – possibly due to the historical influence of the CSP ! and ? operators. Low-level Message Passing Interface (MPI) is another example of prominent two-sided operations. In that case the argument is better efficiency since it authorizes zero-copy message passing in shared memory and better control over buffering. We will try to demonstrate over the course of this book that client anonymity one-sided communication, with asynchronous rendezvous-based semantics, is the choice for abstraction, reuse, determinism, and scalability.

1.2.4 Synchronization

Synchronization always boils down to waiting for something: a given event or a piece of data.

Control-based mechanisms provide primitives that allow one to explicitly block the course of execution. The programmer makes use of a dedicated instruction to wait for some conditions or the occurrence of some events. One of the main purposes of such control-based interaction is often to avoid a busy wait. The well-known *select with guards* statement is the best example, as for instance in CSP or Ada. In such cases, a select is a rather complex control structure that also embodies features such as process termination and non-deterministic choice. Moreover, the guard capacity to include rendezvous-based communications leads to a very complex semantics for the programmer, and a rather difficult implementation in distributed environments; cf. for instance the polling nature of the Ada select [75]. The problem arises from the need to select among several calls from remote clients, themselves entitled to withdraw their calls. This book proposes a clear answer to avoid such trouble: systematic asynchronous calls that consistently allow for selection on a *local* pending queue. We will identify that feature as *locally blocking services*.

If one adds *non-blocking services* and *pending-queue inspection*, it further authorizes the building of select-like capacity, but still without any polling. While highly expressive and useful for synchronization problems (reader-writers, philosophers, etc.), such non-blocking primitives are intrinsicly non-deterministic.

While select statements in channel languages deal with messages being awaited, RPC frameworks deal with *requests* of procedure execution. For instance, the Ada `Select` statement operates on *process entry points*, which are very similar to procedure declarations. In that case, the synchronization turns out to be a *blocking service*: a process waits for a remote call to occur on a given procedure. Upon the remote call, the procedure is executed; we say that the *service occurred* to reflect the server nature of such a process. In the quest for powerful synchronization primitives, selection can also be based on the caller identity, breaking the caller anonymity and somehow returning to two-sided communications. Some languages (e.g., Concurrent C [74]) even authorized selection, and as such synchronization, based on the value of effective parameters.

Overall, the select statement is an instruction to *filter* upon pending communications, and trigger the appropriate control flow. As there is no reason to wait for a unique communication, filtering can be achieved on several procedure calls or messages. This is the case in frameworks such as the join-calculus [70], functional nets [127], or the Polyphonic C# [28]. They are still control-based synchronizations, and rather demanding with respect to programmer skill.

Dataflow synchronization is an important step in the direction of more manageable, but also more efficient distributed systems.

The idea is rather simple and powerful: let us trigger operations just based on the data availability. The programmer should say no more than the functional dependencies between computations. Deriving from applicative languages, dataflow evaluations naturally allow parallel evaluation; see for instance the Sisal language [44, 147] for an attempt to achieve numerical dataflow in a functional setting. Also worthly mention is the top role played by dataflow synchronization in current processor architectures.

Our focus (and belief) being on explicit distribution and parallelism, the dataflow idea turns into a language construct: *a future*.

Definition 1.5 (Future)
> *A reference to a value unknown at creation, to be automatically filled up by some activity.*
> *An automatic wait upon a strict operation on a future.*

To the best of our knowledge, MultiLisp [83] invented the imperative face of dataflow synchronization with a reference to a value yet to be determined, a future value. While still in an imperative setting, synchronization becomes more data oriented: a strict operation on an unknown future will beblocked until the data is available. While MultiLisp is in a functional and shared memory setting, an important contribution of this book will be to generalize this idea with respect to two aspects: objects and distribution.

Aspect **Synchronization** taking value in

- Control
- Filtering patterns (select, join, blocking service)
- Dataflow
- Future

1.2.5 Reactive vs. Proactive vs. Synchronous

This section attempts to address a common belief: reactive systems have to be synchronous.

Informally, a *reactive system* is a system where an input causes an output. Somehow inherent to the reactive nature of such a computer system is the external environment to react to. A system, or a component, is reactive only because there is an external world to the system under consideration. A more complete and demanding definition is:

Definition 1.6 (Reactive system)
  A system is reactive if it always reacts quickly enough with respect to the occurrences of the stimuli and the dynamics of the environment.

An interesting presentation of synchronous reactive systems is given in [112], from which this definition was inspired. Also, note that a reactive system is in general continuously reacting to its environment, in a kind of infinite loop.

A reactive system is for instance a plane autopilot. In that case the environment is made of sensors (inputs such as speed, position, etc.) and commands (outputs such as actions on elevator, flaps, and landing gear). Other typical examples are production lines (e.g., chemical plants), or command/control infrastructures (e.g., Air Traffic Control Systems). Such critical reactive systems without doubt call for formal treatment and verification.

Another type of reactivity can be considered, just induced by *interactivity*. Any user of a graphical interface knows that feeling of un-reactivity when clicks produce no reaction, or even worse, reactions so late that they produce undesired effects. If such systems are usually unquantified and dealt with informally, they fall under the scope of reactive systems. One sometimes oppose *reactive vs. interactive*, for in the later the environment (the user) has synchronization abilities: it can wait. However, we believe it is rather a matter of specifying the limits of what is an acceptable reaction time; like a user, a chemical plant under control can also wait for a limited amount of time.

The model and technology underneath could be the same, only the constraints and demands for formal proofs are different. By analogy with real-time constraints, one could talk about "*hard*" and "*soft reactivity.*"

In the reactive system definition above, it must be clear that the "environment" can also be a computer system, potentially reactive itself. As a consequence, the *compositional* capacity of any reactive model is a central aspect. Air Traffic Control Systems are typical examples of a complex hierarchy of reactive systems. Composability is unavoidable in order to master complexity.

To deal with reactivity, *synchronous models* are first placed under the *synchrony hypothesis* [29, 30]. We informally provide the following definition.

Definition 1.7 (Synchrony hypothesis)
  1. *Functional execution and communication time are both considered as null.*
  2. *The entire system is placed under a unique global clock, usually a logical clock, defining global instants.*
     Reactivity occurs at each instant.

In a first step, the hypothesis above allows designers to concentrate on the system functionalities in a deterministic framework, asserting qualitative properties in a discrete-time domain within global instants. In a second step, synchronous reactive systems must test the validity of the first part of the definition: checking that functional execution and communication time are close enough to nullity, producing in practice an effective reactive system.

We would like to avoid a common misconception, and highlight an important idea: reactivity is not tight to the synchronous paradigm. One can perfectly consider that communications do take time and that no global clock exists, as WAN systems require, and still seek reactivity and determinism. Indeed, there are already important bodies of work achieving reactivity and verification in an asynchronous framework; for instance, LOTOS (Language of Temporal Ordering Specifications) [92, 157], the ELECTRE language [54], and the CADP tool [72] dedicated to specifying and verifying asynchronous finite-state systems.

Returning to the focus of this book, i.e., systems based on asynchronous method calls, it is perfectly possible to seek both reactivity and determinism with such activities. While method executions do take time (functional execution in the definition above), they can be neglected if this time is small enough compared to constraints of the environment being controlled (very much like the first part of the synchrony hypothesis). The granularity of reactivity for an activity receiving requests is just up to the request treatment. Locally, an activity can be seen as reacting instantaneously, provided the non-interruptible request treatment is small enough, and the proper priority is programmed: based on the pending request state, one picks up the next input to deal with. This accounts for the *pro-active* nature of activities that we propose: they can decide, with a granularity under the control of the programmer, what is the most important action to undertake next.

The second issue, being capable of verifying global system properties in the framework of asynchronous activities, falls within the scope of techniques to verify asynchronous finite-state systems. Within the ASP model, some advances have already been made to formalize such capacity, and to develop effective techniques [37, 38].

A pitfall arises: the capability of limiting the size of buffering, i.e., the size of pending requests. Indeed, in the absence of the synchrony hypothesis, message transmission and relative speed of processors are unbounded; potentially there is an infinite delay between the sending of a request and its treatment. This makes it possible for a given activity to flood others with requests, leading to bad behavior and also potentially infinite systems. A synchronous system actually provides a kind of automatic *feedback loop*, through the implementation of instants, with the consequence that processes stay in-sink and flooding due to relative speed cannot occur. However, with the appropriate programming patterns such a risk can be overcome in asynchronous systems, and verification achieved statically. A simple example of an asynchronous program with bounded pending queues will be given in this book (Fibonacci example,

Sec. 5.4, page 80). The next step is to use *composable* modeling and verification. Parametric asynchronous automata make this possible, and represent an exciting perspective.

To conclude, as the ASP framework proposes asynchronous and determinate systems, one can expect in the future practical systems that are asynchronous, large scale, and reactive, in the sense of producing control and command for critical environments.

1.3 Objects

In the previous section, we mentioned parallel processes, message or remote procedure communications, and dataflow synchronization. What arises from these concepts when objects come into play?

1.3.1 Object vs. Remote Reference and Communication

Let us start with a fairly basic shift: Remote Procedure Call (RPC) to Remote Method Invocation (RMI, e.g., Java RMI). Method in the RMI acronym denotes the object paradigm. But the major shift is not in the terminology moving from procedure to method. In truth, the move comes from the target: a method call has a peculiar parameter, the target object, hence the dot notation. When turning a call such as `ro.foo (p);` into a communication, `ro` represents – identifies – a remote entity. It is also the case in a concurrent object language like ABCL [161], where a message-oriented syntax like `[T <== M]` allows us to explicitly name the target remote object (T here). In contrast RPC requires a specific parameter, a handle, to represent the remote target (e.g., `foo(ro_handle, p);`). As a consequence, references to objects are somehow unified with references to remote entities. So far, the shift is rather syntactical.

Aspect **Object RMI** taking value in
- Yes
- No

1.3.2 Object vs. Parallel Activity

We mentioned above that references to objects are unified with references to remote entities. However, the decisive question is between objects and activities. Is the very notion of object unified with activity, or with process? Is a reference to a remote object also a reference to a remote activity?

Let us first put aside threads for which the answer is clearly no, even in object-oriented languages such as Java or C#. If threads are somehow reified, some basic features of threads are encapsulated in a class, but this does not go very far. The activities that proceed from a thread are indeed orthogonal to other objects; a thread goes through many objects, several threads can cross the same object at the same time. In short, in such languages a thread is an object, but every object is not, and cannot become, a thread.

Let us also put aside models such as Java RMI. A Java remote object is not by essence an activity. The fact that several threads can execute several remote method calls simultaneously within a remote object does reveal that facet. When writing ro.foo (p);, what ro identifies is not a remote activity, but just a remote object. This has several consequences, along with the presence of sharing between remote objects that prevents them from being a unit of computational migration; we will return to this point.

On the contrary, the notion of object can be unified with the notion of activity. Then, an activity *is* an object. A remote reference to an object becomes also a remote reference to an activity. This is the case in the functional framework of Actors [9, 11]. An activity is identified with an actor, and a so-called *acquaintance* is just a reference to a remote activity. In the context of imperative object languages, such a concept, merging an activity and a remote entity, is an *active object*.

A final question remains: are all objects activities? The actor language answer to that question is yes, leading to what is called *uniform actor models*. All objects are active. Although theoretically interesting, we believe that solution not to be effective and practical. We prefer the so-called *non-uniform* models, where only some objects are turned into active objects. The capacity for the programmer to specifically pinpoint the active objects reflects the role of activities in explicit parallelism: one has to decide what and where the activities are, a feature most needed for efficiency and large-scale distribution.

Aspect **Object Activity** taking value in

- Yes, all objects (uniform)
- Yes, some objects (non-uniform)
- No

To summarize a key point, in the framework of *object activity* a reference to a remote object is also a reference to a remote activity.

1.3.3 Object vs. Synchronization

Finally, let us offer a quick overview of dataflow synchronization in an object world.

When activities are remote objects, asynchronous method calls are a first move to decoupled computations and envision scalability. As a method call can return a value, a dataflow synchronization can naturally be added to object languages: each result of an asynchronous call can be viewed as a future. It will be updated upon reception of the result, after the remote method execution. In the meantime, any attempt to use the unknown future will be blocked.

For instance, when `ro` is a remote object, the execution of the call
`v = ro.foo(p);` will not block the current activity. Such systematic asynchronous semantics for remote calls leads to `v` being automatically a future.
As for MultiLisp, any strict operation on an unknown future, e.g., in the current object context a `v.bar()` method call, will be blocked until the future
is filled up. But also the distributed nature of large scale systems has to be
taken into account: such automatic futures must also be generalized references, passing from one address space to another. In the following example,
where both `ro1` and `ro2` are remote objects:

```
v1 = ro1.foo(p);
v2 = ro2.foo(v1);
```

at the time of the second remote call, `v` is most likely still a future. Nevertheless, the call should proceed asynchronously.

Overall, we will call such an object-oriented dataflow synchronization *wait-by-necessity* [49]. In short, wait-by-necessity is not only dataflow synchronization, but also automatic future creation and transmission between activities.

Definition 1.8 (Wait-by-necessity)
> *Automatic and transparent creation of future objects upon*
> *remote method invocations.*
> *Futures as generalized references passed between distributed activities.*
> *Automatic wait upon strict operations on future objects.*

The systematic and implicit characteristic of wait-by-necessity is decisive.
It accounts for a lot of its flexibility, dynamicity, and as such efficiency. The
burden of decoupling applications for the sake of scalability is partially shifted
from the user to the system – after the initial effort of identifying activities
and partitioning the application. To ensure true wait-by-necessity, passing a
future in a communication parameter is no longer a strict operation, neither
returning a future as the result of a remote call; the future value per se is
not immediately needed, and it is not even clear that the target activity will
ever need it. Wait-by-necessity implies first-class futures: they can be passed
around between activities, and the update mechanism has to take that into
account.

Many opportunities arise with such a principle. They will be examined in
depth during the course of this book.

Aspect **Wait-by-necessity** taking value in
• Yes
• No

Aspects	Possible Values:
Activity	Process
	Expression evaluation
	Actor
	Active object
Sharing	Yes
	Some
	No
Communication Base	Channel
	RPC
Communication Passing	Generalized reference
	Copy and deep copy
	copy–restore
	Lazy copy
	Copy of activities (mobility)
Communication Timing	Synchronous
	Asynchronous with rendezvous
	Asynchronous FIFO preserving
	Asynchronous without guarantee
Synchronization	Control
	Filtering patterns (select, join, blocking service)
	Dataflow
	Future
Object RMI	Yes
	No
Object Activity	Yes, all objects (uniform)
	Yes, some objects (non-uniform)
	No
Wait-by-necessity	Yes
	No

Table 1.1. Aspects of distribution, parallelism, and concurrency

1.4 Summary and Orientation

Table 1.1 summarizes the various aspects discussed in the course of this introduction. For all of them, the typical values identified are recorded. They will be used in the related bibliography section (Chap. 2) to classify a few languages and calculi.

Let us briefly provide a quick overview of the ASP calculus in terms of the analysis above.

We believe in objects as a powerful abstraction for mastering the complexity of distribution. ASP relies on *active objects*; a reference to a remote object is equivalent to a reference to a remote activity. Seeking both large-scale distributed systems and determinism, there is no sharing. This allows one to avoid low level interleaving, and besides turns active objects into a unit of computational mobility (see Chap. 12).

Communication is based on pure remote method invocation, with copy semantics of parameters; of course active objects are passed by reference. For the sake of scalability and low-coupling, such communication is systematically asynchronous. However, the ASP calculus does not feature messages freely floating in communication media: the semantics enforces direct transmission to the target context. In practice, this means that there is a short rendezvous phase between the caller and callee for transmitting the request; after this hand-shake each one continues its execution asynchronously. Being systematically asynchronous means one cannot decide on the synchronous or asynchronous semantics on a per method basis. Hence, interacting entities are really asynchronous objects, and the interactions between them are fully uniform.

With respect to synchronization between active objects, we extensively use the object dataflow principle: wait-by-necessity. The resulting futures will be first-class value, passing between activities.

As already mentioned, we believe in non-uniform models: not all objects are active objects. Why not exploit the more canonical actor model? Even with wait-by-necessity, uniform models with every single object being an asynchronous entity are not realistic: they are far too non-deterministic in essence, or there are far too much synchronizations to add. Moreover, such fine-grain parallelism cannot be implemented efficiently. As a final argument, it is still possible to define applications with all objects being active when appropriate – a uniform actor model is still at hand when needed.

With respect to control-based synchronization, there is no complex select instruction. Rather, a *service* primitive allows one to selectively serve within a list of method calls, specified as parameters. It is a synchronization primitive as it will block if there is no such pending request. It is a fully local operation, as it acts solely on the local queue of requests already received.

Table 1.2 summarizes the fundamental characteristics of ASP.

ASP is the first object calculus featuring active objects with full-blown wait-by-necessity, together with confluence and determinism. Furthermore, the calculus encompasses all strategies for future update (lazy to the most eager). As such, proofs of confluence and determinism are valid for any of those strategies.

Aspects	Values:
Activity	Active object
Sharing	No
Communication Base	RPC
Communication Passing	Generalized reference to activities and futures
	Deep copy of objects
	Copy of activities (mobility)
Communication Timing	Asynchronous with rendezvous
Synchronization	Blocking service
	Future
Object RMI	Yes
Object Activity	Yes, some objects (non-uniform)
Wait-by-necessity	Yes

Table 1.2. Aspects of ASP

Formalisms and Distributed Calculi

This second chapter provides a broad overview of formalisms and languages used for distribution, parallelism, and concurrency.

We successively study basic formalisms (such as the λ- and π-calculus), concurrent calculus, and finally formalisms with some object concepts.

Among distributed, concurrent, or parallel languages, mainly those benefiting from a formal definition will be analyzed in this chapter. Programmatic and algorithmic issues related to distributed systems are covered at large in [155]. With respect to concurrent programming, see for instance [16, 108]. Finally, for a comprehensive study of parallel programming languages and associated environments, see [148] or [149] and [59].

2.1 Basic Formalisms

This section reviews the main calculi and formalism from which most of the (formally described) concurrent languages and calculi have been derived.

Figure 2.1 provides an informal classification of calculi considering the different concurrency principles.

2.1.1 Functional Programming and Parallel Evaluation

the λ-calculus and pure functional languages provide a simple framework for designing parallel languages. In fact, it is well known that the λ-calculus is confluent [22] whatever evaluation strategy is chosen. In other words, the absence of side effects allows one to evaluate expressions composing the programs in any order. A parallel evaluation of functional languages is both deterministic and deadlock free.

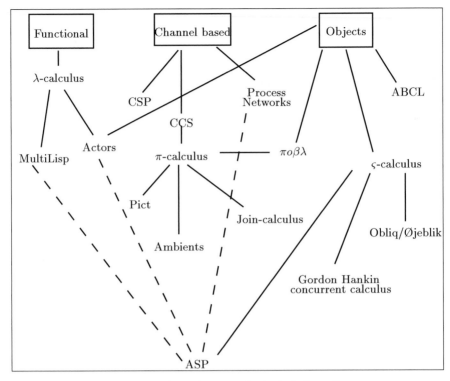

Fig. 2.1. Classification of calculi (informal)

We recall below the syntax of the λ-calculus:

$$M, N ::= x \qquad \text{variable}$$
$$| \; \lambda x.M \quad \text{abstraction}$$
$$| \; (MN) \quad \text{application}$$

Functional languages are directly inspired and modeled by the λ-calculus. Figure 2.2 gives an example of a binary tree in CAML (a classical functional language). This example is composed of the declaration of a `btree` type, and two functions, one for adding an element and one checking if an element is in the tree. This example is written in a purely functional style and does not contain any side effect. Consequently, the function `insert` has to return the whole tree which could be inefficient in a distributed implementation. As this example is purely functional, any execution of these functions can be performed in parallel without loss of determinacy.

The parallel functional evaluators have been widely studied, see for example [101] for a lazy parallel evaluation, or [84] for a survey of parallel functional programming.

```
type 'a btree = Empty | Node of 'a * 'a btree * 'a btree;;

let rec member x btree =
  match btree with
       Empty -> false
     | Node(y, left, right) -> if x = y then true else
         if x < y then member x left else member x right;;

let rec insert x btree =
  match btree with
       Empty -> Node(x, Empty, Empty)
     | Node(y, left, right) ->
         if x <= y then
             Node(y, insert x left, right)
         else
             Node(y, left, insert x right);;
```

Fig. 2.2. A binary tree in CAML

2.1.2 Actors

Actors [9, 10, 11] are a typical example of the *uniform object activity* aspect: each actor is a rather functional process. Actors interact by asynchronous *message passing*. Instead of having an internal state, actors can change their *behavior*, i.e., their reaction to received messages.

Agha, in [9], presented an actor language. More formal syntax, operational semantics, equivalence, and bisimulation techniques for actors are given in [10] and [11]. Actors are based on a functional language but are organized in an object-based style. An actor is an object for which each method is written in a purely functional language. Communication is ensured by a mailbox mechanism and thus is asynchronous. Fairness is an important requirement of actor specification. According to Agha, fairness is a realistic hypothesis that provides semantical properties. Characteristics specific to actors are:

- An actor may *send* a message to another actor; send(a,v) creates a message with receiver a and contents v and sends it.
- An actor may *change* its own behavior. During a message treatment, an actor *must* specify its new behavior (which can be the same as before the message treatment) by the primitive become(b).
- An actor may *create* other actors with the primitives newaddr() for creating an address and initbeh(a,b) for initializing an actor behavior.

While actors are originally based on a purely functional paradigm, some actor languages (e.g. Thal [103]) use imperative constructs for local behavior in order to provide efficient execution on standard computers. However, since the semantics of imperative sequential programs can be represented in the lambda-calculus using store-passing style translations (see, for example, [135]), this optimization is semantically not significant though of pragmatic importance.

The history-sensitive aspect of actors is performed by the *become* primitive. In other words, the state of an actor is specified by its behavior. This means that the behavior of an actor at invocation time (on message sending) may differ from its behavior at execution time (on message reception). In ASP, such behavior modification will be forbidden and replaced by an imperative aspect allowing objects to modify their state (their data). These two approaches are somewhat opposite. Indeed, Agha and others store the state of the actors inside their functions, while in ASP the state is only stored in the data part of objects (field).

Table 2.1 defines the syntax of an actor language. This syntax only includes the primitives that are characteristic of an actor language.

```
⟨act program⟩ ::= ⟨behavior definition⟩* (⟨command⟩)

⟨behavior definition⟩ ::= (define (id {(with identifier ⟨pattern⟩)}*)
                                   ⟨communication handler⟩*)

⟨communication handler⟩ ::= (Is-communication⟨pattern⟩ do ⟨command⟩)

⟨command⟩ ::= let ⟨let binding⟩* ⟨command⟩
            | (if ⟨expression⟩ then ⟨command⟩ else ⟨command⟩)
            | (send ⟨expression⟩ ⟨expression⟩)
            | (become ⟨expression⟩)
```

Table 2.1. The syntax of an Actors language [9]

```
(define (Factorial ())
   (Is-Communication (a eval (with customer ≡ c)
                             (with number ≡ n)) do
       (become Factorial)
       (if (NOT (= n 0))
          (then (send x 1))
          (else (let (x (new FactCust (with customer c)
                                      (with number n)))
                  (send Factorial (a eval (with customer x)
                                          (with number n-1)))))))))
(define (FactCust (with customer ≡ m)
                  (with number ≡ n))
   (Is-Communication (a number k) do
      (send m n*k)))
```

Fig. 2.3. A factorial actor [9]

A notion of futures for actors is also presented in [9]. A λ-calculus-based actor calculus is presented in [10, 11]. Actors are presented as an open system: they can receive messages from outside actors. These articles specify an operational semantics, an operational equivalence, and operational bisimulation techniques for actors.

Figure 2.3 defines an actor computing a factorial that distributes the work to customers. More precisely, a chain of `FactCust` objects is created. Each customer performs one multiplication and forwards the result to the following customer, thus each call to factorial first creates a `FactCust` actor and recursively calls the `Factorial` actor with the newly created customer, for $n - 1$.

In [105], an actor-like concurrent language is presented but is more related to typing theory and can capture "message not understood" errors. It is based on ML-like typing of record calculus. Indeed, this article considers that a concurrent object-oriented programming language is an assemblage where records are added to a concurrent calculus (*à la* π-calculus). Actor semantics can also be built out of the pi-calculus by adding typing restrictions [12, 128].

Aspects	Possible Values:
Activity	Actor
Sharing	No
Communication Base	Channel
Communication Passing	Generalized reference
Communication Timing	Asynchronous, with a fairness guarantee
Synchronization	Filtering patterns (futures can exist at a higher level)
Object RMI	No
Object Activity	Yes, all objects (uniform)
Wait-by-necessity	No

Table 2.2. Aspects of Actors

A popular actor inspired language in current use is E [62], which is particularly useful for scripting P2P systems. It offers *capabilities* for secure distribution. Other systems use a library approach to provide actor functionalities in a conventional language such as Java (see for example, the *Actor Foundry* [8]).

Table 2.2 summarizes the fundamental aspects of Actors. Most of these characteristics are a direct consequence of the uniform model of Actors and of the fact that communications are performed with message passing and pattern matching on message reception. Communications are asynchronous but a fairness hypothesis ensures that every sent message will finally be delivered; however, some implementations of actors ensure a FIFO preserving communication timing.

2.1.3 π-calculus

π-calculus is one of the most popular calculi modeling communications. Compared to actors, π-calculus does not have a built-in notion of object, nor a notion of object identity. Moreover, in its original version π-calculus offers synchronous communications.

π-calculus activities are expressions that communicate synchronously with channels. The expressive power and the concept of mobility in π-calculus come from the possibility to send channels along other channels: the first class entities of π-calculus are the channels.

CCS [117] was introduced by Milner; in this book, we decided to focus on π-calculus which can be considered as an extension of CCS. π-calculus is a concurrent calculus based on communications over channels and introduced by Milner et al. [119, 120, 144]. It is a very small calculus where channels are first-class entities and communication is due to synchronization between a process performing an output on a channel and another process performing a blocking input on the same channel. Channel names are first-class entities and can be passed over channels.

Several versions of π-calculus exist and π-calculus syntax can be presented in different ways. We will use the syntax of Table 2.3 and present the main variants of π-calculus below.

$P, Q ::= \mathbf{0}$	nil
$\mid P \vert Q$	parallel composition
$\mid (\nu x.P)$	restriction of name x
$\mid \tau.P$	unobservable action
$\mid x(y).P$	input
$\mid x\langle y\rangle.Q$	output
$\mid [x = y].Q$	name matching
$\mid P + Q$	choice
$\mid !P$	replication

Table 2.3. The syntax of π-calculus

Informally,

- $x\langle y\rangle.Q$ sends y along channel x and, after synchronization with a process $x(z).P$ listening on channel x, continues as Q. Similarly and synchronously, $x(z).P$ receives y on channel x and continues as P where z is replaced by y.
- $\nu x.P$ creates a fresh channel x with lexical scope P.
- $P \vert Q$ corresponds to the parallel composition of two processes; $!P$ is an infinite number of P processes running in parallel.
- $P + Q$ denotes an external choice: as soon as P can be reduced, Q is discarded, or vice versa.

- Name matching only exists in some variants of π-calculus. In that case $[x = y].Q$ executes Q if x and y are the same channel.

Table 2.5 defines an operational semantics for (synchronous) π-calculus without matching similar to the one that can be found in [119]. From the structural congruence relation defined in Table 2.4, a reduction relation $\rightarrow$ can be defined ($\{y \leftarrow z\}$ denotes the substitution of y by z).

$P \equiv Q$ if P is obtained from Q by change of bound names (alpha conversion)

$$P + \mathbf{0} \equiv P, \ P + Q \equiv Q + P, \ P + (R + R) \equiv (P + Q) + R$$

$$P|\mathbf{0} \equiv P, \ P|Q \equiv Q|P, \ P|(R|R) \equiv (P|Q)|R$$

$$(\nu x.(P|Q)) \equiv P|(\nu x.Q) \text{ if } x \notin fn(P), \ (\nu x.\mathbf{0}) \equiv \mathbf{0}, \ (\nu y.(\nu x.P)) \equiv (\nu x.(\nu y.P))$$

$$!P \equiv P|!P$$

Table 2.4. π-calculus structural congruence

In Table 2.5 the TAU rule is associated to unobservable actions. REACT is the (synchronous) communication rule between two processes. PAR means that except for the reaction rule, processes evolve asynchronously. RES allows reduction inside a binder. STRUCT expresses that the terms are reduced modulo structural equivalence; for example, one can reorder processes in order to allow the reaction between two processes. The use of the rules STRUCT and REACT with bound channels allows the restriction scope of these channels to be changed, this mechanism is sometimes called *scope extrusion*.

Most of the π-calculus derived languages and calculi presented below do not include name matching. Name matching makes different equivalence relations on π-calculus [69] equivalent, but this is not directly linked to the subject of this study.

Some variants of π-calculus exclude the choice operator mainly for simplicity.

Nearly all π-calculus theoretical developments are based on the definition of one or several bisimulation relations. The main idea of bisimulation is to define an equivalence between terms based on (potentially infinite) reduction. In very short, two terms are bisimilar if every reduction performed on one term (e.g., receiving z on the channel x) can be performed on the other term, and the two terms after reduction are still bisimilar. Bisimulation definition and techniques are based on a *coinduction* principle. Several variants of bisimulation relations exist which are more or less discriminating (this also depends

TAU:

$$\tau.P + M \to P$$

REACT:

$$(x(y).P + M)|(x\langle z\rangle.Q + N) \to P\{\!|y \leftarrow z|\!\}|Q$$

PAR:
$$\frac{P \to P'}{P|Q \to P'|Q}$$

RES:
$$\frac{P \to P'}{(\nu x.P) \to (\nu x.P')}$$

STRUCT:
$$\frac{P \to P' \wedge P \equiv Q \wedge P' \equiv Q'}{Q \to Q'}$$

Table 2.5. π-calculus reaction rules

on the variant of π-calculus on which it is applied). The study of bisimulation is beyond the scope of this book, see for example [144] for a rather complete study of π-calculus variants and some bisimulation relations and techniques.

Variants of π-calculus

Polyadic π-calculus [118] allows one to send/receive several channels on a channel (i.e., $x(y).P$ becomes $x(y_1 \ldots y_n).P$). Polyadic π-calculus can be encoded in monadic π-calculus; thus, polyadic π-calculus is mainly useful for introducing the concept of sorts in π-calculus.

π-calculus can be either synchronous or asynchronous. Asynchrony is obtained by disallowing an output prefix. This means that output messages do not have any continuation; that is to say, $x\langle y\rangle.Q$ is replaced by $x\langle y\rangle$ in the syntax above. Asynchronous π-calculus without a choice operator was first proposed by Honda and Tokoro in [90] and Boudol in [35]. Synchronous π-calculus can be encoded in asynchronous π-calculus, but behavioral equivalence differs in synchronous and asynchronous π-calculus. Translation from asynchronous π-calculus to synchronous π-calculus is a convenient model for programming languages where synchronized communications are built upon asynchronous primitives.

Merro and Sangiorgi introduce a (variant of) "local π-calculus" (Lπ) in [115] which forbids the use of a received channel for input or name matching. In [143], Sangiorgi extends this calculus with the capacity of sending processes through channels (LHOπ: Local Higher Order π-calculus) and shows the compilation from LHOπ to Lπ. A more general compilation of the HOπ (Higher Order π-calculus) into the π-calculus was presented in [141].

PICT is a language based on π-calculus and is briefly described in Sect. 2.2.2.

Linear and Linearized Channels

Linear and linearized channels use typing techniques to provide confluence for some π-calculus terms. A channel with a linear type [104] can only be used once in input and once in output. Thus communication over a linear channel can not be affected by a third process.

Nestmann and Steffen in [124] introduce a generalization of linear channels: "linearized" channels which can be reused after a "unique" usage. This article aims at ensuring, with typing techniques, that at any time only one communication is possible through a given channel.

Communication over linear and linearized channels is deterministic. Thus π-calculus terms only communicating over linear and linearized channels are confluent. This technique seems to be a convenient criterion for deciding statically whether a π-calculus program is deterministic or not.

What is Mobility?

In [119], Milner classifies mobility in three main categories:

(A) *processes* move, in the physical space of *computing sites*;
(B) *processes* move, in the virtual space of *linked processes*;
(C) *links* move, in the virtual space of *linked processes*.

π-calculus adopts the choice (C) and Milner considers that (B) can be reduced to (C). This book partly follows this idea and will not focus on the site where an activity is placed but will rather adopt choice (B) because ASP calculus is based on the notion of activities rather than channels.

Even if some kinds of channels can be implemented in ASP and communicated between processes, this book will be more focused on the concurrency aspects than on mobility of names as presented by Milner. However, a notion of mobility *à la* Milner is intrinsic to ASP through the mobility of global references to some objects: ASP global references can be transmitted between processes.

With respect to the concept of physical place, we consider that the interaction between physical location and the methodology of communication is beyond the scope of this study. Consequently, Chap. 12 will introduce migration in ASP by considering that the content of an activity moves to another activity.

In short, to come back to Milner's classification, this book rather adopts the choice (B) and considers that it can be easily reduced to (A) in practice.

Table 2.6 summarizes the fundamental characteristics of synchronous π-calculus. Of course asynchronous π-calculus features asynchronous communication timing without guarantee. The absence of a buffer for storing messages prevents the existence of other communication timing in π-calculus. Indeed, asynchronous with rendezvous communication would require distinguishing message reception and message treatment which is not compatible with the fact that messages cannot be stored and only an acknowledgment can be returned to the sender. Moreover, asynchronous FIFO preserving communication timing cannot be performed by a simple syntactic modification of π-calculus; for example, asynchronous π-calculus forbids an activity to send several messages. Moreover, the control synchronization can be complemented with simple name matching, if such a primitive is allowed.

Aspects	Values:
Activity	Expression evaluation
Sharing	No
Communication Base	Channel
Communication Passing	Generalized reference
	Copy of activities (mobility of activities) in HOπ
Communication Timing	Synchronous
Synchronization	Control
Object RMI	No
Object Activity	No
Wait-by-necessity	No

Table 2.6. Aspects of π-calculus

2.1.4 Process Networks

Process Networks are mainly characterized by process-based activities communicating with asynchronous FIFO preserving channels (buffers). They feature dataflow synchronization and determinacy but are rather restrictive on the patterns of communications that can be expressed.

The Process Networks of Kahn and others [99, 100, 159] are explicitly based on the notion of *channels* between processes, performing *put* and *get* operations on them. Each process is an independent sequential computing station (no shared memory). They are linked with channels (one to one or one to many) behaving like unbounded FIFO queues making the communications asynchronous.

One Process Network channel can link at most one source process and many destinations. The destinations do not split the channel output, but each one reads every value put in the channel (a kind of broadcast). The reading on a channel is performed by a blocking *get* primitive. The order of reading on channels is fixed by the source program. Process Networks provide *deterministic* parallel processes, but require that the order of service is predefined and two processes cannot send data on the same channel.

Figure 2.5 shows the example of the sieve of Eratosthenes written in Process Networks. Note that all communications are performed through explicit and blocking PUT and GET operations which impose a lot of (not always necessary) synchronizations. The behavior of this example is rather simple: an INTEGER process generates integers which pass through as many FILTER processes as prime numbers found. Integers finally arriving at the SIFT process are used to spawn a new FILTER process and sent to the OUTPUT. Figure 2.4 shows the graph of processes when two prime numbers have been found.

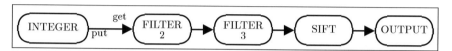

Fig. 2.4. Execution of the sieve of Eratosthenes in Process Networks

Table 2.7 summarizes the fundamental characteristics of Process Networks. The dataflow synchronization aspect is a direct consequence of the blocking *get* primitive.

Aspects	Values:
Activity	Process
Sharing	No
Communication Base	Channel
Communication Passing	Copy
Communication Timing	Asynchronous FIFO preserving
Synchronization	Dataflow
Object RMI	No
Object Activity	No
Wait-by-necessity	No

Table 2.7. Aspects of Process Networks

2.1.5 ς-calculus

We conclude our basic formalisms with the sequential ς-calculus, at the root of the proposed theory of distributed objects.

```
Process INTEGERS out QO
    Vars N; 1 → N;
    repeat INCREMENT N; PUT(N,QO) forever
Endprocess;

Process FILTER PRIME in QI out QO
    Vars N;
    repeat GET(QI) → N;
            if (N MOD PRIME)≠0 then PUT(N,QO) close
    forever
Endprocess;

Process SIFT in QI out QO
    Vars PRIME; GET(QI) → PRIME;
    PUT(PRIME,QO);   emit a discovered prime
    doco channels Q;
      FILTER(PRIME,QI,Q); SIFT(Q,QO);
    closeco
Endprocess;

Process OUTPUT in QI;
    repeat PRINT(GET(QI)) forever
Endprocess

Start doco channels Q1 Q2;
    INTEGERS(Q1);SIFT(Q1,Q2); OUTPUT(Q2);
    closeco;
```

Fig. 2.5. Sieve of Eratosthenes in Process Networks [100]

Abadi and Cardelli [3, 1, 2] present a calculus for modeling object-oriented languages: ς-calculus. The main contribution of [3] deals with typing in object calculi. Even if this aspect is important, it will not be studied in this book. Indeed in our case, classical typing could be considered as orthogonal with concurrency.

Abadi and Cardelli studied both functional and imperative behavior, starting from an object-based functional calculus (no classes) without typing, then adding imperative aspects and most importantly studied typing. A class-based object calculus can also be translated to ς-calculus; an example of translation is defined in [3]. ς-calculus is a base calculus for several parallel calculi (e.g., Øjeblik [114], the concurrent object calculus of [78], etc.).

ASP calculus is based on an untyped imperative ς-calculus (**impς**-calculus). In [3], several equivalent variants of **impς**-calculus. The ASP calculus is closer to **impς$_f$**-calculus are discussed. The basic **impς**-calculus syntax is described in Table 2.8.

We present below the semantics of **impς**-calculus as defined in [3]. It is based on the following syntactic constructs (:: stands for the concate-

$a, b \in L ::= x$	variable
$\mid [m_j = \varsigma(x_i)a_i]^{i \in 1..n}$	object definition
$\mid a.m_i$	method invocation
$\mid a.l_i \Leftarrow \varsigma(x)b$	method update
$\mid clone(a)$	superficial copy
$\mid let\ x = a\ in\ b$	let

Table 2.8. The syntax of **impς**-calculus [3]

nation of lists and $+$ the update of an entry in an association map):

ι	store location (e.g., an integer)
$v ::= [m_i = \iota_i]^{i \in 1..n}$	result (m_i distinct)
$\sigma ::= \{\iota_i \mapsto \langle \varsigma(x_i)b_i, S_i \rangle\}^{i \in 1..n}$	store (ι_i distinct)
$S ::= \{x_i \mapsto v_i\}^{i \in 1..n}$	stack (x_i distinct)
$S \vdash \diamond$	well-formed store judgment
$\sigma \bullet S \vdash \diamond$	well-formed stack judgment
$\sigma \bullet S \vdash a \rightsquigarrow v \bullet \sigma'$	term reduction judgment

The semantics presented by Abadi and Cardelli is a big-step, closure-based semantics; it is based on three different judgments, and the reduction rules are presented in Table 2.11. Well-formedness judgments are defined in Tables 2.9 and 2.10.

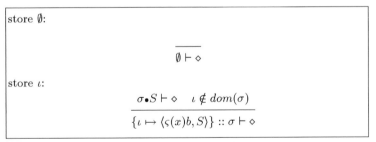

Table 2.9. Well-formed store

Gordon et al. presented a substitution-based semantics of **impς**-calculus (small step and big step), and proved their equivalence with Abadi and Cardelli closure-based semantics in [79, 80]. We based our semantics on the operational semantics of [79] because it is more intuitive and concise than the one of Abadi and Cardelli. However, such a semantics is based on a substitution that is more difficult to implement efficiently.

stack $\emptyset$:

$$\frac{\sigma \vdash \diamond}{\sigma \bullet \emptyset \vdash \diamond}$$

stack x:

$$\frac{\sigma \bullet S \vdash \diamond \quad \iota \notin dom(\sigma)}{\sigma \bullet \left(\{x \mapsto [m_i = \iota_i]^{i \in 1..n}\} :: S\right) \vdash \diamond}$$

Table 2.10. Well-formed stack

x:

$$\frac{\sigma \cdot (S :: \{x \mapsto v\} :: S') \vdash \diamond}{\sigma \bullet (S :: \{x \mapsto v\} :: S') \vdash x \rightsquigarrow v \bullet \sigma}$$

object:

$$\frac{\sigma \bullet S \vdash \diamond \quad \forall i \in i..n, \ \iota_i \notin dom(\sigma)}{\sigma \bullet S \vdash [m_j = \varsigma(x_i)a_i]^{i \in 1..n} \rightsquigarrow [m_j = \iota_i]^{i \in 1..n} \bullet \{\iota_i \mapsto \langle \varsigma(x_i)a_i, S \rangle^{i \in 1..n}\} :: \sigma}$$

select:

$$\frac{\begin{array}{c} \sigma \bullet S \vdash a \rightsquigarrow [m_i = \iota_i]^{i \in 1..n} \bullet \sigma' \\ \sigma'(\iota_j) = \langle \varsigma(x_j)a_j, S' \rangle \quad x_j \notin dom(S') \quad j \in 1..n \\ \sigma' \bullet (x_j \mapsto [m_i = \iota_i]^{i \in 1..n} :: S') \vdash a_j \rightsquigarrow v \bullet \sigma'' \end{array}}{\sigma \bullet S \vdash a.m_j \rightsquigarrow v \bullet \sigma''}$$

update:

$$\frac{\sigma \bullet S \vdash a \rightsquigarrow [m_i = \iota_i]^{i \in 1..n} \bullet \sigma' \quad j \in 1..n \quad \iota_j \in dom(\sigma')}{\sigma \bullet S \vdash a.m_j \Leftarrow \varsigma(x)b \rightsquigarrow [m_i = \iota_i]^{i \in 1..n} \bullet \left(\{\iota_j \mapsto \langle \varsigma(x)b, S \rangle\} + \sigma'\right)}$$

clone:

$$\frac{\sigma \bullet S \vdash a \rightsquigarrow [m_i = \iota_i]^{i \in 1..n} \bullet \sigma' \quad \forall i \in 1..n, \ \iota_i \in dom(\sigma') \wedge \iota_i' \notin dom(\sigma')}{\sigma \bullet S \vdash clone(a) \rightsquigarrow [m_i = \iota_i']^{i \in 1..n} \bullet \left(\{\iota_i' \mapsto \sigma'(\iota_i)\} + \sigma'\right)}$$

let:

$$\frac{\iota \sigma \bullet S \vdash a \rightsquigarrow v' \bullet \sigma' \quad \sigma' \bullet \left(\{x \mapsto v'\}\right) :: S \vdash b \rightsquigarrow v'' \bullet \sigma''}{\sigma \bullet S \vdash let \ x = a \ in \ b \rightsquigarrow v'' \bullet \sigma''}$$

Table 2.11. Semantics of **impς**-calculus (big-step, closure based)

Note that Gordon et al. [79, 80] also present compilation and CIU (Closed Instance of Use) equivalence on imperative objects. Moreover Gordon and Rees also present a bisimilarity equivalence of the typed object calculi of Abadi and Cardelli in [81]. These aspects deal with the equivalence of *static* terms. In this book, we will not use this framework because, to be as general as possible, we are interested in relations that are still defined on (partially) reduced terms. Indeed, this book is rather a study of parallel reduction than a study of (statically) equivalent programs.

Figure 2.6 presents an example of a prime number sieve expressed in ς-calculus. It mainly follows the same principle as the Process Network sieve, cloning a new *sieve* object for each prime number found.

$Sieve \triangleq [m = \varsigma(s)\,\lambda(n)$
$\qquad\qquad let\ sieve' = clone(s)$
$\qquad\qquad in \quad s.prime := n;$
$\qquad\qquad\qquad s.next := sieve';$
$\qquad\qquad\qquad s.m{\Leftarrow}\varsigma(s')\,\lambda(n')$
$\qquad\qquad\qquad\qquad if(n'\ mod\ n) = 0$
$\qquad\qquad\qquad\qquad then\ [\,]$
$\qquad\qquad\qquad\qquad else\ sieve'.m(n');$
$\qquad\qquad\qquad [\,],$
$\qquad\quad prime = \varsigma(x)\,x.prime,$
$\qquad\quad next = \varsigma(x)\,x.next];$

$\Leftarrow$ denotes the method update: modifies the body of a method.

The sieve can be used in the following way:

$for\ i\ in\ 2..99\ do\ sieve.m(i)$ $\qquad$ initializes primes ≤ 100

$sieve.next.next.prime$ $\qquad\qquad$ returns the third prime

Fig. 2.6. Sieve of Eratosthenes in ς-calculus [3]

Figure 2.7 presents a binary tree class example. It has been slightly modified: types were removed. $\lambda x.b$ and $(a\ b)$ denote abstraction and application of λ-calculus.[1]

Concurrent extension of ς-calculus will be presented in Sect. 2.2.

2.2 Concurrent Calculi and Languages

2.2.1 MultiLisp

To our knowledge, MultiLisp is the first language to define the concept of a *future* and the automatic dataflow synchronization that follows from this notion.

---

[1] λ-terms can be encoded in ς-calculus.

$$
\begin{aligned}
binClass \triangleq [new = \\
\varsigma(z)\,[isleaf = \varsigma(s)\,z.(isleaf\ s), \\
lft = \varsigma(s)\,z.(lft\ s), \\
rht = \varsigma(s)\,z.(rht\ s), \\
consLft = \varsigma(s)\,z.(consLft\ s), \\
consRht = \varsigma(s)\,z.(consRht\ s)], \\
isLeaf = \lambda(self)\,true, \\
lft = \lambda(self)\,self.lft \\
rht = \lambda(self)\,self.rht \\
consLft = \lambda(self)\,\lambda(newlft) \\
((self.isleaf := false).lft := newlft).rht := self, \\
consRht = \lambda(self)\,\lambda(newrht) \\
((self.isleaf := false).lft := self).rht := newrht]
\end{aligned}
$$

Fig. 2.7. Binary tree in ς-calculus [3]

Halstead defined MultiLisp [83], a language with *shared memory* and *futures*. The construct $(future\ X)$ immediately returns a future for the value of X and concurrently evaluates X. A future without a value associated to it is said to be *undetermined*; it becomes *determined* when its value has been computed. The combination of shared memory and side effects prevents MultiLisp from being determinate.

The main parallelism primitive is a *PCALL* that performs an implicit *fork* and *join* and evaluates its arguments concurrently: $(PCALL\ F\ A\ B)$ concurrently evaluates F, A, and B to f, a, and b; and applies f to the arguments a and b.

In MultiLisp, as the addition operator + needs a value of its arguments, the two following expressions yield essentially the same parallelism:

```
(+ (future A) (future B))
```

```
(pcall + A B)
```

Halstead classifies the programming languages by specifying whether they have explicit parallelism, side effects, and shared memory. For example, CCS is characterized by explicit parallelism, side effects and no shared memory, and MultiLisp by explicit parallelism, side effects and shared memory.

According to Halstead [83], the fact that no data is shared between different threads (no shared memory) is one of the failings of CSP. But the interleaving of processes accessing and modifying data can also be considered as disturbing for the programmer as different interleaving between the threads can lead to different results (MultiLisp is not deterministic). Another drawback of CSP pinpointed by Halstead is that it leads to non-uniform access to data. Indeed local accesses can be performed classically, whereas accesses to data belonging to another process need a communication through channels. In ASP no memory is shared but the copying of shared data is implicit. Consequently, concerning the non-uniform access to data in ASP, the programmer only has to know that objects sent between activities are deeply copied and to deal with the coherence of these deep copies if necessary.

Katz and Weise [102] studied the interactions between futures and continuations and problems arising when those two functionalities are mixed. Flanagan and Felleisen gave a semantics formalization of futures in MultiLisp in [66].

Table 2.12 summarizes the fundamental characteristics of MultiLisp. Most of the items of this classification have a poor signification because of the multithreaded aspect of MultiLisp.

Aspects	Values:
Activity	Expression evaluation
Sharing	Yes
Communication Base	No communication
Communication Passing	No communication
Communication Timing	No communication
Synchronization	Future
Object RMI	No
Object Activity	No
Wait-by-necessity	No

Table 2.12. Aspects of MultiLisp

2.2.2 PICT

PICT [132] is a language based on π-calculus. It is based on an asynchronous π-calculus without choice and name matching. Thus it features asynchronous communications through channels, and PICT activities are based on expressions.

A core language of PICT is presented in [131] and is used to create more complex objects able to encode classical features. For example, synchronization, locks, choice, and a lot of other primitives can be derived from the core calculus. Typing (sub-typing and type inference) of PICT and higher level features (than π-calculus) are also presented in [132].

From a general point of view, PICT is designed to be used to experiment with new designs of concurrent object structures (like, for example, the one in [131]). Only a few primitives provide the possibility of writing simple objects and their typing. No specific concurrency mechanism for objects has been implemented inside PICT.

$Val ::= Id$	Variable
$[\ Label\ Val\ ...\ Label\ Val\ ]$	Record
$\{\ Type\ \}\ Val$	Polymorphic package
$(\ rec\ :\ \mathbf{T}\ Val\ )$	Rectype value
$String$	String constant
$Char$	Character constant
$Bool$	Boolean constant
$Label ::= \langle empty \rangle$	Anonymous label
$Id\ =$	Explicit label
$Pat ::= Id\ :\ Type$	Variable pattern
$\_\ :\ Type$	Wildcard pattern
$Id\ :\ Type\ @\ Pat$	Layered pattern
$[\ Label\ Pat\ ...\ Label\ Pat\ ]$	Record pattern
$\{\ Id\ <\ Type\ \}\ Pat$	Package pattern
$(\ rec\ :\ \mathbf{T}\ Pat\ )$	Rectype pattern
$Abs ::= Pat\ =\ Proc$	Process abstraction
$Proc ::= Val\ !\ Val$	Output atom
$Val\ ?\ Abs$	Input prefix
$Val\ ?\ *\ Abs$	Replicated input prefix
$(\ Proc\ |\ Proc\ )$	Parallel composition
$(Dec\ Proc\ )$	Local declaration
$\mathbf{if}\ Val\ \mathbf{then}\ Proc\ \mathbf{else}\ Proc$	Conditional

Table 2.13. A syntax for PICT [132]

Table 2.13 presents the syntax of the PICT language. The main constructors introduce communication (input and output), parallel composition, records, and pattern matching. Note that name matching does not belong in PICT, there is no choice operator, and that replicated processes are necessarily guarded by an input. The presence of records and pattern matching may allow some kind of subtyping and structured programming. *Rectype* is useful to define and type recursive data structures; Package is used to implement polymorphism.

In [130] the presented syntax is slightly different, mainly by the fact that replicated input is removed and somehow replaced by a def primitive allowing the introduction a declaration.

Figure 2.8 shows a simple Fibonacci example in PICT using some high-level primitives. This example automatically forks one process for calculating each $fib(i)$ because def declaration creates a kind of replicated input process.

Figure 2.9 shows a factorial example written in the core PICT calculus; it is much longer than the example in Fig. 2.8 because it does not use some derived forms also presented in [130] that greatly simplify programming in PICT.

Table 2.14 summarizes the fundamental characteristics of PICT.

```
def fib[n:Int r:!Int] =
  if (|| (== n 0) (== n 1)) then
     r!1
  else
    r!(+ (fib (- n 1)) (fib (- n 2)))

run printi!(fib 7)
```

Fig. 2.8. A simple Fibonacci example in PICT [130]

```
run
(def fact [n:Int r:!Int]=
   (new br:^Bool
      ( {- calculate n=0 -}
        ==![n0 (rchan br)]
      | {- is n=0? -}
        br?b =
          if b then
            {- yes: return 1 as result -}
            r!1
          else
            {- no ... -}
          (new nr:^Int
            ( {- subtract one from n -}
              -![n 1 (rchan nr)]
            | nr?nMinus1 =
              {- make a recursive call to compute fact(n-1) -}
              (new fr?f =
                ( fact!nMinus1 fr]
                | fr?f =
                    {- multiply n by fact(n-1) and send the result
                       on the original result channel r -}
                    *![f n (rchan r)]
              ))))))
  new r:^Int
    ( fact![5 r]
    | r?f = printi!f )
```

Fig. 2.9. A factorial example in the core PICT language [130]

Aspects	Values:
Activity	Expression evaluation
Sharing	No
Communication Base	Channel
Communication Passing	Generalized reference
Communication Timing	Asynchronous without guarantee
Synchronization	Filtering patterns (pattern matching)
Object RMI	No
Object Activity	No
Wait-by-necessity	No

Table 2.14. Aspects of PICT

2.2.3 Ambient Calculus

Ambient calculus [47] is a calculus describing the movement of processes through the explicit notion of *location*: processes execute at an identified place called location. Ambients are convenient for modeling movements through administrative domains (e.g., through firewalls). Consequently ambients naturally feature some kind of mobility as ambients can be moved from one location (an ambient) to another.

An ambient is defined by the following characteristics.

- An ambient is a bounded place.
- Ambients can be nested and can be moved as a whole.
- Computation takes place inside ambients, and can control the ambient itself (e.g., make it move).

The actions of ambients are also called *capabilities*. The capability *in m* allows entry into the ambient m, the capability *out m* allows exit out of m, and the capability *open m* allows the opening of m.

The syntax of ambient calculus is defined in Table 2.15 (n are names, P, Q are processes, and M are capacities).

$$
\begin{array}{rll}
P, Q ::= & (\nu n)P & \text{restriction} \\
& \mathbf{0} & \text{inactivity} \\
& P|Q & \text{composition} \\
& !P & \text{replication} \\
& n[P] & \text{ambient} \\
& M.P & \text{action} \\
\\
M ::= & in\ n & \text{can enter } n \\
& out\ n & \text{can exit } n \\
& open\ n & \text{can open } n
\end{array}
$$

Table 2.15. The syntax of Ambient calculus

Some communication primitives can be added to ambients in a somewhat orthogonal way (in a π-calculus style): $(x).P$ performs an input action that can interact with an asynchronous output action $\langle M \rangle$. Such interactions are only *local* to an ambient. Indeed, long-range communications may need to cross firewalls and should not happen automatically. According to Cardelli and Gordon, long-range communications should be performed by the movement of a "messenger" ambient. With such communication primitives, ambients can encode the asynchronous π-calculus.

Operational semantics is based on the three following rules:

$$n[in\ m.P|Q]|m[R] \rightarrow m[n[P|Q]|r]$$

$$m[n[out\ m.P|Q]|r] \rightarrow n[P|Q]|m[R]$$

$$open\ n.P|n[Q] \rightarrow P|Q$$

and a local communication rule:

$$(x).P|\langle M \rangle \rightarrow P\{x \leftarrow M\}$$

Mobility in π-calculus is a mobility of names: names can be communicated over channels whereas mobility in ambients consists in moving ambients themselves. Thus the notions of mobility in these two calculi are not incompatible; in fact inside each ambient a mobility of names is possible, e.g., by using an encoding of the asynchronous π-calculus.

A strong contribution of [47] concerns the expressiveness of Ambients. This paper also contains many examples of ambients. As such, Fig. 2.10 shows an example of theencoding of locks in ambients [47] and Fig. 2.11 illustrates an encoding of named channels useful to encode the π-calculus in Ambients.

$$acquire\ n.P \triangleq open\ n.P$$
$$release\ n.P \triangleq n[\ ]|P$$

Fig. 2.10. Locks in ambients [47]

$buf\ n$	$\triangleq$	$n[!open\ io]$	a channel buffer
$(ch\ n)$	$\triangleq$	$(\nu n)\,(buf\ n\,|\,P)$	a new channel
$n(x).P$	$\triangleq$	$(\nu p)\,(io[in\ n.(x).p[out\ n.P]]\,|\,open\ p)$	channel input
$n\langle M \rangle$	$\triangleq$	$io[in\ n.\langle M \rangle]$	async channel output

Fig. 2.11. Channels in ambients [47]

Note that a meaningless term of the form $n.P$ can arise during reduction, and a type system like the one described in [46] is necessary to avoid such an anomaly.

Table 2.16 summarizes the fundamental characteristics of Ambients. Note that references to ambients are generalized but can only be used locally: for example, before entering an ambient m, another ambient n has first to move in order to be at the same level as m.

Aspects	Values:
Activity	Expression evaluation
Sharing	No
Communication Base	Channel
Communication Passing	Generalized reference, with local effect
	Copy of ambient (mobility)
Communication Timing	Synchronous
Synchronization	Control
Object RMI	No
Object Activity	No
Wait-by-necessity	No

Table 2.16. Aspects of Ambients

2.2.4 Join-calculus

The join-calculus [70, 68, 67] is an asynchronous calculus with mobility and distribution. Synchronization in the join-calculus is based on *filtering patterns* over channels. From the communication point of view, join-calculus can be seen as an asynchronous π-calculus with powerful message receivers (called triggers): a process can be triggered by the presence of several messages simultaneously.

The join-calculus syntax is composed of processes (P), definitions (D), and join patterns (J) as described in Table 2.17.

The join-calculus semantics is based on a reflexive chemical abstract machine (RCHAM) and can be summarized by the rules of Table 2.18. Each rule (of the form $J \triangleright P$) defines a reaction that can occur upon the simultaneous presence of several messages specified by the join pattern J. If the messages are simultaneously pending ($J\sigma$ on the right of $\vdash$) then those messages are consumed and become the term $P\sigma$ defined by the reaction rule. σ is a substitution of names that can be used to unify arguments of pending messages with formal parameters defined in the reaction rule.

Figure 2.12 shows an example of a reference cell in join-calculus. It is based on three channels. *put* and *get* are sent back on κ_0 and will the become

$P ::=$	$\mid x\langle \tilde{y} \rangle$	message emission
	$\mid \mathbf{def}\ D\ \mathbf{in}\ P$	definition of ports
	$\mid P \mid P$	parallel composition
	$\mid \mathbf{0}$	null process
$D ::=$	$J \triangleright P$	rule matching join pattern J (trigger)
	$\mid D \wedge D$	connection of rules
	$\mid \mathbf{T}$	empty definition
$J ::=$	$x\langle \tilde{y} \rangle$	message pattern
	$\mid J \mid J$	joined patterns

Table 2.17. The syntax of the join-calculus

$\vdash P \mid P' \leftrightarrow \vdash P, P'$	
$\vdash \mathbf{0} \leftrightarrow \vdash$	
$\mathbf{T} \vdash \leftrightarrow \vdash$	
$\vdash \mathbf{def}\ D\ \mathbf{in}\ P \leftrightarrow D\sigma \vdash P\sigma$	σ creates fresh channels
$J \triangleright P \vdash J\sigma \longrightarrow J \triangleright P \vdash P\sigma$	

Table 2.18. Main rules defining evaluation in the Join calculus

accessible in order to write or read values in the cell. s remains local and is used to store the value contained by the cell.

$$\mathbf{def}\ mkcell\langle v_0, \kappa_0 \rangle \triangleq \left(\begin{array}{ll} \mathbf{def} & get\langle \kappa \rangle \mid s\langle v \rangle \triangleright \kappa\langle v \rangle \mid s\langle v \rangle \\ \wedge & set\langle u, \kappa \rangle \mid s\langle v \rangle \triangleright \kappa\langle \rangle \mid s\langle u \rangle \\ \mathbf{in} & s\langle v_0 \rangle \mid \kappa_0 \langle get, set \rangle \end{array} \right)$$

Fig. 2.12. A cell in the join-calculus [68]

Table 2.19 summarizes the fundamental characteristics of the join-calculus.

2.2.5 Other Expressions of Concurrency

Several other concurrent languages exist, most of them being derived from the basic formalisms. Some of them are object oriented, but in general no unification of objects and activities is clearly identified.

CML

In [136], Reppy presents an extension of SML (Standard ML) called CML (Concurrent ML) for concurrent programming in SML. CML is a threaded

Aspects	Values:
Activity	Expression evaluation
Sharing	No
Communication Base	Channel
Communication Passing	Generalized reference
Communication Timing	Asynchronous without guarantee
Synchronization	Filtering patterns (join)
Object RMI	No
Object Activity	No
Wait-by-necessity	No

Table 2.19. Aspects of the Join-Calculus

language. The synchronization is performed by a `sync` operator which synchronizes on an event. An event is either a *basic event*, i.e., a communication, or an event built by combining several basic event. In the base language, the communications are synchronous but a mailbox (request queue) mechanism can be easily implemented with a buffered channel.

Kell-calculus

Stefani [152] has introduced a calculus that is able to model hierarchical components, especially sub-components control. The *kell-calculus* is based directly on the π-calculus with the possibility to have joins inside triggers (as in *distributed join-calculus* – DJoin [68]).

The **M**-calculus [145] is somehow a preliminary version of the kell-calculus. The kell-calculus is also intended to overcome the limitations of the **M**-calculus presented in [152].

Steele Shared Memory Non-interference

Steele [151] expressed a programming model ensuring the confluence of programs by analyzing (mainly dynamically) the shared memory accesses in order to ensure non-interference. But it is based on a shared memory mechanism with asynchronous threads and not on possibly distributed programs.

Montanari Tile-Based Semantics

Montanari et al. introduced *tile-based semantics* [43, 64] which is based on rewrite rules in side effects. This theoretical framework (based on double categories) has been applied to give a semantics to located CCS in [64]. We think such a framework could be used to provide a modular semantics for ASP.

Functional Nets

Functional nets [127] is a language based on join patterns. It consists of two kinds of functions: synchronous and asynchronous. Asynchronous functions correspond to channels with an asynchronous communication timing as in asynchronous π-calculus. Synchronous functions have a synchronous communication timing and thus a value can be returned by such function (the caller awaits for the result before continuing execution). Only the leftmost operand of a fork or a join operator can return a result. In other words, all operands except the leftmost one must be asynchronous functions. Functional nets also feature an object-oriented view with records.

2.3 Concurrent Object Calculi and Languages

2.3.1 ABCL

ABCL [161, 162] features active objects in an imperative object-oriented language. Placing itself in a uniform model where all objects are viewed as active, it does not have shared objects per se. The communication is RPC, and more specifically based on remote method invocation (object RMI). The language features both synchronous and asynchronous communications, and a *select* construct for filtering and waiting for specific message patterns. Table 2.20 summarizes the fundamental aspects of ABCL.

Figure 2.13 (inspired from [161]) presents a simple bounded buffer in ABCL. The *script* part defines the object behavior: what messages the active object accepts and what actions it performs upon reception. Somehow the script specifies the object activity, with the specificity that the object is initially waiting for a message (it is "dormant"); the buffer initially waits for a put or get message. The *select* construct allows one to suspend the activity (turning to the "waiting" mode) in order to selectively wait for some message pattern:

```
(select
      (=> [:message-pattern ...]  where constrains ... actions ...)
             .
             .
             .
      (=> [:message-pattern ...]  where constrains ... actions ...)
)
```

The where part specifies conditions for the message to be treated. This selective wait is close to the select statements found in languages such as CSP [88] and later on in Ada [91]. In the buffer case, a single message is waited for in each select instruction. On reception of an expected message, the object returns to the "active" mode, treating the message.

```
[object Buffet
   (state declare-the-buffer-state )
   (script

      (=> [:put elt]      ; Put an element in the buffer
        (if full
           then (select    ; Waits for a [:get] message
                   (=>[:get] remove-from-storage-and-return )
              )
        )
        store-elt
      )

      (=> [:get]          ; Get an element from the buffer
        (if empty
           then (select   ; Waits for a [:put ...] message
                   (=>[:put elt] send-elt-to-get-caller )
              )
           else remove-from-buffer-send-it-to-get-caller
        )
      )
   )
]
```

Fig. 2.13. Bounded buffer in ABCL [161]

One must notice the *quasi-parallel* nature of ABCL activities: several method activations can exist at the same time, but at most one of them is executing at any given time. This has to be compared to languages with *parallel activities* where several executions (threads) are actually going on simultaneously in the same code. Of course, the other end of the spectrum is *sequential activity* as proposed in ASP: at any time a single method activation, a single thread, a single stack, exist within the object.

The principle of this classification (*sequential, quasi-parallel, parallel activities*) was initially proposed in [160].

Getting back to the code in Fig. 2.13, one can notice the *monitor* [87] nature of this activity: at most one method of the object is executing, while the other activations are suspended on some conditions, respecting a kind of *mutual exclusion*. In the case of a monitor, *condition variables* authorize the expression of wait conditions. For ABCL, the select construct permits to wait for specific messages. ABCL seems to get away with the signaling of monitors at the cost of some code duplication. Instead of signaling after a put that a potentially blocked get can be resumed, the code for putting in an empty buffer is given within the get method. Furthermore, such synchronization can be classified as *mainly centralized*: the synchronization code and object activity is somehow gathered in the script construct, but still mixed up with some functional aspects (code for put and get here). Finally, the mechanism by which a request is treated can be classified as *explicit message acceptance*: there is an instruction that can be placed in the control flow to wait for and execute a request, e.g., the $=>$[:get] in the buffer code. This will be close to the Serve primitive of ASP (Fig. 4.2, page 71). Another alternative, used in other languages, is an *implicit message acceptance* where the programmer expresses conditions for accepting a message, but no specific construct authorizes triggering it at a given point in code. An implicit message acceptance authorizes the programming of activity in a declarative style. However, as an explicit message acceptance is rather a primitive construct, and as it also authorizes the construction of declarative abstractions, we believe a concurrent calculus or language should provide an explicit message acceptance primitive.

```
     ; Synchronous communication:
     ; send and wait for message execution
     ; Originally called:  Now Type Message Passing
 x := [T  <== M]
         ; Current activity send a message M to T
         ; wait for message execution and return value,
         ; which is stored in x

     ; Asynchronous one-way communication:
     ; send and does not wait for
     ; message execution, no reply
     ; Originally called:   Past Type Message Passing
 [T  <= M]
         ; Current activity send a message M to T
         ; no wait

     ; Asynchronous communication with explicit future:
     ; send and does not wait for message execution,
     ; reply to be sent later in  x
     ; Originally called:  Future Type Message Passing
 [T  <= M $ x]
         ; Current activity send a meessage M to T
         ; non-blocking, the result will be put
         ; asynchronously in x
 ...
 (ready? x)
         ; Test if x is still awaited
```

Fig. 2.14. The three communication types in ABCL

An important contribution of ABCL was the introduction of three different communication semantics. The language specifies with dedicated syntax three communication timings for an object to send a message to another. From synchronous to asynchronous, ABCL features synchronous communication, asynchronous one-way communication, and asynchronous communication with explicit future. Figure 2.14 presents the corresponding syntax and intuitive semantics. In the last communication type, an explicit future variable can be specified for the reply to be stored. The `ready?` primitive permits one to explicitly test the availability of a value in a future. A future object in ABCL is in fact a queue. It is explicitly declared ((`Future` ... `x` ...)), and access to it has to be explicit (`[:next-value]`, `[:all-value]`), which of course can be blocking.

An interesting ABCL feature is the capacity to explicitly specify and manipulate the object address where to send a reply. The general syntax for sending a message is in fact the following:

```
[T  <= M  @ dest ]
```

where the variable `dest` specifies where to send the result. For such a communication with a reply, the caller is not interested in the result, but indeed it has to be sent to the `dest` object. Of course, the communication remains non-blocking. Furthermore, the general syntax for accepting a message and returning a reply is:

```
(=> [:M ...] @ dest ... [ dest  <= result ] )
```

An object receiving a message also receives explicitely the destination where it is suppose to send back the result. Turning explicit the reply destination, makes it possible to explicitly *delegate* calls to other objects. For instance, if the message acceptation above is changed into:

```
(=> [:M ...] @dest ... [ T2  <= M  @ dest ] )
```

the call is delegated to the object `T2`, specifying that the reply still has to be sent to the same `dest` object. In that case the reply will be delivered directly, without going through the middle object. Section 10.1 will discuss the possibility to add explicit delegation to ASP and compare it to the implicit delegation existing in ASP because of the first-class futures.

ABCL also features *express mode* message passing: if an object is active and dealing with an *ordinary* message, an express message will suspend the ongoing activity in order for it to be treated right away. By default the suspended treatment will be resumed at the end of the express message treatment. The `atomic` primitive authorizes an object to protect itself against express messages for the execution of a set of instruction. Several versions of the ABCL language were further developed, for instance ABCL/R [158] offers reflective improvements.

The ABCL language is rather significant as one of the first imperative object-oriented languages inspired by the Actors paradigm. Moreover it takes a different approach to the one proposed here (also in an imperative setting) in considering that all objects are active (uniform model). In ABCL, parallelism is induced by asynchronous communications; even if objects are systematically active, doing standard synchronous communication (now type message passing) does not raise any parallelism in itself. While programming, one has to decide for each call its synchronous or asynchronous nature. The control of parallelism is at the fine granularity of each communication. By contrast, ASP will adopt the control of parallelism at the global level of each object, in a non-uniform active object model.

Table 2.20 summarizes the fundamental characteristics of ABCL.

Aspects	Values:
Activity	Active object
Sharing	No
Communication Base	RPC
Communication Passing	Generalized reference
Communication Timing	Synchronous, and
	Asynchronous FIFO preserving
Synchronization	Control
	Filtering patterns (select)
	Future
Object RMI	Yes
Object Activity	Yes, all objects (uniform)
Wait-by-necessity	No

Table 2.20. Aspects of ABCL

2.3.2 Obliq and Øjeblik

Obliq [45] is a language based on the ς-calculus that expresses both parallelism and mobility. Obliq is an object language based on threads communicating with a shared memory (all references to objects are generalized). Thus accesses to objects are strongly concurrent except for serialized objects which can only be accessed by one thread. Figure 2.15 gves an example of a prime number sieve in Obliq.

Øjeblik [123, 41, 114] is a sufficiently expressive subset of Obliq which has a formal semantics. The main results on Øjeblik concern migration but Øjeblik does not take distribution into account.

Øjeblik and Obliq semantics is based on threads (*fork* and *join* operators) and all references are global when necessary: When an object reference is passed through the network, a local reference becomes a global reference. As a consequence these languages are based on a shared memory mechanism. Calling a method on a remote object leads to a remote execution of the method

```
let sieve =
{ m =>
    meth(s, n)
      print(n);
      let s0 = clone(s);
      s.m := meth(s1,n1)
                  if (n1 % n) is 0 then ok
                  else s0.m(n1)
                  end
              end;
    end};

  print the primes <100
  for i=2 to 100 do sieve.m(i) end;
```

Fig. 2.15. Prime number sieve in Obliq

but this execution is performed by the original thread (or more precisely the original thread is blocked). Thus the parallelism is only based on threads, and is independent of the location of the objects performing operations.

We present in Table 2.21 an untyped syntax of Øjeblik, see [123] for the detailed semantics of Øjeblik.

$a, b \in L ::= s, x, y$	variable
$\mid [m_j = \varsigma(s_i, \tilde{x}_j)a_i]^{i \in 1..n}$	object definition
$\mid a.m_i\langle \tilde{b} \rangle$	method invocation
$\mid a.l_i \Leftarrow \varsigma(s, \tilde{x})b$	method update
$\mid a.clone$	superficial copy
$\mid a.alias\langle b \rangle$	object aliasing
$\mid a.surrogate$	object surrogation
$\mid a.ping$	object identity
$\mid let\ x = a\ in\ b$	let
$\mid fork\langle a \rangle$	thread creation
$\mid join\langle a \rangle$	thread destruction

Table 2.21. The syntax of Øjeblik

In Øjeblik the notion of argument of a method is introduced: a method has two formal parameters, one is the object itself (*self/this/...*), the other is a function parameter. Such an extra argument is only necessary in the context of remote method calls. Indeed, in a local context, a method call can return a function (e.g., a λ-term) that will be applied to the argument, whereas in the case of remote method invocations, the execution of the method is performed on the distant object. In Obliq and in most of the distributed calculi the place where a method is executed has a strong influence on its behavior. For example, in a concurrent object calculus like Obliq, it can be useful to protect the state of the object from outside modifications (`protected` keyword explained below). For such protected objects, returning a function and performing operations "inside" the object[2] are not equivalent because only the later solution can modify the state of the invoked object (without losing coherence of the objects or introducing locks). We will see in Part II that in ASP, the argument of methods will also be used as it is deep copied in order to preserve a given topology of links between objects.

In Obliq, the interferences between threads can be limited by serialized objects: if an object is *serialized*, then, at any time, only one thread is inside this object. In other words, a second thread entering an object is blocked until the first one has finished. Serialization may be guaranteed with a mutex. An operation is *self-inflicted* if it addresses the current self. Authorizing reentrant mutexes allows self-inflicted operations to be performed for serialized objects. This allows recursion but not mutual recursion (no call-back).

An Obliq object can be *protected*, as in [122, 123]: "based on self infliction, objects are protected against external modification." That means that for the protected objects, only self-inflicted update cloning and aliasing are allowed. In Øjeblik every object is *protected* and *serialized*.

Migration

In Obliq and Øjeblik migration is the composition of cloning and aliasing:

$$surrogate = \varsigma(s)s.alias\langle s.clone \rangle$$

This composition is deeply studied in Øjeblik, see for example [123].

In [123], Nestmann et al. present different semantics for forwarding and updating. The effect of authorizing (or not) some operations to pass (or not) through the forwarders is studied.

Table 2.22 summarizes the fundamental characteristics of Obliq and Øjeblik. Note that synchronization comes from two aspects: thread destruction and serialization.

The complexity of object interactions that occurs in Obliq and Øjeblik (serialization, self-infliction, protection) is typical of a language without object activity. The orthogonality of activities and objects lead to complex interactions.

2.3.3 The $\pi o \beta \lambda$ Language

Inspired by POOL [14, 15] Jones designed a concurrent object-oriented calculus named $\pi o \beta \lambda$ [95, 96, 94, 97]. $\pi o \beta \lambda$ can be considered as a rather synchronous language where communications are synchronous and asynchrony

---

[2] Or more precisely, inside a thread belonging to the object invoked.

Aspects	Values:
Activity	Process
Sharing	Yes
Communication Base	RPC
Communication Passing	Generalized reference
	Copy of activity (mobility) as cloning+aliasing
Communication Timing	Synchronous
Synchronization	Control
Object RMI	Yes
Object Activity	No
Wait-by-necessity	No

Table 2.22. Aspects of Obliq and Øjeblik

only comes from the possibility to return a result before the end of execution of a method, thus activating two objects at the same time. All references to objects are generalized but objects are protected against external modification; consequently references are shared but not internal states.

The highly synchronous aspect of $\pi o\beta\lambda$ can be summarized by the following facts:

- Only one method of a given object can be active at any time. Using the Obliq vocabulary, one could say that every object is serialized.
- As in Obliq, the calling method is blocked until a result is returned by the called object.

In practice every object is *active* if it is evaluating a method, *waiting* if it is waiting for the result of a method call, or *quiescent* if it has no method currently evaluated. An object only becomes active if it is quiescent and receives a method call or if it is waiting and receives the result of the invoked method.

There is no direct notion of thread in $\pi o\beta\lambda$. Instead, parallelism comes from two facts:

- A function can return a value before the end of its execution. In that case, the calling method obtains the result and can continue its execution while the called function terminates its computation (which will have no consequence on the returned value).
- A function can delegate the task of returning a value to another object by using the *yield* or *commit* or *delegate*[3] primitive. In that case, this object is no longer blocked and the result is directly returned from the last object to the first caller.

These features will have to be compared with automatic and transparent updates of futures in ASP.

Figure 2.16 shows an example of a $\pi o\beta\lambda$ binary tree.

---

[3] The *yield* primitive of [95, 96] is called *commit* in [110] and *delegate* in [97].

```
class T0
var K:NAT, V:ref(A), L:ref(T), R:ref(T)

method Insert(X:NAT, W:ref(A))
    if K=nil then (K:=X ; V:=W ; L:=new(T) ; R:=new(T))
    else if X=K then V:=W
        else if X<K then L!Insert(X,W)
            else R!Insert(X,W);
    return

method Search(X:NAT):ref(A)
    if K=nil then return nil
    else if X=K then return V
        else if X<K then return L!Search(X)
            else return R!Search(X)
```

Fig. 2.16. Binary tree in (a language inspired by) $\pi o\beta\lambda$ [110]

A sufficient condition is given for increasing the concurrency of $\pi o\beta\lambda$ programs without losing confluence, this condition is based on a program transformation. The principle is that an operation can be safely exchanged with a return statement, provided the operation does not *interfere* with the result to be returned. The interference can concern both dataflow aspects – the operation should not affect the result – and control flow ones – the operation should terminate and cannot invoke methods on public objects (because such calls could interfere with calls performed by the caller object which should occur later).

Under this condition, one can return a result from a method before the end of its execution; then the execution of the method continues in parallel with the caller thread. This sufficient condition is expressed by an equivalence between original and transformed program. $\pi o\beta\lambda$ can be translated to (dialects of) the π-calculus (e.g., [94]). From such a translation, Sangiorgi [142] and Liu and Walker [110, 111] proved the correctness of transformations on $\pi o\beta\lambda$ described in [97].

An operational semantics of $\pi o\beta\lambda$ is defined in [97]; this definition seems to be the most adapted to the aspects considered in this book.

Figure 2.17 shows an example with the result of such a transformation applied to the program of Fig. 2.16. Consequently, these two programs behave identically.

There is an equivalent version of the calculus (defining, for example, the sieve of Eratosthenes), with a very different syntax in [95].

Table 2.23 summarizes the fundamental characteristics of $\pi o\beta\lambda$. As for ABCL, all objects are active (uniform), but synchronous communications create awaiting activities, and necessitate a quiescent destination object. Conse-

```
class TO
var K:NAT, V:ref(A), L:ref(T), R:ref(T)

method Insert(X:NAT, W:ref(A))
    return ;
    if K=nil then (K:=X ; V:=W ; L:=new(T) ; R:=new(T))
    else if X=K then V:=W
            else if X<K then L!Insert(X,W)
                    else R!Insert(X,W)

method Search(X:NAT):ref(A)
    if K=nil then return nil
    else if X=K then return V
            else if X<K then commit L!Search(X)
                    else commit R!Search(X)
```

Fig. 2.17. $\pi o \beta \lambda$ parallel binary tree, equivalent to Fig. 2.16 [110]

quently, $\pi o \beta \lambda$ active objects are strongly synchronous. Communication timing is synchronous with early return which is in between "Synchronous" and "Asynchronous FIFO preserving."

Aspects	Values:
Activity	Active object
Sharing	No
Communication Base	RPC
Communication Passing	Generalized reference
Communication Timing	Synchronous with early return
Synchronization	Control
Object RMI	Yes
Object Activity	Yes, all objects (uniform)
Wait-by-necessity	No

Table 2.23. Aspects of $\pi o \beta \lambda$

Note that another view of $\pi o \beta \lambda$ could consist in considering activities based on threads which would change the above classification and make it more similar to the one of Øjeblik. Such a classification would be closer to the semantics of $\pi o \beta \lambda$ based on translation into the π-calculus but does not correspond to the original semantics given by Jones.

2.3.4 Gordon and Hankin Concurrent Calculus: concς-calculus

concς-calculus is an archetype of a model where threads are orthogonal to objects. Threads are asynchronous between them, but method calls within a thread are synchronous. This is highlighted by the fact that threads and objects coexist in every term of **concς**-calculus.

Results:
$$u, v \in L ::= x \quad \text{variable}$$
$$\mid p \text{ name}$$
Denotations:
$$d ::= [m_j = \varsigma(x_i)a_i]^{i \in 1..n} \text{ object}$$
Terms:
$$a, b \in L ::= u \qquad\qquad\qquad \text{result}$$
$$\mid p \mapsto d \qquad\qquad \text{denomination}$$
$$\mid u.m_i \qquad\qquad \text{method invocation}$$
$$\mid u.l_i {\Leftarrow} \varsigma(x)b \quad \text{method update}$$
$$\mid clone(u) \qquad \text{superficial copy}$$
$$\mid let\ x = a\ in\ b \text{ let}$$
$$\mid a\ \mathsf{l}\ b \qquad\qquad \text{parallel composition}$$
$$\mid (\nu p)a \qquad\qquad \text{restriction}$$

Table 2.24. The syntax of **concς**-calculus [78]

Gordon and Hankin [78] proposed a concurrent object calculus: a parallel composition l is added to the ς-calculus. Every object has a name: there is a *denomination* operator. The syntax of **concς**-calculus is given in Table 2.24 In such a calculus, a method is executed by the thread that has invoked it. Moreover, objects need to be declared as separate processes that do not perform computation. As a consequence, the notions of object and of executing threads are clearly separate (one could define objects and threads in different spaces).

Moreover a type system is necessary to distinguish terms from expressions as a denominated object can only be a process, but an expression can either be a top-level process (thread) or be included inside another expression. In other words, a denomination $(p \mapsto d)$ cannot be used as an expression, it should only appear on the left side of a parallel composition $(a\ \mathsf{l}\ b)$.

Note that an additional synchronization mechanism has to be added to the calculus (via mutexes).

Jeffrey [93] introduced a modified version of Gordon and Hankin's concurrent object calculus, and added the notion of *location* in order to make this calculus distributed.

Table 2.25 summarizes the fundamental characteristics of Gordon and Hankin calculus.

Aspects	Values:
Activity	Process
Sharing	Yes
Communication Base	RPC
Communication Passing	Generalized reference
Communication Timing	Synchronous
Synchronization	Control
Object RMI	Yes
Object Activity	No
Wait-by-necessity	No

Table 2.25. Aspects of **concς**-calculus

2.4 Synthesis and Classification

This chapter has reviewed some classical concurrent calculi and languages. We tried to organize a rich set of intertwined languages into a few basic aspects. Table 2.26 summarizes the main aspects of a few calculi and languages.

Among the languages discussed above, we identified three featuring mobility: LHOπ, Ambients, Obliq, and Øjeblik. Note that Silvano Dal Zilio [163] uses a notion of mobile processes different from ours. He classifies mobile processes into those featuring a mobility of names which are called "*labile processes*," and processes with a notion of explicit movement and explicit locations like Ambients calculus, called "*motile processes*." Such a classification explains why the standard π is often credited with capturing mobility, which in fact is only the mobility of names (*lability*). From this point of view, π-calculus is *labile*, while Ambients are *motile*.

The purpose of our study is to examine the impact of different models on the programming paradigm, and especially the methodology to deal with concurrency. From this point of view, Ambients calculus and π-calculus are not very much apart; they both use expression evaluation and channels as fundamental concepts. With respect to locations, we will first fully abstract them away in the core calculus. Then, we will consider true mobility, "*motile processes*," using the following two-step approach. First, activity identities are considered to be locations; this is consistent with the fact that an identity is directly used to communicate, to find, another activity. Second, a mobility is captured with the deep copy of an activity, and its incarnation with a new identity. This view is rather in accordance with an effective implementation of process mobility. Changing identity/location upon mobility allows us to take into account another practical aspect of mobile processes: localization strategy. Finally, that approach makes it possible to study the impact of mobility on formal semantics, convergence, and determinism (see Chap. 12).

Determinism being an important focus, let us point out the few languages with some convergence or deterministic properties: namely, π-calculus linear channels, Process Networks. π-calculus is by essence non-determinate, but some programs can be identified as deterministic based on the linear nature of all their channels. On the contrary, Process Networks offer a framework where the programming model enforces determinism; a Process Network program cannot be non-deterministic. It is generally acknowledged that not all concurrent applications must be deterministic; indeed there are some well-known good non-deterministic ones. So the Process Networks approach is probably too dogmatic to be practical. ASP, also featuring determinism, offers a solution somehow in between π-calculus linear channels and Process Networks. There is some part of the ASP programming model that guarantees determinism (e.g., out of order future updates are still determinate), while fully deterministic programs will require extra properties. A specific chapter will identify *"non confluent features"* (Chap. 11, page 143).

In the following parts of this book, the ASP calculus will be presented, both informally and formally. Chapter 21, page 245, will further compare a posteriori most of the languages and calculi presented here with ASP.

Languages Aspects	Functional			Channel Based		Object	
	ASP	Actors	MultiLisp	π-calculus	Process Networks	πoβλ	Obliq Øjeblik
Activity	Active object	Actor	Exp.	Exp.	Process	Active object	Process
Sharing	No	No	Yes	No	No	No	Yes
Communication Base	RPC	Channel	No com.	Channel	Channel	RPC	RPC
Communication Passing	GR:activities+futures Deep copy of objects Copy of activities (mobility)	GR	No com.	GR	GR only in reconfiguration Copy	GR	GR Copy of Activity (mobility as cloning+aliasing)
Communication Timing	Asynchronous with rendezvous	Asynchronous (fairness)	No com.	Synchronous	Asynchronous FIFO preserving with early return	Synchronous	Synchronous
Synchronization	Blocking service Future	Filtering Patterns	Future	Control	Dataflow Blocking service	Control	Control
Object RMI	Yes	No	No	No	No	Yes	Yes
Object Activity	Yes, non-uniform	Yes, uniform	No	No	No	Yes, uniform	No
Wait-by-necessity	Yes	No	No	No	No	No	No

Exp. = Expession evaluation   No com.= No communication   GR = Generalized Reference

Table 2.26. Summary of a few calculi and languages

Part II

ASP Calculus

This part presents and defines the calculus named *ASP: Asynchronous Sequential Processes*.

ASP models an object-oriented language with asynchronous communications, futures, and sequential execution within each parallel process. ASP starts from a purely sequential and classical object calculus (**imp**ς-calculus) [3] and extends it with two parallel constructors: *Active* and *Serve*. *Active* turns a standard object into an active one, executing in parallel and serving requests in the order specified by the *Serve* operator.

Method calls on active objects are asynchronous: performing a method call on an active object adds a new entry to the pending request queue of the destination. The results of asynchronous calls are represented by *futures* until the corresponding response is returned. Automatic synchronization of processes comes from *wait-by-necessity* [49]: a wait automatically occurs upon a strict operation (e.g., a method call) on a future. This synchronization mechanism is natural because the real value of an object is *only needed* to perform a strict operation on it. A second form of synchronization exists in ASP: when serving a new request, an activity is blocked if no matching request is found in the request queue.

The passing of *futures* (results of asynchronous calls) between processes, both as method parameters and as method results, is an important feature of ASP. As futures can proliferate, a strategy must be specified to choose when and how a future value has to be updated. Therefore, in practice many strategies can be implemented (e.g., eager, lazy): the ASP calculus captures all the possible update strategies, and thus the demonstrated properties are valid for all of them. While communication is asynchronous, a given process is insensitive to the moment when a result comes back. This is a powerful characteristic of the convergence property exhibited in Part III.

Chapter 3 presents the underlying object calculus inspired by the **imp**ς-calculus. The syntax and informal semantics of ASP are provided in Chap. 4. A few standard examples are given in Chap. 5.

3

An Imperative Sequential Calculus

The ASP calculus starts from an imperative sequential object calculus à la Abadi and Cardelli. Only a few characteristics have been changed between the original **impς**-calculus and ASP sequential calculus.

- Because arguments passed to an active object method will play a particular role, a parameter is added to every method as in [123]: in addition to the "self" argument of the methods (noted x_j and representing the object on which the method is invoked – self), an argument representing a parameter object can be sent to the method (y_j in the syntax below).
- Method update is not included in the ASP calculus because we do not find it necessary, and it is possible to express updatable methods in ASP calculus anyway (e.g., updatable fields containing lambda expressions). Moreover, adding updatable methods would not raise any theoretical problems.[1] Section 10.3 (page 141) will further discuss the expression of method update in ASP.
- As in [79], during the reduction, *locations* (reference to objects in a store) can be part of terms in order to simplify the semantics. The locations should not appear in source terms.

3.1 Syntax

The abstract syntax of the ASP calculus is defined in Table 3.1:

- l_i are field names,
- m_j are method names,
- ς is a binder for method parameters,
- a location ι is an entry in the store defined below,

---

[1] But, in the parallel case, updating methods would unnaturally modify the meaning of requests that have already been sent but are not executed yet.

- in the following, l_i, $i \in 1..n$, range over fields names,[2] and m_j, $j \in 1..m$, over method names. In practice, there is one integer n and one integer m for each object, but as there is no ambiguity we will simply denote all these numbers by n and m.

$a, b \in L ::= x$	variable
$\quad \mid [l_i = b_i; m_j = \varsigma(x_j, y_j)a_j]_{j \in 1..m}^{i \in 1..n}$	object definition
$\quad \mid a.l_i$	field access
$\quad \mid a.l_i := b$	field update
$\quad \mid a.m_j(b)$	method call
$\quad \mid clone(a)$	superficial copy
$\quad \mid \iota$	location (not in source terms)

Table 3.1. Syntax of ASP sequential calculus

As an example, a point object could be defined in the following way:

$$Point \triangleq [x = 0, \, y = 0, \, color = [R = 0, G = 0, B = 0; print = \ldots];$$
$$getX = \varsigma(s,p)s.x, \, setX = \varsigma(s,p)s.x := p, getColor = \varsigma(s,p)s.color, \ldots]$$

An object without fields will be denoted by $[; m = \varsigma(z, x) \ldots]$.

let $x = a$ *in* b and sequence $a; b$ can be easily expressed in this sequential calculus and will be used in the following:

$$let \; x = a \; in \; b \triangleq [; m = \varsigma(z, x)b].m(a)$$

$$a; b \triangleq [; m = \varsigma(z, z')b].m(a)$$

Lambda expressions can be encoded as follows (strongly inspired by [3]):

$$\lambda x.b \triangleq [arg = [], val = \varsigma(x, y)b\{x \leftarrow x.arg\}]$$
$$(b \; a) \triangleq (clone(b).arg := a).val([])$$

A simple way of expressing (mutually) recursive *let* in the case where a and b are objects (e.g., lambda abstractions) is defined below:

$$\begin{aligned} let \; x = a \; and \; y = b \; in \; c \triangleq \; &let \; o = [x = [], y = []] \; in \\ &let \; x = a\{x \leftarrow o.x, y \leftarrow o.y\} \; in \\ &let \; y = b\{x \leftarrow o.x, y \leftarrow o.y\} \; in \\ &o.x := x; o.y := y; c \end{aligned}$$

This solution only works if mutual references are only accessed by methods of a and b, and a and b are not active,[3] but this simplified expression will be

---

[2] $i \in 1..n$ classically represents $i \in \mathbb{N} \cap [1, n]$.

[3] Another encoding will be provided for mutually dependent active objects in Chap. 5.

sufficient for the sequential terms used in the rest of this book. Note that this expression also allows to modify the value stored in x: $x := a'$.

The general definition of (mutually) recursive *let* is much more complex (see for example [36] for a typing analysis of recursive objects).

For example, we will neither use nor try to give a semantics to the following term:

$$let\ x\ =\ [f = y]\ and\ y = [g = x]\ in\ \ldots$$

Moreover, methods with zero and more than one argument are also easy to encode in the sequential calculus and will also be used in this study. For example, $foo = \varsigma(s)\ldots$ and $o.foo()$ will respectively denote the definition and the invocation of a method foo with zero argument.

Finally, we also use in the following integers and boolean and their associated operations. For example we will use $if\ldots then\ldots else\ldots$ statements, integer comparisons $(<, >, \ldots)$ and classical operations on integers and booleans $(+, not, \ldots)$. Integers and booleans can be either added to the sequential calculus or encoded into the sequential calculus (e.g., Church integers).

3.2 Semantic Structures

Let $locs(a)$ be the set of locations occurring in a and $fv(a)$ the set of variables occurring free in a. The *source terms* (initial expressions) are *closed* terms $(fv(a) = \emptyset)$ without any location $(locs(a) = \emptyset)$; such terms are also called *static terms*. Locations appear when objects are put in the store.

3.2.1 Substitution

The substitution of b by c in a is written: $a\{\!\!\{b \leftarrow c\}\!\!\}$. Substitutions are denoted by $\theta ::= \{\!\!\{b \leftarrow c\}\!\!\}$. Multiple substitutions are applied from left to right: $a\theta\theta' = (a\theta)\theta'$.

In method calls (INVOKE), substitution is applied in a classical way on bounded variables: formal parameter x is replaced by the location of the argument without replacing inside binders $\varsigma(x, z)$ or $\varsigma(z, x)$.

An *injective* substitution of some locations by other locations that do not appear in the involved term will also be called a *renaming*. A renaming is in fact an alphaconversion of locations. Renamings will be useful to define equivalence relations between terms.

3.2.2 Store

Reduced objects are objects with all fields reduced to a location:

$$o ::= [l_i = \iota_i; m_j = \varsigma(x_j, y_j)a_j]_{j \in 1..m}^{i \in 1..n}$$

A *store* σ is a finite map from locations to reduced objects:

$$\sigma ::= \{\iota_i \mapsto o_i\}$$

The domain of σ, $dom(\sigma)$, is the set of locations defined by σ.

Let $\sigma :: \sigma'$ append two stores with disjoint locations (*store append*). When the domains are not disjoint, $\sigma + \sigma'$ updates the values defined in σ' by those defined in σ (*store update*). It is defined on $dom(\sigma) \cup dom(\sigma')$ by:

$$(\sigma + \sigma')(\iota) = \sigma(\iota) \ \text{ if } \iota \in dom(\sigma)$$
$$\sigma'(\iota) \text{ otherwise}$$

The operator $+$ will be used, for example, to update the value associated to a location.

Note that $\sigma :: \sigma'$ is equal to $\sigma + \sigma'$ but specifies that $dom(\sigma) \cap dom(\sigma') = \emptyset$.

3.2.3 Configuration

Let a *configuration* (a, σ) be a pair (expression, store): the store σ associates values to some locations that can appear in a. $\vdash (a, \sigma)$ OK denotes a *well-formed configuration* (no free variable and σ defines every useful location):

Definition 3.1 (Well-formed sequential configuration)

$$\vdash (a, \sigma) \text{ OK} \Leftrightarrow \begin{cases} locs(a) \subseteq dom(\sigma) \wedge fv(a) = \emptyset \\ \forall \iota \in dom(\sigma), \ locs(\sigma(\iota)) \subseteq dom(\sigma) \ \wedge \ fv(\sigma(\iota)) = \emptyset \end{cases}$$

Let $\equiv$ be the equality between configurations modulo renaming of locations:

Definition 3.2 (Equivalence on sequential configurations)

$$(a, \sigma) \equiv (a', \sigma') \Leftrightarrow \exists \theta, \ (a\theta, \sigma\theta) = (a', \sigma')$$

3.3 Reduction

Table 3.2 defines a small-step, substitution-based operational semantics ($\rightarrow_S$) for the sequential calculus. It gives reduction rules for:

- object creation (STOREALLOC),
- field access (FIELD),
- method invocation (INVOKE),

- field update (UPDATE),
- and shallow clone (CLONE).

This semantics is very close to the one defined in [80]. Table 3.2 applies one rule on the point of reduction represented by the unique occurrence of • in the following *reduction contexts*:

$$\mathcal{R} ::= \bullet \mid [l_i = \iota_i, l_k = \mathcal{R}, l_{k'} = b_{k'}; m_j = \varsigma(x_j, y_j)a_j]_{j\in 1..m}^{i\in 1..k-1, k'\in k+1..n}$$
$$\mid \mathcal{R}.m_i \mid \mathcal{R}.m_j(b) \mid \iota.m_j(\mathcal{R}) \mid \mathcal{R}.l_i := b \mid \iota.l := \mathcal{R} \mid clone(\mathcal{R})$$

The reduction contexts allow us to specify the order of reductions inside the sequential terms. For example, to evaluate a field update, the object to be updated is first evaluated, then the new value of the field is also evaluated, and finally the field update is performed.

$\mathcal{R}[a]$ denotes the substitution inside a reduction context, that is to say $\mathcal{R}[a]$ is the term obtained by replacing the only hole of $\mathcal{R}$ by the sub-term a:

$$\mathcal{R}[a] = \mathcal{R}\{\!\!\{\bullet \leftarrow a\}\!\!\}$$

In $\mathcal{R}[a]$, a is the sub-term that has to be reduced by the next elementary sequential reduction, and $\mathcal{R}$ is the rest of the term (the context) that is neither useful nor modified by the next elementary reduction.

STOREALLOC:

$$\frac{\iota \notin dom(\sigma)}{(\mathcal{R}[o], \sigma) \rightarrow_s (\mathcal{R}[\iota], \{\iota \mapsto o\} :: \sigma)}$$

FIELD:

$$\frac{\sigma(\iota) = [l_i = \iota_i; m_j = \varsigma(x_j, y_j)a_j]_{j\in 1..m}^{i\in 1..n} \quad k \in 1..n}{(\mathcal{R}[\iota.l_k], \sigma) \rightarrow_s (\mathcal{R}[\iota_k], \sigma)}$$

INVOKE:

$$\frac{\sigma(\iota) = [l_i = \iota_i; m_j = \varsigma(x_j, y_j)a_j]_{j\in 1..m}^{i\in 1..n} \quad k \in 1..m}{(\mathcal{R}[\iota.m_k(\iota')], \sigma) \rightarrow_s (\mathcal{R}[a_k\{\!\!\{x_k \leftarrow \iota, y_k \leftarrow \iota'\}\!\!\}], \sigma)}$$

UPDATE:

$$\frac{\begin{array}{c}\sigma(\iota) = [l_i = \iota_i; m_j = \varsigma(x_j, y_j)a_j]_{j\in 1..m}^{i\in 1..n} \quad k \in 1..n \\ o' = [l_i = \iota_i, l_k = \iota', l_{k'} = \iota_{k'}; m_j = \varsigma(x_j, y_j)a_j]_{j\in 1..m}^{i\in 1..k-1, k'\in k+1..n}\end{array}}{(\mathcal{R}[\iota.l_k := \iota'], \sigma) \rightarrow_s (\mathcal{R}[\iota], \{\iota \rightarrow o'\} + \sigma)}$$

CLONE:

$$\frac{\iota' \notin dom(\sigma)}{(\mathcal{R}[clone(\iota)], \sigma) \rightarrow_s (\mathcal{R}[\iota'], \{\iota' \mapsto \sigma(\iota)\} :: \sigma)}$$

Table 3.2. Sequential reduction

3.4 Properties

Initial Configuration

To evaluate a source term a, we create an *initial configuration* $(a, \emptyset)$ containing this term and an empty store. Then, this configuration can be evaluated following the reduction $\rightarrow_S$.

Well-formedness

As a first correctness property, it is easy to show that reduction preserves well-formedness.

Property 3.3 (Well-formed sequential reduction)

$$\vdash (a, \sigma) \,\text{OK} \,\wedge\, (a, \sigma) \rightarrow_S (b, \sigma') \quad \Longrightarrow \quad \vdash (b, \sigma') \,\text{OK}$$

This property is proved by case analysis on the applied sequential rule and checking that every referenced location exists in the store. It is necessary to ensure that every accessed object exists in the store; for example, when evaluating $\iota.l_0$, Property 3.3 ensures that the accessed object referenced by ι exists in the store.

Sequential Determinism

A first result toward determinism is to ensure that a sequential reduction is deterministic. Indeed, the reduction contexts fully specify the order of reduction. Consequently, a sequential reduction is deterministic up to the choice of freshly allocated locations:

Property 3.4 (Determinism)

$$c \rightarrow_S d \,\wedge\, c \rightarrow_S d' \Rightarrow d \equiv d'$$

In fact, at most one reduction can be made on each configuration. The only choice is the name of locations created by the rules STOREALLOC and CLONE.

4

Asynchronous Sequential Processes

We introduce here the ASP calculus which is based on *activities*, each one including a single *active object*. After providing the main principles of ASP, we present two new syntactic constructs: *Active* and *Serve*. We conclude this chapter with a detailed informal semantics.

4.1 Principles

Each ASP object is either *active* or *passive*. There is one active object at the root of each activity. Activities execute instructions concurrently (potentially in parallel), and interact only through method calls. Method calls toward active objects are always *asynchronous*. Synchronization is due to *wait-by-necessity* on the result of an asynchronous method call (data-driven synchronization).

An *activity* is a single process (a single execution thread) associated with a set of objects put in a store. Among them one is *active* and every *request* (method call) sent to the activity is actually sent to this object. The activity serves/executes each of the received requests one after another. As such, an activity also contains the pending requests (requests that have been received and are still pending) and the responses to the requests for which the execution is finished (values of the results). *Passive* (non-active) objects are only referenced by objects belonging to the same activity, but any object can reference active objects: ASP activities do not share memory. Figure 4.1 shows an example of an objects topology in a configuration containing four activities.

The principles of asynchronous method calls is the following: when an object sends a request to an activity, it is stored in a request queue and a *future* is associated to this request. Such a request is called *pending*. Later on this request will be *served* (i.e., taken into the request queue in order to be evaluated); it becomes a *current request* . When the service is finished, a value is associated to the result of this request and the association between the future corresponding to this request and the calculated value is stored in

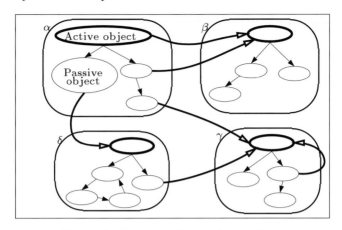

Fig. 4.1. Objects and activities topology

a *future values list*. Such requests are called *served requests*. Afterward, the distant reference to the future may be *updated* by the calculated value. A *future* represents the result of a method call to an active object that has not yet been returned.

The activation of a given object a ($Active(a, m)$) creates a new activity whose active object is a copy of a. If a method m is provided, it specifies the active object activity (a sort of main), else, by default, when $m = \emptyset$ the object activity is a FIFO service of requests. $Serve(M)$ performs a blocking service of requests targeted at a method belonging to M and received by the current active object.

For example, with the point object defined in Sect. 3.1, $Point.getColor()$ will perform a classical method call with synchronous semantics. In the term $let\ p = Active(Point, \emptyset)\ in\ let\ col = p.getColor()\ in\ p.setX(2); col.print()$, every method call to object p will be asynchronous. $p.setX(2)$ will trigger the execution of the method in the activity of p and continues the local evaluation in parallel. Execution will be blocked when one tries to perform a strict operation on the result of an asynchronous method before the end of its execution. Such blocking states are called *wait-by-necessity*. In the preceding example, $col.print()$ is a strict operation on the object col ; if the result of $getcolor$ has not been returned by the active object p, then the local activity is stuck until this result is replied.

Unlike many other concurrent calculi based on ς-calculus (e.g., Obliq [45]), in ASP, the requests are not executed by the process that performs the method call, but by the processes associated to the destination of the request.

4.2 New Syntax

In Table 4.1, we extend the sequential calculus by adding the possibility to create an active object and to serve a request.

$a, b \in L ::= \dots$		
	$\lvert Active(a, m_j)$	Activates object: deep copy + activity creation,
		m_j is the activity method or $\emptyset$ for FIFO service
	$\lvert Serve(M)$	Serves a request among a set of method labels,
	$\lvert a \Uparrow f, b$	a with continuation b (not in source terms)

where M is a set of method labels used to specify the request that has to be served:

$$M = m_{k_1}, \dots, m_{k_h}$$

Table 4.1. Syntax of ASP parallel primitives

A parallel configuration is a set of activities; each activity contains several fields that will be introduced informally in Sect. 4.3 just below, and formally defined in Chap. 6:

$$P, Q ::= \alpha[a_\alpha; \sigma_\alpha; \iota_\alpha; F_\alpha; R_\alpha; f_\alpha] \parallel \beta[\dots] \parallel \dots$$

To summarize, the whole syntax of the ASP source terms is given in Table 4.2.

$a, b \in L ::= x$	variable,
$\lvert [l_i = b_i; m_j = \varsigma(x_j, y_j)a_j]_{j \in 1..m}^{i \in 1..n}$	object definition
$\lvert a.l_i$	field access
$\lvert a.l_i := b$	field update
$\lvert a.m_j(b)$	method call
$\lvert clone(a)$	superficial copy
$\lvert Active(a, m_j)$	activity creation
$\lvert Serve(m_{k_j})^{j \in 1..h}$	service primitive

Table 4.2. Syntax of ASP calculus

4.3 Informal Semantics

In every activity α, a *current term* a_α represents the current computation. Every activity has its own *store* σ_α which contains one active and many passive objects. It also contains *pending requests* which store the pending method calls, and a *future list* which stores the result of finished requests.

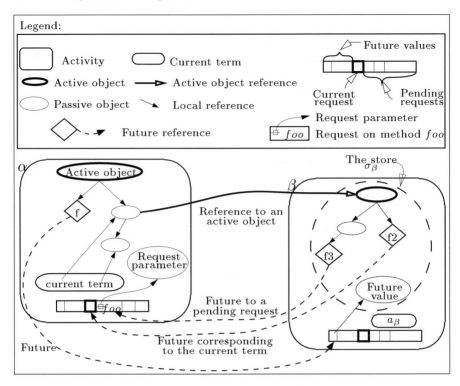

Fig. 4.2. Example of a parallel configuration

Figure 4.2 shows a representation of a configuration consisting of two activities (α and β). It contains three references to futures: one calculated (f), one current (f_2), and one pending (f_3). The active objects are bold ellipses; the futures references are diamonds; the futures values, the current future, and the pending requests are merged in the bottom rectangles: calculated future values are on the left, the current future is represented by a bold rectangle, and pending requests are on the right. The continuation does not appear in the diagrams.

4.3.1 Activities

The *Active* operator ($Active(a, m_j)$) creates a new activity α with the object a at its root. The object a is copied as well as all its dependencies (deep copy) in the new activity, to prevent distant references to passive objects. The second argument of the *Active* operator is the name of a method which will be called as soon as the object is activated. This method is called the *service method* as it usually specifies the order of requests that the activity should serve. If no service method is specified, a *FIFO* service will be performed: the requests will be served in the order they arrived in the activity. Note that in Fig. 4.2, in case of a FIFO service, the current request (bold square) progresses from left to right in the queue. When the service method terminates, no more requests are treated, and there is no more intrinsic activity. The activity conceptually ends.

The remote references to the active object of activity α will be denoted by $AO(\alpha)$. $AO(\alpha)$ acts as a proxy for the active object of activity α.

4.3.2 Requests

The communications between activities are due to method calls on active objects and returns of corresponding results. A method call on an active object ($Active(o, \emptyset).foo()$) consists in atomically adding an entry to the *pending requests* of the callee, and associating a *future* (an identifier representing the result of the request) to the response. From a practical point of view, this atomicity is guaranteed by a *rendezvous* mechanism (the request sender waits for an acknowledgment before continuing its execution). The arguments of requests and the values of futures are deeply copied when they are transmitted between activities; this prevents sharing, i.e., distant reference to passive objects. Active objects are transmitted with a reference semantics.

4.3.3 Futures

A *future* is a unique identifier representing the reply to a request between the moment when the request is sent and put in a queue, and the moment when the result of the request is sent and updated. A *future update* consists in replacing the reference to the future by a copy of the future value. Of course, a deep copy occurs, again to prevent sharing.

Futures are generalized references that can be manipulated classically while no strict operation is performed on the object they represent. In Fig. 4.2, the futures f_2 and f_3 denote pointers to not yet computed requests while f is a future pointing to a value already computed by the activity β.

An operation on an object is *strict* if it needs to access the content of the object: the only strict operations are field and method access, field update, and clone. For example, transmitting an object as a method parameter is not a strict operation, including in a request.

A wait-by-necessity occurs when one tries to perform a strict operation on a future. This wait-by-necessity can only be released by *updating* the future.

The fact that futures are first-class entities is sometimes called "automatic continuation." We avoid using this terminology in this book as it may be confusing.

4.3.4 Serving Requests

The primitive *Serve* can appear at any point in source code. Its execution stops the current activity until a matching request is found in the pending requests. A *matching request* is a request on one of the method labels specified as parameter of the *Serve* primitive. For semantics specification reasons, we introduced the operator ⇑ which allows us to save the continuation of the request we are currently serving while we serve another one.

Note that with such a mechanism there can be several requests being served at the same time. More precisely, an activity always serves at most one request if *Serve* operations are only performed by the activity method or the method recursively called by this method, because in that case, no $Serve(M)$ is performed while a request is being served.

When the execution of a request is finished, the corresponding future is associated to the newly calculated value (*future value*). Then, the execution continues by restoring the stored continuation. The term that had served the finished request continues its execution (it becomes the current term). The *future list* maps futures to their values within the activities that computed them. As a future value can contain references to other futures, a future value is called *partial* if its dependencies contain futures references.

Note that a field access on an active object is forbidden (it would nearly always be non-deterministic) and an activity trying to access a field of an active object is irreversibly stuck (like an access to a non-existing field).

However, one can syntactically transform a field access (field update) into a call to a getter method (setter method). Provided such a call is treated as a normal request, inserted in the pending queue and normally served, this allows one to deal adequately with remote fields.

5

A Few Examples

This chapter presents four examples illustrating the ASP calculus. First, Sect. 5.1 presents a simple binary tree. Then, Sects. 5.2 and 5.4 present two examples: a sieve of Eratosthenes and a Fibonacci number computation, inspired by process networks. Section 5.3 gives a brief idea of the possible translations from process networks to ASP. Finally, Sect. 5.5 outlines how a more complex program (a bank account server) could be implemented in ASP.

Lambda expressions, integers and comparisons (Church integers, for example), booleans and conditional expressions, and methods with many parameters can be expressed in ASP as shown in Sect. 3.1. The definition of classes (*new* method etc.) has already been proposed by Abadi and Cardelli in the **impς**-calculus [3].

Some examples below use mutually recursive definitions of activities which can be expressed as follows:

$$
\begin{array}{ll}
let\ x = Active(a, s_1) & \triangleq let\ srv\ =\ Active([x = [], y = []; \\
and\ y = Active(b, s_2)\ in\ c & \qquad getX = \varsigma(s)s.x, \\
& \qquad getY = \varsigma(s)s.y, \\
& \qquad setX = \varsigma(s, x, y)(s.x := Active(a, s_1); s.x), \\
& \qquad setY = \varsigma(s, x, y)(s.y := Active(b, s_2); s.y), \\
& \qquad service = \varsigma(s)Serve(setX); Serve(setY); \\
& \qquad\qquad\qquad Repeat(Serve(getX); Serve(getY)) \\
& \qquad], service) \\
& \quad in \\
& \quad [; m = \varsigma(s, x, y)c].m(\\
& \qquad\qquad srv.setX(srv.getX(), srv.getY()), \\
& \qquad\qquad srv.setY(srv.getX(), srv.getY()))
\end{array}
$$

The principle is to use futures to mutually set references between the two active objects. Of course strict operations must not be done on the mutually recursive variables (here x and y) during initialization of objects a and b. For example, if a and b are only objects, x and y must not be accessed strictly in the fields of these objects. Indeed such accesses would always lead to a deadlock.

5.1 Binary Tree

Figure 5.1 shows an example of a simple parallel binary tree where each object can be turned into an active object. The binary tree has two methods: *add* and *search*.

add stores a new key at the right place and creates two empty objects. Note that in the parallel case, objects are activated as soon as they are created.

search searches for a key in the tree and returns the value associated with it or an empty object if the key is not found.

new is the method invoked to create a new object.

This example is parameterized by a factory able to create sequential (sequential binary tree) or active (parallel binary tree) objects.

$BT \triangleq [new = \varsigma(c)[empty = true, left = [], right = [], key = [], value = [],$
$\qquad\qquad search = \varsigma(s, k)(c.search\ s\ k), add = \varsigma(s, k, v)(c.add\ s\ k\ v)],$
$\qquad search = \varsigma(c)\lambda s\ k.if\ (s.empty)\ then\ []$
$\qquad\qquad\qquad\qquad else\ if\ (s.key == k)\ then\ s.value$
$\qquad\qquad\qquad\qquad else\ if\ (s.key > k)\ then\ s.left.search(k)$
$\qquad\qquad\qquad\qquad else\ s.right.search(k),$
$\qquad add = \varsigma(c)\lambda s\ k\ v.if\ (s.empty)\ then(s.right := Factory(s);$
$\qquad\qquad\qquad\qquad\qquad\qquad s.left := Factory(s); s.value := v;$
$\qquad\qquad\qquad\qquad\qquad\qquad s.key := k; s.empty := false;\ s)$
$\qquad\qquad\qquad else\ if\ (s.key > k)\ then\ s.left.add(k, v)$
$\qquad\qquad\qquad else\ if\ (s.key < k)\ then\ s.right.add(k, v)$
$\qquad\qquad\qquad else\ s.value := v;\ s\qquad]$
where: $Factory(s) \triangleq s.new$ in the sequential case and
$\qquad Factory(s) \triangleq Active(s.new, \emptyset)$ for the concurrent binary tree.

Fig. 5.1. Example: a binary tree

In the case of the parallel factory, the following term:

$let\ tree = (BT.new).add(3, 4).add(2, 3).add(5, 6).add(7, 8)in$
$\qquad [a = tree.search(5), b = tree.search(3)].b := tree.search(7)$

creates a binary tree, puts in parallel four values in it, and then searches three in parallel. The third value is used to modify the field b. Finally, it always reduces to $[a = 6, b = 8]$.

Note that as soon as a request is delegated to another active object, a new one can be handled. Moreover, when the root of the tree is the only object reachable and from only one activity, the result of all parallel calls is deterministic. Determinism properties will be detailed in Chap. 8.

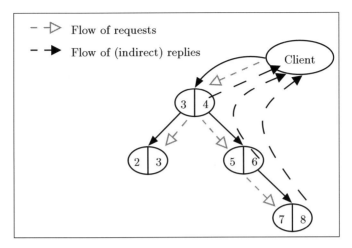

Fig. 5.2. Topology and communications in the parallel binary tree

Figure 5.2 illustrates the parallel binary tree and the flow of requests and replies that occur for the example term given above.

5.2 Distributed Sieve of Eratosthenes

Let us translate in ASP the distributed sieve of Eratosthenes described in [100] and shown in Fig. 2.5, page 32.

In [100], the sieve was performed by several processes linked by channels, a process for each prime number n. The process associated with the prime number n receives numbers and forwards only the ones that are not divisible by n. We tried to apply the same methodology and create one activity by prime number. We first consider a "pull" version: the process that performs a *get* on a channel becomes a request sending, and each *put* on the same channel consists in serving this request. The corresponding request is called *get* in our example (see Fig. 5.4). *Repeat* performs an infinite loop and will be defined in Sect.6.2 (page 89). Figure 5.3 defines a "pull" sieve of Eratosthenes in ASP.

The *Integer* object generates all integers. There is one *Sieve* object for each prime number n. In order to reply to the *get* request, the *Sieve* object n takes the next integer returned by its parent's *get* request and forwards it provided it is not divisible by n, or else it asks its parent for another number. The *Sift* object represents the main object (*print(n)* denotes the output of integer n). When a new prime is found, a new *Sieve* in inserted between the *Sift* and the former last *Sieve*.

$let \ Integer = Active([n = 1; get = \varsigma(s)(s.n := s.n + 1; s.n)], \emptyset) \ in$
$let \ Sieve = [parent = [], prime = 0; init = \varsigma(s, par)s.parent := par,$
$\qquad get = \varsigma(s)let \ n = parent.get() \ in$
$\qquad\qquad if(n \ \text{MOD} \ s.prime \neq 0) \ then \ n \ else \ s.get()] \ in$
$let \ Sift = [source = Integer;$
$\qquad act = \varsigma(s)Repeat(let \ n = s.source.get() \ in$
$\qquad\qquad print(n); Sieve.prime := n;$
$\qquad\qquad s.source := Active(clone(Sieve.init(s.source)), \emptyset))] \ in$
$Active(Sift, act)$

Fig. 5.3. Example: sieve of Eratosthenes (pull)

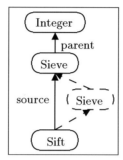

Fig. 5.4. Topology of sieve of Eratosthenes (pull)

Another Formulation

In the preceding example, every object always replies to a *get* request. In other words, a new possible prime number is pulled by a process when it needs it. Thus, the program will be evaluated sequentially and the pipelining that could be performed on the example of Kahn and MacQueen cannot occur here. The following implementation of the sieve allows such pipelining and parallelism (see the topology in Fig. 5.6). The program in Fig. 5.5 defines such a "push" sieve of Eratosthenes in ASP. In this formulation, each *Sieve* object pushes each potential prime number in the request queue of the next sieve.

With this formulation, every *Sieve* object keeps a reference on the *Display* object. Some conflicts could occur between the sending of results to the display. Here, determinism is ensured by the fact that as soon as a new *Sieve* is created, the preceding one somewhat "promises" not to use its reference to *Display* any more. But the fact that this reference will no longerbe used could only be verified by a (complex) control flow analysis.

$let \; Sieve = [N = 0, prime = 0; next = []; put = \varsigma(s, n)s.N := n,$
$\quad act = \varsigma(s)Serve(put); Display.put(s.N);$
$\qquad\qquad s.prime := s.N; s.next := Active(s, act);$
$\qquad\qquad Repeat(Serve(put));$
$\qquad\qquad if \; (s.N \; \textsc{mod} \; s.prime \neq 0) \; then \; s.next.put(s.N))] \; in$
$let \; Integer = [n = 1; first = Active(Sieve, act);$
$\qquad act = \varsigma(s)Repeat(s.n := s.n + 1; s.first.put(s.n))] \; in$
$\quad Active(Integer, act)$
where $Display$ is an object collecting and printing the prime numbers.

Fig. 5.5. Example: sieve of Eratosthenes (push)

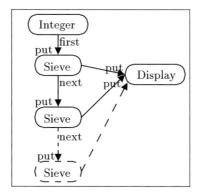

Fig. 5.6. Topology of sieve of Eratosthenes (push)

5.3 From Process Networks to ASP

These two encodings of the sieve of Eratosthenes suggest the translation
sketched in Fig. 5.7.

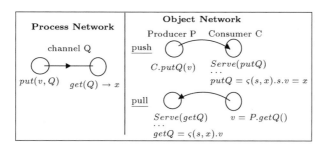

Fig. 5.7. Process Network vs. object network

The translation from a process network to an ASP term is performed either
by a *push* strategy allowing pipelining (we call a method *put* on the destination

of the channel), or by a *pull* strategy (the destination calls a method *get* on the source of the channel). Section 21.1.3 further details the translation and comparisons between ASP and Process Networks.

5.4 Example: Fibonacci Numbers

Consider the Process Network that computes the Fibonacci numbers in [129]. Let us write an equivalent program in ASP. Figure 5.8 describes the set up of processes that computes the Fibonacci numbers, and Fig. 5.9 shows the corresponding program.

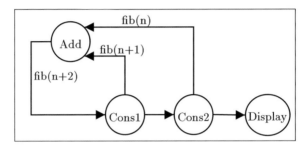

Fig. 5.8. Fibonacci number processes

$$
\begin{aligned}
&let\ Add = Active([n1 = 0, n2 = 0; \\
&\qquad\qquad service = \varsigma(s) \\
&\qquad\qquad\qquad Repeat(Serve(set1); Serve(set2); Cons1.snd(s.n1 + s.n2)), \\
&\qquad\qquad set1 = \varsigma(s, n)s.n1 := n, set2 = \varsigma(s, n)s.n2 := n], service) \\
&and\ Cons1 = Active(\\
&\qquad\qquad [; service = \varsigma(s)\,(Add.set1(1); Cons2.snd(1); Repeat(Serve(snd))) \\
&\qquad\qquad snd = \varsigma(s, n)(Add.set1(n); Cons2.snd(n))], service) \\
&and\ Cons2 = Active(\\
&\qquad\qquad [; service = \varsigma(s)\,(Add.set2(0); Display.snd(0); Repeat(Serve(snd))) \\
&\qquad\qquad snd = \varsigma(s, n)(Add.set2(n); Display.snd(n))], service)
\end{aligned}
$$

Fig. 5.9. Example: Fibonacci numbers

Display receives the list of Fibonacci numbers. Initialization consists in sending 0 ($fib(0)$) and 1 ($fib(1)$) from *Cons2* and *Cons1* respectively. Contrary to the other examples, this program is rather synchronous because there is at most two pending requests in each activity (except the *Display*).

It is a good example of a program based on an asynchronous model that somehow behaves in a synchronous manner, still exhibiting asynchronous communications and parallelism. Indeed, such a program is deterministic.

5.5 A Bank Account Server

Let us imagine a bank application server. Figure 5.10 gives the set up of the different objects, this application should provide the following characteristics:

- A client activity sends a request to a unique *central service* to get a statement of an account.
- The central service dispatches the request to the appropriate activity corresponding to the regional database of the client.
- Further, based on the client device type (browser, PDA, etc.) the central service requests the formatting of the data (the statement) from the appropriate presentation server. Some advertising could be added.
- The final result has to be sent to the client.

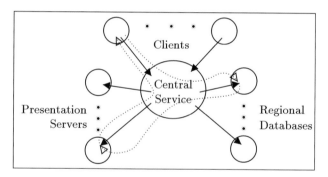

Fig. 5.10. Topology of a bank application

Figure 5.11 defines the central service object. The client calls the *getStatement* request on the central service, which receives the account number and device type of the client. The central service asks for the statement from the appropriate regional database and sends it to the right presentation server before returning the result to the client as a reply to its initial request.

The other involved objects are not detailed here. The regional databases have to be able to serve the request *getStatement(accountNumber)*. The presentation servers will serve *getPresentation(statement)* requests. The client will obtain the statement of his account by calling *CentralServer.getAccount(ID, device)* where *ID* is its account number and *device* the kind of device it is using.

$$
\begin{array}{l}
let\ CentralService\ =\ [\ldots; \\
\quad regionalDatabase = \varsigma(s, ID)\ldots, \\
\quad presentationServer = \varsigma(s, device)\ \ldots, \\
\quad act = \varsigma(s, \_)Repeat(Serve(getStatement)), \\
\quad getStatement = \varsigma(self, ID, device) \\
\qquad let\ state = (self.regionalDatabase(ID)) \\
\qquad\qquad\qquad\qquad\qquad\qquad .getStatement(ID) \\
\quad in\quad (self.presentationServer(device)) \\
\qquad\qquad\qquad\qquad\qquad .getPresentation(state)\ \ ]
\end{array}
$$

Fig. 5.11. Example: bank account server

Note that at the end of the *getStatement* evaluation, the result sent to the client might contain several futures coming from regional database and presentation server; in other words, clients can obtain a *partial result*. Thus, by writing a classical object-oriented program, one obtains a parallel and somewhat lazy execution: remaining parts of the result will be automatically brought and updated in the client activity as they are calculated.

Part III

Semantics and Properties

This part is first dedicated to the formal definition of ASP: Chap. 6 defines ASP small step parallel reduction composed of six reduction rules. ASP properties are then presented in the following three chapters: basic properties (Chap. 7), confluence (Chap. 8), and determinacy (Chap. 9).

The results derived in this part can be summarized by the following simple assertions:

- *The execution is insensitive to the moment when futures are updated.*
- *The execution is only characterized by the ordered list of activities that have sent requests to a given activity.*
- Several approximations can be performed in order to characterize programs behaving deterministically. *For example, every program communicating over a tree behaves deterministically.*

Our objective in this book is not necessarily to focus only on deterministic calculi but more generally to provide a minimal characterization of execution. Even if deterministic behavior is not always needed, we think that a calculus with a well-identified source of non-determinism (concurrency between activities sending requests to the same destination) and consequently a very small characterization of execution (ordered list of identifiers of request senders in each activity) is a key characteristic of a practical and powerful distributed calculus.

6

Parallel Semantics

This chapter describes the formal semantics of ASP. First, Sect. 6.1 defines semantic structures and extends the sequential semantic structures defined in Sect. 3.2. Then, in Sect. 6.2 the parallel reduction rules of ASP are presented in Table 6.2 and each rule is explained. ASP parallel reduction uses the sequential rules of Table 3.2 to define the local reduction occurring inside each activity. Finally, Sect. 6.3 extends the sequential well-formedness property.

6.1 Structure of Parallel Activities

In the following, there are three distinct name spaces allocated dynamically: activities ($\alpha, \beta \in Act$), locations (ι), and futures (f_i). Locations are local to an activity: two occurrence of the same location will correspond to the same object only if these references belong to the same activity.[1] One also have three statically defined name spaces for fields names, method names, and variables.

A future is characterized by its identifier f_i, the source activity α, and the destination activity β of the corresponding request (the activity that receives and handles the request): ($f_i^{\alpha \to \beta}$). The identifier f_i must be chosen in order to ensure that $f_i^{\alpha \to \beta}$ is unique for the whole configuration. For example, one can choose to associate the identifier f_i to the ith request received by β,[2] or equivalently to the ith request sent by α.

Each activity $\alpha[a; \sigma; \iota; F; R; f]$ is characterized by:

- a *current term* ($a = b \Uparrow f_i^{\gamma \to \alpha}, b'$) to be reduced: a contains the terms corresponding to the different requests being treated separated by $\Uparrow$. The left part b is the term currently evaluated, the right one ($f_i^{\gamma \to \alpha}, b'$) is

---

[1] The locality of locations ensures the absence of sharing in ASP.

[2] Thus ensuring that f_i is locally unique in the destination activity.

the continuation: the future and term corresponding to a request that has been stopped before the end of its execution (because of a *Serve* primitive evaluated inside another service). Of course, b' can also contain continuations.

- a *store* (σ) that contains all the objects of the activity α. It can be considered as the memory associated to the activity α.
- an *active object location*: ι is the location of the active object of activity α; thus $\sigma(\iota)$ is the active object of activity α.
- *future values*: $F = \{f_i^{\gamma \to \alpha} \mapsto \iota\}$ is a list associating, for each served request, the corresponding future $f_i^{\gamma \to \alpha}$ and the location ι where the result of the request (also called future value) is stored.
- *pending requests*: $R = \{[m_j; \iota; f_i^{\gamma \to \alpha}]\}$, a list of pending requests. A request can be seen as the "reification" of a method call [150].
  Each request $r ::= [m_j; \iota; f_i^{\alpha \to \beta}]$ consists of:
  - the name of the *target method* m_j (invoked method),
  - the location of the *argument* passed to the request ι,
  - the *future* identifier which will be associated to the result $f_i^{\alpha \to \beta}$.
- a *current future*: $f = f_i^{\gamma \to \alpha}$, the future associated with the request currently served. To simplify notations, f will denote any future ($f ::= f_i^{\gamma \to \alpha}$).

Empty parts of activities will be denoted by $\emptyset$. $\emptyset$ designates an empty list (future values or pending requests), or an empty current future (when no request is currently treated).

A parallel configuration is a set of activities:

$$P, Q ::= \alpha[a; \sigma; \iota; F; R; f] \parallel \beta[a'; \sigma'; \iota'; F'; R'; f'] \parallel \cdots$$

Configurations are identified modulo the reordering of activities.

Adding a request r at the end of the pending requests (R) will be denoted by $R :: r$, and taking the first request (r) at the beginning of the pending requests by $r :: R$. Similarly, $F :: \{f_i \mapsto \iota\}$ adds a new future association to the future values.

In the store, one has either objects or global references:

$$o ::= [l_i = \iota_i; m_j = \varsigma(x_j, y_j)a_j]_{j \in 1..m}^{i \in 1..n} \quad \text{reduced object}$$
$$| AO(\alpha) \qquad\qquad\qquad\qquad \text{active object reference}$$
$$| fut(f_i^{\alpha \to \beta}) \qquad\qquad\qquad \text{future reference}$$

$fut(f_i^{\alpha \to \beta})$ references the future $f_i^{\alpha \to \beta}$ corresponding to a request from activity α to activity β. $AO(\alpha)$ references the active object in activity α. $AO(\alpha)$ and $fut(f_i^{\alpha \to \beta})$ act as "proxies" to a remote activity or to a future object. As they are valid across activities, references to active objects and futures are called *generalized references*.

From a practical point of view, when a reference to a future is encountered in an activity, the activity that may know the corresponding value can easily be contacted because it is encoded in the future reference (β in $f_i^{\alpha \to \beta}$). Of course, the same holds for activities (α in $AO(\alpha)$).

6.2 Parallel Reduction

The terms below define the infinite loop *Repeat* and the FIFO service that will be used when no service method is specified. A *FifoService* service method serves the requests in the order they arrived:

$$Repeat(a) \triangleq [repeat = \varsigma(x)a; x.repeat()].repeat()$$
$$FifoService \triangleq Repeat(Serve(\mathcal{M}))$$

where $\mathcal{M}$ is the set of all method labels. Note that $\mathcal{M}$ only needs to contain all the method labels of the concerned (active) object.

Object activation and terms containing a continuation are added to the reduction contexts as follows:

$$\mathcal{R} ::= \dots \mid Active(\mathcal{R}, m_j) \mid \mathcal{R} \Uparrow f, a$$

These reduction contexts extend the ones of Sect. 3.3 and allow us to perform reduction inside *Active* primitives and continuation terms. In the case of continuation, the reduction context specifies that only the left part of a continuation term can be reduced. The right part will only be accessible after an ENDSERVICE rule.

For specifying complex service policies one may need a *Repeat . . . Until . . .* statement:

$$Repeat\ a\ Until\ b \triangleq [repeat = \varsigma(x)a; if\ (not(b))\ then\ x.repeat()].repeat()$$

6.2.1 More Operations on Store

Before defining the parallel reduction rules, we need to define three more operations on stores:

- deep copy: $copy(\iota, \sigma)$,
- merge: $Merge(\iota, \sigma, \sigma')$,
- copy and merge: $Copy\&Merge(\sigma, \iota\ ;\ \sigma', \iota')$.

The last one combines the two first and will be used to "send" objects from one activity to another.

Deep Copy

The operator $copy(\iota, \sigma)$ creates a store containing the deep copy of $\sigma(\iota)$. The deep copy is the smallest store satisfying the rules of Table 6.1. It is the part of the store σ that contains the definition of ι ($\sigma(\iota)$) and recursively all objects referenced by ι. The deep copy stops when a generalized reference is encountered. In that case, the new store contains the generalized reference itself. In Table 6.1, the first two rules specify which locations should be present in the created store, and the last one means that the codomain is similar in both the copied and the original store.

$$\iota \in dom(copy(\iota, \sigma))$$

$$\iota' \in dom(copy(\iota, \sigma)) \Rightarrow locs(\sigma(\iota')) \subseteq dom(copy(\iota, \sigma))$$

$$\iota' \in dom(copy(\iota, \sigma)) \Rightarrow copy(\iota, \sigma)(\iota') = \sigma(\iota')$$

Table 6.1. Deep copy

A more operational definition would consist in marking the location ι at the root of the copy and recursively all the locations that are referenced by marked locations (all locations contained in $\sigma(\iota')$ if ι' is marked). When a fix-point is reached, $copy(\iota, \sigma)$ is the part of store defining marked locations.

The part of store defined by a deep copy is independent: it references only locations defined in $copy(\iota, \sigma)$ (and generalized references). In other words, if a store is well-formed and contains a location then the deep copy starting at this location is well-formed as well:

$$\vdash (\iota, \sigma) \text{ OK} \Rightarrow \vdash (\iota, copy(\iota, \sigma)) \text{ OK}$$

Consequently, a deep copy can be safely sent between activities without risk of transgressing the absence of sharing property (the only shared references are generalized references: futures and active objects).

Figure 6.1 shows an activity α and the deep copy of a location ι. The deep copy is inside the dotted area.

Merge

Let us define a function $Merge$ which merges two stores. It creates a new store, independently merging σ and σ' except for ι which is taken from σ':

$$Merge(\iota, \sigma, \sigma') = \sigma'\theta + \sigma$$
$$\text{where } \theta = \{\!\!\{ \iota' \leftarrow \iota'' \mid \iota' \in dom(\sigma') \cap dom(\sigma) \backslash \{\iota\}, \iota'' \text{ fresh} \}\!\!\}$$

This function will be useful for appending a part of store σ' at a given location ι of another store σ avoiding collision with the existing store σ.

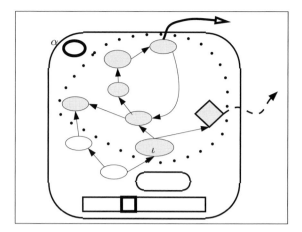

Fig. 6.1. Example of a deep copy: $copy(\iota, \sigma_\alpha)$

Copy and merge

The following operator deeply copies the part of σ starting at location ι in to σ' under the location ι' avoiding collisions (only ι' can be updated):

Definition 6.1 (Copy and merge)

$$Copy\&Merge(\sigma, \iota \; ; \; \sigma', \iota') \triangleq Merge(\iota', \sigma', \; copy(\iota, \sigma)\{\iota \leftarrow \iota'\})$$

The following property is a consequence of the preceding definitions. It states that σ' is unchanged by $Copy\&Merge(\sigma, \iota'' \; ; \; \sigma', \iota')$ (except ι', which can be updated):

Property 6.2 (Copy and merge)

$$\iota \in dom(\sigma') \wedge \iota \neq \iota' \Rightarrow \sigma'(\iota) = Copy\&Merge(\sigma, \iota'' \; ; \; \sigma', \iota')(\iota)$$

6.2.2 Reduction Rules

Table 6.2 describes the reduction rules corresponding to a small-step semantics of the ASP calculus. The grayed values are unchanged and unused by reduction rules. A description of these rules is given in the following:

LOCAL

Inside each activity, a local reduction can occur following the rules of Table 3.2 ($\rightarrow_S$). Note that sequential rules concerning the strict operations, i.e., FIELD, INVOKE, UPDATE, CLONE[3] are stuck when the target location is a generalized

---

[3] The cloning of a future is considered as a strict operation for deterministic behavior reasons (cf. Sect.A.6 page 286 for more details).

LOCAL:

$$\frac{(a,\sigma) \to_S (a',\sigma') \qquad \to_S \text{ does not clone a future}}{\alpha[a;\sigma;\iota;F;R;f] \parallel P \longrightarrow \alpha[a';\sigma';\iota;F;R;f] \parallel P}$$

NEWACT:

$$\frac{\gamma \text{ fresh activity} \quad \iota' \notin dom(\sigma) \quad \sigma' = \{\iota' \mapsto AO(\gamma)\} :: \sigma}{\sigma_\gamma = copy(\iota'',\sigma) \quad Service = (\text{if } m_j = \emptyset \text{ then } FifoService \text{ else } \iota''.m_j())}$$

$$\alpha[\mathcal{R}[Active(\iota'',m_j)]];\sigma;\iota;F;R;f] \parallel P \longrightarrow$$
$$\alpha[\mathcal{R}[\iota'];\sigma';\iota;F;R;f] \parallel \gamma[Service;\sigma_\gamma;\iota'';\emptyset;\emptyset;\emptyset] \parallel P$$

REQUEST:

$$\frac{\sigma_\alpha(\iota) = AO(\beta) \quad \iota'' \notin dom(\sigma_\beta) \quad f_i^{\alpha \to \beta} \text{ new future} \quad \iota_f \notin dom(\sigma_\alpha)}{\sigma'_\beta = Copy\&Merge(\sigma_\alpha,\iota' \; ; \; \sigma_\beta,\iota'') \quad \sigma'_\alpha = \{\iota_f \mapsto fut(f_i^{\alpha \to \beta})\} :: \sigma_\alpha}$$

$$\alpha[\mathcal{R}[\iota.m_j(\iota')];\sigma_\alpha;\iota_\alpha;F_\alpha;R_\alpha;f_\alpha] \parallel \beta[a_\beta;\sigma_\beta;\iota_\beta;F_\beta;R_\beta;f_\beta] \parallel P \longrightarrow$$
$$\alpha[\mathcal{R}[\iota_f];\sigma'_\alpha;\iota_\alpha;F_\alpha;R_\alpha;f_\alpha] \parallel \beta[a_\beta;\sigma'_\beta;\iota_\beta;F_\beta;R_\beta :: [m_j;\iota'';f_i^{\alpha \to \beta}];f_\beta] \parallel P$$

SERVE:

$$\frac{R = R' :: [m_j;\iota_r;f'] :: R'' \quad m_j \in M \quad \forall m \in M, m \notin R'}{\alpha[\mathcal{R}[Serve(M)];\sigma;\iota;F;R;f] \parallel P \longrightarrow \alpha[\iota.m_j(\iota_r) \Uparrow f, \mathcal{R}[[]];\sigma;\iota;F;R' :: R'';f'] \parallel P}$$

ENDSERVICE:

$$\frac{\iota' \notin dom(\sigma) \quad F' = F :: \{f \mapsto \iota'\} \quad \sigma' = Copy\&Merge(\sigma,\iota \; ; \; \sigma,\iota')}{\alpha[\iota \Uparrow (f',a);\sigma;\iota;F;R;f] \parallel P \longrightarrow \alpha[a;\sigma';\iota;F';R;f'] \parallel P}$$

REPLY:

$$\frac{\sigma_\alpha(\iota) = fut(f_i^{\gamma \to \beta}) \quad F_\beta(f_i^{\gamma \to \beta}) = \iota_f \quad \sigma'_\alpha = Copy\&Merge(\sigma_\beta,\iota_f \; ; \; \sigma_\alpha,\iota)}{\alpha[a_\alpha;\sigma_\alpha;\iota_\alpha;F_\alpha;R_\alpha;f_\alpha] \parallel \beta[a_\beta;\sigma_\beta;\iota_\beta;F_\beta;R_\beta;f_\beta] \parallel P \longrightarrow}$$
$$\alpha[a_\alpha;\sigma'_\alpha;\iota_\alpha;F_\alpha;R_\alpha;f_\alpha] \parallel \beta[a_\beta;\sigma_\beta;\iota_\beta;F_\beta;R_\beta;f_\beta] \parallel P$$

Table 6.2. Parallel reduction (used or modified values are non-gray)

reference. Only REQUEST allows one to invoke an active object method, and REPLY may transform a future reference into a real object (ending a wait-by-necessity)[4].

NEWACT

This rule activates an object. A new activity γ is created containing the deep copy of the object $\sigma(\iota)$, an empty pending requests queue, and no future values. A generalized reference to the created activity $AO(\gamma)$ is stored in the source activity α. The other references to ι in α are unchanged (still pointing

---

[4] To be precise, an update can also transform a future reference into another future reference.

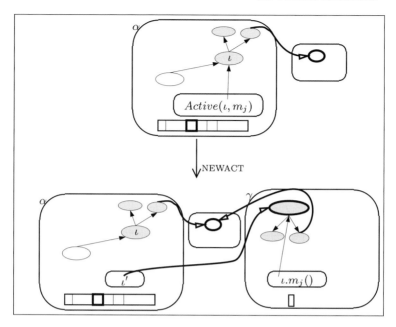

Fig. 6.2. NEWACT rule

to a passive object) because it seems more intuitive to us and it follows the ProActive behavior.

m_j specifies the service method (the first method executed). The service method has no argument and should perform *Serve* instructions. If no method m_j is specified, a FIFO service is performed as a default behavior. When the execution of the service method is finished, the activity does not execute any more operations. Afterward, it is only useful for updating the values of futures which have already been calculated; such an activity only performs REPLY operations.

Note that in $Active(Active(\iota, m_j), \emptyset)$, the left activity is reduced in two steps into a reference to an activity $\gamma \{\iota'' \mapsto AO(\gamma)\}$, and γ acts as a forwarder for the activity β, first created by α (see Fig. 6.3):

$$Active(Active(\iota, m_j), \emptyset) \longrightarrow \begin{array}{c} Active(\iota', \emptyset) \\ \sigma_\alpha(\iota') = AO(\beta) \end{array} \longrightarrow \begin{array}{c} \iota'' \\ \sigma_\gamma(\iota') = \sigma_\alpha(\iota') = AO(\beta) \\ \sigma_\alpha(\iota'') = AO(\gamma) \end{array}$$

where $\sigma_\alpha(\iota')$ is no longer reachable at the end of reduction.

REQUEST

This rule sends a new request from the activity α to the activity β (Fig. 6.4). A new future $f_i^{\alpha \to \beta}$ is created to represent the result of the request; a reference to this future is stored in α. A request containing the name of the method,

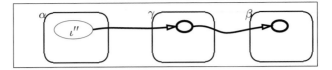

Fig. 6.3. A simple forwarder

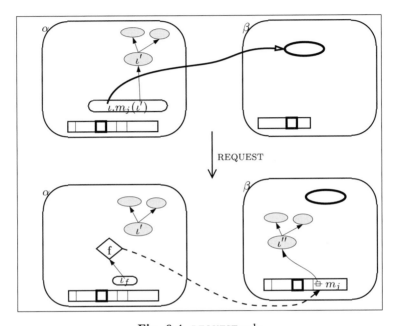

Fig. 6.4. REQUEST rule

the location of a deep copy of the argument (which is stored in σ_β), and the associated future $[m_j; \iota''; f_i^{\alpha \to \beta}]$ is added to the pending requests R_β.

The REQUEST rule does not take into account the particular case when only one activity is involved: $\alpha = \beta$. This case corresponds to an asynchronous method call on the same activity (which is different from a sequential method call on the active object). The following rule, trivially deduced from the general one, could be added to deal with this particular case:

REQUEST $\alpha = \beta$:

$$\frac{\sigma_\alpha(\iota) = AO(\alpha) \quad \iota'' \notin dom(\sigma_\alpha) \quad f_i^{\alpha \to \alpha} \text{ new future} \quad \iota_f \notin dom(\sigma_\alpha)}{\iota'' \neq \iota_f \quad \sigma'_\alpha = Copy\&Merge(\sigma_\alpha, \iota' \; ; \; \{\iota_f \mapsto fut(f_i^{\alpha \to \alpha})\} :: \sigma_\alpha, \iota'')}$$

$$\overline{\alpha[\mathcal{R}[\iota.m_j(\iota')]; \sigma_\alpha; \iota_\alpha; F; R; f]|||Q \longrightarrow \alpha[\mathcal{R}[\iota_f]; \sigma'_\alpha; \iota_\alpha; F; R :: [m_j; \iota''; f_i^{\alpha \to \alpha}]; f]|||Q}$$

In the sequel, we will focus only on the general REQUEST rule; even if the particular case $\alpha = \beta$ is not a strict application of the general rule, it can be studied without any technical difficulty.

From a practical point of view, the atomicity of this operation can be ensured by a rendezvous: the caller process or thread waits for an acknowledgment from the callee activity before continuing its execution. If the future identifier is created by the callee, it can be returned inside the acknowledgment message. If created by the caller, the future identifier is sent along with the argument and the target method name.

Chapter 18 will discuss the possibility to remove the rendezvous phase and study the semantical consequences of such a modification.

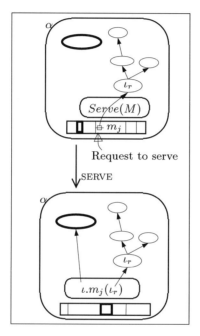

Fig. 6.5. SERVE rule

SERVE

When a call to a *Serve* primitive is encountered, the SERVE starts the service of a new request (Fig. 6.5). The current reduction is stopped and stored as a continuation (future f, expression $\mathcal{R}[[]]$), and the oldest request concerning one of the labels specified in M is selected and served: the current term to be evaluated is a call to the method $(\iota.m_j(\iota_r))$. If no such request exists, the activity is stuck until a matching request is found in the pending requests.

ENDSERVICE

When the current request is finished (current term is a location), ENDSERVICE associates the location of the result to the current future f. The response is (deep) copied to prevent post-service modification of the value and the next current term and current future are extracted from the continuation (Fig. 6.6).

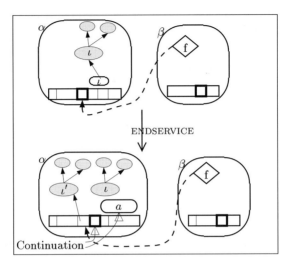

Fig. 6.6. ENDSERVICE rule

REPLY

This rule updates a total or partial future value (Fig. 6.7). It replaces a reference to a future by its value. Deliberately, it is not specified when this rule should be applied. It is only required that an activity α contains a reference to a future $f_i^{\gamma \to \beta}$, and another one (β) has calculated the corresponding result. Also, some operations (e.g., INVOKE) need the real object value of some of their operands. Such operations may lead to wait-by-necessity, which can only be resolved by the update of the future value. Also note that a future $f_i^{\gamma \to \beta}$ can be updated in an activity different from the origin of the request ($\alpha \neq \gamma$) because of the capability to transmit futures inside the value of a method call parameter and inside returned values (future values).

A future can also be updated in the same activity in which it has been calculated ($\alpha = \beta$) leading to the following particular case:

REPLY $\alpha = \beta$:

$$\sigma_\alpha(\iota) = fut(f_i^{\gamma \to \alpha}) \quad F_\alpha(f_i^{\gamma \to \alpha}) = \iota_f \quad \sigma'_\alpha = Copy\&Merge(\sigma_\alpha, \iota_f \; ; \; \sigma_\alpha, \iota)$$

$$\overline{\alpha[a_\alpha; \sigma_\alpha; \iota_\alpha; F_\alpha; R_\alpha; f_\alpha] \parallel P \longrightarrow \alpha[a_\alpha; \sigma'_\alpha; \iota_\alpha; F_\alpha; R_\alpha; f_\alpha] \parallel P}$$

After an update, a future cannot be removed from the future values because the future might have proliferated in other activities; reference counting could be used to perform garbage collection of futures [106, 65]. See

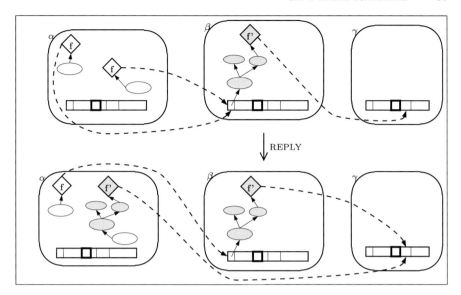

Fig. 6.7. REPLY rule

Chap. 20 for more details.

Note that SERVE, LOCAL, and ENDSERVICE are local rules (involving a single activity). NEWACT only creates an activity and thus the only communication rules are REQUEST and REPLY. These two rules require a kind of synchronization between two activities because both activities are involved in the same rule at the same time. Concerning the REPLY rule, this synchronization has no consequence because no operation on the activity that has calculated the result can be the consequence of sending a reply. Concerning REQUEST, this synchronization both ensures a FIFO point-to-point order and that, when the caller continues its execution, the request has been put in the request queue of the callee. Note that even if such synchronization has some consequences on the semantics and on the possible interleaving of communications in ASP, the activities remain strongly asynchronous because the synchronization does not involve the current term (or the main thread) of the callee.

Initial Configuration

An *initial configuration* consists of a single activity, called the *main activity*; the current term of this configuration is the source term a: $\mu[a; \emptyset; \emptyset; \emptyset; \emptyset; \emptyset]$. This activity will never receive any request. It can only communicate by sending requests or receiving replies.

6.3 Well-formedness

This section defines well-formed terms, that is, terms for which every local or generalized reference is well defined.

First, in the following, we will denote by $\alpha \in P$ the fact that α is an activity of the configuration P.

Let $ActiveRefs(\alpha)$ be the set of active objects referenced in α and $FutureRefs(\alpha)$ the set of futures referenced in α:

$$ActiveRefs(\alpha) = \{\beta | \exists \iota \in dom(\sigma_\alpha), \sigma_\alpha(\iota) = AO(\beta)\}$$

$$FutureRefs(\alpha) = \{f_i^{\beta \to \gamma} | \exists \iota \in dom(\sigma_\alpha), \sigma_\alpha(\iota) = fut(f_i^{\beta \to \gamma})\}$$

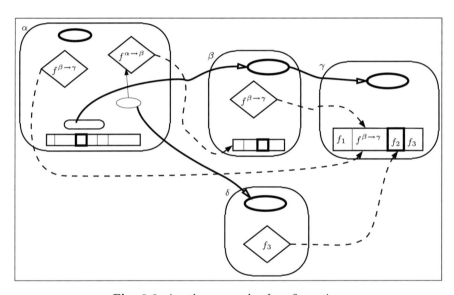

Fig. 6.8. Another example of configuration

For example, in Fig. 6.8, one has, for the activity α:

$$ActiveRefs(\alpha) = \{\beta, \delta\}$$

$$FutureRefs(\alpha) = \{f^{\alpha \to \beta}, f^{\beta \to \gamma}\}$$

Definition 6.3 (Future list) *Let $FL(\gamma)$ be:*

- *the list of futures that have been calculated,*
- *the current futures (the one in the activity and all those in the continuation of the current expression), and*
- *futures corresponding to pending requests of activity γ.*

Then:

$$FL(\gamma) = \{f_i^{\beta \to \gamma} | \{f_i^{\beta \to \gamma} \mapsto \iota\} \in F_\gamma\}$$
$$:: \{f_\gamma\} :: \mathcal{F}(a_\gamma)$$
$$:: \{f_i^{\beta \to \gamma} | [m_j, \iota, f_i^{\beta \to \gamma}] \in R_\gamma\}$$
$$where \quad \begin{cases} \mathcal{F}(a \Uparrow f, b) = f :: \mathcal{F}(b) \\ \mathcal{F}(a) = \emptyset & \text{if } a \neq a' \Uparrow f, b \end{cases}$$

The futures list is depicted by the rectangles at the bottom of each activity and in the legend of Fig. 4.2 page 72.

For example, in Fig. 6.8, the futures list of the activity γ is:

$$FL(\gamma) = \{f_1, f^{\beta \to \gamma}, f_2, f_3\}$$

A parallel configuration is *well-formed* if all local configurations are well-formed (in the sense of Definition 3.1 page 66), every referenced activity exists, and every future reference points to a future that has been or is being calculated, or corresponds to a still pending request:

Definition 6.4 (Well-formedness)

$$\vdash P \text{ OK} \Leftrightarrow \forall \alpha \in P \begin{cases} \vdash (a_\alpha, \sigma_\alpha) \text{ OK} \\ \vdash (\iota_\alpha, \sigma_\alpha) \text{ OK} \\ \beta \in ActiveRefs(\alpha) \Rightarrow \beta \in P \\ f_i^{\beta \to \gamma} \in FutureRefs(\alpha) \Rightarrow f_i^{\beta \to \gamma} \in FL(\gamma) \end{cases}$$

Sequential well-formedness Property 3.1 can be translated into the parallel reduction case. Indeed, it is easy to show that **parallel reduction preserves well-formedness**:

Property 6.5 (Well-formed parallel reduction)

$$\vdash P \text{ OK} \wedge P \longrightarrow P' \quad \Longrightarrow \quad \vdash P' \text{ OK}$$

Of course, as initial configurations are well-formed, every term obtained during reduction is also well-formed.

7

Basic ASP Properties

This chapter gives some properties on the topology of objects, first between activities (Sect. 7.2) and then inside an activity (Sect. 7.3). The first section introduces new notation and hypothesis that will be used in the sequel of this book (mainly Chap. 7, 8, and 9).

Figure 7.1 shows the dependencies between properties and definitions given in this book.

7.1 Notation and Hypothesis

In the following, α_P denotes the activity α of configuration P.

We suppose that the *freshly allocated activities are chosen deterministically*: the first activity created by α^1 will have the same identifier for all the possible executions. This condition is necessary to avoid renaming activities. Indeed the renaming of activities leads to complicated considerations to be sure that renamed activities are equivalent. For example, two activities could be exchanged such that this would make compatible[2] two configurations that do not converge. To simplify this we have chosen to consider that activities are named deterministically. However, for example, one could safely add a renaming of activities to equivalence modulo future updates of Sect. 8.2 without technical difficulty. The main interest in renaming activities seems to be the case where, after a set of undeterministically interleaved requests, a term always reaches the same state, and then behaves deterministically. As this case is not studied in this book, and in order to keep the following framework as simple as possible, we impose a deterministic naming of activities. Just recall that activities could be renamed provided this renaming avoids making compatible two configurations that are not confluent.

---

[1] An activity is always created by another one.

[2] Compatibility will be defined in Sect. 8.1

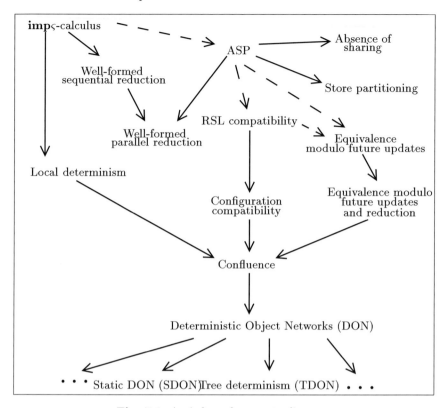

Fig. 7.1. An informal property diagram

In order to ensure a deterministic choice of activity names, an activity could be characterized by a list of integers. When an activity [1.2.5] creates its fifth activity, this activity is called [1.2.5.5]. Of course, a more concise (but somewhat equivalent) notation should be used in practice. In the following, to keep the notation concise, we still use $\alpha, \beta, \gamma, \delta \ldots$ for activity names.

Moreover, we consider that the equivalent activities have the same identifier in equivalent configurations (i.e., if P and Q are equivalent, the activity corresponding to α_P in the configuration Q is α_Q). In practice, this is directly ensured by the facts that configurations to be compared are always derived from the same source terms, and the freshly allocated activities are chosen deterministically.

Let us specify the choice of fresh futures $f_i^{\alpha \to \beta}$. We consider that the future identifier f_i is the name of the invoked method indexed by the number of requests that have already been received by β. Thus if the fourth request received by β comes from γ and concerns method foo, its future identifier will actually be $foo_4^{\gamma \to \beta}$. In the following, for notational simplicity, both m_j

and f will denote method labels. Consequently, futures will still be denoted $f_i^{\alpha \to \beta}$, but when necessary, f will be characterized by a method name. Note that this choice doss not contradic the preceding definitions and ensures that f_i is unique for any destination activity (and $f_i^{\alpha \to \beta}$ is globally unique).

$\xrightarrow{*}$ will denote the transitive closure of $\longrightarrow$, and $\xrightarrow{T}$ will denote the application of rule T of Fig. 6.2 page 92 (e.g., LOCAL, REPLY, etc.). For example, $\xrightarrow{\text{REPLY*}}$ will denote any number (≥ 0) of applications of the REPLY rule.

Potential Services

Let $\mathcal{M}_{\alpha P}$ be a *static approximation*[3] of the set of M that can appear in the $Serve(M)$ instructions of αP. Thus $\mathcal{M}_{\alpha P}$ is a set of sets of method labels. In other words, for a given source program P_0, for each activity α created, consider that there is a set $\mathcal{M}_{\alpha P_0}$ such that if α will be able to perform a $Serve(M)$ then $M \in \mathcal{M}_{\alpha P_0}$. More formally, for each configuration P, the set M_0 of sets of methods potentially served can be defined as follows:

$$P_0 \xrightarrow{*} P \wedge a_{\alpha P} = \mathcal{R}[Serve(M)] \Rightarrow M \in M_0$$

However, only an over-approximation of the set of such *potential services* is needed for the following. Thus the set of potential services $\mathcal{M}_{\alpha P}$ associated with a given activity α and a given configuration P is defined as follows:

Definition 7.1 (Potential services)
Let P_0 be an initial configuration. $\mathcal{M}_{\alpha P}$ is any set verifying:

$$P \xrightarrow{*} P' \wedge a_{\alpha P'} = \mathcal{R}[Serve(M)] \Rightarrow \exists M' \in \mathcal{M}_{\alpha P}, \ M \subseteq M'$$

This definition states that for any service performed by α there must be, in the potential services, an over-approximation of the set of method labels served by this service primitive.

Note that for any activity the set of all method labels of a program P_0 is a correct but very imprecise potential service ($\mathcal{M}_{\alpha P_0} = \mathcal{M}$). This is the only valid potential service for a FIFO service policy. Actually, the set of methods defined in the active object of activity α would be a more precise approximation but it would not produce any benefit.

For example, let P_0 be a source program and α be an activity created by this program that may serve either some requests on m_1 and m_2 ($Serve(m_1, m_2)$), or some requests on m_3 ($Serve(m_3)$). It will be characterized by $\mathcal{M}_{\alpha P_0} = \{(m_1, m_2), (m_3)\}$. Consequently, we will say that requests on method m_3 and on method m_1 *do not interfere*. Two requests are *non-interfering* (for an activity) if they cannot be served by the same service instruction (performed by this activity).

---

[3] For example, it could be approximated and verified statically by classical static analysis or typing techniques that are not studied here.

A static approximation is needed because a *Serve* primitive can be present in an object received as a request parameter. Thus if one had a dynamic characterization of potential services $\mathcal{M}'_{\alpha P}$, the service of a new request could modify $\mathcal{M}'_{\alpha P}$ and, as a consequence, the following potential services would be changed and that would break the properties of the compatibility relation. Indeed, Sect. 8.4 will prove that if two requests are not in the same potential service, they cannot interfere and can be safely exchanged in the pending request queue. If the potential service could be changed while those same requests are pending, this could make them interfere and would invalidate most of the properties of Chaps. 8 and 9. To summarize, if the potential services could be changed dynamically, the request sending between requests that are *currently* interfering would not be the only source of concurrency in ASP.

7.2 Object Sharing

In ASP, a shared reference would have been an object that would be referenced by objects belonging to different activities. The syntax of intermediate terms guarantees that there are no shared references in ASP (Fig.7.2) except generalized references: namely, future and active object references.

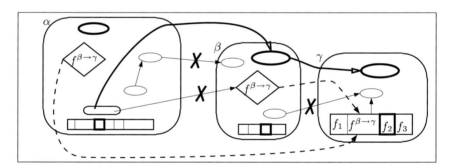

Fig. 7.2. Absence of sharing

In other words, the only generalized references are the active objects and the future references. No memory is shared because future values can only be deeply copied when they are updated in another activity (and thus are immutable in the activity that has calculated them), and active objects are only accessible through asynchronous method calls. This property on topology is strongly related to the fact that the only communications between activities are the sending of requests and the updates of futures, and implies the use of deep copy in the sending of requests and the receiving of replies.

Note that this property is actually syntactic: it is directly ensured by ASP syntax where locations are local to an activity. As a consequence, deep copies are necessary to maintain the well-formedness of ASP configuration without losing the absence of sharing.

Consequently, it is adequate to have unique locations names locally, i.e., inside an activity: if some memory could be shared between activities then a location identifier local to an activity would not be sufficient.

7.3 Isolation of Futures and Parameters

The following property states that the value of each future and each request parameter is situated in an isolated part of a store. Figure 7.3 illustrates such isolation of a future value (on the left) and a request parameter (on the right).

Property 7.2 (Store partitioning)
Let:

$$ActiveStore(\alpha) = copy(\iota_\alpha, \sigma_\alpha) \cup \bigcup_{\iota \in locs(a_\alpha)} copy(\iota, \sigma_\alpha)$$

At any stage of computation, each activity has the following invariant:

$$\sigma_\alpha \supseteq \left(ActiveStore(\alpha) \bigoplus_{\{f \mapsto \iota_f\} \in F_\alpha} copy(\iota_f, \sigma_\alpha) \bigoplus_{[m_j; \iota_r; f] \in R_\alpha} copy(\iota_r, \sigma_\alpha) \right)$$

where $\bigoplus$ is the disjoint union.

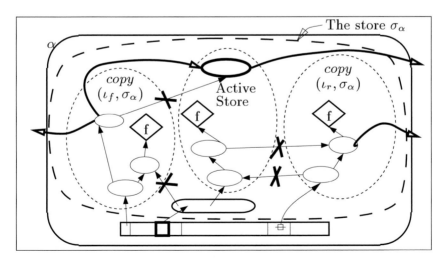

Fig. 7.3. Store partitioning: future value, active store, request parameter

This invariant is proved by checking it on each reduction rule. The part of σ_α that does not belong to the preceding partition may be freely garbage collected. The only modifications allowed on the partitions containing the futures and the parameters is the update of a calculated future value. Consequently, only the current store ($ActiveStore(\alpha)$) contains mutable objects.

In an equivalent calculus, one could consider that, instead of a single store by activity, one might have a local store and specialized stores for each future value and each method parameter. In that case, one would need to add two REPLY rules: one that updates futures inside a future value and another that updates futures inside a method parameter. As wait-by-necessity can only occur on an object belonging to the active store. These two rules are not necessary to obtain a coherent calculus, but without them, we could not express all the future update strategies.

8

Confluence Property

Confluence properties relieve the programmer from studying the interleaving of instructions and communications. Very different treatments have been performed to ensure the confluence of calculi, languages, or programs. Linear channels in π-calculus [124, 104], non-interference properties in shared memory systems [151], Process Networks [99], or Jones' technique for creating deterministic concurrency in $\pi o \beta \lambda$ [95] are typical examples. But none of them deals with a concurrent, imperative, object language with asynchronous communications.

This chapter starts by defining a notion of compatibility between configurations (Sect. 8.1) and an equivalence relation on configurations (Sect. 8.2). These two important definitions will lead us to a strong confluence property in Sect. 8.4. Section 8.3 gives some properties of the equivalence relations defined in Sect. 8.2. The key property of this chapter states that the execution of a set of processes is only determined by the order of arrival of requests (Sect. 8.4); asynchronous replies can occur in an arbitrary order without any observable consequence.

The proofs, some technical details, and the specification of equivalence can be found in Appendices A and B, and also in [51, 86].

8.1 Configuration Compatibility

This section introduces the concept of compatibility between configurations that is a prerequisite for the confluence of terms presented in Sect. 8.4. Informally, two configurations are compatible if, for all activities present in both, the served, current, and pending requests of one is a prefix of the equivalent list in the other. Moreover, if two requests cannot interfere, that is to say if no $Serve(M)$ can concern both requests, then these requests can be safely exchanged. The compatibility definition is justified by the fact that the order of evaluation is entirely defined by the order of request sending. More precisely, Theorem 8.10 states that the order of activities sending requests to a given activity determines the behavior of the program. Or in other words, that compatible configurations are confluent. This means that the *future updates and imperative aspects of ASP do not act upon the final result of evaluation.* This property can be considered as the main contribution of this study.

Definition 8.1 (Request Sender List)
The request sender list (RSL) is the list of request senders in the order the requests have been received and indexed by the invoked method.
The ith element of $RSL(\alpha)$ is defined by:

$$(RSL(\alpha))_i = \beta^f \text{ if } f_i^{\beta \to \alpha} \in FL(\alpha)$$

The list of futures that have or will be calculated by the activity α is $FL(\alpha)$ and has been defined in Sect. 6.3 page 98. The RSL list is obtained from *futures* associated to *served requests, current requests,* and *pending requests.* Moreover, if n requests have been received by α, then for each i between 1 and n, $(RSL(\alpha))_i$ is well defined. It is important to note that the order of this list is the order of request *arrivals*; thus, for example, some entries corresponding to already served requests can appear after some current or pending requests inside the RSL. This is because requests are not always treated in their arrival order nor finished in their treatment order.

In the examples, for simplicity of notation, in an activity β we will denote by $\delta.foo(b)$ when there is ι such that $\iota.foo(b)$ and $\sigma_\beta(\iota) = AO(\beta)$. The example in Fig. 8.1 shows four activities. This state (calculated, current, and pending futures of activity δ) is obtained with the following sequence:

- the activity β invokes a bar request on the activity δ: $\delta.bar()$, the corresponding future is $bar_1^{\beta \to \delta}$,
- α performs a $\delta.foo()$, future: $foo_2^{\alpha \to \delta}$,
- γ performs two consecutive $\delta.gee()$, futures: $gee_3^{\gamma \to \delta}$, $gee_4^{\gamma \to \delta}$,
- α performs a $\delta.foo()$, future: $foo_5^{\alpha \to \delta}$,
- β performs a $\delta.foo()$, future: $foo_6^{\beta \to \delta}$,
- β performs a $\delta.bar()$, $bar_7^{\beta \to \delta}$,
- γ performs a $\delta.gee()$, future: $gee_8^{\gamma \to \delta}$.

Meanwhile, δ has finished first the service of a request *foo*, then of a request *bar*. Then, it has served a request *gee*, and while serving *gee* it has served another *gee* request.

In this example, the RSL of the activity δ is:

$$RSL(\delta) = \beta^{bar} :: \alpha^{foo} :: \gamma^{gee} :: \gamma^{gee} :: \alpha^{foo} :: \beta^{foo} :: \beta^{bar} :: \gamma^{gee}$$

Let $RSL(\alpha)\big|_M$ represent the *restriction* of $RSL(\alpha)$ to the set of labels M. In the example of Fig. 8.1, one has:

$$RSL(\delta)\big|_{foo,bar} = \beta^{bar} :: \alpha^{foo} :: \alpha^{foo} :: \beta^{foo} :: \beta^{bar}$$

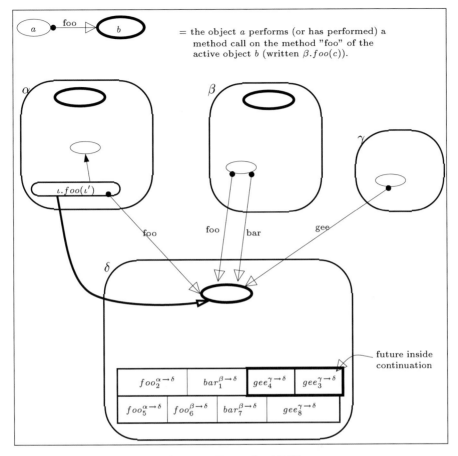

Fig. 8.1. Example of RSL

For a FIFO service, and if no service is performed while another request is being served, the order of requests cannot be changed when they are served. Thus the RSL is directly obtained from the concatenation of the future values (in the order they have been calculated), the unique current future, and the pending requests in the order they arrived. Finishing the current service (ENDSERVICE) and serving a new request (SERVE) will respectively put the current future at the end of the futures values, and take the first pending request future as the current future. Indeed if $f_n^{\beta \to \alpha}$ is the current future, then $f_1^{\delta \to \alpha} \ldots f_{n-1}^{\gamma \to \alpha}$ correspond to calculated futures and $f_{n+1}^{\delta \to \alpha} \ldots$ correspond to pending requests.

Definition 8.2 (RSL comparison $\trianglelefteq$)

RSLs are ordered by the prefix order on activities:

$$\alpha_1{}^{f_1}\ldots\alpha_n{}^{f_n} \trianglelefteq \alpha_1'{}^{f_1'}\ldots\alpha_m'{}^{f_m'} \Leftrightarrow \begin{cases} n \leq m \\ \forall i \in [1..n], \alpha_i = \alpha_i' \end{cases}$$

Two RSLs are compatible if they are comparable (they have a least upper bound). That means that one of the two RSLs is simply the beginning of the other one.

Definition 8.3 (RSL compatibility: $RSL(\alpha) \bowtie RSL(\beta)$)

Two RSLs are compatible if they have a least upper bound or equivalently if one is a prefix of the other:

$$RSL(\alpha) \bowtie RSL(\beta) \Leftrightarrow RSL(\alpha) \sqcup RSL(\beta) \text{ exists}$$
$$\Leftrightarrow (RSL(\alpha) \trianglerighteq RSL(\beta)) \vee (RSL(\beta) \trianglelefteq RSL(\alpha))$$

Two configurations are said to be *compatible* if all the restrictions of their RSL that can be served are compatible. Suppose that configurations to be compared derive from the same term: there is a P_0 such that $P_0 \overset{*}{\longrightarrow} P$ and $P_0 \overset{*}{\longrightarrow} Q$. Then the compatibility of P and Q is defined by:

Definition 8.4 (Configuration compatibility: $P \bowtie Q$)

If P_0 is a configuration such that $P_0 \overset{*}{\longrightarrow} P$ and $P_0 \overset{*}{\longrightarrow} Q$:

$$P \bowtie Q \Leftrightarrow \forall \alpha \in P \cap Q, \forall M \in \mathcal{M}_{\alpha_{P_0}}, RSL(\alpha_P)\big|_M \bowtie RSL(\alpha_Q)\big|_M$$

Intuitively, this means that RSLs are in a compatible state if the application of *Serve* operations that will be performed will lead to the same execution because the same requests will be served in the same order.

Following the RSL definition (Definition 8.1) the configuration compatibility only relies on the arrival order of requests; the future list (FL) order (Definition 6.3), potentially different on served and current requests, does not matter. Indeed, the behavior of an activity is fully determined by the arrival order of requests.

In the general case, *Serve* operations can be performed while another request is being served; then the relation between RSL order and FL order can only be determined by a precise study. If no *Serve* operation is performed while another request is being served (only the service method performs *Serve* operations), then all the restrictions (to potential services) of the RSL and the FL are in the same order. In the FIFO case, the FL order and the RSL order are the same.

Observe that the restriction of RSLs in Definition 8.3 is only useful for that part of the RSL containing pending requests. If two calculated futures are exchanged (even if they correspond to different labels) they correspond to two requests that have been served in a different order. And thus, they correspond to a non-confluent program. Indeed, these two services could have modified the state of the object concurrently. In fact, such exchanged futures mean that there are two RSLs (perhaps in another activity) that are not compatible.

For example, if the method foo sets a field to the value 1 and the method bar sets the same field to the value 2, then, if the calculated futures are $\{foo_1^{\alpha \to \gamma} :: bar_2^{\alpha \to \gamma}\}$, the field has the value 2. Whereas if the calculated futures are $\{bar_2^{\alpha \to \gamma} :: foo_1^{\alpha \to \gamma}\}$ then the field has the value 1 even if there is no $Serve(foo, bar)$.[1] Such a configuration can be obtained if the service method performs a $Serve(foo); Serve(bar)$ in one case and $Serve(bar); Serve(foo)$ in the other case; for example, because the activity that has created this activity has a non-deterministic behavior. In that case it is this source activity that can have two different RSLs (leading to the two service methods) that are not compatible.

Figure 8.2 extends the example of Fig. 8.1. It shows only the pending requests of δ. In this example we will focus only on pending requests and we will not detail the other parts of RSLs. Figure 8.2 provides (the pending requests' part of) four examples of compatible RSLs. Suppose the potential services of the activity δ are:

$$\mathcal{M}_{\delta_{P_0}} = \{\{foo, bar\}, \{foo, gee\}\}$$

that is to say, the only calls to $Serve$ primitive are $Serve(foo, bar)$ and $Serve(foo, gee)$. The two RSLs corresponding to pending requests at the bottom of the diagram are:

$$RSL_3(\delta) = \ldots \alpha^{foo} :: \gamma^{gee} :: \beta^{foo} :: \gamma^{gee} :: \beta^{bar}$$

$$RSL_4(\delta) = \ldots \alpha^{foo} :: \beta^{foo} :: \gamma^{gee} :: \beta^{bar} :: \beta^{bar}$$

Then all the configurations having the RSLs at the bottom of the diagram are compatible. For example, for RSL_3 and RSL_4:

$$RSL_3(\delta)\big|_{bar, foo} = \ldots \alpha :: \beta :: \beta \bowtie \ldots \alpha :: \beta :: \beta :: \beta = RSL_4(\delta)\big|_{bar, foo}$$

$$RSL_3(\delta)\big|_{gee, foo} = \ldots \alpha :: \beta :: \gamma :: \gamma \bowtie \ldots \alpha :: \beta :: \gamma = RSL_4(\delta)\big|_{gee, foo}$$

8.2 Equivalence Modulo Future Updates

This section briefly defines an equivalence relation on terms that is insensitive to future updates. This equivalence relation could also be called *equivalence modulo replies* because it states that two configurations that only differ by applying some REPLY rules are equivalent.

---

[1] Moreover, in that case, the two RSLs are the same!

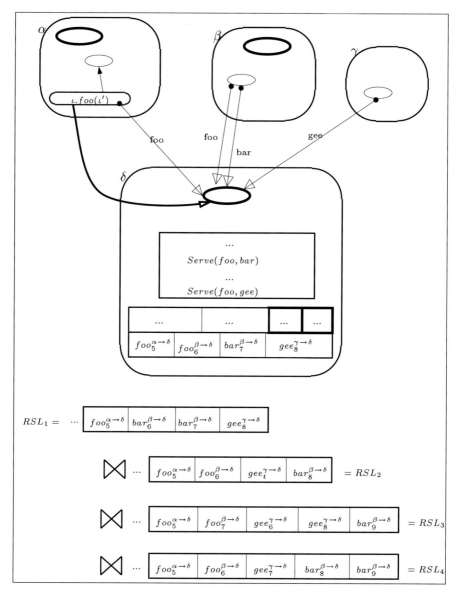

Fig. 8.2. Example of RSL compatibility

First, let us generalize the equivalence relation ≡ defined previously (Definition 3.2 page 66). Let ≡ now denote the equivalence of parallel configurations modulo the renaming of locations and futures. Furthermore, let ≡ also take into account the RSL compatibility. The equivalence on pending requests allows them to be reordered provided the compatibility of RSLs is maintained: requests that cannot interfere (because they can not be served by the same

Serve primitive) can be safely exchanged. Modulo these allowed permutations, equivalent configurations are composed of equivalent pending requests in the same order.

8.2.1 Principles

Let us now introduce an equivalence relation that is insensitive to the update of futures.

Equivalence modulo future updates ($P \equiv_F Q$) is an extension of $\equiv$ authorizing the update of some calculated futures. This is equivalent to considering a reference to a future already calculated (but not locally updated) as equivalent to a local reference to the (part of the store which is the) deep copy of the future value. Or, in other words, a future is equivalent to a part of the store if this part of the store is equivalent to the store which is the (deep copy of the) future value (provided the updated part does not overlap with the remainder of the store).

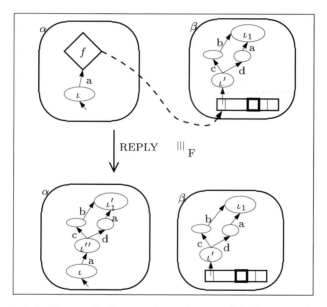

Fig. 8.3. Two equivalent configurations modulo future updates

Figure 8.3 shows two equivalent configurations. The bottom configuration is obtained by updating the future f (applying a REPLY rule). Arrows still represent references but are labeled with field names.

The main principles of the formal definition of $\equiv_F$ are given below.

Let L be a path in the tree formed by the term a that follows references inside the local store. Paths contain field access, dereferencing, etc., but are insensitive to the dereferencing of a future reference. Following a path inside α is denoted by $\overset{\alpha}{\mapsto}_L$; and following a path starting in α and containing future references and thus possibly inside different activities is denoted by $\overset{\alpha*}{\mapsto}_L$.

First let us illustrate what "insensitive to the dereferencing of a future reference" means. In Fig. 8.3, in the bottom configuration $\sigma_\alpha(\iota) = [a = \iota'']$. Then in the bottom configuration:

$$\alpha \overset{\alpha}{\mapsto}_{...} \iota \overset{\alpha}{\mapsto}_{ref.a} \iota''$$

which corresponds in the top one to (with $F_\beta(f) = \iota'$):

$$\alpha \overset{\alpha}{\mapsto}_{...} \iota \overset{\alpha*}{\mapsto}_{ref.a} \iota'$$

Here, $\iota \overset{\alpha}{\mapsto}_{ref.a} \iota''$ follows one arrow whereas $\iota \overset{\alpha*}{\mapsto}_{ref.a} \iota'$ follows three arrows including a future reference.

8.2.2 Alias Condition

An important and necessary condition to define a sound equivalence relation between configurations is that aliased objects are the same in both configurations. This condition, called the *alias condition*, states that alias[2] existing in one configuration can also exist in the second one. It can be formalized as follows:

> *Aliases existing in P_1 also exist in P_2 if P_1 and P_2 verify the following relation:*

$$\exists L_1, L_2 \begin{cases} \alpha \overset{\alpha}{\mapsto}_{L_1} \iota_1' \\ \alpha \overset{\alpha}{\mapsto}_{L_2} \iota_1' \end{cases} \text{in } P_1 \;\Rightarrow\; \exists L, L', L_1', L_2', \iota' \begin{cases} L_1 = L.L_1' \\ L_2 = L'.L_2' \\ L_1' \neq \emptyset \\ \alpha \overset{\alpha*}{\mapsto}_L \iota' \overset{\beta}{\mapsto}_{L_1'} \iota_1 \\ \alpha \overset{\alpha*}{\mapsto}_{L'} \iota' \overset{\beta}{\mapsto}_{L_2'} \iota_1 \end{cases} \text{in } P_2$$

Consider two configurations P_1 and P_2 that should be equivalent; the preceding implication states that: if two different paths L_1 and L_2 lead to the same object (ι_1') in the first configuration (without following future references) then the same paths lead to the same final object (ι_1) in the second configuration. However, in the second configuration, one can follow future references provided that in the last activity (β) covered by both paths, two different paths go from the same location (ι') to the final object.

Conversely, one must also verify that aliases of the second configuration also exist in the first one.

---

[2] We mean by "alias" that the same object can be referenced by two different objects.

For example in Fig. 8.3, the bottom configuration shows two paths $L_1 = ref.a.ref.c.ref.b$ and $L_2 = ref.a.ref.d.ref.a$ leading to the same location (ι_1') without following future references. That is:

$$\exists L_1, L_2 \; \alpha \overset{\alpha}{\mapsto}_{...} \iota \overset{\alpha}{\mapsto}_{L_1} \iota_1' \wedge \alpha \overset{\alpha}{\mapsto}_{...} \iota \overset{\alpha}{\mapsto}_{L_2} \iota_1'$$

In the top configuration, one can verify that the same two paths L_1 and L_2 lead to a single location ι_1 with the constraint that in the last activity covered by these paths, the two paths are aliased i.e.:

$$\exists L, L', L_1', L_2', \iota' \begin{cases} L_1 = L.L_1' \wedge L_2 = L'.L_2' \wedge L_1' \neq \emptyset \\ \alpha \overset{\alpha}{\mapsto}_{...} \iota \overset{\alpha*}{\mapsto}_{L} \iota' \overset{\beta}{\mapsto}_{L_1'} \iota_1 \\ \alpha \overset{\alpha}{\mapsto}_{...} \iota \overset{\alpha*}{\mapsto}_{L'} \iota' \overset{\beta}{\mapsto}_{L_2'} \iota_1 \end{cases}$$

This relation is verified with $L = L' = ref.a.ref$, $L_1' = c.ref.b$, and $L_2' = d.ref.a$. Consequently, aliases of the bottom configurations also exist in the top configuration.

Actually, only the last part of the alias is necessary and a "minimal" alias condition could also be specified as: if two locations are aliased then there is a *minimal* pair of aliased paths (containing no other alias), and these aliased paths correspond to a pair of aliased paths *in a unique activity* in the equivalent configuration. This condition is illustrated by the rightmost part of the alias condition:

$$\iota' \overset{\beta}{\mapsto}_{L_1'} \iota_1 \wedge \iota' \overset{\beta}{\mapsto}_{L_2'} \iota_1$$

But such a definition would be more difficult to formalize as it requires both a definition of minimal alias paths and a specification of the activity where alias must occur in the equivalent configuration.

The necessity of the alias condition is illustrated in Fig. 8.4. Indeed, the alias condition avoids identifying the configurations Q_0 and Q'. The alias existing in α in configuration Q' exists neither in Q_0 nor in Q. However, all the paths that exist in Q_0 also exist in Q'; thus the alias condition is necessary for specifying equivalence modulo future updates.

8.2.3 Sufficient Conditions

As explained informally in this section, two configurations only differing by some future updates (applications of some REPLY rules) are equivalent:

$$P \xrightarrow{\text{REPLY}} P' \Rightarrow P \equiv_F P'$$

More precisely, we have the following sufficient condition for equivalence modulo future updates:

$$\left(P_1 \xrightarrow{\text{REPLY}} P' \wedge P_2 \xrightarrow{\text{REPLY}} P' \right) \quad \Rightarrow \quad P_1 \equiv_F P_2$$

But this condition is not necessary as it does not deal with mutual references between futures.

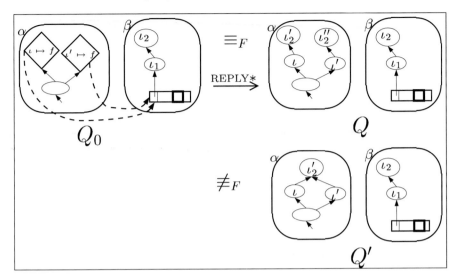

Fig. 8.4. An example illustrating the alias condition

Definition 8.5 (Cycle of futures)

A configuration contains a cycle of futures if some futures values are mutually dependent: each future value references another future, finally leading to a cycle.

A cycle of futures is a set of future identifiers $\{fut(f_i^{\gamma_i \to \beta_n})\}$ such that $\beta_0 \dots \beta_n$ verify:

$$\begin{cases} \left(\forall i,\, 0 < i \leq n,\, fut(f_{i-1}^{\gamma_{i-1} \to \beta_{i-1}}) \in copy(F_{\beta_i}(fut(f_i^{\gamma_i \to \beta_i})), \sigma_{\beta_i})\right) \\ fut(f_n^{\gamma_n \to \beta_n}) \in copy(F_{\beta_0}(fut(f_0^{\gamma_0 \to \beta_0})), \sigma_{\beta_0}) \end{cases}$$

In Fig. 8.5 the two bottom configurations are equivalent but there is no configuration P' such that:

$$P_1 \xrightarrow{\text{REPLY}} P' \wedge P_2 \xrightarrow{\text{REPLY}} P'$$

Indeed all configurations derived from P_1 will only contain future f_1 and, similarly, all configurations derived from P_2 will only contain future f_2.

In this example, one can still prove the equivalence of P_1 and P_2 simply because of the transitivity of $\equiv_F$, and P_1 and P_2 are derived by REPLY rules from a common configuration; but, in the general case, it is difficult to exhibit this common configuration when one only knows the configurations P_1 and P_2. Even more generally, it seems difficult to infer which futures must be "unupdated" to find a common source configuration. Consequently a definition of future equivalence based on paths rather than simple applications of the REPLY rule seems necessary. Appendix A formally defines the equivalence modulo future updates, and exhibits and proves its main properties.

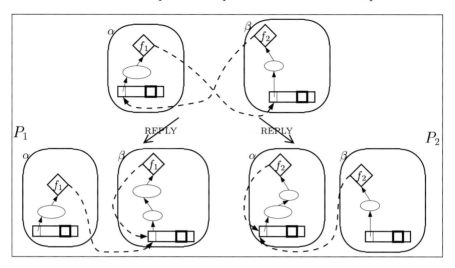

Fig. 8.5. Updates in a cycle of futures

8.3 Properties of Equivalence Modulo Future Updates

In the following, some important properties of $\equiv_F$ are exhibited. Let T be any parallel reduction:

$$T \in \{\text{LOCAL}, \text{NEWACT}, \text{REQUEST}, \text{SERVE}, \text{ENDSERVICE}, \text{REPLY}\}$$

Then let us denote by $\Longrightarrow$ the reduction $\longrightarrow$ preceded by some applications of the REPLY rule.

Definition 8.6 (Parallel reduction modulo future updates)

$$\overset{T}{\Longrightarrow} \quad = \quad \begin{array}{c} \xrightarrow{\text{REPLY}*}\overset{T}{\longrightarrow} \; \textit{if } T \neq \text{REPLY} \\ \xrightarrow{\text{REPLY}*} \qquad \textit{if } T = \text{REPLY} \end{array}$$

Informally, this reduction allows us to achieve any replies necessary for the application of another transition. If the rule is REPLY then $\Longrightarrow$ represents any number of applications of the REPLY rule (including zero). The following property is verified:

Property 8.7 (Equivalence modulo future updates and reduction)

$$P \xrightarrow{T} Q \;\wedge\; P \equiv_F P' \;\; \Rightarrow \;\; \exists Q',\, P' \overset{T}{\Longrightarrow} Q' \;\wedge\; Q' \equiv_F Q$$

This important property states that if one can apply a reduction rule on a configuration then, after several REPLY rules, a reduction using the same rule can be applied on any equivalent configuration. The proof consists in verifying that, after several REPLY rules, the application of the same rule on the same activities is possible and applying a given rule preserves equivalence (see Sect. A.6 for details).

The following corollary states that one can actually apply several REPLY rules before the reduction $P \xrightarrow{T} Q$ without any effect on Property 8.7:

Property 8.8 (Equivalence and generalized parallel reduction)

$$P \xRightarrow{T} Q \ \wedge \ P \equiv_F P' \ \Rightarrow \ \exists Q', P' \xRightarrow{T} Q' \ \wedge \ Q' \equiv_F Q$$

In the following sections, we present sufficient conditions for confluence of ASP configurations.

8.4 Confluence

Two configurations are said to be *confluent* if they can be reduced to equivalent configurations.

Definition 8.9 (Confluent configurations: $P_1 \ \curlyvee \ P_2$)

$$P_1 \curlyvee P_2 \Leftrightarrow \exists R_1, R_2, \begin{cases} P_1 \xrightarrow{*} R_1 \\ P_2 \xrightarrow{*} R_2 \\ R_1 \equiv_F R_2 \end{cases}$$

The next property states that if, from a given term, one obtains two compatible configurations ($\bowtie$, Definition 8.4, page 110), then these configurations are confluent.

Theorem 8.10 (Confluence)

$$\begin{cases} P \xrightarrow{*} Q_1 \\ P \xrightarrow{*} Q_2 \implies Q_1 \curlyvee Q_2 \\ Q_1 \bowtie Q_2 \end{cases}$$

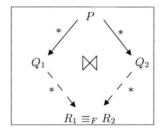

Fig. 8.6. Confluence

Let us recall that configuration compatibility ($\bowtie$) only relies on the order of *sender activities for received requests* and on *potential services*. Two such compatible configurations (Figure 8.6) can always be reduced to equivalent configurations modulo future updates.

Note that if there is no cycle of futures we obtain the direct equivalence (Fig. 8.7).

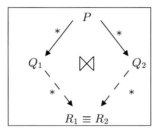

Fig. 8.7. Confluence without cycle of futures

The principles of the confluence theorem can be summarized as: concurrency can only originate from the application of two interfering REQUEST rules on the same destination activity; for example, the order of updates of futures never has any influence on the reduction of a term. The only constraint on the moment when a REPLY must occur is a wait-by-necessity on that future. In fact even if this theorem is natural, it allows a lot of asynchronism and proves that the mechanism of futures is rather powerful, especially in an imperative calculus.

Furthermore, the order of requests does not matter if they cannot be involved in the same *Serve* primitive; thus if some requests on different methods do not interfere (cannot be served by the same *Serve(M)* primitive), then they can be safely exchanged. This is expressed by the compatibility relation.

On the contrary, consider two requests R_1 and R_2 on the same method of a given destination activity. If in a configuration Q_1, R_1 is before R_2, and in another configuration Q_2, R_2 is before R_1, then the configurations obtained from Q_1 and Q_2 will never be equivalent.

In other words, $Q_1 \bowtie Q_2$ is a necessary condition for Q_1 and Q_2 to be confluent modulo future updates. Of course, another equivalence relation could be found for which our compatibility between terms would not be necessary for confluence. For example, consider a strictly functional server which has no internal state and only serves requests by replying with the same result whatever his history is. Such a server could be considered as deterministic even if it receives requests in an undetermined order.

The proof of Theorem 8.10 is presented in Appendix B. It is rather long but the key idea is that if two configurations are compatible, then there is a way to perform missing sending of requests in the right order. Thus the configurations can be reduced to a common one (modulo future updates equivalence). See Appendix B and [86] for more details about this proof.

Concerning field access to active objects, recall that field accesses and updates on active objects are forbidden (stuck). We stated that such accesses should be replaced by getter and setter (Sect.4.3.4, page 74) but those new methods have to be served and can interfere with other requests. Consequently, introducing and serving getter and setter introduces new potential services and potentially non-determinism.

9

Determinacy

The objective of this chapter is to identify deterministic sub-calculi of ASP. A specification of a set of terms called DON (*Deterministic Object Networks*), is given in Sect. 9.1. DON terms behave deterministically and can be seen as a generalization of Process Networks. Then several approximations of this property are presented, these approximations providing a means of deciding statically the deterministic nature of programs. A first static approximation of DON terms is presented in Sect. 9.2. Then Sect. 9.3 studies the case of tree topology of activities. Finally, Sect. 9.4 shows some examples of deterministic ASP programs. A discussion on the different strategies for serving requests, with respect to determinism, concludes this chapter.

Note that even if the hypothesis that activities names are chosen deterministically is a necessary prerequisite for characterizing compatible configurations, this hypothesis is not necessary for a program to behave deterministically.

9.1 Deterministic Object Networks

The work of Kahn and MacQueen on process networks [100] suggested to us the possibility to define the DON properties that ensure determinacy of some programs. In process networks, the determinacy is ensured by the facts that channels have only one source, and destinations read the data independently (values are broadcast to all destination processes). And, most importantly, the order of reading on different channels is fixed for a given program, and the reading of an entry in the buffer is a blocking primitive.

In ASP, where *Serve* is a blocking primitive, non-determinism cannot appear directly because of the delay needed to send a request; in other words, one cannot create non-determinism by testing the presence of a pending request. But if at a point in time, two activities can send concurrently a request on a given method to the same activity, then a conflict appears and the reduction is not confluent. More generally, a conflict also appears when the two activities send requests on two different method labels m_1 and m_2, but those two methods appear in the same $Serve(M)$, ($m_1 \in M$ and $m_2 \in M$). Consequently, the only non-confluent aspect of ASP is the conflict between interfering requests sent to the same destination.

In other words, if at any time two activities cannot send concurrently to the same third activity a request; or if such requests concern two methods that do not appear in the same $Serve(M)$; then there is no interference and the reduction is confluent.

In order to formalize this principle, Deterministic Object Networks (DON) are defined below.

Definition 9.1 (DON)
A configuration P, derived from an initial configuration P_0, is a Deterministic Object Network, $DON(P)$, if it cannot be reduced to a configuration where two interfering requests can be sent concurrently to the same destination activity:

$$DON(P) \Leftrightarrow \left(\begin{matrix} P \xrightarrow{*} Q \Rightarrow \forall \alpha \in Q, \ \forall M \in \mathcal{M}_{\alpha P_0}, \exists^1 \beta \in Q, \exists m \in M, \\ a_\beta = \mathcal{R}[\iota.m(\ldots)] \wedge \sigma_\beta(\iota) = AO(\alpha) \end{matrix} \right)$$

where $\exists^1$ means "there is at most one."

A program is a deterministic object network if at any time of any possible reduction, for each potential service M of α, at most one activity can send a request to α on a method of M.

The first example of a sieve of Eratosthenes, Fig. 5.4 page 78, verifies the $DON(P)$ property, and it is easy to verify this statically because in Fig. 5.4 the object dependence graph forms a tree.

The second example, Fig.5.6 page 79, seems much more difficult to verify because in Fig. 5.6 the object dependence graph is no longer a tree. This comes from the fact that all sieve objects keep a reference to the $Display$ object. However, dynamically, at each time a single one will be able to send a request on $Display$, and thus the second sieve of Eratosthenes is also a DON configuration. This reflects the very dynamic nature of the DON definition. It has been done intentionally, in order to first capture as many programs as possible.

From the definition of DON one can easily conclude that DON terms always reduce to compatible configurations:

Property 9.2 (DON and compatibility)

$$DON(P) \wedge P \xrightarrow{*} Q_1 \wedge P \xrightarrow{*} Q_2 \Rightarrow Q_1 \bowtie Q_2$$

Indeed, RSL compatibility comes from the fact that $DON(P)$ implies that two activities are not able to send requests that can interfere to the same third activity: namely, the uniqueness of request sender (β) for every target (α) for every potential service.

This can be proved by contradiction: if two incompatible RSLs were obtained in an activity γ, we would have two requests R_1 and R_2 at the same place in the two RSLs. Moreover, we would have $R_1 = [foo, \iota, f_{1i}^{\alpha \to \gamma}]$ and $R_2 = [bar, \iota', f_{2i'}^{\beta \to \gamma}]$ and $foo \in M$ and $bar \in M$ for a given $Serve(M)$. Then there would exist another term Q' such that $P \xrightarrow{\quad} Q'$ and in Q' the two concurrent requests R_1 and R_2 could be sent concurrently from β and γ to the activity α:

$$a_\beta = \mathcal{R}[\iota.foo(\ldots)] \wedge \sigma_\beta(\iota) = AO(\alpha)$$

and

$$a_\gamma = \mathcal{R}[\iota'.bar(\ldots)] \wedge \sigma_\gamma(\iota') = AO(\alpha)$$

As a consequence P would not be a DON term. □

Thus, the reduction of DON terms always leads to the same RSLs, for all orders of request sending: requests are always served in the same order.

Therefore, the set of DON terms is a deterministic sub-calculus of ASP:

Theorem 9.3 (DON determinism)

$$\begin{cases} DON(P) \\ P \xrightarrow{*} Q_1 \\ P \xrightarrow{*} Q_2 \end{cases} \implies Q_1 \curlyvee Q_2$$

Figure 9.1 illustrates the fact that the term that does not verify the DON definition can lead to undeterministic behavior. In P two requests can be sent concurrently to δ, and we obtain two configuration P_1 and P_2 that are not confluent (they have incompatible RSLs).

As explained before, the two examples of sieve of Eratosthenes (Figs. 5.3 and 5.5) are both DON and thus their execution is deterministic.

This section showed that one can identify a sub-calculus (DON terms) of ASP that is deterministic and inspired by Process Networks. The similarities between DON terms and Process Networks are further studied in Sect. 21.1.3. The idea is that, for a DON term, a *channel* is a set $M \in \mathcal{M}_\alpha$ for a given activity α. At any time, only one activity can send requests on this channel (because of the DON definition); remember that the process networks are based on the uniqueness of the sender for each channel. Such ASP channels have a behavior similar to the Process Networks ones, and one could simulate such channels by Process Networks channels. It is important to note that this definition of channels can be considered as a first step toward a static approximation of DON: if one can statically determine such channels and prove that two channels never interfere in the same *Serve* primitive of the same activity, then one obtains a confluent sub-calculus that is statically verifiable. Such a sub-calculus is presented in the next section.

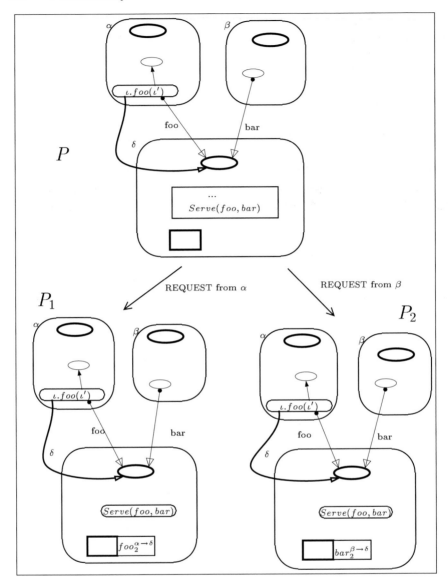

Fig. 9.1. A non-DON term

9.2 Toward a Static Approximation of DON Terms

The DON definition is dynamic. However, it could be approximated by statically determining the set of active objects that can send a request on method m of activity α. This means that one has first to statically decide whether an object is active or not (by static analysis). Note also that a static approximation of reachable configurations Q is needed. Such static analyses have been (heavily) studied in the literature (see for instance [60, 139]). Our objective is not to detail a static analysis of ASP, but rather to explain how such an analysis could ensure confluence statically.

More precisely, suppose one has a static over-approximation of activities: $\dot\alpha, \dot\beta, \dots$ ensuring that, dynamically, abstract activities can only be merged. That is to say, objects statically identified inside the same abstract activity *must* belong to the same dynamic activity.

Moreover, let $\mathcal{G}(P_0)$ be an *approximated call graph* (source activity, target activity, method label) between abstract activities; that is an, approximation of potential method calls between activities. More formally:

If dynamically a request on the method foo can be sent from α to β, and $\dot\alpha$ and $\dot\beta$ are the static approximations of activities α and β then $(\dot\alpha, \dot\beta, foo) \in \mathcal{G}(P_0)$:

$$P \xrightarrow{*} Q \wedge a_{\alpha_Q} = \mathcal{R}[\iota.foo(\iota')] \wedge \sigma_{\alpha_Q}(\iota) = AO(\beta) \Rightarrow (\dot\alpha, \dot\beta, foo) \in \mathcal{G}(P)$$

Consequently, the following property is an approximation of DON terms:

Definition 9.4 (Static DON) *A program P_0 is a Static Deterministic Object Network $SDON(P_0)$ if it verifies:*

$$SDON(P_0) \Leftrightarrow \left(\left\{ \begin{array}{l} (\dot\alpha, \dot\beta, m_1) \in \mathcal{G}(P_0) \\ (\dot\alpha', \dot\beta, m_2) \in \mathcal{G}(P_0) \Rightarrow \forall M \in \mathcal{M}_{\dot\beta_{P_0}}, \{m_1, m_2\} \not\subseteq M \\ \dot\alpha \neq \dot\alpha' \end{array} \right. \right)$$

where $\forall\beta, M \in \mathcal{M}_{\beta_P} \Rightarrow M \in \mathcal{M}_{\dot\beta_P}$.

Of course, Static DON terms are DON terms and behave deterministically:

Property 9.5 (Static approximation)

$$SDON(P_0) \Rightarrow DON(P_0)$$

Theorem 9.6 (SDON determinism)
SDON terms behave deterministically:

$$\begin{cases} SDON(P) \\ P \xrightarrow{*} Q_1 \\ P \xrightarrow{*} Q_2 \end{cases} \implies Q_1 \curlyvee Q_2$$

For example, as explained informally in Sect.9.1 page 122, the pull version of the sieve of Eratosthenes is an SDON term whereas the push version is not (contrarily to Fig. 5.6, in Fig. 5.4 the object dependence graph forms a tree).

Despite the convenient static approximation of DON terms presented here, the dynamic nature of the DON property is rather intrinsic and unavoidable: active objects are created dynamically; the dependencies between objects can evolve over time; over different periods, different activities can send requests to a given activity. These changes in object topology can be related to reconfigurations in Process Networks [100].

9.3 Tree Topology Determinism

In this section a much simpler static approximation of DON terms is performed. It has the advantage of being correct even in the highly interleaving case of FIFO services.

A *request flow graph* is a graph where nodes are activities and there is an edge between two activities if one activity has previously sent requests to another one ($\alpha \rightarrow_R \beta$ if α has sent a request to β). Such a graph only grows with time.

It is easy to prove that if, at every step of the reduction, the request flow graph is a tree, then the term verifies the DON definition. Indeed, at any time a unique activity can send a request to a given one. Thus, for each $\alpha \in Q$, $RSL(\alpha)$ contains occurrences of at most one activity (the same activities for all possible reductions): $RSL(\alpha) = \beta :: \beta :: \beta \ldots$. Then for all Q and R such that $P \xrightarrow{*} Q \wedge P \xrightarrow{*} R$, Q and R are compatible ($Q \bowtie R$) as they can only differ by the existing activities and the length of their RSLs (of course, $\beta :: \beta \bowtie \beta :: \beta :: \beta$). As a consequence:

Theorem 9.7 (Tree determinacy, TDON)

If, at every step of the reduction, the request flow graph forms a set of trees then the reduction is deterministic (TDON).

This property can also be seen as an approximation of SDON determinism in the case where the names of the invoked methods are abstracted away. Indeed if one does not care about name of method, all requests sent to a given activity are merged and all potential services become $\mathcal{M}$, the set of all method labels, in which case a channel is simply a link between two activities on which a request can be sent.

What is important here is to see that while the request flow graph forms a tree, the reduction is deterministic. Indeed, on a global synchronization, one can reset the request flow graph to an empty one. Then, in order to prove that a term is confluent, one only has to study determinism at moments when the request flow graph is not a tree. For example, consider a program that first, creates and communicates over a set of activities forming a tree, performs a global synchronization step, and finally communicates over another tree. Such a program results in a deterministic behavior.

9.4 Deterministic Examples

9.4.1 The Binary Tree

The binary tree of Fig. 5.1 page 76 verifies Theorem 9.7 and thus behaves deterministically provided that, at each time, at most one client can add new nodes.

Figure 9.2 illustrates the evaluation of the term:

$$let\ tree = (BT.new).add(3,4).add(2,3).add(5,6).add(7,8)\ in$$
$$[a = tree.search(5), b = tree.search(3)].b := tree.search(7)$$

This term behaves in a deterministic manner whatever order of replies occurs.

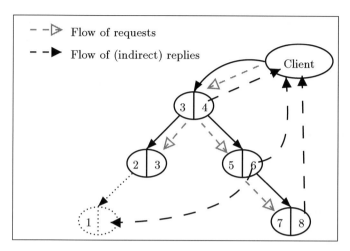

Fig. 9.2. Concurrent replies in the binary tree case

Now consider that the result of a preceding request is used to create a new node (dotted lines at bottom left of Fig. 9.2):

$$let\ tree = (BT.new).add(3,4).add(2,3).add(5,6).add(7,8)\ in$$
$$let\ Client = [a = tree.search(5), b = tree.search(3)]\ in$$
$$Client.b := tree.search(7);\ tree.add(1, Client.a)$$

Remember that future updates can occur at any time. For instance, the value associated to the result of $tree.search(5)$ is not needed, neither by the client nor by the leave created with key 1. Consequently, a future update occurs directly from node number 5 to node number 1 as soon as the result of $tree.search(5)$ is not updated before the creation of node number 1.

9.4.2 The Fibonacci Number Example

To show the application of DON and SDON theorems (Theorem 9.3 and 9.6), let us examine the Fibonacci number example of Section 5.4 page 80.

In the following, we will show that this example is fully deterministic but does not verify a tree topology. This example is a very convenient way of comparing the different approximations performed in this chapter. We will first show that Fibonacci numbers example leads to compatible configurations, we will then show that it is easier to prove that Fibonacci numbers verify the

DON property, and we will conclude by showing that the SDON definition is even easier to verify. Of course, the more easily the property can be verified the fewer the number of programs verify it.

Compatibility

Figure 9.3 shows the Fibonacci number example of Fig. 5.9 with the RSLs inside the bottom rectangles of each activity.

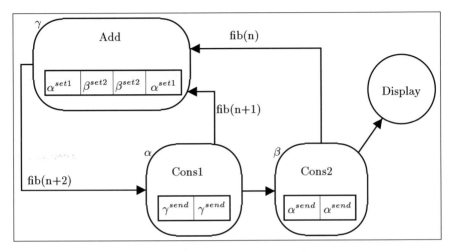

Fig. 9.3. Fibonacci number RSLs

The most interesting activity is the one containing the *Add* object (activity γ); we will focus on this one. In the most general case, its RSL is of the form:[1]

$$RSL(\gamma) = \emptyset \mid \beta^{set2} \mid \alpha^{set1} \mid$$
$$\alpha^{set1} :: \beta^{set2} :: RSL(\gamma) \mid \beta^{set2} :: \alpha^{set1} :: RSL(\gamma)$$

The potential services of activity γ are:

$$\mathcal{M}_{\gamma ExempleFibo} = \{\{set1\}, \{set2\}\}$$

Thus, in all possible executions, one has:

$$RSL(\gamma)\big|_{set1} = \alpha^*$$

$$RSL(\gamma)\big|_{set2} = \beta^*$$

---

[1] One could find a more precise form for the RSL but it is not our purpose here.

As a consequence, all the configurations obtained in the Fibonacci number example have compatible RSLs and thus are compatible. Finally, the Fibonacci number example is deterministic. However, it seems difficult to prove formally and statically that the RSL has the general form given above.

Fibonacci Example Is a DON

By comparison, let us prove that the Fibonacci number example verifies the DON definition. To reach that goal, we must verify that at each time only one activity can send a request on these potential services:

$$\mathcal{M}_{\gamma ExempleFibo} = \{\{set1\}, \{set2\}\}$$

Thus we will consider separately the request on $set1$ and on $set2$.

One can easily verify that only $Cons1$ invokes the $set1$ method on the Add object (program Fig.5.9, page 80). Thus, for the activity α:

$$\forall \delta \in Fibo \neq \alpha, \, a_\delta = \mathcal{R}[\iota.set1(\ldots)] \wedge \sigma_\delta(\iota) = AO(\gamma) \text{ is impossible}$$

and:

$$\exists^1 \alpha, \, a_\alpha = \mathcal{R}[\iota.set1(\ldots)] \wedge \sigma_\alpha(\iota) = AO(\gamma)$$

Similarly, only $Cons2$ invokes the $set2$ method on the Add object:

$$\exists^1 \beta, \, a_\beta = \mathcal{R}[\iota.set2(\ldots)] \wedge \sigma_\beta(\iota) = AO(\gamma)$$

Thus Theorem 9.3 states that the Fibonacci number example has a deterministic behavior.

This example shows that the DON property is, to our mind, an interesting first step toward the *static detection of confluent programs*. On the other hand, complex control-flow information is necessary to find the possible RSLs, and this is much more difficult to determine statically. The DON determinism is somewhat intermediate between the highly control-flow-based confluence property based on potential RSL and the totally static approximation provided by SDON. Indeed to verify the DON property one must consider the potential reductions for a given program, but the precise interleaving of request sending is not necessary. However, for a DON but not an SDON term one must guarantee that some synchronization prevents two interfering method calls from being sent concurrently.

SDON Approximation

More statically, and less precisely, from a static approximation of active objects and method calls, it seems easy to verify the SDON property (when it is true).

Indeed, Fig. 5.8 page 80 shows the result of what could be a static approximation of the set of activities involved in a Fibonacci program and of an associated method call (with labeled arrows linking processes). Once again, let us focus on the *Add* object. Two activities can send requests on the γ activity but these requests concern two different methods that cannot interfere in the same *Serve* primitive. In other words, Fig. 5.8 shows that the Fibonacci example follows the SDON definition (Definition 9.4):

$$\left(\left\{ \begin{array}{l} (\dot{\alpha}, \dot{\gamma}, set1) \in \mathcal{G}(P_0) \\ (\dot{\beta}, \dot{\gamma}, set2) \in \mathcal{G}(P_0) \\ \dot{\alpha} \neq \dot{\beta} \end{array} \right. \right) \Rightarrow \forall M \in \{\{set1\}, \{set2\}\}, \{set1, set2\} \not\subseteq M$$

This time, Theorem 9.6 is sufficient to prove the determinacy of the Fibonacci example, and illustrate the fact that the SDON determinacy is the most easily verified one (direct from Fig. 5.8).

Details on the static analysis of ASP calculus are beyond the scope of this book, but are a promising avenue toward deciding statically the determinate nature of distributed programs.

9.5 Discussion: Comparing Request Service Strategies

FIFO service is, to some extent, the worst case with respect to determinism, as any out-of-order reception of requests will lead to non-determinism.

By contrast, a request service *by source activity* (e.g., of the form $Serve(\alpha)$) is entirely confluent. More precisely, if no FIFO service were allowed, and the service determined by method label ($Serve(M)$ service primitive) were replaced by a service determined by the source activity of requests ($Serve(\alpha)$ service primitive), then the resulting calculus would be fully confluent. Indeed, the request service order would be the same whatever the interleaving of request arriving. This aspect is not developed here but could be very interesting if the order of activities sending a request to a given one was known. Such a calculus would be somewhat similar to process networks where *get* operations are performed on a given channel, and a channel only has one source process. However, specifying in a language from whom a sever accepts (serves) requests is no longer considered a general option as clients must remain anonymous for the sake of modularity.

Even if the DON definition allows a great flexibility for the general case, it seems difficult to find a more precise static property for FIFO services than the tree determinacy (Theorem 9.7). Indeed, FIFO services enforce a merging of all possible method labels which systematically reduces SDON to the tree topology. Of course, if a static analysis revealed some information about synchronization between processes then the tree topology would not be a necessary condition for determinacy. Nevertheless, even in this case one could probably identify several tree topology phases separated by (local or global) synchronization phases.

10

More Confluent Features

This chapter presents confluent features that can be added to ASP. In some sense these features already exist in ASP but all the constructs presented here appear to be very convenient, and a specific syntax is indeed very useful. Of course, in the beginning of this book, some other confluent constructors have already (and classically) been added to ASP core syntax (e.g., the *let ... in* primitive), but the features detailed in this chapter are strongly linked to concurrency and should be discussed in detail.

10.1 Delegation

First of all, it must be stressed that, due to first class futures, delegation is mostly useless. However, delegation points can be explicitly provided by the programmer for optimization purpose.

Principles of Explicit Delegation

In $\pi o\beta\lambda$, for example, a function can delegate the task of returning a value to another object by using the *yield* primitive. In that case, this object is no longer blocked and the result is directly returned from the last object to the first caller. In ASP, we can introduce a new primitive *delegate* that is similar to the *yield* primitive in $\pi o\beta\lambda$. But in our case, the expressive power of this primitive is much less important; indeed, in ASP, delegating only means leaving to another activity the task to give a value to the current future. In other words, a *delegate* primitive delegates the service of the current request to a new activity. In ASP, as futures are first-class objects, the value replied by an activity can be a future corresponding to another request, thus leading to some kind of implicit delegation.

Let *delegate(a)* denote the delegate primitive.

Contrarily to the $\pi o\beta\lambda$ case, in ASP, as in the ς-calculus, we impose that the returned value is the last value computed by a method. Consequently, we consider that *delegate* is the last primitive of a request. Performing the computation after returning a result from a request could also be specified in ASP and would not pose any technical difficulty.

delegate does not have any effect in the sequential case and is ignored.

Reduction Rules

The behavior of a *delegate(a)* primitive is described by the following two reduction rules (Table 10.1):

Parallel DELEGATE:

$$\frac{\sigma_\alpha(\iota) = AO(\beta) \quad \iota'' \notin dom(\sigma_\beta)}{\sigma'_\beta = Copy\&Merge(\sigma_\alpha, \iota' \; ; \; \sigma_\beta, \iota'') \quad f_\emptyset \text{ new future}}$$

$\alpha[\mathcal{R}[delegate(\iota.m_j(\iota'))]; \sigma_\alpha; \iota_\alpha; F_\alpha; R_\alpha; f_i^{\gamma \to \alpha}] \parallel \beta[a_\beta; \sigma_\beta; \iota_\beta; F_\beta; R_\beta; f_\beta] \parallel P \longrightarrow$
$\quad \alpha[\mathcal{R}[[]]; \sigma_\alpha; \iota_\alpha; F_\alpha; R_\alpha; f_\emptyset] \parallel \beta[a_\beta; \sigma'_\beta; \iota_\beta; F_\beta; R_\beta :: [m_j; \iota''; f_i^{\gamma \to \alpha}]; f_\beta] \parallel P$

Sequential DELEGATE:

$$\sigma_\alpha(\iota) = [l_i = \iota_i; m_j = \varsigma(x_j, y_j)a_j]_{j \in 1..m}^{i \in 1..n} \quad k \in 1..m$$

$\alpha[\mathcal{R}[delegate(\iota.m_j(\iota'))]; \sigma_\alpha; \iota_\alpha; F_\alpha; R_\alpha; f_\alpha] \parallel P \longrightarrow$
$\quad \alpha[\mathcal{R}[a_k \{\!\{ x_k \leftarrow \iota, y_k \leftarrow \iota' \}\!\}]; \sigma_\alpha; \iota_\alpha; F_\alpha; R_\alpha; f_\alpha] \parallel P$

Table 10.1. Rules for delegation (DELEGATE)

In the parallel case this rule means that delegation consists in letting β give the reply to the current request in α (corresponding to future $f_i^{\gamma \to \alpha}$). Then α replaces the current future by a dummy one or an empty future that can be directly garbage collected ($f_\emptyset$). α will continue its preceding computation by performing an unnecessary ENDSERVICE. In the sequential case, DELEGATE is a local rule that performs a sequential method call (*delegate* is ignored).

The first rule could also be replaced by a single rule delegating its future to another activity and restoring the stored continuation. This would avoid creating an unnecessary future but would necessitate consideration of request sending and restoration of continuation in the same rule. Consequently, the first rule of Table 10.1 could be replaced by the following one:

Parallel DELEGATE:

$$\frac{\sigma_\alpha(\iota) = AO(\beta) \quad \iota'' \notin dom(\sigma_\beta)}{\sigma'_\beta = Copy\&Merge(\sigma_\alpha, \iota' \; ; \; \sigma_\beta, \iota'') \quad \mathcal{R} \text{ does not contain any continuation}}$$

$\alpha[\mathcal{R}[delegate(\iota.m_j(\iota'))] \Uparrow (f, a); \sigma_\alpha; \iota_\alpha; F_\alpha; R_\alpha; f_i^{\gamma \to \alpha}] \parallel$
$\quad \beta[a_\beta; \sigma_\beta; \iota_\beta; F_\beta; R_\beta; f_\beta] \parallel P \longrightarrow$
$\alpha[a; \sigma_\alpha; \iota_\alpha; F_\alpha; R_\alpha; f] \parallel \beta[a_\beta; \sigma'_\beta; \iota_\beta; F_\beta; R_\beta :: [m_j; \iota''; f_i^{\gamma \to \alpha}]; f_\beta] \parallel P$

Actually, this rule corresponds to both REQUEST and ENDSERVICE rules. The condition "$\mathcal{R}$ does not contain any continuation" ensures that the term a

corresponds to the service that has to be restored (the one that triggered the service which performs the delegation).

In both cases, a new REPLY rule is needed to allow an activity that is not the original target of the request to answer it. Consequently a new mechanism for finding the activity that has calculated the value of a future is necessary.[1]

Consequently, the REPLY rule must be changed into the following one (notice that only the destination activity associated to the future is different):

Generalized REPLY:

$$\frac{\sigma_\alpha(\iota) = fut(f_i^{\gamma\to\delta}) \quad F_\beta(f_i^{\gamma\to\delta}) = \iota_f \quad \sigma_\alpha' = Copy\&Merge(\sigma_\beta, \iota_f \; ; \; \sigma_\alpha, \iota)}{\alpha[a_\alpha; \sigma_\alpha; \iota_\alpha; F_\alpha; R_\alpha; f_\alpha] \parallel \beta[a_\beta; \sigma_\beta; \iota_\beta; F_\beta; R_\beta; f_\beta] \parallel P \longrightarrow \\ \alpha[a_\alpha; \sigma_\alpha'; \iota_\alpha; F_\alpha; R_\alpha; f_\alpha] \parallel \beta[a_\beta; \sigma_\beta; \iota_\beta; F_\beta; R_\beta; f_\beta] \parallel P}$$

Of course, such a rule is still valid in the calculus without delegation. In the calculus presented up to now, one has necessarily $\delta = \beta$ while no delegation is performed, but one could imagine that a future value is stored in several activities (e.g., as soon as a future is updated), then such a rule would be really useful. Strategies for updating futures will be further discussed in Chap. 17.

Introducing this rule requires a slight modification of the definition of well-formed configurations (Definition 6.4) to take into account the fact that a future value may be calculated in an activity that is not the destination activity of the original request.

Definition 10.1 (Well-formedness)

$$\vdash P \text{ OK} \Leftrightarrow \forall \alpha \in P \begin{cases} \vdash (a_\alpha, \sigma_\alpha) \text{ OK} \\ \vdash (\iota_\alpha, \sigma_\alpha) \text{ OK} \\ \beta \in ActiveRefs(\alpha) \Rightarrow \beta \in P \\ f_i^{\beta\to\gamma} \in FutureRefs(\alpha) \Rightarrow \exists \delta, \; f_i^{\beta\to\gamma} \in FL(\delta) \end{cases}$$

Figure 10.1 shows an example of explicit delegation. α has sent a request to β which has delegated the reply to γ. Finally the future value associated to future f_1 is known by γ.

Implicit Delegation in ASP

As stated at the beginning of this section, delegation is implicitly handled in ASP thanks to first-class futures.

The behavior of the DELEGATE reduction is automatically simulated in ASP by the application of the following rules: one REQUEST, one ENDSERVICE, and several REPLY rules. In that case the reply is not delegated to another activity but we have two futures that are chained: a future value is a reference to another future.

---

[1] In the absence of delegation the activity that calculates the value associated to the future is encoded in the future identifier.

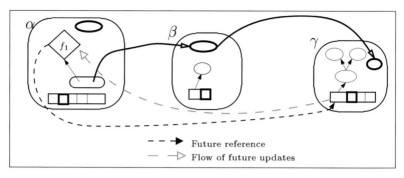

Fig. 10.1. Explicit delegation in ASP

To simulate the fact that β delegates to γ the service of a request sent by α (with associated future: $f_i^{\alpha \to \beta}$), a new future $f_j^{\beta \to \gamma}$ is created and the value associated to $f_i^{\alpha \to \beta}$ is simply $fut(f_j^{\beta \to \gamma})$:

REQUEST:

$$\frac{\sigma_\beta(\iota) = AO(\gamma) \quad \iota'' \notin dom(\sigma_\gamma) \quad f_i^{\beta \to \gamma} \text{ new future} \quad \iota_f \notin dom(\sigma_\beta)}{\sigma_\gamma' = Copy\&Merge(\sigma_\beta, \iota' ; \sigma_\gamma, \iota'') \quad \sigma_\beta' = \{\iota_f \mapsto fut(f_i^{\beta \to \gamma})\} :: \sigma_\beta}$$

$$\beta[\mathcal{R}[\iota.m_j(\iota')]; \sigma_\beta; \iota_\beta; F_\beta; R_\beta; f_i^{\alpha \to \beta}] \parallel \gamma[a_\gamma; \sigma_\gamma; \iota_\gamma; F_\gamma; R_\gamma; f_\gamma] \parallel P \longrightarrow$$
$$\beta[\mathcal{R}[\iota_f]; \sigma_\beta'; \iota_\beta; F_\beta; R_\beta; f_i^{\alpha \to \beta}] \parallel \gamma[a_\gamma; \sigma_\gamma'; \iota_\gamma; F_\gamma; R_\gamma :: [m_j; \iota''; f_i^{\beta \to \gamma}]; f_\gamma] \parallel P$$

ENDSERVICE:

$$\frac{\iota_f' \notin dom(\sigma_\beta) \quad F_\beta' = F_\beta :: \{f_i^{\alpha \to \beta} \mapsto \iota_f'\} \quad \sigma' = Copy\&Merge(\sigma_\beta', \iota_f ; \sigma_\beta'', \iota_f')}{\beta[\iota_f \Uparrow (f', a); \sigma_\beta'; \iota_\beta; F_\beta; R_\beta; f_i^{\alpha \to \beta}] \parallel P \longrightarrow \beta[a; \sigma_\beta''; \iota; F_\beta'; R; f'] \parallel P}$$

Then future $fut(f_i^{\beta \to \gamma})$ becomes an alias for future $f_i^{\delta \to \beta}$, and this alias information must be transmitted to all the potential users of the result by the REPLY rules, e.g., α:

REPLY:

$$\frac{\sigma_\alpha(\iota) = fut(f_i^{\alpha \to \beta}) \quad F_\beta'(f_i^{\gamma \to \beta}) = \iota_f}{\sigma_\beta''(\iota_f') = fut(f_i^{\beta \to \gamma}) \quad \sigma_\alpha' = \{\iota \to fut(f_i^{\beta \to \gamma})\} + \sigma_\alpha}$$

$$\alpha[a_\alpha; \sigma_\alpha; \iota_\alpha; F_\alpha; R_\alpha; f_\alpha] \parallel \beta[a_\beta; \sigma_\beta''; \iota_\beta; F_\beta'; R_\beta; f_\beta] \parallel P \longrightarrow$$
$$\alpha[a_\alpha; \sigma_\alpha'; \iota_\alpha; F_\alpha; R_\alpha; f_\alpha] \parallel \beta[a_\beta; \sigma_\beta''; \iota_\beta; F_\beta'; R_\beta; f_\beta] \parallel P$$

Consequently this new primitive does not add much expressive power but has important implementation consequences. Indeed such a primitive should greatly lower the number of replies and avoid most of the REPLY rules consisting of simple aliasing of futures (replies stating that the value associated to a future is another future). In a real language these unnecessary communications can be avoided at the cost of explicit programming, and as such the usage of a delegate primitive can be useful.

Figure 10.2 shows the flow of future updates that occurs in case of implicit delegation. α has sent a request to β which has replied with the future

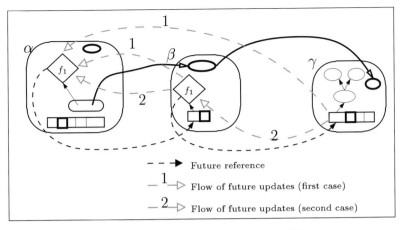

Fig. 10.2. Implicit delegation in ASP

corresponding to another request sent to γ. Compared to explicit delegation, implicit delegation requires one more reply rule, and consequently one more communication. Note that two flows of replies are possible depending on the order in which reply rules are applied; this order can be specified by a future update strategy (see Chap. 17).

10.2 Explicit Wait

It is sometimes necessary to perform an explicit synchronization, in order to wait until a future is updated. This can be performed in ASP by accessing any field of an object that can be a future. In practice, a *waitFor* primitive performing a wait-by-necessity on any kind of object is more convenient and easier to understand than accessing a particular field. This primitive can easily be encoded in ASP by the following transformation:

$$[\![l_i = b_i; m_j = \varsigma(x_j, y_j)a_j]_{j\in1..m}^{i\in1..n}]\!] \triangleq [wait = [], l_i = b_i; m_j = \varsigma(x_j, y_j)a_j]_{j\in1..m}^{i\in1..n}$$

$$[\![waitFor(a)]\!] \triangleq a.wait$$

The principle is to consider an implicit field, called *wait*, for each object. The *waitFor* primitive just accesses that implicit field.

As a consequence, such a primitive does not compromise the confluence property.

10.3 Method Update

Updating the methods of objects is nearly always possible in object calculi (e.g., basic ς-calculus objects do not contain fields, and thus in **imp**ς-calculus method update is added as the main imperative feature). This feature is generally not directly present in object languages even if it can be simulated. We chose not to include method update in our basic calculus, but as this feature does not compromise sequential properties like determinacy (Property 3.4), adding method update does not modify the semantics. There are two ways of adding method update in ASP.

First, method update can be expressed by updatable fields containing functions (encoding of lambda expressions). But this solution still have two drawbacks:

- Considering the sequential framework, there is no "self" parameter to lambda terms.
- Considering the parallel a framework, such method cannot be called directly from other activity because the other activity cannot access a field.

Those two problems can be solved by creating an updatable field and a method consisting in calling the lambda expression encoded in the field:[2]

$$[foo\_field = \lambda self.\lambda y.body, foo = \varsigma(x,y)\,((x.foo\_field\ x)\ y)]$$

Then updating a method becomes (if b is of the form $\lambda self.\lambda y.body$):

$$x.foo \Leftarrow b \triangleq x.foo\_field := b$$

Finally, calling such methods is unchanged.

Second, method update could be added directly as in the classical **impς**-calculi [3, 80], this would simply add one sequential rule for updating methods.

Method update is useful as soon as one wants to modify the behavior of an (active) object. For example, we will see that this is a valuable solution for handling migration. The main drawback of method update is that it may seem unnatural to be able to modify the body of a pending request. Indeed, method update can change the meaning of a request between the moment when it is put in a queue and the moment when it is treated.

Somehow, for an active object, this is like changing its already planned future. This might seem to tangle determinism, but indeed it is not the case. If an active object belongs to a configuration behaving deterministically, the change of its future was "planned," and was bound to occur before the service of the corresponding requests. So even with method update an active object belonging to a deterministic configuration cannot avoid its destiny; ASP determinism still applies in the presence of method update.

---

[2] The encoding of lambda terms and applications has already been defined, see Sect. 3.1, page 64.

Non-Confluent Features

Serving the oldest requests from different sources can introduce non-determinism in ASP. But some features, very useful in practice, introduce non-determinism even in a tree topology. Indeed, the behavior of the primitives presented in the text of this chapter is highly dependent on the time needed to communicate a request or a future even if there is no concurrent communication. For instance, such primitives enable to testing of the availability of a future value or a request. In such configurations the confluence properties presented in this book do not apply.

11.1 Testing Future Reception

In the preceding chapter, we presented a primitive *waitFor* allowing us to perform an explicit wait-by-necessity on any object. This primitive did not compromise confluence properties. A primitive much more powerful than *waitFor* allows us to determine whether a future has been updated or not. Of course the result returned by this primitive is highly dependent on the communication time and on the time necessary to treat a request. This primitive will be denoted by $awaited(a)$ which returns *true* if a is a *future* and *false* otherwise. It is described by the following two sequential rules.[1]

WAITT:

$$\frac{\sigma(\iota) = fut(f_i^{\alpha \to \beta})}{(\mathcal{R}[awaited(\iota)], \sigma) \to_S (\mathcal{R}[true], \sigma)}$$

---

[1] These rules are classified as sequential because they are local to an activity and are involved in the sequential reduction, but, of course, they could also be added to the parallel reduction.

WAITF:

$$\frac{\sigma(\iota) \neq fut(f_i^{\alpha \to \beta})}{(\mathcal{R}[awaited(\iota)], \sigma) \to_S (\mathcal{R}[false], \sigma)}$$

With this new primitive, no confluence property can be expressed but the counterpart of the loss of properties is a better expressive power concerning synchronization and scheduling of computations. For example, it allows one to perform computations in a different order depending on the order of reception of replies. It may also lower the number of times of wait-by-necessity, and consequently could allow the programmer to avoid some deadlocks.

A Simple Example: Synchronization on Available Futures

Suppose two activities referenced by *alpha* and *beta* are able to compute the Fibonacci number $fib(n)$, and the current activity wants to use that result as a parameter of a call to a method *foo*. The following term uses the first $fib(n)$ that is calculated to compute $foo(fib(n))$ and finally stores the result in *s.result*:

$let\ f_1 = alpha.fib(n)\ in$
$let\ f_2 = beta.fib(n)\ in$
   $Repeat$
      $if\ not(awaited(f_1))\ then\ s.result := foo(f_1)$
         $else\ if\ not(awaited(f_2))\ then\ s.result := foo(f_2)$
   $Until\ (not(awaited(f_1)) \vee not(awaited(f_2)))$

Of course, if the two activities do not calculate the same value for $fib(n)$, then the final value of *s.result* is non-deterministic. Here, if $fib(n)$ has the expected behavior, the overall execution leads to a deterministic value, but this example reveals the potential non-determinacy induced by the *awaited* primitive.

11.2 Non-blocking Services

Another non-confluent feature consists in serving a request only if it is in the request queue. The primitive $ServeWithoutBlocking(M)$ behaves like $Serve(M)$ if there is a request on a method belonging to M in the request queue but has no effect otherwise. As a consequence, if there is no request to be served, the activity is not blocked as it would be in the case of the primitive $Serve(\ldots)$. The reduction rules for non-blocking services are:

SERVEWBSERVE:

$$\frac{R = R' :: [m_j; \iota_r; f'] :: R'' \quad m_j \in M \quad \forall m \in M, m \notin R'}{\alpha[\mathcal{R}[ServeWithoutBlocking(M)]; \sigma; \iota; F; R; f] \parallel P \longrightarrow \\ \alpha[\iota.m_j(\iota_r) \Uparrow f, \mathcal{R}[[]]; \sigma; \iota; F; R' :: R''; f'] \parallel P}$$

SERVEWBCONTINUE:

$$\frac{\forall m \in M, m \notin R}{\alpha[\mathcal{R}[ServeWithoutBlocking(M)]; \sigma; \iota; F; R; f] \parallel P \longrightarrow \\ \alpha[\mathcal{R}[[]]; \sigma; \iota; F; R; f] \parallel P}$$

The first rule serves a request on a method belonging to M if such a method is found in the pending requests queue. The second rule just continues the local execution if no request to be served is in the pending requests queue.

Like the possibility to check the availability of a response to an asynchronous method call, the non-blocking service is a highly non-confluent feature, but allows the programmer to perform more complex services and to specify in a simple manner some scheduling policy.

11.3 Testing Request Reception

An even more general feature consists in testing the presence of a request in the request queue. We introduce the predicate $inQueue(M)$ that returns true when there is a request on a method of M in the request queue.

INQUEUET:

$$\frac{\exists m \in M, m \in R}{\alpha[\mathcal{R}[inQueue(M)]; \sigma; \iota; F; R; f] \parallel P \longrightarrow \alpha[\mathcal{R}[true]; \sigma; \iota; F; R; f] \parallel P}$$

INQUEUEF:

$$\frac{\forall m \in M, m \notin R}{\alpha[\mathcal{R}[inQueue(M)]; \sigma; \iota; F; R; f] \parallel P \longrightarrow \alpha[\mathcal{R}[false]; \sigma; \iota; F; R; f] \parallel P}$$

Of course, such a primitive allows encoding of the $ServeWithoutBlocking$ primitive:

$$ServeWithoutBlocking(M) \triangleq if \; inQueue(M) \; then \; Serve(M) \; else \; []$$

This new expression is not atomic: unlike the definition of the preceding section, several reductions are necessary to serve one request or to continue execution. Consequently, other reductions may be interleaved inside this nonblocking service. But this does not have any noticeable consequence on the behavior of programs.

The primitive $inQueue$ is more general than $ServeWithoutBlocking$ and allows sophisticated expressions of synchronization and service policies at the expense of some transparency. With such a powerful primitive one can express what we call *abstractions for concurrency control*: various patterns allowing the programmer to define specific synchronizations of concurrent programs. The next section presents the expression of such an abstraction.

11.4 Join Patterns

Join patterns, as in join-calculus (cf. Sect. 2.2.4), allows one to express the fact that an action can be the consequence of the simultaneous presence of several messages. Of course, the *inQueue* primitive allows us to express the service of a request as the consequence of the simultaneous presence of several pending requests $(inQueue(M_1) \land inQueue(M_2))$, but it is not possible to directly collect the arguments of several method calls in the ASP calculus.

From another point of view, the core calculus (which verifies the confluence property) allows us to collect the arguments of several methods. Indeed, several request arguments can be collected sequentially (by sequentially serving those requests), and, as the sequential execution is entirely deterministic, this will have the same effect as if the arguments were collected simultaneously. Moreover, the notion of inner services (the service of a new request while another one is being served) allows us to consider that, inside an inner service, several requests are being served. Consequently, using both *inQueue* primitives and imbricated requests seems to be adequate for simulating join patterns.

A less obvious aspect concerning the join patterns is setting the replies to those different requests, and more precisely setting which service must give a significant reply in the case of inner services. In the case of ASP, a first answer is trivial: all served requests must give a reply. But in the join-calculus, one generally considers that there is only one action for all the messages involved in a given join pattern. In ASP, it would mean that only one request must give a significant result.

11.4.1 Translating Join Calculus Programs

The join-calculus example of Fig. 2.12 (page 43) expresses a cell in join calculus. Of course, an activity encoding a cell can be encoded in a more object-oriented way, but in order to illustrate the possibility of encoding join patterns in ASP, Fig. 11.1 adopts a join pattern approach. We chose to express this example in a rather systematic translation in order to give hints about the possibility of translating the join-calculus in ASP.

In this example:

- the fields are used to store the values sent as arguments of the request,
- the join patterns are programmed with expressions involving *inQueue* primitives,

$$Cell \triangleq Active([s_v = [], set_v = [];$$
$$set = \varsigma(this, v)this.set_v := v$$
$$s = \varsigma(this, v)this.s_v := v$$
$$get = \varsigma(this)[]$$
$$srv = \varsigma(this)Repeat(if\ inQueue(s) \wedge inQueue(set)\ then$$
$$this.setcell()$$
$$if\ inQueue(s) \wedge inQueue(get)\ then$$
$$this.getcell()),$$
$$setcell() = \varsigma(this)(Serve(set); Serve(s); thisActivity.s(this.set_v)),$$
$$getcell() = \varsigma(this)(Serve(get); Serve(s); thisActivity.s(this.s_v); this.s_v))$$

Fig. 11.1. A join-calculus cell in ASP

- the request service is used both to dequeue the pending requests, and to store the arguments of these requests in the fields of the active object.

Contrarily to the join-calculus example (Fig. 2.12), the entity s is not a private channel in the cell of Fig. 11.1: local elements in ASP are fields and methods that are never served; but using fields to replace the local channel s would lead to a trivial implementation of cells that would not illustrate the possibility of expressing join patterns.

The cell object of Fig. 11.1 is used as follows:

$$Cell.s([]); Cell.set([x = 2]); Cell.get()$$

11.4.2 Extended Join Services in ASP

We introduce here new primitives that could be specified or programmed in order to program with join patterns or join services within ASP.

The essence of a join pattern is to execute specific code on receipt of specific messages. In order to fully express such a concept in a method-based language, one would need a construct where a piece of code can be specified as a parameter. For instance, the following construct

$$Join((m_1, m_2, M_1), (m_1, m_3, M_2), ...)$$

could express that upon recept of requests onto both methods m_1 and m_2, then a method named M_1 is executed, and the result of that method is used to set the result of requests m_1 and m_2 themselves, if they exist – ano alternative is to define a construct with a unique method returning a value and playing the role of the join body, along the lines of what is done in the Polyphonic C# [28]. Mechanisms to transmit the effective parameters of m_1 and m_2 to the code M_1 can also be used, either extending the syntax above, or using reification. However, specifying a semantics for such new primitives seems tedious.

As a consequence, we just provide here a primitive that sequentially serves several requests upon their simultaneous presence. The full primitive above can be simulated with the one below at the expense of manually encoding some switching upon the requests being received.

More specifically, we introduce the new primitive $Join(...)$ that takes a set of lists of method labels. $Join((m_1, m_2), (m_1, m_3))$ serves either m_1 then m_2, or m_1 then m_3, but only starts upon the simultaneous presence of m_1 and m_2, or m_1 and m_3. For instance, here is an example below together with its translation:

$$Join((m_1, m_2), (m_1, m_3)) \triangleq let\ served = false\ in$$
$$Repeat$$
$$if\ (inQueue(m_1) \wedge inQueue(m_2))\ then$$
$$(Serve(m_1);\ Serve(m_2);\ served := true)$$
$$else\ if\ (inQueue(m_1) \wedge inQueue(m_3))\ then$$
$$(Serve(m_1);\ Serve(m_3);\ served := true)$$
$$Until(served = true)$$

Let us now generalize this translation to k patterns joining n_k requests:

$$Join((m_{11}, m_{12}, \ldots, m_{1n_1}), (m_{21}, \ldots, m_{2n_2}), \ldots (m_{k1}, \ldots, m_{kn_k})) \triangleq$$
$$let\ served = false\ in$$
$$Repeat$$
$$if\ (inQueue(m_{11}) \wedge inQueue(m_{12}) \wedge \ldots \wedge inQueue(m_{1n_1}))\ then$$
$$(Serve(m_{11});\ Serve(m_{12}); \ldots Serve(m_{1n_1});\ served := true)$$
$$else\ if\ (inQueue(m_{21}) \wedge \ldots \wedge inQueue(m_{2n_2}))\ then$$
$$(Serve(m_{21}); \ldots Serve(m_{2n_2});\ served := true)$$
$$else\ if\ (inQueue(m_{k1}) \wedge \ldots \wedge inQueue(m_{kn_k}))\ then$$
$$\ldots$$
$$(Serve(m_{k1}); \ldots Serve(m_{kn_k});\ served := true)$$
$$Until(served = true)$$

Of course, such a Join primitive is by its essence highly non-confluent as it tests request reception and branches upon that information.

The Join pattern above serves methods in an order specified by the construct usage. $Join((m_1, m_2), (m_1, m_3))$ always serves m_1 first, and only after m_2 or m_3 has also been received. Another non-confluent feature would be a barrier pattern where the order of services is not fully fixed by the construct usage but is rather influenced by the request arrival order.

Let us call such a primitive $Barrier$. It takes a single list of method names as its parameters. For instance, in the following example

$$Barrier(m_1, m_2, ..., m_n)$$

a single request is served for each of the m_i, and each service occurs as soon as possible, i.e., in the order of the request arrival.

Note that the following barrier call

$$Barrier(m_1, m_2)$$

is different from two successive calls to the service primitive:

$$Serve(m_1, m_2); \; Serve(m_1, m_2)$$

The latter can lead to the servicing of two m_1 or two m_2. The former always leads to the servicing of a single m_1 and a single m_2, in any order. The *barrier* construct helps efficiency and latency reduction. An example of its usage is provided in Sect. 16.2.3 (Fibonacci), page 211.

Several other join patterns can be imagined. For instance one can program a mixture of the two above: when the concurrent branches permit, the methods are executed as soon as possible, i.e., upon arrival. A construct like

$$JoinBarrier((m_1, m_2, m_3), (m_4, m_2, m_5))$$

would then have the following behavior: whenever the first occurence of the request aimed at m_2 arrives, it is served immediately in that setting. On the contrary, serving a request aimed at m_1 also requires one aimed at m_3, similarly for m_4 and m_5.

We believe the number of useful patterns for concurrency control is indeed unbounded. As a consequence, such patterns, we call *abstractions for concurrency control*, should be programmable in a flexible and reusable manner in a concurrent language, rather than being a primitive construct. Caromel [48] analyzes the requirements to achieve that flexibility in a language. Within a calculus, ASP provides such a capability.

12

Migration

ASP is a calculus suited for expressing *distributed* objects: as references to active objects are global, each activity can be placed on a different machine. However, the core ASP calculus did not explicitly include a primitive for moving activities between different machines. This chapter discusses and introduces such primitives for computational mobility.

ASP also does not include the notion of *a location* where an activity lives. The calculus is on purpose location-less: convergence and determinism are valid whatever the physical location of activities. As this chapter deals with studying computational mobility, in essence a change in location, we will consider migration as a very practical two-step operation:

1. a deep-copy of an activity, followed by
2. a kind of reincarnation in a new activity.

Indeed, this is exactly what needs to be achieved in practice for moving activities (threads) from one machine to another. Studying these operations will provide important feedback on the impact of migration on confluence.

However, it is important to note that the solution presented in this chapter totally loses the state of the current term that triggered the execution. In other words, if migration is performed during a request service, this request will have no result. The continuation of the current term is lost too. Making an activity responsible for finishing the current service in a sound way is much more complicated and will not be studied here.

12.1 Migrating Active Objects

This section presents a solution for migrating an activity. This solution moves all the useful objects (starting with the active one) and the pending requests. Inside the old activity, a forwarder active object replaces the previous one.

The *Active* primitive can be used to create a new activity with the active object of the current activity at its root; this creates a clone of the initial activity, potentially at a different location, hence moving an active object. However, this cannot be considered as an expression of mobility because it does not move the pending requests nor the existing references to the activity; thus received and pending requests will still be treated in the old activity. Unceasingly forwarding (in FIFO order) all the requests in the request queue to the newly created activity transfers both pending and new requests to the migrated activity. The old activity acts as a *forwarder*. This old activity still holds future values for previously finished requests. Thus it is also useful for storing and replying to previously computed future values.

This methodology first requires that there is a mechanism for obtaining the location of the active object of the current activity. This means introducing a new primitive: *thisActivity*. If it is the active object that triggers the migration *thisActivity* $\triangleq$ *this*. Otherwise, we would need either to add a new operator *thisActivity* to our calculus that reduces to ι_α in an activity α or to maintain a field named *thisActivity* in all objects.[1]

Then one could migrate an object by calling *thisActivity.Migrate*() and adding the following method to the active object:

$$Migrate = \varsigma(this)\,let\ newao = Active(this, sevice)\ in$$
$$(CreateForwarders(newao); FifoService)$$

where *service* is the service method to be executed when the activity has migrated, and *CreateForwarders(newao)* replaces the body of each method of the current active object by a forwarded call:

$$CreateForwarders(newao) \triangleq \forall m_j,\ m_j \Leftarrow \varsigma(x,y)newao.m_j(y)$$

This necessitates having updatable methods in ASP like those introduced in Sect. 10.3.

Automatically, all pending requests and all requests that will be received in the future will be forwarded to the newly created activity. Such work is clearly strongly related to the Øjeblik assertion [41]:

$$surrogate = \varsigma(s)s.alias\langle s.clone\rangle$$

This mechanism creates a chain of method calls due to forwarding and a chain of futures for transmitting the reply as shown in Fig. 12.1.

In Fig. 12.1, one has two forwarders β_1 and β_2 finally pointing to activity β (the active object of activity β has migrated twice). Consequently, each request

---

[1] This last solution seems difficult to write because it requires a lot of additional treatment on activation, on object creation, on arguments of requests, and with more difficulty on future updates (because of their transparent and automatic aspect).

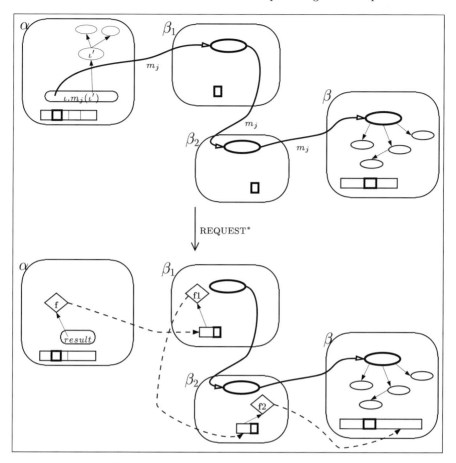

Fig. 12.1. Chain of method calls and chain of corresponding futures

(e.g., m_j) sent to activity β_1 is actually forwarded twice and a chain of aliased futures will be created: f, f_1, and f_2 all represent the future associated to the same original request. The value of f is a reference to the future f_1, which value is a reference to the future f_2, which value will be the real result of the request.

12.2 Optimizing Future Updates

With such a mechanism, the chain of asynchronous method calls is associated to a chain of futures. This means that a lot of replies are necessary to update the result corresponding to a request. Even if it is not straightforward to remove the forwarding, it seems possible to shorten the reply mechanism.

The number of replies could be lowered by using *delegation*. Indeed forward-based migration seems to be a very classical application for the *delegate* mechanism detailed in Sect. 10.1. Each forwarded method call becomes a delegated method call to the migrated activity and the future associated to the request is of the form $f_i^{\alpha \to \beta}$ where β is the activity to which the original request has been sent (the activity before migration). Recall that the delegation mechanism implies the usage of a new REPLY rule stating that a future can be updated from an activity that is not the original source of the request. Here, it is the activity after migration which calculates the future value.

By applying such a strategy, each method becomes a delegated (forwarded) method call:

$$CreateForwarders(newao) \triangleq \forall m_j,\, m_j \Leftarrow \varsigma(x, y)\, delegate(newao.m_j(y))$$

This methodology applied to the example of Fig. 12.1 would lead to future f directly pointing to the pending request of activity β.

12.3 Migration and Confluence

Concerning confluence properties, the encoding of migration presented here only uses confluent features; indeed *thisActivity* primitive does not compromise confluence because it is a purely local rule that cannot interfere with another local rule.

The unique rendezvous used for sending a request to an object that has not migrated is transformed into several rendezvous between the sender, the forwarders, and the destination. If all requests are sent to the same forwarder then the FIFO order is preserved and we obtain an asynchronous FIFO communication instead of an asynchronous communication with rendezvous. Chapter 18 will show that this is still sufficient for ensuring determinism in most cases.

However, some requests may become concurrent because they are sent to different instances of the same (migrated) object. For example, the same activity may send concurrently two requests to an object before and after migration. In Fig. 12.1, the order of reception of two requests $\beta_1.m_j$ and $\beta.m_j$ is not guaranteed, even if both requests come from the same activity α. This does not strictly compromise the confluence property (Property 8.10 page 118) because the forwarder and the migrated active object are two concurrent activities; thus a request sent directly to β may interfere with another forwarded by β_1.

From a higher level point of view, one might like to merge the forwarder and migrated object as a single entity because all these different activities *represent* the same effective activity. Let *entity* refer to the set consisting of a migrated active object and all its forwarders. In this context, if all requests sent to an entity are actually sent to the same activity then the confluence properties are still ensured, or else some requests sent to the same entity may overtake themselves.

Contrarily to the preceding chapter, confluence problems that can arise in the case of migration are not directly due to communication time. Here, concurrency can be expressed in terms of interfering requests even if two requests coming from the same activity and sent to the same entity can become concurrent. Such considerations are strongly related to the loss of rendezvous in communication (see Chap. 18).

In order to implement migration, several localization protocols can be used. They are presented in the part dedicated to the implementation strategies, namely Part V, Sect. 16.1.4, page 192.

13

Groups

Group communications are crucial for scalability. The group concept is used in a wide spectrum of frameworks, from network multicast to message services in Web-oriented middleware (e.g., JMS [85]). We are aiming here at a group concept fitting within a typed and object world.

Being in a framework with method-based communications, we are seeking a group on which methods can be called. In the same way one can call methods on a given object, and it should be possible to call the same methods on a group of such objects, without restrictions on the method signatures. As we will see, this implies the dynamic and automatic creation of groups, for instance upon a group call on a method returning a result. In short, we propose in this chapter a very dynamic and unrestricted form of *typed group communications*.

Further, groups of active objects can be proposed. Indeed, this is made possible by the systematic asynchronous communication that is at the root of ASP. With respect to practical large-scale distributed systems, this feature is crucial for hiding latency. In one perspective, it produces opportunities for distributed and parallel components.

The chapter first studies the typed group notion for any objects, in the framework of the ς-calculus. A second section proposes groups of active objects, featuring asynchronous group calls and groups of futures. Finally, the implication on confluence and determinism is analyzed. We study the consequences over group behavior of an important semantic variation: *group atomicity*.

13.1 Groups in an Object Calculus

This section introduces and defines the semantics of a new constructor for creating groups of objects in ASP. $Group(a_1, \ldots, a_n)$ creates a new entity formed by the objects $a_1, \ldots, a_n$. These objects can be either active or passive. The semantics of groups is first defined as a simple extension of local reduction rules. Then, a purely syntactic formulation for groups without field update is defined.

Group Constructor

The syntax of ASP is extended as follows (a_k, $k \in 1..l$,range over the objects of the created group):

$$a, b \in L ::= \ldots, \qquad \text{ASP without groups}$$
$$| \ Group(a_k)^{k \in 1..l} \quad \text{group constructor}$$

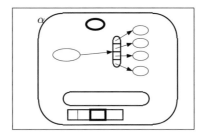

Fig. 13.1. A group of passive objects

The $Group(a_k)^{k \in 1..l})$ primitive creates a group of l objects with the a_k. Figure 13.1 illustrates a group of four passive objects.

Groups as an Extension of Local Semantics: A Group Proxy

Let us first define a new kind of object that can be kept in the store: a group proxy ($Gr(\ldots)$) is a particular object made of a group of objects. Following the store principle, a group can be stored if it only contains objects that are reduced (to a location):

$$o ::= \ldots \qquad \text{reduced object, or active object or future reference}$$
$$| Gr(\iota_k)^{k \in 1..l} \quad \text{group of references}$$

Reduction contexts are extended as follows. Evaluation of a group constructor is performed from left to right:

$$\mathcal{R} ::= \ldots | \ Group(\iota_k, \mathcal{R}, b_{k'})^{k \in 1..m-1, k' \in m+1..l}$$

Then one must add new rules for evaluation of groups. A simple approach specifies reduction rules for groups as an extension of the sequential calculus semantics. Table 13.1 expresses the reduction rules which consist in creating, for all constructors that are stuck when applied to a group, a new group built by performing the required operation on each object of the group. For example, performing a method call on a group creates a new group with the results of the method calls performed on each object of the group. The "Store group" rule is similar to STOREALLOC: it puts a reduced group in the store.

Store group:

$$\frac{\iota \notin dom(\sigma)}{(Group(\iota_k)^{k \in 1..l}, \sigma) \rightarrow_G (\iota, \{\iota \mapsto Gr(\iota_k)^{k \in 1..l}\} :: \sigma)}$$

Field access:

$$\frac{\sigma(\iota) = Gr(\iota_k)^{k \in 1..l}}{(\mathcal{R}[\iota.l_i], \sigma) \rightarrow_G (Group(\iota_k.l_i)^{k \in 1..l}, \sigma)}$$

Field update:

$$\frac{\sigma(\iota) = Gr(\iota_k)^{k \in 1..l}}{(\mathcal{R}[\iota.l_i := \iota'], \sigma) \rightarrow_G (Group(\iota_k.l_i := \iota')^{k \in 1..l}, \sigma)}$$

Invoke method:

$$\frac{\sigma(\iota) = Gr(\iota_k)^{k \in 1..l}}{(\mathcal{R}[\iota.m_j(\iota')], \sigma) \rightarrow_G (Group(\iota_k.m_j(\iota'))^{k \in 1..l}, \sigma)}$$

Table 13.1. Reduction rules for groups

These rules do not interfere with local or parallel reduction, and thus do not compromise confluence properties. Indeed, these rules only allow reduction of those terms that would otherwise be stuck.

The semantics expresses that a single instruction results in performing l operations (one for each member of the group). If members of the group are passive objects then these operations are performed sequentially.

In the case of a method call toward a group object, the same argument is sent to all objects of the group. However, we could imagine a new primitive taking two groups and sending to each object of the destination group an object of the parameter group (this supposes that the size (l) of the parameter group would be equal to the size of the target group).

At this point, operations on groups are similar to *map* operations on functional languages, but are performed automatically on some particular kinds of objects.

A Purely Syntactic Formulation

The expression of group semantics given above is based on a modification of local reduction rules. We give below a purely syntactic encoding of groups that allows us to keep the original ASP semantics.

The following syntactic encoding of groups is based on the hypothesis that every field of a group object is replaced by a method with no argument, recall that this was already the case in the **impς**-calculus [3].

The following solution is not adequate for encoding groups with updatable fields, but provides a purely syntactic encoding of groups that does not require an extension of the local semantics. As for dealing with fields of active objects, setters and getters could be added to objects belonging to a group in order to allow field updates inside a group of objects.

The function $Group(a_1, \ldots, a_n)$ creates a group of objects (active or not), and returns for each method call on a group object a new group formed by the results of the method calls to each object of the group:

$$let \ Group = \lambda a_1 \ldots a_n.[\ g_1 = a_1, \ldots, g_n = a_n,$$
$$\forall j, \ m_j = \varsigma(x, y) Group(x.g_i.m_j(y))]$$

The following of this chapter is based on the first formulation but is generally valid for both. To be precise, only the reduction rule for atomic group communication (Table 13.2) is based on a modification of the semantics. However, a complex formulation for atomic group communications in the case of the purely syntactic encoding could also be found.

13.2 Groups of Active Objects

The above definitions of groups of objects allow us to define groups of (references to) active or passive objects. Even groups where some of the objects are active and some others are passive can be defined. However, groups are mainly useful when dealing with active objects; in that case groups provide a new abstraction for the parallel evaluation of terms.

Let us define the creation of a group of active objects: $ActiveGroup(a_1, \ldots, a_n, m)$ creates a group of references to an activity built by activation of objects $a_1, \ldots, a_n$. It is not restrictive to suppose that the same service method is invoked on every activated object:

$$ActiveGroup(a_1, \ldots, a_n, m) \triangleq Group(Active(a_1, m), \ldots, Active(a_n, m))$$

Sending a request to such an active object consists, in fact, in sending one request to each of the n objects of the group. The result of this invocation is stored in a group containing only references to futures. These futures will be naturally updated by the classical REPLY rule, in any order.

Note that accessing a field of a group where some of the objects are active necessarily leads to a stuck configuration.

Figure 13.2 shows a group of active objects and the result after a request sent to this group of active objects. The configuration on the right is obtained from the leftmost one by applying one $\to_G$ rule, four REQUEST rules for sending one request to each member of the group and associating a future to this request, and one local reduction to store the object consisting of the group of futures.

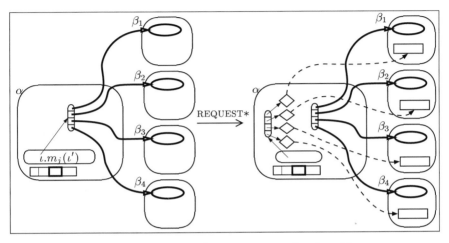

Fig. 13.2. Request sending to a group of active objects

Let us now study the behavior of $Active(Group(a_1, \ldots, a_n), m)$ and compare it to $ActiveGroup(a_1, \ldots, a_n, m)$.

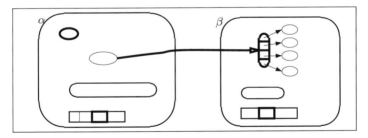

Fig. 13.3. An activated group of objects

$Active(Group(a_1, \ldots, a_n), m)$ creates a group of *passive* objects and activates this group.

Figure 13.3 shows an activated group of passive objects, to be compared to the configuration of Fig. 13.2 consisting of a group of four active objects.

Each request sent to the activated group will trigger n *sequential* method invocations during the request service, one on each object of the group. The result of a request to such an activated group is a single future whose value is a group of objects.

If $m = \emptyset$ then this group activity performs a FIFO service.

If $m \neq \emptyset$ then the service method m is taken in the first object of the group. If this method terminates, then the service method of the second object of the group is executed, etc.

$Active(Group(a_1, \ldots, a_n), m)$ groups are much less asynchronous than those created by the *ActiveGroup* primitive. More generally, groups of active objects provide a convenient and structured pattern for parallel evaluation.

Note that a group of active objects can also be turned into an active entity. In that case, the group of active objects becomes a global reference that can be shared between activities. It is a very useful first step toward updatable groups that can dynamically change membership and still provide the same view to all.

To summarize, we distinguish the following connections between groups and active objects:

- Activated groups of objects: asynchronous remote invocation of a group of objects:
$$Active(Group(a_1, \ldots, a_n), s)$$

- Groups of active objects: asynchronous remote invocation on group of active objects:
$$ActiveGroup(a_1, \ldots, a_n, s) = Group(Active(a_1, s), \ldots, Active(a_n, s))$$

- Activated groups of active objects: asynchronous remote control and invocation on a group of active objects:
$$Active(ActiveGroup(a_1, \ldots, a_n, s))$$

13.3 Groups, Determinism, and Atomicity

First, all confluence and determinism properties apply to groups because all rules added for groups are local ones and do not interfere with other local rules. This is mainly due to the fact that such rules only apply when other local rules are stuck.

Of course, if all members of a group of active objects know a given active object and can send it some requests, these requests will arrive concurrently, potentially creating non-determinism. In other words, the objects of a group of active objects cannot be considered as a single object, even if syntactically they are accessed like a unique object.

Atomicity

A classical feature of group communication is the atomicity of the communication; that is to say, the communication to all the active objects of a group is atomic (it cannot be interleaved with other communications or reductions). The above definition of groups does not guarantee atomicity. This has an important consequence concerning confluence as atomicity guarantees that, if several activities can send requests to a group of active objects, then these requests will be in the same order in all the request queues of all the destination activities.

A simple solution to obtain atomicity of group communications consists in using an *activated group of active objects*. Indeed, if all objects of the group object are only stored in one activity, the group of objects has only one entry point and interleaving of requests only occurs in one activity: the one containing the activated group of active objects. The main drawbacks of this solution are that it requires an additional activity and that the group is only accessed through the common activated group activity.

The following presents a solution for ensuring atomicity based directly on reduction rules, and thus avoiding the drawbacks of this approach.

Let us first denote $\xrightarrow{\text{REQUEST}_{\alpha \to \beta}}$ as the application of the REQUEST rule with sender α and destination β.

In the following, we replace the "Invoke method" rule of Table 13.1 by the one defined in Table 13.2. This rule encapsulates as many request sendings as there are active objects in the group, and creates a new group containing all the futures corresponding to requests to active objects and classical method calls concerning passive objects. We obtain a partially evaluated method call where method calls to active objects have all been forced to occur during the same rule: atomicity is ensured by the fact that $\xrightarrow{\text{REQUEST}_{\alpha \to \beta_k}}$ forces a given request sending to be performed inside the same reduction rule.

Atomic group REQUEST:

$$\sigma(\iota) = Group(\iota_k)^{k \in 1..l}$$

$\forall k \in i..l$, if $\iota_k = AO(\beta_k)$ then

$$\alpha[\mathcal{R}[\iota_k.m_j(\iota')]; \sigma_{k-1}; \iota; F; R; f] \parallel P_{k-1} \xrightarrow{\text{REQUEST}_{\alpha \to \beta_k}}$$
$$\alpha[\mathcal{R}[a_k]; \sigma_k; \iota; F; R; f] \parallel P_k$$

else $\quad a_k = \iota_k.m_j(\iota') \ \wedge \ \sigma_k = \sigma_{k-1} \ \wedge \ P_k = P_{k-1}$

$\alpha[\mathcal{R}[\iota.m_j(\iota')]; \sigma_\alpha; \iota; F; R; f] \parallel P_0 \longrightarrow \alpha[\mathcal{R}[Group(a_k)^{k \in 1..l}]; \sigma_l; \iota; F; R; f] \parallel P_l$

Table 13.2. Atomic reduction rules for groups

In practice, this strategy for ensuring atomicity will be implemented with a distributed protocol.

Without atomicity, to maintain determinism in the case of local method calls, one had to maintain sequentiality of method calls, which was not necessarily a good solutions if objects of the group were active. With atomic communications, in a group call, all requests toward active objects are sent first, then the calls to local objects are achieved in sequencel, from left to right. Of course, in practice such a group request would be implemented in parallel to hide latency.

Confluence and Atomicity

Concerning confluence, atomicity may turn confluent some programs that were not confluent with non-atomic groups. Indeed atomicity increases synchrony of communications, and can prevent some interleaving between requests.

We present below an example of a program behaving deterministically if communications are atomic. It is based on two activities α_1 and α_2 sending requests foo_1 and foo_2 to a group of objects β_i. When β_0 serves foo_1 it allows α_2 to send the request foo_2 (by sending a request bar).

The corresponding program is sketched in Fig. 13.4.

$$
\begin{aligned}
&let\ \beta_1 = [\ldots\ foo_1 = \varsigma(s)(\alpha_2.bar();\ldots), foo_2 = \varsigma(s)\ \ldots]\\
&\quad\ldots\\
&and\ \beta_4 = [\ldots\ foo_1 = \varsigma(s)\ldots, foo_2 = \varsigma(s)\ \ldots]\\
&and\ betas = ActiveGroup(\beta_1, \beta_2, \beta_3, \beta_4)\\
&and\ \alpha_1 = Active([\ldots\ main = \varsigma(s)betas.foo_1()\ldots])\\
&and\ \alpha_2 = Active([\ldots\ bar = \varsigma(s)betas.foo_2()\ldots])\ \ in\\
&\quad\alpha_1.main()
\end{aligned}
$$

Fig. 13.4. A confluent program if communications are atomic

Figure 13.5 shows a possible configuration corresponding to the execution of the program of Fig. 13.4. Note that all the requests foo_1 and foo_2 necessarily arrive in the same order in all the activities β_i of the group of active objects. This is due to the fact that when foo_1 is served in β_1 the semantics ensures that the request foo_1 has been received by all the activities of the group. Consequently, the confluence theorem (Theorem 8.10, page 118) ensures that the program of Fig. 13.4 *behaves deterministically if group communications are atomic.*

Now, let us consider the case of non-atomic communications. In this case, nothing ensures that when the request bar is served by α_2, the foo_1 requests have been received by all the active objects of the group. Consequently, some

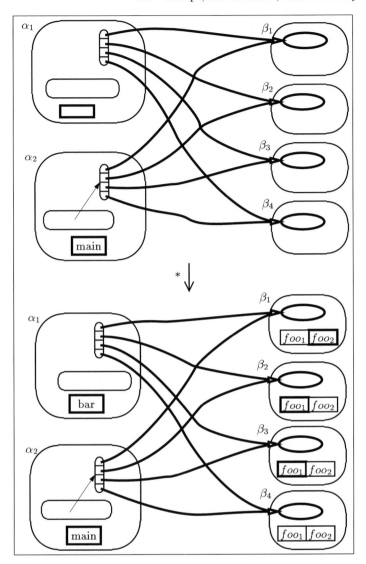

Fig. 13.5. Execution with atomic group communications

of the activities of the group may receive out-of-order requests. In fact, only β_1 is certain to receive foo_1 before foo_2. Finally, *without the guarantee of atomicity*, the program of Fig. 13.4 *does not behave deterministically* because RSL compatibility is not ensured.

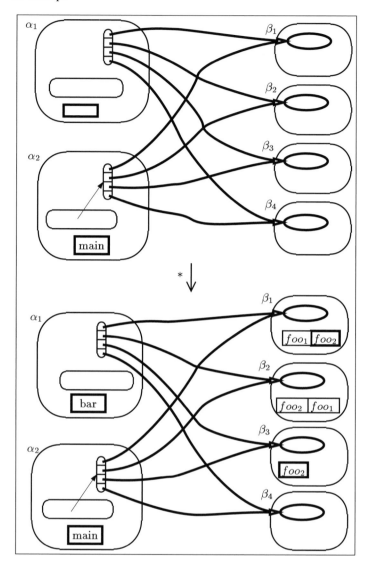

Fig. 13.6. An execution without atomic group communications

Figure 13.6 illustrates a possible configuration during the execution of the program of Fig. 13.4 without atomicity in group communications. This figure shows that the order of requests and even the presence of requests in the request queue is not guaranteed to be identical in all group members and a lot of different and incompatible configurations can be obtained.

However, let us imagine that the β_i active objects in the program of Fig. 13.4 are performing the following service: $Serve(foo_1); Serve(foo_2)$. In this case, even without group atomicity, the program is deterministic. This demonstrates that non-atomic groups can also produce determinism, and are also useful. Indeed, being less synchronous, they can be implemented more efficiently.

14

Components

Taking advantage of the ASP properties, this chapter demonstrates how to build hierarchical, distributed, and deterministic components. This could be considered as a first study in order to reach out a calculus modeling asynchronous and distributed components. This chapter provides:

- a formal syntax for the description of components on top of ASP,
- a semantics based on a static deployment of components into a plain ASP configuration,
- a characterization of deterministic components and deterministic composition of components.

As an extension of composite components, it is demonstrated how groups can be used to design *parallel* components. Finally, the chapter exhibits how *out-of-order future updates* enables a low coupling between components.

14.1 From Objects to Components

Recall that $\mathcal{M}_{\alpha P_0}$ is the set of M (M is itself a set of method labels) that can appear in the $Serve(M)$ instructions of a given activity α of a program P_0. In the following, the program P_0, which corresponds to the source program for the system of components, will be omitted. We consider a simple component model defined as follows.

Definition 14.1 (Primitive component)
A primitive component is defined from an activity α (a root active object and a set of passive objects), a set of Server Interfaces *(SIs), and a set of* Client Interfaces *(CIs).*

Each server interface SI_i is a subset of the served methods.

$$SI_i \subseteq \bigcup_{M \in \mathcal{M}_{\alpha P_0}} M$$

Served methods that do not belong to an interface correspond to asynchronous calls that can only be internal to a component.

A client interface (CI_j) is a reference to an(other) activity contained in any attribute (field) of the active object: $CI_j = l_i$ where l_i is a field of the active object. More formally, we define a primitive component as follows:

$$PC ::= C_n < a, srv, \{SI_i\}^{i \in 1..k}, \{CI_j\}^{j \in 1..l} >$$

where a is an ASP term corresponding to the object to be activated and its dependencies (passive objects), srv is the service method of the object a, each SI_i is a set of method labels (as defined above), and each CI_j is a field name of the root object defined by a, C_n is the name of the defined component.

Server Interface 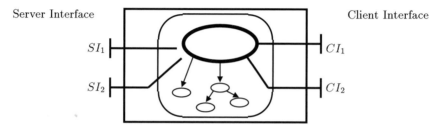 Client Interface

Fig. 14.1. A primitive component

This definition is only valid for primitive components based on a single activity, and for which the client interfaces are fields of the active object. It could be extended in order to deal with multi-activity components and generalized client interfaces.

14.2 Hierarchical Components

Composite components can be built from primitive components by interconnecting some components and exporting some SIs and CIs.

Definition 14.2 (Composite component)
A composite component is a set of components (either primitive (PC) or composite (CC)) exporting some server interfaces (some SI_i), some client interfaces (some CI_j), and connecting some client and server interfaces (defining a partial binding (CI_i, SI_j)). Such a component is given a name C_n. CC is a composite component and C either a primitive or a composite one:

$$CC ::= C_n \ll \quad C_1, \ldots, C_m; \{(C_{i_p}.CI_{j_p}, C_{i'_p}.SI_{j'_p})\}^{p \in 1..k};$$
$$\{C_{i_q}.CI_{j_q} \to CI_q\}^{q \in 1..l}; \{C_{i_r}.SI_{j_r} \to SI_r\}^{r \in 1..l'} \gg$$

$$C ::= PC \mid CC$$

where each C_i is the name of one included component C_i (i $\in$ 1..m), supposed to be pairwise distinct; each exported SI is only bound once to an included component, and each internal client interface $(C_i.CI_j)$ appears at most one time:

$$\forall p, p' \in 1..k, \forall q, q' \in 1..l, \forall r, r' \in 1..l' \begin{cases} p \neq p' \Rightarrow C_{i_p}.CI_{j_p} \neq C_{i_{p'}}.CI_{j_{p'}} \\ q \neq q' \Rightarrow C_{i_q}.CI_{j_q} \neq C_{i_{q'}}.CI_{j_{q'}} \\ C_{i_p}.CI_{j_p} \neq C_{i_q}.CI_{j_q} \\ r \neq r' \Rightarrow SI_r \neq SI_{r'} \end{cases}$$

Only client interfaces that are not bound can be exported, and only explicitly renamed interfaces are exported. Interfaces that are neither explicitly exported nor bound will be unused.

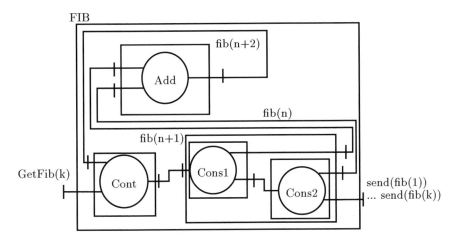

Fig. 14.2. Fibonacci as a composite component

Figure 14.2 represents a component version of the Fibonacci example of Sect. 5.4. A primitive component *Add* can be built up from active object *Add*. *Cons1* and *Cons2* have been assembled in a composite component (composed of two primitive components). A controller component *Cont* has been added. It exports a server interface $(ComputeFib(k))$ taking an integer k and forwards $k-1$ times its input to *Cons1*. According to the program of Sect. 5.4, *Cons2* sends *send* requests on the client interface. These components are interconnected in a single composite component FIB, exporting a server interface $ComputeFib(k)$ and producing $Fib(1)\dots Fib(k)$ on a client interface $send(i)$.

Figure 14.3 presents a component definition for the Fibonacci numbers example, the ASP terms are strongly similar to the example of Fig. 5.9, and the deployment of such a component corresponds to Fig. 14.2. This example uses a new operator, $Repeat_k(a)$, which evaluates k times the term a ($Repeat_k$ can be

$$C_{Fibo} \ll C_{add} < [n1 = 0, n2 = 0, Cont = [];$$
$$srv = \varsigma(s)Repeat(Serve(set1); Serve(set2);$$
$$s.Cont.snd(s.n1 + s.n2)),$$
$$set1 = \varsigma(s, n)s.n1 := n, set2 = \varsigma(s, n)s.n2 := n],$$
$$srv,$$
$$\{\{set1\}, \{set2\}\},$$
$$\{Cont\} >,$$
$$C_{cont} < [CI = [];$$
$$srv = \varsigma(s)Serve(GetFib),$$
$$GetFib = \varsigma(s, k)Repeat_k(Serve(snd)),$$
$$snd = \varsigma(s, k)s.CI.snd(k)],$$
$$srv,$$
$$\{\{GetFib\}, \{snd\}\},$$
$$\{CI\} >,$$
$$CC \ll C_{cons1} < [add = [], out = [];$$
$$srv = \varsigma(s)(s.add.set1(1); s.out.snd(1); Repeat(Serve(snd)))$$
$$snd = \varsigma(s, n)(s.add.set1(n); s.out.snd(n))],$$
$$srv,$$
$$\{\{snd\}\},$$
$$\{add, out\} >,$$
$$C_{cons2} < [add = [], out = [];$$
$$srv = \varsigma(s)(s.add.set2(0); s.out.snd(0); Repeat(Serve(snd)))$$
$$snd = \varsigma(s, n)(s.add.set2(n); s.out.snd(n))],$$
$$srv,$$
$$\{\{snd\}\},$$
$$\{add, out\} >;$$
$$\{C_{cons1}.out \rightarrow C_{cons2}.\{snd\}\};$$
$$\{C_{cons2}.out \rightarrow Displ, C_{cons1}.add \rightarrow Add1, C_{cons2}.add \rightarrow Add2\};$$
$$\{C_{cons1}.\{snd\} \rightarrow In\} \gg;$$
$$\{CC.Add1 \rightarrow C_{add}.\{set1\}, CC.Add2 \rightarrow C_{add}.\{set2\},$$
$$C_{add}.Cont \rightarrow C_{cont}.\{snd\}, C_{cont}.CI \rightarrow CC.In\};$$
$$\{CC.Displ \rightarrow Display\};$$
$$\{C_{cont}.GetFib \rightarrow GetFib\} \gg$$

Fig. 14.3. A definition of Fibonacci components

encoded in core ASP calculus). This component can only work once, modifying it to serve any number of *GetFib* requests is not difficult but would make the above example longer without showing any particularity of the component model, and thus we only present here the simplified version.

14.3 Semantics

We define here a static translation: from a definition of a composite component we produce a set of activities, i.e., an ASP configuration. Each primitive component is translated into an activity, all composite components entirely disappear at execution. The bindings at the component level are translated into genuine active object references stored in active object fields.

In order to obtain a well-configured and running set of active objects from a given composite, the idea is to apply the following functions or steps:

- from a server interface of a composite, a function recursively descends a binding to get the corresponding final primitive,
- from a client interface of a composite, a function recursively descends a bindings to get the corresponding final primitive,
- form a given composite component, using the two functions above, a list of bindings to be achieved between the inner primitive components is established,
- for each primitive component, an activity using the ASP primitive `Active` is created,
- each binding (SI,CI) is translated into the form of a field update with an active object reference, before activating the object:
$Object_i.CI_j := activeObject_k$ and $activeObject_i = Active(Object_i)$.

After these steps, the configuration carries on its execution as a standard ASP system, only made of a set of activities.

Let us detail those steps, starting with the three first ones. The two functions $getCI$ and $getSI$ recursively get the primitive component corresponding to an interface, and $Bind$ establishes the set of bindings between primitive components.

The functions $getCI$ and $getSI$ are defined on the server and client interfaces and follow the bindings corresponding to the interfaces exported by a composite component. This definition enters recursively into the definition of the composite components and thus necessarily terminates by reaching a primitive one.

$$getSI \ : \ C.SI \times C \ \rightarrow \ C$$
$$getSI(C.SI_j, PC) = C$$
$$\forall CC = C \ll C_1, \ldots C_i \ldots, C_n; \ldots; \ldots; \{..C_i.SI_{j'} \rightarrow SI_j..\} \gg$$
$$getSI(C.SI_j, CC) = getSI(C_i.SI_{j'}, C_i)$$

$$getCI \ : \ C.CI \times C \ \rightarrow \ \mathcal{P}(C.CI)$$
$$getCI(C.CI_j, PC) = C.CI_j$$
$$\forall CC = C \ll C_1, \ldots, C_n; \ldots; ExportedCI; \ldots \gg$$
$$getCI(C.CI_j, CC) = \{getCI(C_i.CI_{j'}, C_i) | C_i.CI_{j'} \rightarrow CI_j \in ExportedCI\}$$

Note that the definitions above require that the first argument of both functions is an interface of the provided component (second argument). Note that the definition of CC ensures the soundness of the above definitions.

The set $Bind(CC)$ defines the set of bindings which must be performed between primitive components in order to deploy the composite component

CC. In the definition below, $Bindings$ is the set of bindings defined by the component CC.

$$Bind \ : \ C \ \to \ \mathcal{P}(C.CI \times C.SI)$$

$$Bind(PC) = \emptyset$$

$$\forall CC = C \ll C_1, .., C_n; Bindingss; ..; .. \gg$$

$$Bind(CC) = \bigcup_{\substack{(C_{i_p}.CI_{j_p}, C_{i'_p}.SI_{j'_p}) \in Bindings \\ C.CI \in getCI(C_{i_p}.CI_{j_p}, C_{i_p})}} \left\{ \left(C.CI, getSI(C_{i'_p}.SI_{j'_p}, C_{i'_p}) \right) \right\}$$

$$\cup \bigcup_{i \in 1..n} Bind(C_i)$$

We define below the deployment of the composite component CC: this static deployment *creates* as many activities as there are primitive components and *binds* their interfaces accordingly.

Let $PC_{i_k} = C_{i_k} < a_k, srv_k, ..., ... >^{k \in 1..N}$ range over primitive components defined inside a CC to be deployed. Consequently, srv_k corresponds to the service method of the component named C_{i_k}.

Let CI_{pq} be some fields label of the primitive components and $c(p,q)$ the index of the primitive component to which this client interface must be bound. The bindings are defined as follows:

$$(C_p.CI_j, C_j) \in Bind(CC) \ \Rightarrow \ \exists q, \, (CI_j = CI_{pq} \wedge c(p,q) = j)$$

Then the term defined in Fig. 14.4 deploys the composite component CC defined above. This deployment is based on the activation of each primitive component object, but before the activation, the different CI fields of the object are assigned a reference to another component, following the bindings calculated previously. Finally primitive component objects are activated and run their own srv_k service method.

$let \ c_{i_1} = Active(((a_1.CI_{11} := c_{c(1,1)}). \, ...).CI_{1n_1} := c_{c(1,n_1)}, srv_1)$
$and \ ...$
$and \ c_{i_k} = Active(((a_k.CI_{k1} := c_{c(k,1)}). \, ...).CI_{kn_k} := c_{c(k,n_k)}, srv_k)$
$and \ ...$
$and \ c_{i_k} = Active(((a_N.CI_{N1} := c_{c(N,1)}). \, ...).CI_{kn_N} := c_{(N,n_N)}, srv_N)$

Fig. 14.4. Deployment of a composite component

The component deployment presented here is very static: in such a framework, components are not runtime entities. Once the configuration is generated, components completely disappear.

A more dynamic and modular approach could be envisioned. Using an active object for each composite component, one can imagine a translation such that components are accessible and reconfigurable at runtime. Such an extension is promising, but beyond the scope of this book. Indeed the preceding definition is sufficient to give a semantics to the definitions of components presented in this chapter.

14.4 Deterministic Components

Using ASP properties, we introduce deterministic assemblages of asynchronous components.

Definition 14.3 (Deterministic Primitive Component (DPC))
A DPC is a primitive component defined from an activity α. It verifies that server interfaces SIs are disjoint subsets of the served method of the active object of α such that every $M \in \mathcal{M}_{\alpha P_0}$ is (partially) included in a single SI_i.

$$\begin{cases} \forall i, k, i \neq k \Rightarrow SI_i \cap SI_k = \emptyset \\ \forall M \in \mathcal{M}_{\alpha P_0}, \forall M_1 \subseteq M, \forall M_2 \subseteq M \ (M_1 \subseteq SI_i \wedge M_2 \subseteq SI_j) \Rightarrow i = j \end{cases}$$

A constructive way of building server interfaces verifying the second condition (every potential service is included in a single SI_i) is to build each SI_i by merging several potential services:

$$SI_i = \bigcup_{\text{for some } M_j \in \mathcal{M}_{\alpha P_0}} M_j$$

DPC ensures that there is no interference between the services on the different interfaces: request sending on different interfaces will not interfere.

Definition 14.4 (Deterministic Composite Component (DCC))
A DCC is

- *either a DPC,*
- *or a composite component connecting some DCCs such that the binding between server and client interfaces is one to one. More precisely the following constraints must be added to the ones of Definition 14.2:*

$$\begin{cases} \text{Each } C_i \text{ is a DCC} \\ \\ \forall p, p' \in 1..k, \forall q, q' \in 1..l, \forall r, r' \in 1..l' \begin{cases} p \neq p' \Rightarrow C_{i'_p}.SI_{j'_p} \neq C_{i'_{p'}}.SI_{j'_{p'}} \\ r \neq r' \Rightarrow C_{i_r}.SI_{j_r} \neq C_{i_{r'}}.SI_{j_{r'}} \\ C_{i'_p}.SI_{j'_p} \neq C_{i_r}.SI_{j_r} \\ q \neq q' \Rightarrow CI_q \neq CI_{q'} \end{cases} \end{cases}$$

One can note the symmetry between the above constraints and the ones of Definition 14.2. General composite components require a given client interface to be connected at most once to the server interfaces, while a deterministic component adds up a symmetrical and reverse constraint: any server interface has to be the target of at most one client interface to avoid the non-deterministic merging of calls.

Of course, the binding between components can be cyclic, still forming a deterministic composite. The deterministic behavior of a DCC is a direct consequence of the DON properties of Chap. 9. Indeed, a DCC assemblage verifies the SDON property: there is no interference between the services on different interfaces inside a primitive component (DPC), and two CIs will not be (non-deterministically) merged to a single SI (DCC). In other words, components provide a convenient abstraction of activities in order to ensure the SDON property.

Property 14.5 (DCC determinism)
DCC components behave deterministically.

Note that the composite components remain deterministic if two CIs from the *same primitive component* are merged to a single SI, due to the purely sequential nature of activities. But this generalization is no longer valid in the case of composite component connections.

14.5 Components and Groups: Parallel Components

Chapter 13 has defined group communications based on *group proxies*. This section puts together components and groups, leading to *parallel components*.

The main principle is to use group proxies to bind a single client interface to a set of server interfaces. The calls on a group proxy being multicasted in parallel to several activities, this will enable configurations to be defined, where a given call is automatically executed in parallel by several activities. More specifically, a client interface of a component can be bound to the server interface of a set of components. Of course, the client interface and the set of server interfaces must all be of compatible type. Figure 14.5 provides an example of such a *composite and parallel component*. The client interface CI_2 of component C_1 is binded to the interface SI_1 of a set of components. All calls leaving from CI_2 will be sent in parallel, multicasted, to all the components on the right. Note that the components being used in parallel do not have to be of the exact same kind[1] (Cp_0 is different from Cp_1 and Cp_2).

Note that the symmetric operation, binding several client interfaces to a single server one, is already possible. It is a rather classical configuration as it corresponds to a given activity being referenced by several activities, all calling the same subset of methods, i.e., the same server interface. Such

---

[1] In that case, the group of components cannot be created with an *ActiveGroup* primitive but must be created by $Group(Active(a_1 \ldots), \ldots, Active(a_n \ldots))$.

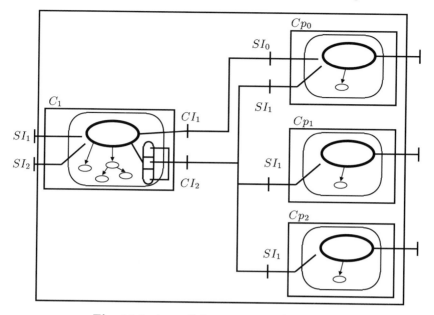

Fig. 14.5. A parallel component using groups

binding is of course highly non-deterministic in general.

With respect to providing a syntax to specify parallel components, one can just authorize *multiple bindings*: a single client interface bound several times to server interfaces of different components using the $\wedge$ connector. For instance:

$$\ll \dots; \dots, (C_1.CI_2, Cp_0.SI_1 \wedge Cp_1.SI_1 \wedge Cp_2.SI_1), \dots; \dots; \dots \gg$$

In this example, the client interface CI_2 of component C_1 is bound to several server interfaces (as illustrated in Fig.14.5). With respect to semantics or more practically generation of active object configuration from components, a group proxy can be used and set in the field corresponding to the client interface $C_1.CI_2$. Of course, the group proxy will contain references to the activities corresponding to the components Cp_0, Cp_1 and Cp_2.

If one wants syntax to express simultaneously multiple components of the same kind with the appropriate binding, then another extension of the component syntax is needed. For instance, it could be something like:

$$\ll \dots, Cp < \dots > N, \dots; \dots, (C_1.CI_1, Cp.SI_1), \dots; \dots; \dots \gg$$

with the meaning that component Cp is instantiated N times, and the client interface CI_1 of component C_1 is bound simultaneously to all the server interfaces SI_1 of the N components Cp. Such component would very much model a parallel code in an *SPMD* style (Single Program Multiple Data): all instantiated components execute the exact same code. The former solution, using a binding to server interfaces of different components, is rather *MIMD* parallelism (Multiple Program Multiple Data): each component can execute its own code.

With respect to determinism, such parallel composites are deterministic provided they respect the conditions of the DCC (Definition 14.4).

14.6 Components and Futures

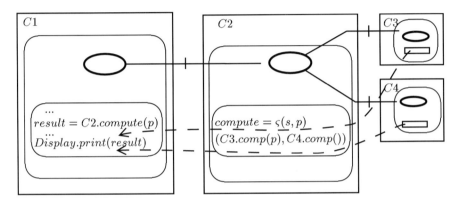

Fig. 14.6. Components and futures

Consider the component assemblage of Fig. 14.6; for the sake of simplicity, components and active object names are identified. In this example, $C1$ calls $C2$ on the interface *compute*, and the result of this call will be printed. $C2$, within the method *compute*, builds a result that includes parts coming from calls to both $C3$ and $C4$.

First of all, all the calls being asynchronous, the coupling between components remains quite low: $C2$ is not blocked while $C3$ and $C4$ are computing their part of the answer. Furthermore, without any explicit continuation or call-back, the part of the result computed by $C3$ and $C4$ will transparently reach $C1$.

This kind of asynchronous assemblage is much more structured and transparent than call-back solutions, and it enables unlimited composition. Moreover, whatever the number of implicit delegations, whatever the depth of the composite, if Definitions 14.3 and 14.4 are ensured, the composition is deterministic.

Perspectives

This chapter has taken advantage of the ASP calculus, mapping components to ASP activities. As a future work, such adaptation of ASP to components should be formally compared to purely component approaches, such as the kell calculus [31].

Another interesting perspective consists in studying the problem of *re-configurations* of such components, which could probably be linked with the reconfiguration within Process Networks.

First of all, out-of-order future updates, presented above at Sect. 14.6, is an important feature not present in Process Networks. We have demonstrated that it enables a very important aspect of composition: low coupling between components.

Besides this intrinsic advantage of ASP, the DON property can be considered as a generalization of Process Networks in an object-oriented framework. Furthermore, Process Networks are actually not too far from asynchronous and distributed components. While Process Networks channels just carry data, component interconnections carry method calls in a much more typed and object-oriented way.

Next chapter studies reconfiguration at the light of Process Networks.

15

Channels and Reconfigurations

This chapter first reviews channels, buffering entities interconnecting activities. We identify intrinsic channels in ASP, and provide an encoding of interconnecting, Process Networks-like, channels. In a second part it reviews the possibilities of reconfigurations that can be implemented in ASP. Reconfiguration consists in changing the branching between activities during the execution of a program.

Internal configuration corresponds to a reconfiguration that is triggered by the activities for which the branching is modified. In contrast, event-based reconfiguration stands for a reconfiguration that occurs because of an external and unpredictable event.

15.1 Genuine ASP Channels

A first step toward the expression of channels in ASP has been presented on Process Networks in Sect. 5.3 (page 79). A general translation for encoding Process Networks channels in ASP will be given in Sect. 15.2 below. What is striking here is that the notion of channels in Process Networks and linear channels in π-calculus come from very different frameworks but could be adapted to ASP through a similar abstraction of *channels*; to some extent, ASP generalizes both π-calculus and Process Networks channel abstractions.

To summarize, this section defines a channel as a pair *(activity, set of method labels)* where if several method labels can be served by the same primitive, then they must belong to the same channel.

The rest of this section formalizes this definition and describes the expressivity of ASP channels.

As in the case of server interfaces for deterministic primitive components, we suppose that we have a partition $\mathcal{C}_i^\alpha$ of method names such that each potential service of α is included in a single channel:

$$\forall i, j, i \neq j \Rightarrow \mathcal{C}_i^\alpha \cap \mathcal{C}_j^\alpha = \emptyset \quad \wedge \quad \forall M \in \mathcal{M}_{\alpha P_0}, \exists i, M \subseteq \mathcal{C}_i^\alpha$$

Then, a channel is a pair $(\alpha, \mathcal{C}_i^\alpha)$. Such a channel has at most one destination activity; and if every channel has a single source activity then the configuration behaves deterministically. Figure 15.1 shows an activity α with two channels and two activities, β and γ, each of them writing on a given channel. This configuration behaves deterministically.

The condition on the partition $\mathcal{C}_i^\alpha$ ($\forall M \in \mathcal{M}_{\alpha P_0}, \exists i, M \subseteq \mathcal{C}_i^\alpha$) is necessary to ensure determinacy. Indeed, if every channel had a single source activity but some distinct channels could be served by the same *Serve* primitive then the configuration might behave non-deterministically. In other words, this condition ensures that there is no interference on the destination side of a channel.

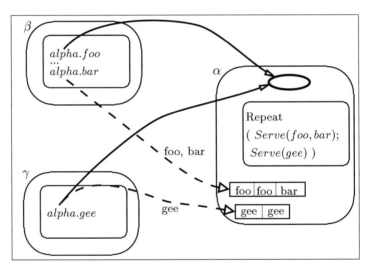

Fig. 15.1. Requests on separate channels do not interfere

This definition of channels allows us to perform a service on a part of the set of methods defining a channel (e.g., some *Serve(foo)* in the example of Fig. 15.1). This feature would correspond to a selective get on a part of a channel. Such a selective get does not exist in Process Networks but does not compromise determinism properties.

Figure 15.2 shows the same configuration as in Fig. 15.1, but a channel is (partially) shared by two source activities. In general, such a configura-

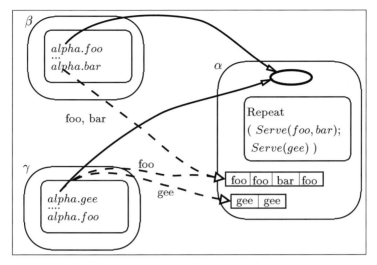

Fig. 15.2. A non-deterministic merge

tion does not behave deterministically. The fact that two activities can send requests on the same channels corresponds to a non-deterministic merge in Process Networks.

The following section formally makes explicit a general translation from Process Networks channels to ASP. It uses interconnecting activities that simulate the Process Networks channels.

15.2 Process Network Channels in ASP

We present here the principles of a translation of Process Networks terms into ASP in the case where each channel has only one destination process. We use and define a *channel object*. Such buffering communication entity is an active object, using asynchronous communications to ensure non-blocking puts, and futures for postponed blocking gets.

A channel is an active object: (1) equipped with two methods *put* and *get*, (2) that performs alternative blocking services on those two methods:

$$Channel \triangleq [value = [];activity = \varsigma(s)Repeat(Serve(put); Serve(get)),$$
$$put = \varsigma(s, val)s.value := val, \quad get = \varsigma(s)s.value]$$

To create a new channel, one just has to activate a *Channel* object by
$$let \ Q = Active(Channel, activity) \ in \dots.$$
Then one can use it with $Q.put(\dots)$ and $Q.get()$. Such channels are first-class entities that can be manipulated with even more expressiveness than process networks ones. Note that the request queue of the channel activity will play the buffering role of a Process Networks channel.

The deposit operation is non-blocking due to the asynchronous nature of *put* method calls. When *put* is served, the next value to be extracted from the channel is stored in the *s.value* field. Then, the channel active object waits for a request to serve on *get*, sending the consumer the *s.value* field value. Note that on the consumer side, upon calling the *get*, a future is obtained right away. So, it is less blocking than a Process Networks `get` that would block instantly, while here the consumer will block only upon a strict use of the value extracted from the channel.

Figure 15.3 shows a *Channel* active object, together with its activity alternating a blocking service on *put*, and a blocking service on *get*. The pending queue bufferizes the channel values within the *put* requests, as well as the pending *get* operations. Several *get* requests can be present in the queue in the case of several consumers on the same channel (usually non-deterministic), or if a single consumer executes several *get* operations without using immediately the values (fully deterministic in that case).

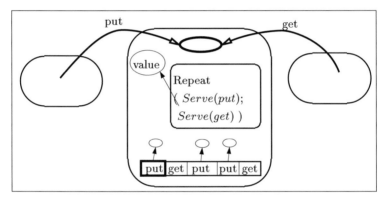

Fig. 15.3. A channel specified with an active object

The declaration of multiple destination channels does not raise any technical difficulty, but is much longer to describe directly. As proposed in [100] we could have a different reference for each activity that can read on a multiple destination channel (different views of the same channel). Actually, a simple solution can be expressed with a new technique proposed in this book: *groups*. A group can be used on the producer side, putting each value to a set of channels. Each consumer will get all values on its own channel.

15.3 Internal Reconfiguration

This book has already proposed a first reconfiguration mechanism that is indeed very transparent: *migration*.

An object has the same behavior before and after migration. As such, migration provides a safe reconfiguration that can be used to solve problems of load balancing, planned maintenance of machines. The migration of an activity can be triggered non-determisistically by an internal non-deterministic activity (a request), or can also be initiated externally from outside the system (operator, other processes, etc.). However, the migration operation presented in this book must be performed by the migrated activity, e.g., when serving a *Migrate* request in the case of a migration triggered from outside. Consequently, the activity can control the moment when the migration occurs thus avoiding the most non-deterministic case: a migration occurring at any point in time.

In components and rather generally in ASP programs, configurable links are usually stored in (updatable) fields of objects. If an attribute reconfiguration is triggered from the inside, then this does not compromise ASP properties like confluence, and the behavior of the activity is predictable and sound.

Such a methodology includes the possibility for an activity to trigger a reconfiguration upon a request service (e.g., with setter and getter methods), and thus to trigger the reconfiguration from the outside but with an internal acknowledgment. However, if requests used for reconfiguration can interfere with other requests then the configuration may not behave deterministically.

Comparing ASP to Process Networks reconfigurations, all computational reconfigurations that are expressed in Process Networks correspond to what is called "internal reconfiguration" here, and can be expressed in ASP. However, with the channel definition of Sect. 15.1, it is not possible to change the destination part of a channel directly: channels can only be reconfigured on the sender side. Consequently, reconfiguring those channels necessarily needs a reconfiguration of the sender. The channels proposed at Sect. 15.2 can be reconfigured from both sides.

In [159], some techniques are developed in order to ensure consistency of representation: it is assumed that once the mutation starts, it continues to completion; that is to say, there is no possibility to affect the newly created process. In ASP this is guaranteed by the fact that computational reconfigurations are internal, and thus performed by the reconfigured activity itself; as no memory is shared, the reconfiguration thread, which is the activity thread itself, cannot be affected by another one.

This kind of internal reconfiguration also applies to ASP components defined in the previous chapter. Once a component configuration is started as an ASP configuration, change in interconnection can occur dynamically (for instance, changing the value of a field referencing an active object). If the ASP configuration respects the DON property, such dynamic changes can be considered as deterministic reconfigurations.

15.4 Event-Based Reconfiguration

A complete expression of a full-fletched event-based reconfiguration is beyond the scope of this book. Nevertheless, this section summarizes the possibilities and the difficulties of such an approach, especially in order to maintain confluence.

First of all, an externally triggered reconfiguration occurs at a non-determinate time. The event triggering the reconfiguration arrives in one active object at a non-determinate time. From that point, the objective is to achieve a determinate reconfiguration, i.e., the reconfiguration is propagated and executed deterministically by other activities.

An event-based reconfiguration will be called determinate if it verifies the following property:

> Once a reconfiguration arrives in the system, we manage to propagate
> a reconfigure request in a determinate manner in all the request queues
> of all activities in the system.

This could be achieved by automatically serving a particular request, called *reconfigure* requests. Indeed, serving a particular request is considered as *internal reconfiguration* (or more precisely, an *event-based reconfiguration internally taken into account*) as stated in the preceding section.

To serve such a reconfigure request as soon as possible, we have to add it to each service primitive of the activity: $Serve(Mi)$ becomes $Serve(Mi, reconfigure)$.

This strategy is sufficient for ensuring a determinate reconfiguration in the case of a tree topology, but a solution for determinate reconfiguration in the case of other topologies, e.g., DAG (Directed Acyclic Graphs) and cycles, is much more difficult.

Another strategy would consist in executing each applicative request in a given configuration: associating to each request the configuration in which it should be executed. Unfortunately, this causes a lot of potentially useless reconfigurations, and is thus inefficient.

At the time of writing, we have found no general and efficient solution allowing a fully determinate reconfiguration to be written in all cases (DAG, cycles). We believe it to be a challenging and promising research avenue.

Part V

Implementation Strategies

16

A Java API for ASP: ProActive

This chapter presents an existing mapping of the ASP calculus in a practical programming language and environment, namely Java [82].

The resulting library, called ProActive, is available in open source with an LGPL license [134]. A few examples of programs are given, mainly those used in the course of this book in the framework of ASP and other calculus.

16.1 Design and API

ProActive is built on top of Java standard APIs – mainly the Java RMI standard interface and the Reflection API. As a consequence it does not require any modification to the standard Java execution environment, nor does it make use of a special compiler, pre-processor, or modified virtual machine.

ProActive features the basic ASP model: active objects, absence of sharing between activities, method-based communications (identified as RMI, Sect.1.3.1 page 14). It also adheres to the ASP communication semantics: communications toward active objects are systematically asynchronous, leading to transparent and first-class futures. This last aspect implies the implementation of distributed future update (see Chap. 17 page 213, for a discussion on the strategies). It is important to note that such full-blown *wait-by-necessity* can be implemented in a standard language, without modifying the compiler, nor the virtual machine. The technique being used relies on Java Reflection, a *runtime Meta-Object Protocol* (MOP) and interception objects [53]. The only constraint resulting for such a non-intrusive implementation of futures is simple: the results of asynchronous methods cannot be of basic types (int, float, etc.), nor final classes. In the first case, standard wrappers have to be used; in the second case, the user just has to define an appropriate wrapper class or interface. Other techniques could be used for implementing futures, for instance *load-time MOP*, as explained in [156].

Besides these basic features, the library also offers:

- *computational mobility*, a way to migrate (weak migration) an activity from one JVM to another one (discussed in Chap. 12, page 151, see also [24]),
- *typed group communications*, under the form of both asynchronous and typed group multicast (Chap. 13, page 157, see also [21]),
- *components*, under the form of asynchronous and hierarchical entities (Chap. 14, page 169, see also [26]),

The library also features some *security*, under the form of *authentication, integrity, confidentiality* (AIC) provided with a Public Key Infrastructure (PKI), and configured outside source code [18] in XML configuration files.

16.1.1 Basic API and ASP Equivalence

Table 16.1 summarizes the relations between the ASP calculus constructors and the ProActive API.

ASP constructors	Java ProActive API
factory = Active(clone(a))	`ProActive.newActive("A", null, Node);`
Active(a, m)	`ProActive.turnActive(obj, Node);`
Serve(M)	`service.blockingServeOldest(String methodName);`
ServeWithoutBlocking(M)	`service.ServeOldest(String methodName);`
inQueue(M)	`service.hasRequestToServe (String methodName);`
waitFor(a)	`ProActive.waitFor(Object);`
awaited (a)	`ProActive.isAwaited(Object);`

Table 16.1. Relations between ASP constructors and ProActive API

The main ProActive primitive, `newActive`, instantiates a given class (e.g., "A") as an active object. The second parameter specifies parameters for the constructor. The third, `Node`, allows one to control the location (the machine and JVM) of where to place the active object (see next section for details). Java being a class-based language, while the ς-calculus is rather object based, the ASP `newActive` equivalent corresponds to an `Active` applied to an ASP factory pattern: a given object is used with a clone to simulate a class.

The second API method to create an active object in ProActive, `turnActive`, is indeed very close to the ASP equivalent: `Active(a,m)`. An existing object is deep cloned and made active: a thread is created as well as a pending request queue. The resulting set (the copy of objects, a thread, a pending queue) is potentially located on a remote JVM (parameter `Node`, see next section).

With respect to service methods, `Serve(M)` ASP primitive has `blockingServeOldest` as a direct equivalent, overloaded with one or several method names as parameters. The non-confluent, non-blocking service, `ServeWithoutBlocking(M)`, see Sect. 11.2 page 144, is just named `serveOldest`.

Finally, the confluent method `waitFor(a)` is identical in both ASP and ProActive, blocking until the parameter object is no longer an awaited future; while the non-confluent `awaited(a)` exists under the name `isAwaited(a)`. In both cases it returns `True` if the object is still an awaited future.

The methods `turnActive` and `newActive`, `waitFor` and `isAwaited` are static methods of the class ProActive, while service methods are defined on an object of type `service` which encapsulates access to the queue of requests.

16.1.2 Mapping Active Objects to JVMs: Nodes

In ASP, activities are specified without any location; indeed the calculus is location-less on purpose: the goal is a framework where the physical place of execution does not affect the behavior. In practice, programmers or deployers need and want to control where to place the activities (machines, processes, or Virtual Machines). This is why there is a need to identify locations in a practical library.

Nodes provide this important capability: a *node* is an object defined in ProActive whose aim is to provide an abstraction for the physical location of a set of active objects. A *node* lives within a JVM, and at any time a JVM hosts one or several nodes. The traditional way to name and handle a node in a simple manner is to associate it with a symbolic name, that is a URL specifying its location, for instance `rmi://lo.inria.fr/Node1`. On creating an active object using the `newActive` primitive:

```
A a = (A) ProActive.newActive("A",params,"rmi://lo.inria.fr/node");
```

the activity is located on the JVM where the node is. Indeed, such a feature provides the extra service (compared to RMI, for instance) allowing one to *remotely create remotely accessible objects*.

Ultimately, one must abstract away from the source code any machine names, creation, registry, and lookup protocols. This is achieved in the ProActive infrastructure with the *Virtual Node (VN)* abstraction. It provides the capacity to capture the distributed nature of an application in a set of virtual nodes. Further, the active objects can be directly created on virtual nodes. For example:

```
A a = (A) ProActive.newActive("A", params, VirtualNodeRenderer);
```

As suggested by the name of the virtual node in this example, VirtualNodeRenderer, such abstraction is often directly related to the application logic. At application deployment, XML configuration files authorize the mapping of virtual nodes onto actual nodes on physical machines and JVMs, see [25] for details.

16.1.3 Basic Patterns for Using Active Objects

Let us take a standard Java class A. The instruction:

```
A a = (A) ProActive.newActive("A", params, Node1);
```

creates a new active object of type A on the JVM identified with Node1. Further, all calls to that remote object will be asynchronous, and subject to the *wait-by-necessity*:

```
v = a.bar (...) ;     // Asynchronous call, no wait
o.gee (v);            // No wait, even if o is a remote
                      // active object and v still awaited

...
v.f (...) ;           // Wait−by−necessity: wait until v
                      // gets its value
```

Futures being first-class entities, there will not be any wait for passing a future to another active object, even if it resides in a remote JVM. In the code above, even if v is still awaited when used as a parameter to a remote call (o.gee (v)), the current active object will not block. Later on, the future v is subject to update both locally and within the active object referenced by o.

16.1.4 Migration

Being able to explicitly locate active objects in a JVM with nodes, the next thing consists in moving them from one JVM to another. In accordance with the conceptual study conducted in Chap. 12 page 151, migration corresponds to the serialization of an activity and its reincarnation at a new location.

More precisely, the following entities are serialized and copied into the new location (physical machine and JVM):

- the active object,
- from it all the reachable passive objects,
- the pending requests,
- all pending futures.

Note that the activity itself, the stack of the corresponding thread, is not in the list above. Actually ProActive implements *weak migration*, for the sake of portability and efficiency.[1]

---

[1] Since Java threads, at the time of writing, are not interruptible and neither serializable, it is either very inefficient or non-portable to offer strong migration.

ProActive static primitive	Migration toward
migrateTo (Node)	the JVM identified by the node
migrateTo (Object)	the current location of another active object

Table 16.2. Migration primitives in ProActive

```
public class SimpleAgent implements Serializable {

  public void moveToNode(Node n) {        // Move to a given node
      ProActive.migrateTo(n);
        logger . error ( "You_should_never_see_this,_report_a_bug,");
        logger . error ( "or _.... strong_migration_has_been_implemented!");
  }

  public void joinFriend(Object friend) {   // Move to join another AO
      ProActive.migrateTo(friend);
  }

  public String whereAreYou () {             // Repplies to queries
      return ("I_am_at_" + InetAddress.getLocalHost ());
      ...
  }
                                // Send information to other agents
  public void sendBestPrice (int myNewBestPrice) {
      ...
        myPeers[i]. receiveBestPrice (myNewBestPrice);
      ...
  }
                                // Receive information from other agents
  public void receiveBestPrice (int newBestPrice) {
      if (newBestPrice < currentBestPrice)
        currentBestPrice = newBestPrice;
  }
  ...
}
```

Fig. 16.1. A simple mobile agent in ProActive

Of course, migration does not impact connectivity between activities. The underlying runtime ensures that requests and replies are transparently conveyed to the current location of the target activity.

To summarize, ProActive provides a way to move an active object from any JVM to any other one. This feature is accessible through a simple migrateTo(...) primitive (see Table 16.2). The primitive is static, and as such always triggers the migration of the current active object. However, the

migrateTo method can be called within a public method of an active object:
the service of a request on such a method will trigger migration. As such,
even in the framework of weak migration, it can be (indirectly) initiated from
another activity. Still, an active object remains responsible for its behavior
since it has to decide by itself to serve such a public migration method.

The code in Fig. 16.1 presents such a mobile active object. The stack being
lost, all code after calls to the migrateTo primitive will never be executed.

One can program a group of mobile agents, everybody migrating from
machine to machine, while still being able to communicate with their peers.

Localization Strategies

In order to ensure the working of an application in the presence of migration,
ProActive provides three mechanisms to maintain communication with mobile
objects:

- servers,
- forwarders,
- the TTL-TTU protocol: a mixed parameterized strategy.

The first one relies on a location sever which keeps track of the mobile
objects in the system; see [121, 58, 154, 5] for details on server-based strategies.
When needed, the server is queried to obtain an up-to-date reference to an
active object. After migrating, an object updates one or several servers with
its new location.

The second strategy uses a fully decentralized technique known as *forwarder* [71, 98, 146, 153, 27]. When leaving a site, an active object leaves
behind a special object, *a forwarder*, which points to its new location. On
receiving a message, a forwarder simply passes it to the mobile object (or the
next forwarder if another migration occurred). Indeed, such a strategy falls
within the scope of *routing protocol*: a valid reference to the target object is
not needed, and the messages are potentially routed along several hosts.

The third one, TTL-TTU, is an original scheme based on a mix between
forwarding and the location server. Featuring Time-To-Live (TTL) forwarders,
and Time-To-Update (TTU) mobile objects, it provides adaptability, performance, and fault tolerance. The main principles are the following:

- upon migration, an active object leaves behind a forwarder,
- after a nominal TTL, a forwarder is subject to self-destruction,
- each active object has a nominal TTU, after which it will inform a localization server of its new location.

For the best performance, a forwarder will update a localization server
before dying. Also, for optimal performances, the TTU parameter is in fact a
double value: besides the time elapsed, the maximum number of hops without
server update is also specified as a protocol parameter.

The protocol allows one to set the values of parameters according to the application behavior, and to the environment. For instance, a LAN or WAN features different latencies, migration, and communication times, and calls for different TTL-TTU values. See [24, 20] for further details.

16.1.5 Group Communications

Group communication in ProActive achieves asynchronous method invocation for a group of remote objects, following the principles and semantics explained in Chap. 13, page 157.

Group communication represents a *typed* group interaction: methods of the active object interface are called on a group, vs. just sending data as for instance in the Java Messaging System (JMS) framework [85]. Moreover, group communication also permits the automatic gathering of replies: a group of replies, initially futures, is dynamically created upon a group call.

Given a Java class, one can initiate group communications using the classical dot notation, hence the typed nature. The typed group being automatically constructed to handle the result of such a collective operation, it provides an elegant and effective way to program *gather* operations.

On a standard Java class A, here is an example of a typical group creation:

Object [][] params = {{...},...,{...}}; // *An array of constructor params*

A ag = (A) ProActiveGroup.newGroup("*A*", params,{node1,...,node2});
                    // *A group of type "A" is created:*
                    // *member AOs are created at once*
                    // *on the specified nodes*

A method invocation on a group has a syntax similar to a standard method invocation:

ag.foo (...) ; // *A group communication*

Such a call is asynchronously propagated to all members of the group in parallel using multithreading. The parameters of the invoked method are deep-copied and broadcast to all the members of the group. As in the ASP basic model, a method call on a group is non-blocking.

A method call on a group yields a method call on each of the group members. Actually, group members can be active objects as illustrated above, but also standard and local Java objects. If a member is a ProActive active object, the method call will be a ProActive call, and if the member is a standard Java object, the method call will be a standard Java method call (within the same JVM).

As already mentioned, an important specificity of the group mechanism is: the *result* of a typed group communication *is also a group*. Let us detail that feature.

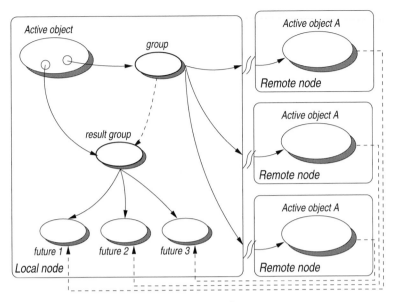

Fig. 16.2. Method call on group

The result group is transparently built at invocation time, with a future for each elementary reply. It will be dynamically updated with the incoming results, thus gathering results, as shown in Fig. 16.2. The *wait-by-necessity* mechanism is also valid on groups: if all replies are awaited the caller blocks, but as soon as one reply arrives in the result group the method call on this result is executed. For instance in

V vg = ag.bar(); // *A method call on a group with result vg:*
...   // *vg is a typed group of "V",*
vg.f() ; // *Also a collective operation, subject to*
         // *wait−by−necessity*

a new f() method call is automatically triggered as soon as a reply from the call **ag.bar()** comes back in the group **vg** (dynamically formed). The instruction **vg.f()** completes when f() has been called on all members of the **vg** group.

Dynamic group manipulation (**add**, **remove** members) is another important feature. The typed group view we have used above corresponds to the functional view of a group of objects. In order to provide a dynamic management of groups, a group-like view is necessary. The interface **Group** extends the Java **Collection** interface which provides management methods like **add**, **remove**, **size**, etc. In order to switch from one representation to the other, two methods are defined:

- the static method **getGroup** returns the group form associated to the given group object;

```
        // Definition of one standard Java object and two active objects
        // Suppose B extends A
A a1 = new A();
A a2 = (A) ProActive.newActive("A", paramsA[], node);
B b  = (B) ProActive.newActive("B", paramsB[], node);


        // Creation of a group of active objects
Object [][] params  = {{...},...,{...}};
A ag1 = (A) ProActiveGroup.newGroup("A", params,{node1,...,node2});


        // An asynchronous one−way group communication
ag1.foo (...) ;
        // An asynchronous group communication with a group as a result
        // vg is a typed group of "V"
V vg = ag1.bar();
    ...
vg.f() ; // Also a collective operation, subject to wait−by−necessity



        // For management purposes, get the group view from the typed view
Group gA = ProActiveGroup.getGroup(ag1);


        // Now, add objects to the group:
        // active and non−active objects can be mixed in the group
gA.add(a1);
gA.add(a2);
gA.add(b);


        // The addition of members to a group immediately reflects
        // on the typed group view (ag1)
        // A method invoked on ag1 will also be called on  a1, a2, b
ag1.foo();
V vg2 = ag1.bar();


        // A new reference to the typed group can also be  built
A ag2 = (A) gA.getGroupByType();
```

Fig. 16.3. Dynamic typed group of active objects

- the method `getGroupByType` defined in the `Group` interface does the opposite.

Figure 16.3 illustrates dynamic group management and summarizes group functionalities.

With such dynamic group manipulation, elements can be dynamically included into a typed group, provided of course their class equals or extends the class specified at group creation. As such, it does authorize and handle *polymorphic* groups. For example, an object of class B (B extending A) can be included in a group of type A (see Fig. 16.3). However, based on Java typing, only the methods defined in class A can be invoked on the group.

Other features are available regarding group communications: for instance, *parameter dispatching* using groups, through the definition of *scatter groups*. One can control and individualize the effective parameter sent to each group member in a group call. Other features are hierarchical groups, group synchronization, and barriers (`waitOne`, `waitAll`, `allArrived`, `allAwaited`, etc.).

See [21] for further details on asynchronous groups and implementation techniques.

16.2 Examples

16.2.1 Parallel Binary Tree

This section presents the *parallel binary tree* example in ProActive. It follows the principles and structure of the ASP binary tree in Fig. 5.1, page 76. The complete package, together with graphical interface, is available at `http://ProActive.ObjectWeb.org`.

Figure 16.4 provides the sequential ProActive version. Note the method `createChildren` at the bottom of class `BinaryTree`. Unlike the `My Type` construct of the language `PolyTOIL` [42], or the *like Current* construction of Eiffel [116], it is difficult in Java to create an object of the same type as the current object without heavy use of the Reflection API. This is the purpose of the method `createChildren` in class `BinaryTree`: it acts as a virtual factory that can just be overridden in heir classes to adjust the type of object being created.

In class `ActiveBinaryTree`, Fig. 16.5, the `createChildren` method is overridden:

- the type is adjusted, creating two sons of the current type (`ActiveBinaryTree`),
- parallelism is added, creating active objects with `newActive` instead of standard Java objects.

Once the root of the tree is created as an active object (Fig. 16.6, parallel version), it ensures that all the objects of the binary tree will be active objects.

At point (1) of the client, `main` in Fig. 16.6, the result of a preceding request is used to create a new object, potentially using a future – remember that future updates can occur at any time. Indeed, the value associated to the result of $res1 = myTree.get(5)$ (point (2) of client) is not needed, neither by the client nor by the leave created with key 1, ($myTree.put(1, res1)$). Consequently, a future update can occur directly from the object number 5 to

```java
public class BinaryTree} {
  protected int key;              // The key contained in this  object
  protected Object value;         // The value contained in this  object
  protected BinaryTree leftTree;  // Left sub-tree
  protected BinaryTree rightTree; // Right sub-tree

  protected boolean isLeaf;       // Convenience instance variable
  // Class invariant:
  // (this . isLeaf == ((this. leftTree ==null) && (this.rightTree==null)))

  public BinaryTree() {           /* Constructor: creates  an empty object */}
    this.isLeaf = true; // On creation, an object has no child
  }
    /* Inserts  a (key, value) pair in current sub-tree */}
  public void put (int key, Object value) {
    if (this.isLeaf) {            // Object This is empty, let's use it
      this.key = key; this.value = value;
      this.isLeaf = false; this.createChildren();
    } else if (key == this.key) {    // Replaces  the current value
      this.value = value;
    } else if (key < this.key) {     // Smaller keys are on the  left
      this. leftTree .put(key, value);
    } else {                      // Greater keys on the  right
      this.rightTree.put(key, value);
    }
  }
    /* Returns  the value  associated  to  a given  key */}
  public ObjectWrapper get (int key) {
    if (this.isLeaf) {            // Reached a leaf, key not found
      return new ObjectWrapper ("null");
    }
    if (key == this.key) {        // Found the object, return value
      return new ObjectWrapper(this.value);
    }
    if (key < this.key) {         // Continue left, smaller keys
      ObjectWrapper res = this.leftTree.get(key);
      return res;
    }                             // Continue right, greater  keys
    ObjectWrapper res = this.rightTree.get(key);
    return res;
  }

  protected void createChildren() {      /* Creates two empty children */}
    this. leftTree  = new BinaryTree();
    this.rightTree = new BinaryTree();
  }
}
```

Fig. 16.4. Sequential binary tree in Java

```
public class ActiveBinaryTree extends BinaryTree {

  protected void createChildren() {
      String s = this.getClass().getName();
      this.leftTree  = (BinaryTree) ProActive.newActive(s, null, null);
      this.rightTree = (BinaryTree) ProActive.newActive(s, null, null);
  }
}
```

Fig. 16.5. Subclassing binary tree for a parallel version

the object number 1 (dotted lines on the bottom left of Fig. 16.7), provided of course the future is not filled up before the final creation of object number 1. Actually, the future update from object number 5 can take place toward any object in between the client and object number 1, depending on the time it occurs and the future update strategy. In any case, such an asynchronous Java program remains deterministic, even when each active object is placed on a different machine.

```
package org.objectweb.proactive.examples.binarytree;

public class Client {

  public static void main (String[] args) {
    BinaryTree tree = null;
    if    ( ... Sequential Version  ... )
      tree = new BinaryTree ();
    else // Parallel Version
      tree =(Tree) ProActive.newActive("ActiveBinaryTree", null, null);

      myTree.put(3, "4");
      myTree.put(2, "3");
      myTree.put(5, "6");
      myTree.put(7, "8");
      ObjectWrapper res1 = myTree.get(5);        // (2)
      ObjectWrapper res2 = myTree.get(3);
      myTree.put(1, res1);                       // (1)
      ...
  }
}
```

Fig. 16.6. Main binary tree program in ProActive

Figure 16.8 shows a screenshot of the binary tree graphical interface. The button *"Automatic Continuations"* permits deactivation first-class futures.

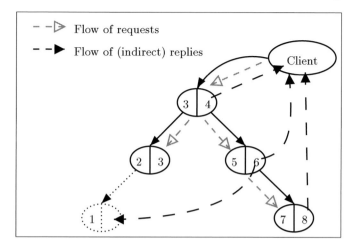

Fig. 16.7. Execution of the parallel binary tree program of Fig. 16.6

One can test and visualize the effect of objects being blocked waiting for future values they do not really need, willing just to pass the future references to others. In such a case, even the parallel binary tree behaves very much sequentially, the root of the tree blocking the entire tree at each `get` request. The observable effect is that the search results arrive sequentially and strictly in order.

Overall, the design is of course a bulky implementation: each object being active is too coarse grain for efficiency. However, we could easily provide a more subtle scheme, such as creating active objects only for a given `depth n` of the tree (so that there cannot be less than a certain number of non-active objects in a given activity). The next section provides such a strategy on another example.

16.2.2 Eratosthenes

Following the ASP Eratosthenes example (Sect. 5.2, page 77), this section proposes a sequential Java version, and a distributed ProActive one. The latter derives from the former, by inheritance.

Both versions are based on an *integer generator* that produces and sends all integers into a chain of prime objects for filtering. As depicted in Fig. 16.9, the architecture is of a *push* nature: an object (`IntegerGenerator`) pushes all integers (actually odd ones) into the first prime. Each prime does the same action with an integer not being a multiple of itself. Figure 16.10 presents the sequential Java version, defined with a single class `Prime`. Following the technique explained in the previous section for a binary tree, it defines a kind of virtual factory, a method named `createPrime`. The filtering of integers is achieved by the method `isPrime`. At point (1) of the method, the integer is passed on to the next prime through a recursive call to `isPrime`. In the

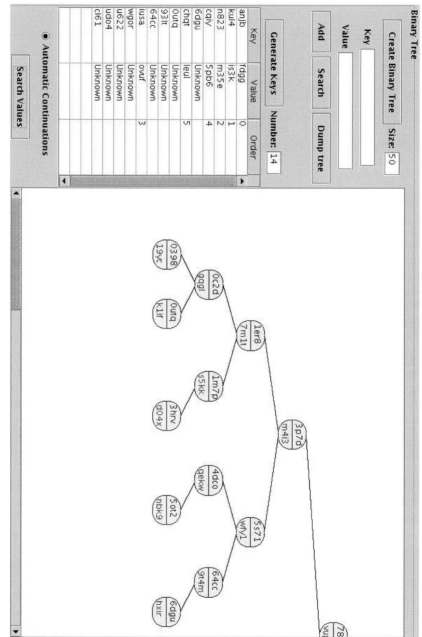

Fig. 16.8. Screenshot of the binary tree at execution

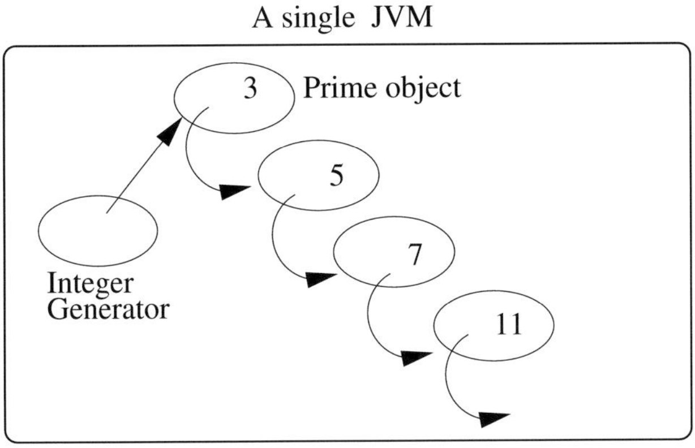

A single JVM

Fig. 16.9. Sequential Eratosthenes in Java

parallel version, this call will sometimes remain synchronous, and sometimes become asynchronous, leading to parallelism.

```
public class Prime {
  private long value;
  private Prime next;

  public Prime (long value) {                    /* Constructor */
    this.value = value;
  }
  public void isPrime (long n) {
    if (n % value == 0) // n is not prime, just drop it
      return;
    if (next == null) { // n is prime
      System.out.println ("New_prime_found:_"+ n);
      next = createPrime (n);
    } else
      next.isPrime(n); // Don't know yet. Pass it to next prime object (1)
  }
  public Prime createPrime (long n) {
    return new Prime (n);
  }
}
```

Fig. 16.10. Sequential `Prime` Java class

The parallel version transforms the prime object into an active object. However, rather than turning all objects active, which would result in too fine-grain parallelism, it applies a strategy for granularity control:

- creating active objects only when it is considered appropriate (effective with respect to parallelism),
- deciding statically or dynamically, based on application or environment criteria.

Figure 16.11 depicts the resulting topology at execution. Each active object can be placed into a specific JVM, on a given machine. Together with a set of non-activated prime objects, this active object forms an activity. References toward activated `ActivePrime` are global, while references toward standard ones are always local within the JVM.

JVM on a given machine

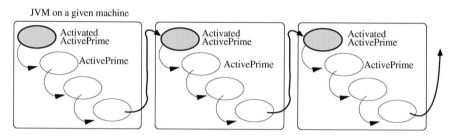

Fig. 16.11. Parallel Eratosthenes in Java ProActive

The program for such explicit granularity control is given at Fig. 16.12. The class `ActivePrime` extends `Prime` and of course redefines the virtual factory `createPrime`. However, compared to the previous binary tree example, active objects are not created in a systematic manner. Rather, one dynamically decides to create a standard, non-active, object (using the standard Java instruction `new`), or an identical but active object using the ProActive primitive `newActive`. In that case, the active object can be placed on a remote JVM, which is dynamically obtained here through the call to a dedicated method (`nextAvailableNode`).

Note than coding alternatives exist, potentially more abstract, using a `Prime interface` and two non-inheriting classes, `Prime` and `ActivePrime`.

The granularity control pattern presented above allows us to tune the amount of parallelism to be used at execution. Of course it applies to applications where there are obviously too many potential parallel actions.

This is to be compared to fine-grained parallel languages based on the generation of many tasks or functions to execute in parallel. Representative examples of such languages are Cilk [33] and lazy threads [76, 77]. Within those languages, a profusion of tasks (function calls that are usually run-to-completion, non-blocking) can be scheduled in parallel. In order to provide both efficiency and adaptation to the actual amount of parallelism available, a runtime implements what is sometimes called Lazy Task Creation (LTC) [77]. This allows excess parallelism to degrade into sequential calls, on the normal stack, without paying the price of allocating useless parallel calls in a

```
public class ActivePrime extends Prime {

  public ActivePrime (long value) {                /* Constructor */
    super(value);
  }
  public Prime createPrime (long n) {
    if ( timeToCreateANewActiveObject() )
      return (Prime)
        ProActive.newActive ("ActivePrime", {n}, nextAvailableNode());
    else
      return new ActivePrime (n);
  }
  public boolean timeToCreateANewActiveObject() {
    ... // Decide statically  or dynamically if there are enough prime objects
    ... // in the current  activity
  }
  public Node nextAvailableNode () {
    ... //Get a new or underloaded ProActive Node (machine+JVM),
    ... //where to locate  the new activity
  }

}
```

Fig. 16.12. Parallel `ActivePrime` class

tree of stacks, called a *cactus stack*. This technique has recently been called in a truthful manner *"sequential degradation"* [138, 137].

To summarize, fine-grained parallel languages execute tasks sequentially when parallelism is not appropriate, relying on a complex runtime system with load-balancing. Conversely, the more imperative frameworks ASP and ProActive authorize and encourage the programmer to explicitly control the amount of parallelism being generated, through the identification of active objects. The language greatly helps the programmer to achieve that control in a simple manner, through a powerful technique:

- dynamic binding toward an active object leads automatically to an asynchronous call (not a *cactus stack*, just a message to an already existing stack),
- while a normal synchronous call is executed toward a standard object (*on stack*).

In some sense, active objects in ASP and ProActive make it very simple to explicitly program sequential degradation or parallel upgrade.

We believe that another difficulty of fine-grained parallel languages is the absence of stateful parallelism: usually tasks are functionals. They cannot hold state as an active object can, taking advantage of it when replying to consecutive requests. This results in a bigger context to pass around at each task creation. This should be compared with a single active object creation, followed by many requests targeted at this activity.

16.2.3 Fibonacci

Following the various ASP Fibonacci examples (Sect. 5.4, page 80), this section proposes a ProActive Java version, potentially distributed over several machines.

Let us remind ourselves that Fibonacci numbers are generated by starting with the value 1 for the two firsts, and then adding the two previous numbers in the sequence to obtain the next one. So, a recursive definition of the Fibonacci sequence is:

```
if n <= 2 fib(n) = 1
if n > 2 fib(n) = fib(n-1) + fib(n-2)
```

So, the beginning of the sequence is :

    1, 1, 2, 3, 5, 8, 13, 21, 34, 55, 89, 144, 233, 377, 610, 987, 1597, ...

The version presented here, like the one in ASP, uses rather a *push* pattern: once initialized, the network of active objects keeps producing new values of the Fibonacci sequence. However, contrarily to a push version of the Eratosthenes sieve, the activities remain in-sink due to the dependencies; a maximum lag of two can occur.

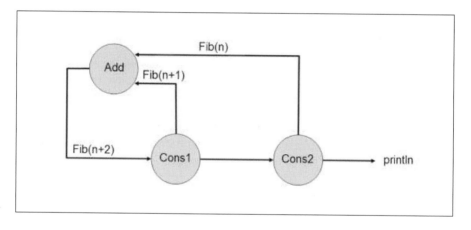

Fig. 16.13. Graph of active objects in the Fibonacci program

Figure 16.13 presents the active objects and the topology at executions. Three active objects are used:

- Add receives fib(n) from Cons2 and fib(n+1) from Cons1, and sends the sum, the result of fib(n+2), back to Cons1,

- Cons1 receives fib(n+2) from Add, and sends it unchanged back to Add, and also to Cons2,
- Cons2 receives fib(n+2) from Cons1, prints that result, and sends fib(n+2), the new fib(n+1), to Add.

```
public static void main(String[] args) {
try {
   Add add = (Add) ProActive.newActive(Add.class.getName(), null);
   Cons1 cons1 =(Cons1) ProActive.newActive (Cons1.class.getName(),null);
   Cons2 cons2 =(Cons2) ProActive.newActive (Cons2.class.getName(),null);
   add.setCons1(cons1);
   cons1.setAdd(add);
   cons1.setCons2(cons2);
   cons2.setAdd(add);
}
      catch (ActiveObjectCreationException e) {
          e.printStackTrace();
      } catch (NodeException e) {
          e.printStackTrace();
      }
}
```

Fig. 16.14. Main Fibonacci program in ProActive

Figure 16.14 presents the main program that creates the three active objects, using the newActive primitive. Then, the topology is established, just using asynchronous method calls on setter methods (the 4 calls setX). This gives to Add a reference to cons1, to Cons1 a reference to both Add and Cons2, and finally provides Cons2 with a reference to Add. At this point, the topology is as depicted in Fig. 16.13; the job of the main is done, and it just terminates itself.

Figure 16.15 provides the full code of the class Add. Compared to previous examples, Fibonacci features a non-FIFO service. In term of programming, a method, runActivity, provides the activity to be carried over by the active object. Compared to ASP where at creation the activity method can be specified in the Active primitive, here the body has to be placed in a fixed-name method; this is a technical choice for the sake of simplicity, which is really not a programming limitation. Any class that needs to specify an activity method just implements the interface RunActive, and provides the body of its runActivity method. An existing method can always be called within runActivity.

Note the initActivity method. It enables us to specify the active object initialization in a separate method. At creation, initActivity is called just

```
public class Add implements Serializable, InitActive, RunActive {
 private Cons1 cons1;
 private BigInteger fibN_1;
 private BigInteger fibN_2;

 public Add() { //Empty noArg constructor
 }
 public void initActivity (Body body) {
       Service service = new Service(body);
       service.blockingServeOldest("setCons1");
 }
 public void runActivity (Body body) {
       Service service = new Service(body);
       while (body.isActive()) {
          service.blockingServeOldest("setFibN_1");
          service.blockingServeOldest("setFibN_2");
          cons1.setFibN(fibN_1.add(fibN_2));
       }
 }
 public void setCons1 (Cons1 cons1) {
       this.cons1 = cons1;
 }
 public void setFibN_1 (BigInteger fibN_1) {
       this.fibN_1 = fibN_1;
 }
 public void setFibN_2 (BigInteger fibN_2) {
       this.fibN_2 = fibN_2;
 }
}
```

Fig. 16.15. The class `Add` of the Fibonacci program

before `runActivity`. In the case of migration, `initActivity` won't be called again, while `runActivity` is to be restarted upon arrival at each new site. Being within the framework of weak migration, `runActivity` is restarted at its beginning (the previous thread state was lost).

Upon initialization, `initActivity` waits and serves a request on `setCons1`, which sets the reference to the active object `Cons1`. The request comes from the main program discussed above. The activity itself, `runActivity`, is an infinite loop repeating two blocking services (`blockingServeOldest`), the addition of $Fib(n-1)$ with $Fib(n-2)$, and one asynchronous call sending the value obtained, $Fib(n)$, to the activity `Cons1`.

Figure 16.16 provides the full code of the class `Cons1`. The initialization is rather similar to the one above, using blocking services to set up references to other active objects, in the current case `Add` and `Cons2`.

```
public class Cons1 implements Serializable, InitActive, RunActive {
 private Add add;
 private Cons2 cons2;
 private BigInteger fibN;

 public Cons1() { //Empty no arg constructor
 }
 public void initActivity(Body body) {
        Service service = new Service (body);
        service.blockingServeOldest ("setAdd");
        service.blockingServeOldest ("setCons2");
 }
 public void runActivity(Body body) {
        Service service = new Service(body);
        add.setFibN_1 (BigInteger.ONE);
        cons2.setFibN_1 (BigInteger.ONE);
        while (body.isActive()) {
            service.blockingServeOldest ("setFibN");
            add.setFibN_1 (fibN);
            cons2.setFibN_1 (fibN);
        }
 }
 public void setAdd (Add add) {
        this.add = add;
 }
 public void setCons2 (Cons2 cons2) {
        this.cons2 = cons2;
 }
 public void setFibN (BigInteger fibN) {
                this.fibN = fibN;
 }
}
```

Fig. 16.16. The class Cons1 of the Fibonacci program

When reaching the iterative part of the activity, the while block of method runActivity, the behavior is rather a kind of forwarder: waiting for a request to receive a Fibonacci value, and forwarding it to the activities add and cons2. However, the value forwarded has the implicit meaning of being $Fib(n-1)$. So, this active object is just a kind of delay gate in a circuit, forwarding at step N the value of step $N-1$ to two other entities.

Finally, the last class, Cons2, is proposed in Fig. 16.17. In its principle, the behavior is very similar to the class above, Cons1, only instead of sending to two activities, one is replaced with printing the value of the Fibonacci suite; one could also use an activity for displaying values, along with what is done in the ASP version (*display* activity, Sect. 5.4, page 80). Besides printing the

```java
public class Cons2 implements InitActive, RunActive {
 private Add add;
 private BigInteger fibN_1;

 public Cons2() { //Empty no arg constructor
 }
 public void initActivity (Body body) {
        Service service = new Service(body);
        service .blockingServeOldest("setAdd");
 }
 public void runActivity (Body body) {
        int k=0;
        Service service = new Service(body);
        add.setFibN_2(BigInteger.ZERO); // starting with 0
        k++;
        while (body.isActive()) {
            service .blockingServeOldest("setFibN_1");
            add.setFibN_2(fibN_1);
            System.out.println("Fib(" + k + ")_=_" + fibN_1);
            k++;
        }
 }
 public void setFibN_1 (BigInteger fibN_1) {
        this.fibN_1 = fibN_1;
 }
 public void setAdd (Add add) {
        this.add = add;
 }
}
```

Fig. 16.17. The class `Cons2` of the Fibonacci program

value of Fib(n), the `Cons2` activity also plays the role of a delay operator, in this case a double delay, forwarding at step N the value of step $N - 2$ to the `Add` activity.

Figure 16.18 presents the execution of the Fibonacci code using IC2D (Interactive Control and Debugging of Distribution), the graphical monitoring tool of the ProActive environment. IC2D features graphical visualization of hosts, Java Virtual Machines, and active objects, including the topology and volume of communications.

In the screen-shot of Fig. 16.18, the Fibonacci program is executed on three different machines. The arrows dynamically depict the topology of the communications. One can see that the `Cons2` active object has several pending requests in its queue – the square dots above its name in the oval symbolizing the active object.

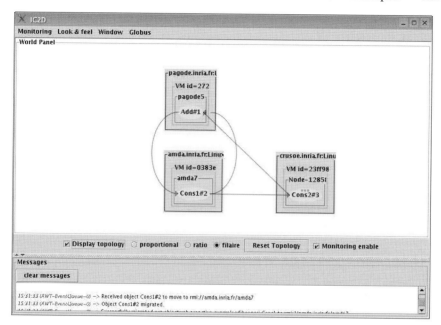

Fig. 16.18. Graphical visualization of the Fibonacci program using IC2D

Let us return to the determinate behavior of this program. In Fig. 16.15, the two blocking services (`blockingServeOldest("...")`) of class `Add` ensure the necessary synchronization. The current programming forces the activity to serve first the request aimed at `"setFibN_1"` (coming from `Cons1`) and then the request aimed at `"setFibN_2"` (coming from `Cons2`). However, that order is not absolutely essential. One could perfectly block-serve the two kinds of requests in the opposite order:

> service.blockingServeOldest(*"setFibN_2"*);
> service.blockingServeOldest(*"setFibN_1"*);
> cons1.setFibN(fibN_1.add(fibN_2));

Indeed, one can even serve the two requests in *any* order, provided the program serves one of each kind before executing the addition (calling the method `add`). Consequently, it is an example where one can use a relaxed join-like operation, as presented and discussed in Sect. 11.4.2, page 147. Namely, we can use the simple `barrier`, where the computation keeps on going after the two requests have been received and served, but in any order:

> service.barrier(*"setFibN_1"*, *"setFibN_2"*);
> cons1.setFibN(fibN_1.add(fibN_2));

Using such a primitive relaxes the program synchronization. However, it is at the expense of easily revealing its determinism. While the resulting program is indeed still determinate, it no longer respects the DON property; this is due to a non-deterministic order of services between `"setFibN_1"` and `"setFibN_2"`.

What brings the entire program back onto a deterministic track is in fact the commutativity of the two methods above. Dealing with such properties in order to qualify a larger class of programs as determinate is a promising prospect.

17

Future Update

A consequence of the confluence property is that the moment when future values are updated has no consequence on the final result of a given execution. This allows us to specify and implement any future update strategy compatible with the ASP REPLY rule.

A general problem that should be solved by this chapter is to determine who needs a future value. Indeed, REPLY rule does not specify which future value is updated and when, but for implementation purposes, this has to be determined.

Two particular and opposite kinds of executions can be distinguished:

- Eager future updates: Future are updated as soon as the future value has been calculated. In such executions, future values do not need to be stored in the activity that has calculated them.
- Lazy future updates: Futures are updated upon demand from another activity that really needs the future value. In such executions, only necessary future updates are performed.

The chapter is organized as follows. First, some general definitions useful for describing a future update strategy are given, then Sect. 17.2.1 presents the most general strategies, starting from the ASP REPLY rule and generalizing it. The remainder of Sect. 17.2 presents several specific future update strategies. Finally, Sect. 17.3 compares the different strategies presented in Sect. 17.2.

17.1 Future Forwarding

First, let us define the set of future references that are transmitted between activities. This set is called FF (Forwarded Futures), and contains triplets (future, future sender activity, future receiver activity):

$$FF ::= \{(f_i^{\alpha \to \beta}, \gamma, \delta)\}$$

with $(f_i^{\alpha \to \beta}, \gamma, \delta) \in FF$ if the future reference $f_i^{\alpha \to \beta}$ has been transmitted from γ to δ. From a more constructive point of view, this means modifying the REQUEST and REPLY rules with the following constraints:

Definition 17.1 (Forwarded futures)
In REQUEST *(sent from α to β),* $f_i^{\gamma \to \delta} \in copy(\iota', \sigma_\alpha) \Rightarrow (f_i^{\gamma \to \delta}, \alpha, \beta) \in FF$
In REPLY *(sent from β to α),* $f_i^{\gamma \to \delta} \in copy(\iota_f, \sigma_\beta) \Rightarrow (f_i^{\gamma \to \delta}, \beta, \alpha) \in FF$

The following property states that the FF set conforms to its intuitive definition, that is to say future references in a given activity correspond either to a future creation, and the current activity is the request sender, or to a forwarded future by another activity, and as such to an entry in FF:

Property 17.2 (Origin of futures)

$$fut(f_i^{\gamma \to \delta}) \in \sigma_\alpha \Rightarrow \alpha = \gamma \vee \exists \beta, (f_i^{\gamma \to \delta}, \beta, \alpha) \in FF$$

where the implication becomes an equivalence as soon as no garbage collection of future references is performed.

The next property is related to the flow of future references. Intuitively, it states that, if an activity gives a future reference, either it is the source activity of the request or it has received this reference from another activity (and thus it belongs to the FF set).

Property 17.3 (Forwarded futures flow)

$$(f_i^{\gamma \to \delta}, \beta, \alpha) \in FF \Rightarrow \beta = \gamma \vee \exists \beta', (f_i^{\gamma \to \delta}, \beta', \beta) \in FF$$

From a practical point of view, the set FF can be constructively built during serialization: when a future reference is serialized in order to be sent to another activity, a corresponding new entry is added to FF. In practice, FF is partitioned and partially stored locally inside each activity. But the part of FF which must be stored inside each activity depends on the chosen strategy.

Figure 17.1 shows an example of the flow of futures. The gray arrows with number show the flow of future references, the black arrows indexed with letters show the resulting future references. The future flow number **1** is a little particular because it corresponds to the future creation and is created by a REQUEST rule involving γ and δ.[1] This figure is, for example, the result of the following execution:

1   Activity γ performs a remote method call on activity δ. Future f_1 is associated to the result of this request.
2   γ sends the future f_1 to β as, for example, the result of a request.
3a β forwards this future reference to α as a part of the result associated to another request.

---

[1] In practice, the future reference can be created either in γ or in δ.

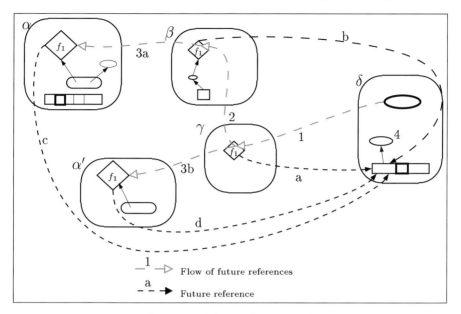

Fig. 17.1. A future flow example.

3b In parallel, γ sends a request to activity α' with future f_1 inside request parameters.

4   Finally, δ calculates a result value to be associated to the future f_1.

Let us suppose that, after those steps, only α and α' perform a strict operation on the future f_1.

   Consequently, references a and b may be garbage collected; however, some strategies, especially based on the forwarding of future values, might prevent their collection. The interaction of a future garbage collector and of future update strategies will not be studied here.

17.2 Update Strategies

This section attempts to offer a comprehensive view of numerous and diverse potential strategies for future updates.

17.2.1 ASP and Generalization: Encompassing All Strategies

A first *strategy* is directly expressed by the ASP calculus rules where no side condition must be verified to apply a REPLY rule and blocking operations are those which really need the value of the accessed object (except *clone* which is considered strict for determinism). The rest of this section defines an even more general strategy by generalizing the future update mechanism.

ASP with the generalized REPLY rule defined below encompasses all strategies and from this general view, every possible strategy can be expressed and implemented. Confluence properties ensure that all those strategies produce equivalent results providing the necessary future values are updated (there is no deadlock).

A first generalization of the REPLY rule has been given in Sect. 10.1 in the context of delegation, where we considered that a future value could be known and given by an activity that was not the target of the original request. Based on the delegation context, this rule can be used jointly with another one, called INFORM. The INFORM rule can communicate a future value to any activity. Consequently, the future value list (F_α) can also store a value associated to a future calculated by another activity. This future value can be used to update a future with the REPLY rule introduced in Sect. 10.1. We obtain the pair of rules described in Fig. 17.1.

Generalized REPLY:

$$\sigma_\alpha(\iota) = fut(f_i^{\gamma\to\delta}) \quad F_\beta(f_i^{\gamma\to\delta}) = \iota_f$$
$$\sigma'_\alpha = Copy\&Merge(\sigma_\beta, \iota_f \; ; \; \sigma_\alpha, \iota)$$

$$\alpha[a_\alpha; \sigma_\alpha; \iota_\alpha; F_\alpha; R_\alpha; f_\alpha] \parallel \beta[a_\beta; \sigma_\beta; \iota_\beta; F_\beta; R_\beta; f_\beta] \parallel P \longrightarrow$$
$$\alpha[a_\alpha; \sigma'_\alpha; \iota_\alpha; F_\alpha; R_\alpha; f_\alpha] \parallel \beta[a_\beta; \sigma_\beta; \iota_\beta; F_\beta; R_\beta; f_\beta] \parallel P$$

INFORM:

$$f_i^{\gamma\to\delta} \notin F_\alpha \quad F_\beta(f_i^{\gamma\to\delta}) = \iota_f$$
$$\iota'_f \notin dom(\sigma_\alpha) \quad \sigma'_\alpha = Copy\&Merge(\sigma_\beta, \iota_f \; ; \; \sigma_\alpha, \iota'_f)$$

$$\alpha[a_\alpha; \sigma_\alpha; \iota_\alpha; F_\alpha; R_\alpha; f_\alpha] \parallel \beta[a_\beta; \sigma_\beta; \iota_\beta; F_\beta; R_\beta; f_\beta] \parallel P \longrightarrow$$
$$\alpha[a_\alpha; \sigma'_\alpha; \iota_\alpha; F_\alpha :: \{f_i^{\gamma\to\delta} \mapsto \iota'_f\}; R_\alpha; f_\alpha] \parallel \beta[a_\beta; \sigma_\beta; \iota_\beta; F_\beta; R_\beta; f_\beta] \parallel P$$

Table 17.1. Generalized future update

These rules allow several activities to know the value of the same future, but in practice only *one* activity needs to have the value of each future. And if this future is no longer referenced then no activity needs to know the associated future value. The definition of well-formed configuration is Definition 10.1 in the delegation section. These rules do not compromise confluence properties and, more precisely, we can prove that:

- The value associated to a future is the same (modulo future update equivalence) in all activities.
- Consequently, updating a future reference from the future value list of different activities leads to equivalent configurations (modulo future update equivalence).

In the following, we will denote by $\text{REPLY}^{\beta\to\alpha}(f_i^{\gamma\to\delta})$ the application of the first rule, and by $\text{INFORM}^{\beta\to\alpha}(f_i^{\gamma\to\delta})$ the application of the second one.

This set of new rules allows us to express the most general strategies. However, even if the general strategies can reveal the most efficient future update, in practice a specific strategy must be chosen; these strategies are presented below. The forward-based strategy (Sect. 17.2.3) is based on the new REPLY and INFORM rules, the other ones can still be expressed using the REPLY rule of the core ASP calculus.

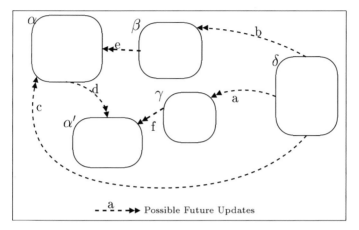

Fig. 17.2. General strategy: any future update can occur

It is difficult to express the future updates that can occur in a generalized strategy. Indeed, Fig. 17.2 shows some future updates that can occur in a generalized strategy for the case presented in Fig. 17.1: future values can be updated from any activity to any other activity. Note that this strategy does not specify which messages or events trigger the future updates and in practice, conditions triggering the update of a future should be more specified.

17.2.2 No Partial Replies and Requests

The simplest strategy forbids sending partial objects either as a result or as a parameter of a request (an object is said to have a *partial* value if it contains direct or indirect references to futures). Thus, a wait automatically occurs when a future has to be sent to another activity; that is to say, in REQUEST and REPLY, *Copy&Merge* is considered as a strict operation.[2]

---

[2] From a practical point of view, the serialization of a future is considered as a strict operation.

With such a strategy, a future only appears in the activity that has sent the request, and the *forwarded futures set is empty*:

Property 17.4 (No forwarded futures)

$$FF = \emptyset$$

The update of the value of a future should be performed as soon as the value is calculated (each ENDSERVICE rule is immediately followed by the corresponding REPLY rule, Table 17.2). This strategy avoids maintaining a future value list, simplifies the update of futures, and minimizes the number of references to futures. But it can lead to avoidable stuck configurations (waste of time) and deadlocks. For example, if α is waiting for a response from β, and this response contains a reference to a future resulting from a request to α, then this strategy leads to a deadlock that could be avoided. As shown in Fig. 17.2, in this strategy, a single application of the REPLY rule is always sufficient to update all references to a given future; and when this future is updated, no other future reference to this future exists. We denote by $A \hookrightarrow B$ the fact that the event or action A triggers the action B.

ENDSERVICE, for future $f_i^{\gamma \to \delta}$ on activity $\delta \hookrightarrow$ REPLY$^{\delta \to \gamma}(f_i^{\gamma \to \delta})$

Table 17.2. No partial replies and requests protocol

This strategy is very restrictive compared to ASP as it can definitively block the execution of some rules that could be evaluated. Thus, the sending of references to futures between activities is important and is possible in all the other strategies.

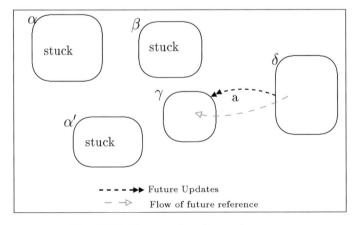

Fig. 17.3. No partial replies and requests

Figure 17.3 shows that when partial replies and requests are forbidden, the execution described in Fig. 17.1 is not possible and α, α', and β are stuck until the future value has been calculated by δ.

This strategy has been implemented in ProActive and this implementation is called "No automatic continuation."

17.2.3 Forward-Based

A second strategy called *forward-based* has also been implemented in ProActive. It allows one to forward futures in request responses and parameters but does not have a future value list: as soon as a response (even a partial one) is calculated, the future is recursively forwarded to every activity that has a reference to it. For this purpose, when a future reference is forwarded to an activity, the sender updates (locally) a list of *forwarded futures activities*: activities needing the future value. When the value is received, it is forwarded to every activity of the local list of *forwarded futures*. This strategy is called *eager* compared to mixed strategies allowed by the ASP calculus. Such an eager strategy minimizes the possibility of stuck configurations and deadlocks because a future is updated as soon as it is available. It is thus more parallel than the preceding one but can generate a lot of references to the same future. Table 17.3 defines the future update phase of the forward-based strategy. As REPLY and INFORM are systematically performed between the same activities, in practice the application of those two rules only requires one communication.

$$
\begin{array}{l}
\text{ENDSERVICE, for future } f_i^{\gamma \to \delta} \text{ on activity } \delta \hookrightarrow \begin{cases} \text{REPLY}^{\delta \to \gamma}(f_i^{\gamma \to \delta}) \\ \text{INFORM}^{\delta \to \gamma}(f_i^{\gamma \to \delta}) \end{cases} \\[4ex]
\text{REPLY}^{\alpha \to \beta}(f_i^{\gamma \to \delta}) \hookrightarrow \forall \beta' \text{ s.t. } (f_i^{\gamma \to \delta}, \beta, \beta') \in FF, \begin{cases} \text{REPLY}^{\beta \to \beta'}(f_i^{\gamma \to \delta}) \\ \text{INFORM}^{\beta \to \beta'}(f_i^{\gamma \to \delta}) \end{cases}
\end{array}
$$

Table 17.3. Forward-based protocol

The *forwarded futures* set can be partitioned into lists of *forwarded futures activities* stored locally in each activity responsible for forwarding the future value:

$$FF_\alpha = \{(f_i^{\gamma \to \delta}, \alpha, \beta') | \exists f_i, \gamma, \delta, \beta'(f_i^{\gamma \to \delta}, \alpha, \beta') \in FF\}$$

The following property states that, in the case where there is no cycle of future,[3] the forward-based strategy is eager and updates all future references.

Property 17.5 (Forward-based future update is eager)
If there is no cycle of future then, for each calculated future $f_i^{\gamma \to \delta}$, the protocol of Table 17.3 terminates with $\forall \beta$, $f_i^{\gamma \to \delta} \notin FutureRefs(\beta)$.

---

[3] Cycle of futures is defined in Definition 8.5 page 116.

This strategy avoids having to maintain a future value list. Indeed, as soon as a future value has been forwarded, the destination has been informed of the future value; thus the source activity does not need to remember the future value (cf. Definition 10.1 of well-formed configurations). From a practical point of view, during the future update phase, the future value is stored temporarily by the future update thread and when this phase ends, it is no longer necessary to store the future value (Property 17.5). Finally, the application of the INFORM rule of Table 17.3 does not require a supplementary communication.

The forward-based strategy, requires that the flow of future updates follows the flow of future reference transmission; and thus some future references can only be updated after several consecutive forwards of future values. Consequently this mechanism may lead to a long future update phase.

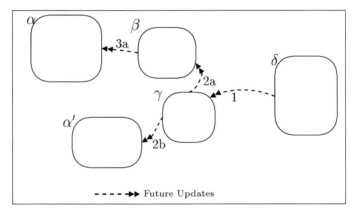

Fig. 17.4. Future updates for the forward-based strategy

Figure 17.4 shows that in the case of the forward-based strategy, future updates follow the flow of transmission of future references. Consequently, no additional message is necessary (only replies). The future is first updated in γ (arrow number **1**), then γ forwards this value to β (**2a**) and α' (**2b**), then β can forward the value to α (**3a**). Consequently, update **3a** must occur *after* updates **1** and **2a**. This illustrates the fact that this future update mechanism may lead to some delay between the moment when the future value is calculated and the moment when it is updated in the activity that really needs the value.

17.2.4 Message-Based

The main drawback of the forward-based strategy is the time spent in the forwarding of future values. Actually the activity that sends (serializes) or receives (deserializes) a new reference to a future can directly contact the activity that should produce the corresponding result. When such a *future forwarded* message is received, basically saying "activity γ might need that future," the target (which has to compute the future value) can update a list of *future receivers*. Then, when the value is calculated, it can be directly sent to future receiver activity; that is to say, to each activity that potentially needs this future value.

$$\text{ENDSERVICE, for future } f_i^{\gamma \to \delta} \text{ on activity } \delta \hookrightarrow$$
$$\begin{cases} \text{REPLY}^{\delta \to \gamma}(f_i^{\gamma \to \delta}) \\ \forall \beta' \text{ s.t. } \exists \beta(f_i^{\gamma \to \delta}, \beta, \beta') \in FF, \text{REPLY}^{\delta \to \beta'}(f_i^{\gamma \to \delta}) \end{cases}$$

Table 17.4. Message-based protocol for future update

Table 17.4 shows the protocol for the message-based future update, sending a future value to all activities that may need it as soon as it is calculated. The *forwarded futures* set is partitioned into *future receivers* lists stored locally in each activity responsible for calculating a future value:

$$FF_\alpha = \{(f_i^{\gamma \to \alpha}, \beta, \beta') | \exists f_i, \gamma, \beta, \beta'(f_i^{\gamma \to \alpha}, \beta, \beta') \in FF\}$$

This strategy needs to send more messages but spend less time updating futures. Moreover, as all future updates are sent from the same activity and the moment when futures are updated has no consequence on execution, all the updates of a given future can be performed in parallel.

Like the preceding strategy, message-based strategy does not need any future value list and is an eager strategy.

Property 17.6 (Message-based strategy is eager)
If there is no cycle of futures then for each calculated future $f_i^{\gamma \to \delta}$, the algorithm of Fig. 17.4 terminates with $\forall \beta$, $f_i^{\gamma \to \delta} \notin FutureRefs(\beta)$.

Figure 17.5 illustrates the message-based future updates. *Future forwarded* messages (gray arrows) are additional messages sent during the transmission of future references. In the figure, they are considered as starting from the activity that *receives the future value*, but as these messages are a consequence of the communication between two activities (involved in a REQUEST or a REPLY rule) they could also be considered as being sent by the activity that forwards the future value.

In order to illustrate the strategy, let us focus on the future reference in α' (indexed by **d** in Fig. 17.1). When γ sends the future reference to α', α' must be added to the list of *future receivers* associated to the future f_1 in δ; thus a *future forwarded* message **4** must be sent by γ or α' to δ. Then, when the future value is calculated, δ *replies* directly to α': the future update indexed by **d**.

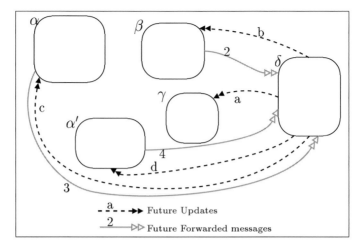

Fig. 17.5. Message-based strategy: future received and update messages

17.2.5 Lazy Future Update

A lazier approach to future update consists in updating a future value only when an activity requires it. The activity in absolute need of a future value (wait-by-necessity) will directly ask for it from the activity computing the future value. In this strategy, the REPLY rule is triggered by a wait-by-necessity on the activity that tries to use the future reference. Contrarily to the preceding strategies, each activity must store and keep in the future value list the results calculated by this activity: a future value may be required at any time. This strategy generates a huge number of future references but only the necessary future updates are performed.

In this strategy, the REPLY rule becomes:

REPLY:

$$\frac{\sigma_\alpha(\iota) = fut(f_i^{\gamma \to \beta}) \quad F_\beta(f_i^{\gamma \to \beta}) = \iota_f}{\sigma'_\alpha = Copy\&Merge(\sigma_\beta, \iota_f ; \sigma_\alpha, \iota) \quad \alpha \text{ is stuck by a wait-by-necessity}}$$

$$\alpha[a_\alpha; \sigma_\alpha; \iota_\alpha; F_\alpha; R_\alpha; f_\alpha] \parallel \beta[a_\beta; \sigma_\beta; \iota_\beta; F_\beta; R_\beta; f_\beta] \parallel P \longrightarrow$$
$$\alpha[a_\alpha; \sigma'_\alpha; \iota_\alpha; F_\alpha; R_\alpha; f_\alpha] \parallel \beta[a_\beta; \sigma_\beta; \iota_\beta; F_\beta; R_\beta; f_\beta] \parallel P$$

Compared to the normal REPLY rule (Table 6.2, page 92), α can receive a future value only if waiting for it (α is in a wait-by-necessity state).

Figure 17.6 illustrates the lazy future update mechanism. When an activity is blocked on an unknown future, it will send a *future needed* message to the target activity of the corresponding request. Future updates (REPLY) only occur in reply to such messages.

For example, when α' needs the future value associated to the future f_1 it sends the message number **2** to δ and requires the future value. When this value is calculated, δ will directly send the future value to α' which will be released of its wait-by-necessity.

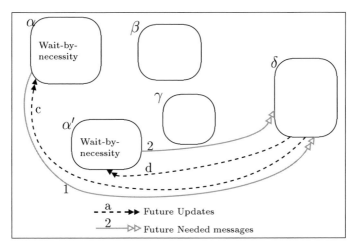

Fig. 17.6. Lazy future update: only needed futures are updated

17.3 Synthesis and Comparison of the Strategies

Figure 17.7 summarizes the future update strategies presented in this chapter. The rest of this section compares the different strategies.

- *No partial replies and requests*: no passing of futures between activities, more deadlocks. Futures are not first-class entities.
- *Eager strategies*: as soon as a future is computed
    - *Forward-based*: each activity is responsible for updating the values of futures it has forwarded.
    - *Message-based*: each forwarding of a future generates a message sent to the activity that computes the future. The activity computing the future is responsible for sending its value to all.
- *Mixed strategy*: future updates can occur at any time between the future computation and the wait-by-necessity. For example, one could implement future updates on inactivity (any stuck configuration).
- *Lazy strategy*: on demand, only when the value of the future is needed (wait-by-necessity on *this* future).

Fig. 17.7. Future update strategies

The strategy forbidding the sending of partial objects between activities is too synchronous and leads to many deadlocks. All the other specified strategies minimize the number of deadlock configurations in an equivalent manner.

Let us compare eager strategies to the *lazy* approach. In eager strategies, we do not need a future value list and avoid a future value garbage collection step; whereas with a lazy strategy, all future values need to be stored until all references to corresponding futures are updated. However, eager strategies may send future values to activities that do not need them, which could result in a waste of time. Moreover the future value is updated as soon as it is calculated, even if it is needed later, and it must either pass through all activities that have forwarded the future, or require the destination activity to perform a lot of updates. To conclude, in eager strategies some time can be wasted updating the future values, but globally the value is updated as soon as possible. Moreover, eager strategies are difficult to adapt to the cases where there are cycles of futures and may lead to live-locks, whereas a lazy strategy is naturally adapted to cycles of futures.

In lazy strategies the minimal number of future updates is performed, but in practice this strategy requires additional communications to be performed upon a wait-by-necessity in order to ask for the future value. Moreover these messages sent upon wait-by-necessity systematically lengthen this synchronization phase, especially in WANs where latency is important.

The two eager strategies have similar characteristics except that in message-based strategy, the activity that is the destination of the request must send to all the future values and may spend a lot of time doing this; whereas the forward-based strategy may require more time to have the future finally updated because the future value has to pass through all activities that have forwarded the future.

Except for the general strategy (Sect. 17.2.1), this chapter did not deal with future updates in the ASP calculus with delegation. Indeed updating futures for a delegated request needs other choices to be made for the employed strategy, leading to at least two sub-strategies for each case studied in this chapter.

Finally, the theoretical results given in Chap. 8 prove the possibility of updating futures independently. In practice, the fact that the execution is insensitive to the moment when futures are updated allows the future update mechanism to be performed by a *separate thread*. Thus, the future update phase and some computational activity can be overlapped. This overlap between asynchronous communications and computations limits the importance of the time spent in communications. Consequently, the fact that the message-based strategy is costly from the request destination point of view has far fewer consequences.

In ProActive, two future update strategies have been implemented: the "No partial replies and requests" and the "Forward-based strategy."

The future update strategies presented in this chapter and their realization are patented [50].

To conclude, choosing a future update strategy often requires a choice to be made between scalability as proposed in the lazy strategy and latency hiding which is maximal for an eager approach.

18

Loosing Rendezvous

The rendezvous phase, which ensures an atomic REQUEST rule, can be considered as time consuming, this chapter studies the impact of this synchronization phase and the possibility to remove it.

This chapter can be considered as strongly related to different articles comparing communication timings in a purely message-based framework [55] and implementing a causal order from a synchronous communication timing by using buffers [113]. The main difference in ASP is that the request reception is clearly distinguished from the request service, the request reception being mostly synchronous but non-blocking, and the request service being strongly asynchronous.

18.1 Objectives and Principles

First, as classified in Sect. 1.2.3, there are two less restrictive *communication timings*:

- Asynchronous without guarantee: this means no guarantee about the order of request receptions and will be briefly studied below.
- Asynchronous FIFO preserving: this guarantee on order still preserves many properties and seems much more promising. However, we will distinguish two sub-categories:
  - Point-to-point FIFO preserving corresponds to the FIFO preserving described in Sect. 1.2.3.
  - One-to-all FIFO preserving is another communication timing that keeps the relative order of message sending but loses the rendezvous. This communication timing corresponds to a sender-based order FIFO preserving instead of the point-to-point FIFO preserving: *FIFO delivery is also guaranteed between requests sent to distinct activities.*

To summarize, from the most asynchronous communication timing to the most property preserving (closest to asynchronous with rendezvous), we have:

- asynchronous without guarantee,
- asynchronous point-to-point FIFO ordering,
- asynchronous one-to-all FIFO ordering.

$$\begin{aligned}
&let \; \delta = Active([\ldots; m_j = \varsigma(s) \ldots]) \; in \\
&\quad let \; \beta = Active\big([; \; foo = \varsigma(s) \, \delta.m_2(); \\
&\qquad\qquad\qquad\qquad\quad Active([; act = \varsigma(s) \, \delta.m_3()], act); \\
&\qquad\qquad\qquad\qquad\quad \delta.m_4() \qquad], \emptyset\big) \; in \\
&\quad\quad Active\big([; act = \varsigma(s) \, \delta.m_1(); \beta.foo(); \delta.m_5()], act\big)
\end{aligned}$$

Fig. 18.1. Example: activities synchronized by rendezvous

Figure 18.1 shows a program that creates four activities communicating asynchronously. This example is designed to show the importance of synchronization resulting from the rendezvous phase. The activity created by the last line of the example will be named α. δ will be the target activity for communications. It defines at least methods m_1, m_2, m_3, m_4, and m_5. α, β, and γ send requests to δ. Method foo of activity β is only invoked by α, and creates an activity named γ.

Figure 18.2 illustrates the execution of the program of Fig. 18.1. It shows the four activities and the communications occurring; the request queue of δ is represented by a graph in order to express all the possible request queues for δ. Two requests are linked in this graph if one is sent before the other in all the executions of the program (with rendezvous). Whether requests have or have not been treated in δ has no consequence here. In this example requests are uniquely characterized by the name of the invoked method. Figure 18.2 considers the case of the "classical" ASP calculus (with rendezvous). For example, the pending requests of δ can be:

- $m_1 :: m_2 :: m_3 :: m_4 :: m_5$, or
- $m_1 :: m_5 :: m_2 :: m_4 :: m_3$.

In this chapter, we will write transformations in order to model different levels of communication timing in ASP. Every translated calculus will verify the ASP properties, but the objective here is to study which of these properties are verified in terms of the original calculus. In other words, to model different communication timing, every activity α will be partitioned into several activities α_i. Trivially, RSL confluence is verified in terms of α_i. However, if we denote by $\alpha^* = \cup \alpha_i$ an *abstract activity* merging all the α_i activities and thus representing the original α, this activity may not verify the RSL confluence property because it is not a real ASP activity and in particular it contains several threads. More generally, we will try to determine which interleaving of operations can occur because of the loss of rendezvous.

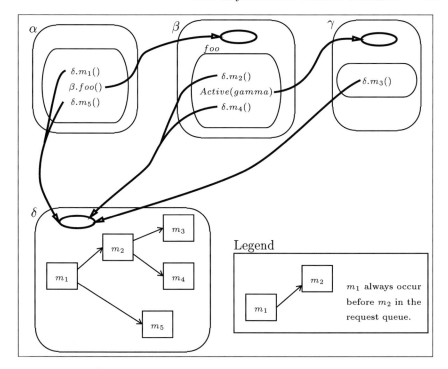

Fig. 18.2. ASP with rendezvous – message ordering

18.2 Asynchronous Without Guarantee

Asynchronous communications without guarantee could be expressed in several ways in ASP.

The most direct way would be to modify the semantic rules: request rule would be split into two rules. A first one would just create a request (the new futures would be necessarily created in the source activity). While this request is not yet taken into account by the destination activity, it would be placed in parallel with the activities. A term would become a set of activities together with transiting messages floating in a medium. A second rule would then incorporate a transiting request into its destination activity. This approach completely modifies the semantics of ASP, and would require a long study of the behavior of this new calculus.

The transiting message could also be simulated in the existing calculus. Indeed instead of having the transiting message, one could create a *carrier activity* for each request. From a very practical point of view this consists in creating a thread for each request sending. We obtain the following encoding that changes the activity creation mechanism:

$$Active'(a) \triangleq let\ act = Active(a, \emptyset)\ in$$
$$let\ trRq = [; \forall m_j, m_j = \varsigma(s, arg)\ act.m_j(arg)]\ in$$
$$[; \forall m_j, m_j = \varsigma(s, arg)\ Active(trRq, \emptyset).m_j(arg)]$$

where m_j ranges over the method labels of the activated object.

A more efficient encoding uses the *delegate* primitive:

$$Active'(a, service) \triangleq let\ act = Active(a, service)\ in$$
$$let\ trRq = [; \forall m_j, m_j := \varsigma(s, arg)\ delegate(act.m_j(arg))]\ in$$
$$[; \forall m_j, m_j := \varsigma(s, arg)Active(trRq, \emptyset).m_j(arg)]$$

In both encodings, $trRq$ is designed to be an object that is used to create a new activity for each sent request, and each instance of $trRq$ corresponds to a transiting request.

Changing all *Active* into *Active'* would result in the *totally asynchronous ASP calculus*. Note that the local passive object associated to each active object and returned by *Active'* acts as a proxy and has the expected behavior when passed between activities.

Once translated into ASP with rendezvous, the program still verifies deterministic properties, but the additional activities created to simulate asynchrony are all independent. The confluence property (Theorem 8.10) states that the execution is characterized by the RSL of all activities. However, as there is one activity for each request, the RSL is equivalent to the ordered list of requests: execution is still characterized by the ordered list of request senders, but a request sender uniquely identifies a request. Then execution is characterized by the order of pending requests in each activity which is much less significant than the RSL confluence in terms of abstract activities. Moreover, no synchronization between those requests allows them to be ordered except wait-by-necessity on the results, and services.

To conclude, even if confluence properties are still verified, they have no signification in terms of the original activities as any request can overtake any other one. In other words, the RSL expressed in abstract activities α^* is not sufficient to characterize execution. Indeed, let α_1 and α_2 be two in-transit messages coming from activity α; $\alpha^* :: \alpha^*$ can correspond either to $\alpha_1 :: \alpha_2$ or to $\alpha_2 :: \alpha_1$.

However, properties dealing with futures are still verified and execution is still *insensitive to the moment when futures are updated*.

Figure 18.3 shows the activities (α_1, α_2, β_1, γ_1, ...) created to simulate totally asynchronous communications in ASP. Each activity corresponds to a request. The resulting requests can appear in any order in δ. This figure illustrates the fact that one activity is created for each sent request.

To summarize, a totally asynchronous ASP calculus is characterized by:

- Execution is still *insensitive to the moment when futures are updated*.

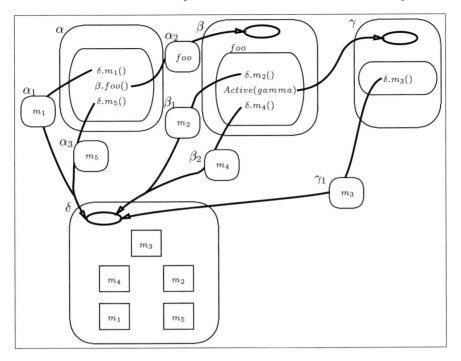

Fig. 18.3. Asynchronous communications without guarantee

- *Request senders are not sufficient* to characterize execution. Execution is characterized by the *complete ordered list of requests* inside each activity (including the invoked method and the arguments).
- Any request sending can overtake any other operation.

Most likely, an ASP determinate program will behave undeterministically with asynchronous without guarantee communications, except of course if all communications are explicitly acknowledged; for example, by systematically performing a wait-by-necessity on each result just before sending the next request. But in that case the program executes rather synchronously.

18.3 Asynchronous Point-to-Point FIFO Ordering

Point-to-point FIFO preserving asynchrony consists in guaranteeing the order of reception of requests coming from the same activity. In other words, the request sending order is preserved for a given couple (sender, receiver). It can be implemented by creating a single thread responsible for sending all requests addressed to the same destination activity.

Compared to the asynchronous without guarantee case, it is more difficult to modify ASP rules in order to express point-to-point FIFO order (e.g., a solution consists in associating a sequence number to each request).

Point-to-point FIFO order could be modeled as follows:

- For each couple (source, destination), associate an activity *queue* responsible for sending requests to the destination. In the modeling below, *thisActivity.Queues⟨destination⟩* returns the unique queue activity corresponding to the couple (*thisActivity, destination*).
- A *queue* activity is similar to the *trRq* defined in the preceding case except that it is designed to ensure the transit of all requests on a given couple (source, destination).
- A proxy object is associated to each destination activity and is stored inside each source activity. Then a request *foo* is sent to activity δ by *thisActivity.Queues⟨δ⟩.foo(arg)*.

This solution supposes one has a primitive *thisActivity* in ASP, and that references to queue activities are stored in the source active object. We suppose one has a *Queues* list which is an association list mapping destination activity references to queue activity references. The encoding of operations on this table is not described here (it does not raise any technical difficulty but would require a rather long development); these operations are the following:

- $d \in Q$: existence of an entry,
- $Q\langle d\rangle$: find an object associated with an entry,
- $Q :: \{d \mapsto b\}$: add a new entry

Here is the encoding of the *queue* method:

$$
\begin{aligned}
queue \triangleq \ &\varsigma(s, dest)\big(if\ (dst \notin s.Queues)\ then\ s.Queues := \\
&s.Queues :: \{dst \mapsto Active([; \forall m_j,\ m_j = \varsigma(s, z)\, \mathcal{D}(dst.m_j(z))], \emptyset)\}); \\
&s.Queues\langle dest\rangle
\end{aligned}
$$

where $\mathcal{D}(a) = a$ if we consider the core ASP calculus, and $\mathcal{D}(a) = delegate(a)$ in the ASP calculus with delegation; m_j ranges over the method labels of the activated object.

Then, let $\mathcal{C}(o)$ be the object o together with the previously defined *queue* method and an empty *Queues* field. The new primitive for creating activities is:

$$
\begin{aligned}
Active'(a, service) \triangleq\ &let\ act = Active(\mathcal{C}(a), service)\ in \\
&[; \forall m_j,\ m_j = \varsigma(s, y) thisActivity.queue(act).m_j(y)]
\end{aligned}
$$

Asynchronous point-to-point FIFO ordering ensures more properties than asynchronous without guarantee ones. Requests between two given activities arrive in the sending order. In other words, an occurrence of an abstract activity α^* in the RSL of δ uniquely corresponds to a queue activity α_δ. Thus, because for each couple (source, destination) only one activity is created, the RSL of the receiver expressed in abstract activities fully characterizes execution. *RSL confluence is still verified in the asynchronous FIFO point-to-point ASP calculus.*

But rendezvous provides additional synchronization that is not guaranteed by point-to-point FIFO ordering as detailed in the following.

Definition 18.1 (Triangle pattern)
A triangle pattern is a configuration such that:

$$\exists \alpha, \beta_1 \ldots \beta_n, \gamma \ s.t. \ \alpha \rightarrow_R \gamma \ and \ then \ \alpha \rightarrow_R \beta_1 \rightarrow_R \ldots \rightarrow_R \beta_n \rightarrow_R \gamma$$

where $\alpha \rightarrow_R \beta$ means α sends requests to β or α creates activity β.

For example, in ASP calculus with rendezvous, the triangle pattern seems useful for initializing activities as it ensures that a particular request (e.g., an initialization request) will be the first received by the destination activity.

Triangle patterns express the *causal ordering* [55] between requests in ASP.

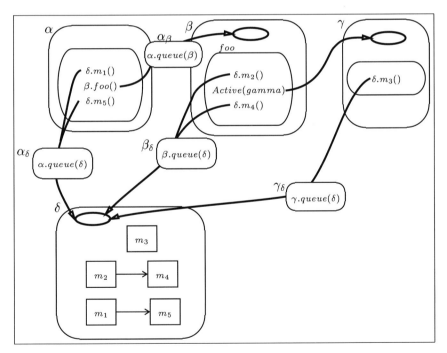

Fig. 18.4. Asynchronous point-to-point FIFO communications

Figure 18.4 shows the activities (α_β, α_δ, β_δ, and γ_δ) containing *Queue* objects associated with each pair (source, destination): α_β is the activity for source α and destination β. Some synchronization is ensured in this communication timing as illustrated in the potential request queues of activity δ. As explained before, this example has been designed to show the consequence of the loss of rendezvous, thus it contains triangle patterns. It shows a maximal number of loss of request reception order compared to the execution with rendezvous.

In the ASP calculus with rendezvous, for the triangle pattern of Fig. 18.4, it is ensured that m_2 and m_3 will be received after m_1. For point-to-point FIFO preserving communications, the triangle pattern is not preserved by the translation defined above. Thus m_2 and m_3 can be received before m_1.

Synchronization in point-to-point FIFO communication timing can also be expressed in the following way:

> Only request reception on the same channel is guaranteed to happen after a previously sent request has been received. But, compared to ASP with rendezvous, this loss of synchronization mainly has consequences for request reception order in the case of the triangle pattern.

More precisely, Charron-Bost et al. [55] also showed that synchronous communications are characterized by the absence of crowns. Crowns enforce some ordering of requests that are not due to causal ordering, and consequently that are not the result of a triangle pattern. Such enforced ordering does not seem useful for writing ASP terms.

To summarize, asynchronous point-to-point FIFO ordering has the following properties:

- Execution is *insensitive to the moment when futures are updated*.
- Execution is characterized by the ordered list of request senders (*RSL confluence*).
- Request reception order is not fully guaranteed, e.g., in the case of the *triangle pattern*.

18.4 Asynchronous One-to-All FIFO Ordering

This section presents an even more synchronous communication timing, getting closer to the rendezvous semantics.

In the point-to-point FIFO preserving case, the requests sent to different activities were sent independently; the following communication timing creates *one single activity* for sending *all requests*. At the implementation level, it corresponds to creating one thread responsible for sending all requests; this is done by the *Queue* active object in the following modeling. Such a *Queue* activity is stored in the *queue* field of each active object:

$$Active'(a, service) \triangleq let\ b = clone(a)\ in$$
$$\left(let\ Queue = [; \forall m_j \in \mathcal{M}_1,\ m_j = \varsigma(s, d, z)\ \mathcal{D}(d.m_j(z))]\ in\right.$$
$$\left. b.queue := Active(Queue, \emptyset)\right);$$
$$let\ act = Active(b, service)\ in$$
$$[; \forall m_j \in \mathcal{M}_2,\ m_j = \varsigma(s, y)(thisActivity.queue).m_j(act, y)]$$

where $\mathcal{D}(a) = a$ if we consider the core ASP calculus, and $\mathcal{D}(a) = delegate(a)$ in the ASP calculus with delegation; $\mathcal{M}_1$ denotes the set of all the method labels that can be called from the activated object (a or b), and $\mathcal{M}_2$ denotes the set of all the method labels of the activated object (a or b).

With this communication timing, the triangle pattern is preserved for request sending: precisely, the triangle pattern between original activities is replaced by another triangle pattern involving some *Queue* activities, but this new triangle still ensures the same synchronization properties as in ASP with rendezvous. One could also verify that crowns cannot exist in such a communication timing. Thus, concerning communication, one-to-all FIFO ordering has the same semantics as ASP with rendezvous.

But a triangle pattern involving activity creation is not maintained by the preceding modeling because activity creation involves a communication that is not a request sending. Consequently, the relative order of requests sent by the created activity (upon creation) and by the activity that triggered this creation is not maintained.

Figure 18.5 shows the *Queue* activities associated to each source activity. All requests sent by a given activity pass through its associated *Queue* activity. The reception order of ASP with rendezvous is almost completely guaranteed. For example, the request reception order is still ensured between m_1 and m_2, but not between m_2 and m_3 because the triangle pattern synchronizing m_2 and m_3 involves one activity creation. Indeed, activity γ is created by β, and it is not ensured that the delivery of message m_2 will happen before γ can itself send messages (m_3).

Note that m_1 necessarily occurs before m_3 because of the *foo* request: the request reception order is ensured between m_1 and *foo* thus m_1 is received by δ before *foo* by β and the *foo* request is treated before the creation of activity γ and the sending of m_3.

Synchronization in one-to-all FIFO communication timing can also be expressed in the following way:

Only request reception is guaranteed to happen after a previously sent request has been received. But compared to ASP core calculus, the loss of rendezvous is only of consequence in the case of activity creation.

If we want to actually get the ASP message ordering, the *Queue* activity can be responsible for creating activities. Indeed suppose method

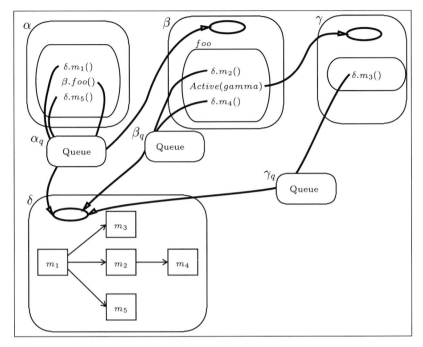

Fig. 18.5. Asynchronous one-to-all FIFO communications

names could be transmitted as method arguments (as *service* in *thisActivity.queue.QActive(b, service)* below); then the following encoding of *Queue* object would ensure the same synchronization as the in ASP calculus with rendezvous:

$$
\begin{aligned}
Active'(a, service) \triangleq\ &let\ b = clone(a)\ \ in \\
&\Big(let\ Queue = [; \forall m_j,\ m_j = \varsigma(s, d, z)]\,\mathcal{D}(d.m_j(z)), \\
&\qquad\quad QActive = \varsigma(s, x, srv)Active(x, srv)]\quad in \\
&\qquad b.queue := Active(Queue, \emptyset)\Big); \\
&let\ act = thisActivity.queue.QActive(b, service)\ in \\
&\quad [; \forall m_j,\ m_j = \varsigma(s, y)(thisActivity.queue).m_j(act, y)]
\end{aligned}
$$

Indeed, the only communication rules in ASP (which are the only rules performing synchronization between activities) are REQUEST, REPLY, and NEWACT. The confluence property of Chap. 8 has shown that REPLY can occur at any time, and the *Queue* activity above orders both REQUEST and NEWACT rules within the same source activity without rendezvous between the original activities.

Consequently, at the implementation level, delegating a thread to perform both activity creation and request sending increases parallelism in ASP without any observable effect. In this case, the possible request queue in activity δ is the same as in Fig. 18.2.

To summarize, one-to-all FIFO ordering communication timing has the following properties:

- Execution is *insensitive to the moment when futures are updated.*
- Execution is characterized by the ordered list of request senders (*RSL confluence*).
- Request reception order is always the *same as in ASP with rendezvous* except in the following case:
  If the *Queue* activity is not responsible for creating activities, then a triangle pattern containing activity creation does not guarantee the same synchronization than ASP with rendezvous.

As just explained, ordering activity creation and message sending with a single thread fully returns to the ASP properties, but still in a more asynchronous way than ASP with rendezvous.

However, some aspects of rendezvous may be useful for certain protocols using very specific ASP properties (e.g., fault tolerance [23]), and a more general approach consists in a soft rendezvous where some local operations (e.g., passive object manipulation) can be performed during the rendezvous phase and some others are considered as more critical and cannot be performed (e.g., request service, activity creation, request sending, etc.).

18.5 Conclusion

In general, as soon as for any couple (sender, receiver) of activities FIFO order is guaranteed, the properties shown in this book, manly confluence and determinacy, are still verified. But the absence of rendezvous nearly always results in a loss of synchronization.

This chapter proved that every communication timing can be simulated in ASP by introducing intermediate activities with a different granularity depending on the required timing:

- Asynchronous communications without guarantee are simulated by creating an activity for each *message*.
- Asynchronous point-to-point FIFO communications are simulated by creating an activity for each couple *(request sender, request receiver)*.
- One-to-all FIFO communications are simulated by creating a dedicated *sender activity* for each request activity. If this activity is also responsible for creating activities, then one obtains a calculus more parallel than ASP but entirely equivalent.

The practical point of view simply consists in replacing the extra activities by additional threads in the modeling described above. For example, point-to-point FIFO communication timing consists in associating one thread to each destination activity in each source activity: one thread for each different acquaintance (proxy).

Except for asynchronous communication without guarantee, the loss of synchronization is only observable in the case of triangle patterns because the additional sender activities alter this pattern. The example presented in this chapter shows different cases of triangle patterns, and demonstrates the consequences of losing rendezvous.

Finally, a good solution for making communications less synchronous but still ensuring ASP properties has been proposed: one-to-all FIFO ordering with one thread responsible for sending requests and creating activities.

19

Controlling Pipelining

In [100], different modes of execution of process networks are presented. The *demand driven mode* activates a process only when one tries to read a value from a channel coming from it. With such an evaluation strategy execution should be fully sequential. This mode is compared to a *parallel mode* of execution where processes producing values continue their execution. This mode provides parallelism and latency hiding, but it can also perform superfluous computations and over-flooding of channels.

Figure 19.1 summarizes the different pipelining strategies presented and analyzed in this chapter.

- *Pure demand driven*: an activity is only activated when another one is waiting for data coming from it.
- *Limited pipelining*: the number of pending requests per sender activity is limited.
- *Unrestricted parallelism*: all activities are executed in parallel without any restriction.

Fig. 19.1. Strategies for controlling parallelism

In fact, all strategies presented here simply consist in determining the order in which ASP reduction rules are applied.

In practice, limiting parallelism can be useful for resource usage control and overall efficiency.

19.1 Unrestricted Parallelism

The classical ASP calculus expresses a fully parallel pipelining. Except when blocked on a wait-by-necessity on services, activities keep serving requests, potentially sending an infinite number of requests. See for example the push version of the sieve of Eratosthenes: Fig. 5.6 page 79.

This supposes that the request queue of each activity is infinite or at least will never be full. The expressiveness of such a calculus is important and it allows a truly parallel computation but can lead to useless computations, and thus some inefficiency. At the semaintic level, it is reflected by the fact that ASP reduction rules can be applied in any order, and each activity performs its own computation without any other synchronization than wait-by-necessity and request service.

19.2 Pure Demand Driven

A pure demand-driven strategy is a truly lazy strategy where wait-by-necessity on a future, besides blocking the current activity, activates the activity that should calculate the future.

This strategy is strongly linked to lazy future update (Sect. 17.2.5) but instead of triggering a REPLY, the wait-by-necessity triggers computations in the destination activity until a value is computed for the awaited future.

It is much more difficult to deal with the other automatic synchronization existing in ASP: namely, request service on a method label that is not in the request queue. Indeed, in that case, it is difficult to know which activity must be activated to send the right request and, moreover, in general this activity is not unique; however, this sender activity is unique in deterministic programs. It would be much simpler in a calculus where a service is determined by the source activity of requests ($Serve(\alpha)$); this service primitive has been further discussed in Sect. 9.5.

Within standard ASP featuring request service on method labels, a demand-driven approach could consist in activating in parallel all activities that can send requests to the stuck activity, for instance all activities handling a generalized reference on the stuck activity. However, this solution is not purely demand driven as some activities will be activated unnecessarily and several activities will be active in parallel.

Finally, a pure demand-driven approach does not seem very adapted to ASP but a partially demand-driven approach can be of use.

19.3 Controlled Pipelining

In addition to the arguments of the preceding section, we do not want to apply a pure demand-driven execution mode in middleware such because ProActive, as it is designed to be distributed over a network, achieve pipelining, and hide latency. But if the length of the request queue could be limited, this would prevent an activity from useless overloading the request queue of another one.

A good solution seems to limit the number of requests each activity can send to another one. Some deadlocks could appear with such a strategy, e.g., if an activity sends a lot of requests on a first method before sending a request on a second method which will be served first. To avoid such potential deadlocks, we should apply a demand-driven approach to solve stuck configurations. This approach has the advantage of benefitting from the parallelism between processes without overloading an activity with requests that may never be served. Figure 19.1 summarizes the different strategies for controlling parallelism.

Garbage Collection

The detailed study of garbage collection for distributed objects is beyond the scope of this book. In this chapter, we simply describe the aspects of garbage collection which are linked to ASP. The objective here is just to give information in order to show how to adapt an existing garbage collector (or at least existing techniques for garbage collection) to the special case of ASP.

Because of the object topology in ASP described in Sect. 7.2, a garbage collection mechanism on ASP can be separated into three concerns: a local garbage collection phase, and the distributed garbage collection of futures and activities. Recall that futures and activities are the only generalized references in ASP. Of course, in practice, the handling of these three concerns should interact.

20.1 Local Garbage Collection

First note that the parameters of requests and values of futures are situated in *isolated* parts of the store and thus could be put in a different store (Property 7.2 page 105).

From that property, local garbage collection can be performed easily: useful objects are referenced by the current term (a_α), the active object (ι_α), the future list (F_α), and the request lists (R_α). They constitute the *roots* of the local object system. Note also that, in the case of a non-incremental garbage collector, the best moment for a garbage collection step seems to be after the ENDSERVICE. Indeed, every object that has only been allocated for serving the preceding request will no longer be useful.

As the global references consist only in futures and active objects, the first step of garbage collection described above is clearly a purely local one and can be performed by classical and well-known techniques.

20.2 Futures

First, one must note that future garbage collecting depends on the future update strategy (Chap. 17).

If a strategy is not eager (*mixed* and *lazy* strategies), then it does not update futures as soon as their values are calculated. Thus, futures have to be kept in the future value list in order to be potentially used later on for update. From a garbage collection point of view, the immediate future reply that occurs in eager strategies (*forward-based*, *message-based*, or even *no partial requests and replies* strategies) is much simpler but it does not allow a future to be updated at any time. We consider this as too restrictive.

Therefore, as the future might have proliferated in many activities, it is difficult to decide in a trivial manner when a future can be removed from the list of future values. In practice, reference counting or any distributed garbage collector mechanism can be used to perform distributed garbage collection of futures. See, for example, [106] and [65] for the study of distributed garbage collectors. Indeed, future references are particular global references, and all frameworks dealing with garbage collection of global references can be applied to the particular case of futures.

20.3 Active Objects

Garbage collection of active objects can be more generally called *garbage collection of activities*. Active object references are also generalized references that can be spread over the different activities. In order to perform garbage collection of active objects one first needs to determine if this active object (or activity) is referenced from "useful" activities (classical garbage collection). The main difficulty arises from cycles of activities. The distributed and dynamic nature of activities makes it difficult to detect useless cycles of activities.

Provided this classical difficulty is dealt with, an activity can be garbage collected if

- it is no longer referenced (classical usefulness),
- the activity no longer contains any pending requests,
- the activity no longer has any proper activity (empty current term with no continuation).

In that case the whole activity *except the future list* can be garbage collected. Of course references to futures contained within this activity can still exist, but their garbage collection is dependent on the constraints described previously.

Part VI

Final Words

21

ASP Versus Other Concurrent Calculi

This chapter compares ASP and the different calculi and languages introduced in Chap. 2. The objective of this chapter is both to compare ASP communications and synchronizations with alternative options, and to discuss how the ASP concepts can be adapted to other calculi. We will also present how tools developed within other calculi could be adapted to ASP.

With respect to shared memory, ASP avoids sharing memory because race conditions prevent determinacy of programs in general. Our objective was to design a calculus with local access within an activity and between activities to be as uniform as possible. However, some copying of data is needed, and the semantics of local and remote communications is somehow slightly different: ASP defines a semantics with implicit data copying upon communication between processes.

The general principle for the design of ASP distributed programs is the following:

- when asynchronism or distribution is needed, an object can easily be made active;
- data exchange between active objects is automatically turned into a copy semantics, and the designer has to take it into account;
- if an object needs to be shared between activities, it can itself just be turned into an active object,

Such a design process is applied until the appropriate sharing, distribution, and granularity are obtained.

21.1 Basic Formalisms

21.1.1 Actors

In relying on the active object concept, the ASP model is rather close to, and was somehow inspired by, the notion of *actors* [10, 11]. Both rely on asynchronous communications, but actors are rather functionals, while ASP is in an imperative and object-oriented setting. While actors interact by asynchronous *message passing*, ASP is based on asynchronous *method calls*, which remain strongly typed and structured, and most importantly more adapted to an object-oriented framework.

From a more fundamental point of view, Actors and ASP differ by the definition of state. In ASP the state is encapsulated in object fields, whereas in Actors the state is encoded in the actor behavior. Furthermore, in the Actors model every actor acts independently and has its own thread, but ASP adopts a less uniform model where only some objects are active, for the sake of granularity control. Generally, the ASP application designer has the possibility and responsibility to achieve this partition for the sake of distribution and parallelism. Thus, starting from very similar objectives, ASP and Actors are very different calculi where a lot of crucial points differ (activity definition, communication base and timing, futures, states, etc.).

ASP future semantics, with the store partitioning property (isolation between the future values, the active store, and the pending requests), accounts for the capacity to achieve confluence and determinism in an imperative setting. Finally, the bisimulation techniques used by Agha et al. in [10, 11] would have been inadequate to obtain the main result presented in the current book: a strong, somehow intrinsic, but dynamic property on processes interacting by asynchronous communications.

To some extent, this study proves the idea introduced in [10, 11]: "The behavior of a component is locally determined by its initial state and the history of its interactions." ASP extends this idea on an imperative language. We take into account a more global history in order to be sensitive only to the order of the message senders instead of the complete history of messages. In other words, we do not need to compare all message contents (arguments of method) in the history of an activity but instead we compare the history of just the message senders (RSL) of *all* activities. Our properties state that in ASP, the history of an activity's interactions is uniquely determined by the RSLs of all activities. The local behavior characterization is still valid in ASP but is not sufficient to obtain the properties of determinism of Chap. 9.

21.1.2 π-calculus and Related Calculi

The ASP calculus could be rewritten in π-calculus [120, 118], but even if such a strategy allowed us to prove some confluence properties on $\pi o\beta\lambda$ this would not be sufficient to prove confluence properties of ASP directly. Indeed, in π-calculus, synchronization is based on channels. On the contrary, ASP relies on a data-driven synchronization over an imperative object calculus, and thus its semantics is different from π-calculus. Indeed, while the synchronization in ASP is implicit, π-calculus imposes explicit synchronization on channels. Thus, writing ASP programs in π-calculus would require knowing the first point where the value of a future is needed, and writing explicit communication for the reception of the replies. An approximation of the first point in a program using a future could be computed statically, but such a static analysis (strictness analysis) requires approximations that are both complicated and imprecise. In general, finding the exact first point using a future is undecidable.

For example, the following code would be problematic (b and c are two boolean variables, $r.bar$ accesses a field of r, performing a wait-by-necessity):

$foo(bool\ b, bool\ c)$
   $r = oa.m()$;   gets a future
   $if\ b\ then\ r.bar$;   subject to wait-by-necessity
   $if\ c\ then\ r = [a = 1, b = 2]$;   creates a local object
   $oa2.bar(r)$;   sends to $oa2$ a possible future
                         possibly awaited

The example above shows that one cannot determine whether a future is already used, if a future is still (or may still be) awaited at a point, and even if a variable contains a future or not.

In the same way, PICT [132, 131] also necessitates channel-based synchronization. Like ASP, PICT is intended to be object oriented, but it does not feature object activity: it is not an active object model.

To conclude, we do not think that translating ASP into π-calculus would simplify our specifications or our proofs. As a consequence, it was more effective to focus directly on ASP rather than obtaining results on translated terms (which will not necessarily provide results on the initial ASP calculus).

However, introducing channels in ASP is possible and could allow us to prove some confluence properties which would probably be more restrictive than the ones shown in this book. We detail below an adaptation of the notion of channels to ASP which could allow one to use π-calculus properties dealing with confluence (e.g., linear channels), and to make precise the relations between π-calculus and ASP channels.

Channels in ASP

Recall that Sect. 15.1 described a notion of channels in ASP as pairs *(activity, set of method label)*.

Under specific restrictions π-calculus channels are called *linear* or *linearized* [124, 104]. The terms communicating over linear channels can be statically proved to be confluent, and such results could be applicable to some ASP terms.

More precisely, if at any time only one activity can send a request on a given channel then the term verifies the DON property, and the program behaves deterministically. In π-calculus such programs would be considered as using only *linearized channels*, and would lead to the same conclusion, determinism. However, a strong difference comes from the fact that in ASP, updates of response along non-linearized channels can be performed which make the ASP confluence property more powerful. Moreover, this definition of channels is more flexible because it can contain several method labels, and then one can wait for a request on any subset of the labels belonging to a channel. In other words, we can perform a *Serve* on a part of a channel without losing determinacy.

Finally, the confluence property principle of ASP is somehow close to linearized channels. However, the ASP confluence property is in general not statically verifiable, and maybe as a consequence it is much more powerful. Several static approximations of ASP confluence can be performed, some of which might probably be close to linear(ized) channels.

21.1.3 Process Networks

The DON property widely used in this study is somewhat inspired by Process Networks. Indeed the ASP channel view introduced in Sect. 21.1.2 can also be compared to Process Networks channels.

The Process Networks of Kahn [99, 100, 159] are explicitly based on the notion of *channels* between processes, performing *put* and *get* operations on them. Process networks provide confluent parallel processes, but require that the order of service is predefined, and two processes cannot send data on the same channel, which is more restrictive and leads to less parallelism than ASP.

As shown in Sect. 5.3 (page 79), the Process Networks channels can be translated in any direction (from a process performing a get to process performing a put: *push*, or in the opposite direction: *pull*). However, this could not be considered as a systematic translation from ASP to Process Networks, because Process Networks channels can be passed in parameter to processes at creation and sometimes used in reconfigurations. In practice, in ProActive, we can use reflection to pass method names as parameters, but the theoretical aspect of this solution has not yet been studied.

Section 15.2 page 183 provided a further analysis and an encoding of Process Networks channels in ASP. It showed that the ASP calculus can encode any Process Network by a DON term.

Comparing ASP and Process Networks Channels

As in the π-calculus case, ASP channels seem more flexible and the confluence property more general.

First, if we consider a channel as a pair *(activity, method label)*, we can perform a wait (*Serve*) on several channels (several labels) at a given program point. This would be expressed in process networks by the possibility to perform a *get* on several channels, and take the first request on one of these channels, thus merging these channels without compromising determinism.

ASP provides a more structured programming model where the causal flow of data can remain in the program structure. For instance, method parameters and results can be used to pass channels between activities whereas Process Networks need process creation or reconfiguration to take a new channel into account.

Furthermore, the fact that future updates can occur at any time counts for a great deal in ASP expressiveness: return channels do not have to verify any constraint. Thus, futures can be seen as hidden and "automatic" transparent channels. These hidden channels are really difficult to simulate in process networks because their existence is based on data-driven synchronization. The hidden channels are somehow revealed by the non-blocking nature of the *get* operation in the channel object above; in Process Networks, *get* blocks right away. Moreover, in ASP, the result from the *get* request can be transmitted to another process even if still awaited. Thus, ASP data-driven synchronization, and more generally the future mechanism, can be considered as one of the most original features of ASP.

21.1.4 ς-calculus

Let us first recall and acknowledge that this book is strongly based on the works of Abadi, Cardelli, Gordon, Hankin and others on **imp**ς-calculus [3, 80, 79].

Proving equivalence between terms can be performed by introducing bisimulation on an object calculus as in [81]. The ASP framework introduces an equivalence relation specific to ASP, and actually some aspects of equivalence modulo future updates are close to bisimulation techniques. But CIU (Closed Instance of Use) equivalence introduced in [81] deals only with static terms. In order to capture the intrinsic properties of the calculus, we are interested in dynamic properties like confluence, thus CIU equivalence is inadequate for ASP. Of course, more static properties could be obtained from the confluence property in order to perform static analysis of programs, but most of such properties would likely be derived from the static approximation of Deterministic Object Networks (SDON) presented in Sect. 9.2.

21.2 Concurrent Calculi and Languages

21.2.1 MultiLisp

With respect to MultiLisp, the shared memory mechanism is the main difference between the two languages, but this difference has strong consequences.

The interleaving occurring due to sharing prevents any general confluence property. Therefore, it seems difficult to compare precisely these two frameworks. Of course, the main common points between ASP and MultiLisp are the existence of futures, and the automatic synchronization upon access to such futures. But futures in MultiLisp are not global references, and as such are much simpler to update than in ASP: they only need to be updated once in the shared memory. Moreover, the creation of a future in MultiLisp must be explicit, contrarily to ASP where a transparent creation occurs automatically upon an asynchronous method call.

21.2.2 Ambient Calculus

Ambient calculus is based on locations (places where a process executes). The objective of this book does not have the same concerns as the ambient framework. One of ASP objective is to abstract away locations, and to provide determinate distributed systems insensitive to location, whereas ambient calculus studies the effect of locations on distributed computations. These two studies could then be considered as complementary. For example, ASP communications could replace π-calculus like communications in ambients, and ambients could be used to study the impact of administrative domains in ASP.

21.2.3 join-calculus

Synchronization in the join-calculus is based on filtering patterns over channels. The translation from channels to ASP objects described in Sects. 21.1.2 and 21.1.3 also applies to join-calculus channels. But this encoding also make the join-calculus inadequate for fully expressing the ASP principles.

With respect to the join-pattern synchronization itself, Sect. 11.4 (page 146) demonstrated the possibility to express join patterns in ASP.

21.3 Concurrent Object Calculi and Languages

Considering concurrent extensions of ς-calculus, Gordon and Hankin [78], and Jeffrey [93] introduced parallel and distributed calculi based on threads and shared memory. As shown in Chap. 2, these calculi are actually very far from ASP characteristics.

21.3.1 Obliq and Øjeblik

Obliq features shared memory and serialized objects, i.e., objects accessed by at most one thread at any time, with synchronous method calls. In ASP, the notion of thread is linked to the activity, and thus every object is "serialized." However, a remote invocation does not stop the current thread. In other words, in ASP there is a unique thread by active object and the parallelism is due to the coexistence of several activities. On the contrary, in Obliq, the notion of thread is not directly linked to the notion of object (there is no object activity). Finally, in ASP data-driven synchronization is the main synchronization feature, and no notion of joining threads is necessary; thus the ASP approach is much less control based. To summarize, the notion of thread is replaced in ASP by the process associated to each activity, and wait-by-necessity for synchronization. Furthermore, data-driven synchronization alleviates the programmer from the explicit insertion of synchronization; thus it seems a very convenient way of programming.

With respect to the confluence, the generalized references for all mutable objects, the presence of threads, and the principle of serialization (with mutexes) make the Obliq and Øjeblik languages very different from ASP. In fact, there is no way of ensuring a confluence property similar to ours in Obliq. For example, to avoid concurrent accesses to shared objects, we would need to remove mutable objects from the calculus, which would contradict one of the main characteristics of ASP: its imperative, stateful, aspect.

21.3.2 The $\pi o \beta \lambda$ Language

In $\pi o \beta \lambda$ [95, 97], a caller always waits for the method result (synchronous method call), which can be returned before the end of the called method (early *return*). In ASP, method calls toward active objects are systematically asynchronous, so more instructions can be executed in parallel: the futures mechanism allows one to continue the execution in the calling activity without having the result of the remote call. A simple and confluent extension to ASP could provide a way to assign a value to a future before the end of the execution of a method. Note that in $\pi o \beta \lambda$ this characteristic is the source of parallelism whereas in ASP this would simply allow an earlier future update (and potentially a shorter wait-by-necessity). In ASP the source of parallelism is the object activation and the systematic asynchronous method calls between activities. The condition given in [97], stating that the result of a method is not modified after being returned, is balanced in ASP by a deep copy of the result (Property 7.2: Store partitioning). Similarly, the *unique reference* condition from the same work is balanced in ASP with the constraints on object topology (no remote reference to passive objects, Fig. 7.2 page 104).

To conclude, $\pi o \beta \lambda$ is one of the calculi most similar to ASP, even if its uniform active object model and its mainly synchronous aspect are different from ASP, finally leading to a different programming methodology. The lack of generalized futures in $\pi o \beta \lambda$ is also an important difference from ASP.

22

Conclusion

With the objective of capturing distribution, concurrency, and parallelism, in object and large-scale systems, we proposed a new calculus named ASP: *Asynchronous Sequential Processes*.

This calculus features asynchronous communications in object-oriented systems, and exhibits confluence properties. Such properties simplify programming as they avoid having to study every possible interleaving of instructions and messages to understand the behavior of a given program.

22.1 Summary

The ASP calculus is based on asynchronous *activities* processing *requests* and responding by mean of *futures*. Inside each activity, the execution is sequential and there is a one-to-one mapping between processes and active objects.

Concerning asynchrony and synchronization, when a process has sent a request, it can perform other operations while the result value is not needed: the result to come is represented by a future. Such futures are first-class entities that can be passed as a parameter and as a result. For synchronization, a rather natural *data-driven synchronization* occurs when a strict operation is performed on a future. This mechanism is called *wait-by-necessity* and the formal study of this data-driven synchronization is one of the main contributions of this book.

Let us summarize the key features of ASP:

- Activities: processes are conducted by active objects.
- A reference to an active object is also a reference to an activity.
- Not all objects are active: a non-uniform active object model.
- Intrinsic guarantee of absence of sharing: deep copy of passive objects.
- Systematic asynchronous method calls: leading to futures.

- Wait-by-necessity:
  - synchronization is performed by an automatic and transparent *data-driven synchronization* occurring when the value of the result associated to a future is really needed;
  - futures are global references: future transmission is not a strict operation.
- A confluence property provides a minimal characterization for execution of ASP terms.

This book also models the following features as extensions of the basic ASP calculus:

- mobility,
- group communication,
- delegation,
- non-confluent features: non-blocking services, testing request and future reception, synchronization patterns (select, join, etc.),
- components and reconfiguration.

With respect to implementation strategies, several techniques and alternatives have been formally proposed and analyzed:

- strategies for future updates,
- solutions for avoiding rendezvous during request sending without losing program properties,
- techniques for controlling the pipelining naturally created by asynchronous communications.

22.2 A Dynamic Property for Determinism

Within ASP, we proved sufficient conditions for partial confluence. Our objective was to provide a formalized and general framework with general properties suitable for open systems, hence the dynamic nature of the properties. From those dynamic properties more static and easily verifiable conditions for confluence can be derived, such as the Static DON property (SDON, Definition 9.4 page 125). Moreover, the properties proved in this book and their formalization already have great practical consequences, as exemplified in the ProActive environment.

ASP ensures a confluence property on compatible terms: two configurations with *compatible* RSLs (Request Sender Lists) are confluent. RSL compatibility is based on a prefix order on sender activities. We proved that execution is only determined by the ordered list of activities sending a request to a given activity; the values of parameters do not have to be taken explicitly into account. What makes ASP properties powerful is that the execution is insensitive to the moment when results of requests are obtained. Consequently, an equivalence relation was introduced to consider a term as equivalent before and after the REPLY reduction (equivalence modulo future update). We defined a sub-calculus of ASP formed of *Deterministic Object Networks* (DON) terms that behave deterministically (Theorem 9.3 page 123). We proved that every program communicating over a tree (Theorem 9.7: Tree determinacy) behaves deterministically, even in the highly concurrent case of a FIFO service.

The following properties summarize the dynamic confluence properties:

- *Execution is fully characterized by the ordered list of request senders*: all execution leading to the same order of requests senders inside each activity is equivalent. Moreover, two requests that cannot be served in the same serve primitive can be safely exchanged.
- *Future updates can occur at any time without affecting the execution*: this allows any future update strategy to be implemented.

Approximations of deterministic programs can be ordered in the following way (from the most general to the most easy to verify statically):

- *Deterministic Object Networks (DON)*: there is no reduction such that two activities can send a request to the same third one *at the same time*, or those two requests cannot be served by the same serve primitive.
- *Static Deterministic Object Networks (SDON)*: if two different activities can possibly send requests to the same third one, *whatever the time*. then these requests cannot be served by the same serve primitive;
- *Tree Deterministic Object Networks (TDON)*: programs communicating over trees.

Note that the proofs detailed in this book can also be adapted to demonstrate other cases of confluence in the ASP or similar calculus. For example, Sect. 9.5 (page 130) discusses the adaptation to the case where the service primitive explicitly specifies the source activity of the request (more detail will be given in Sect. B.4).

From the basic dynamic DON theorem, together with advances in static analysis, many other static properties can be devised.

22.3 ASP in Practice

ProActive is a Java API implementing the ASP model which has been presented in Chap. 16. One of our objectives is to be able to use in practice the properties proved on ASP. For example, the fact that the moment when a future is updated is not observable in ASP can be used to choose any strategy for updating futures in ProActive. Different future update strategies have been studied in Chap. 17.

Several features for concurrency and distribution can be added to the core ASP calculus; Part IV studied some of these features and their relations with confluence (e.g., group communications in Chap. 13). Typically, all the features sensitive to the time needed for communications, that is to say features testing a communication reception and not blocking if this communication has not occurred, compromise the general confluence property.

The semantics of ASP is based on an *asynchronous with rendezvous* communication timing; this necessitates a synchronization step upon sending requests. Such a rather synchronous communication timing can be partially avoided by simply ensuring a FIFO order between outgoing requests and active object creations, as shown in Chap. 18.

22.4 Stateful Active Objects vs. Immutable Futures

Even if ASP is a new calculus it has been greatly inspired by most existing concurrent languages and calculi (e.g., the ς-calculus model of objects, the DON property strongly related to process networks, and which can also be linked with linear channels of π-calculus).

The properties of ASP illustrate the fact that futures in an imperative language are rather powerful and convenient. What actually provides confluence in ASP is the balance between asynchronous communications and synchronizations due to the wait-by-necessity. Of course the topology of objects stating that we can only access an activity through its active object is also important (absence of sharing). Out-of-order replies and data-driven synchronization also provide a convenient way of programming parallel and distributed applications. Indeed, the programmer only has to ensure that the result *can* be calculated at the moment when the value is needed to avoid deadlocks; that is to say, there exists an order for performing computations ensuring that this result is calculated.

Active objects and *futures* are two fundamental entities of the theory being proposed. Let us summarize their duality.

Both active objects and futures are global references. As such, they are the key to distribution. But an active object is a stateful and mutable entity, while a future is somehow an immutable, single-assignment, variable. An active object provides state for the sake of locality and scalability, a future provides a global constant value for the sake of parallelism. Before a future value is set, no computation in any part of the system can change its value. Active objects originate, of course, in the object paradigm, while futures spring from function calls, actually method calls leading to requests.

Futures are not without relation to *I-structures* [17]. As a data structure for parallel computing, an I-structure follows a write-once, read-many principle. In ASP, each call to an active object automatically gives rise to a kind of I-structure.

Another difference lies in the passing semantics. While active objects enjoy a reference semantics, futures virtually feature both copy and reference semantics. Passing a future to another activity corresponds to passing a deep copy of its value if it turns out as an object, or to passing a reference if it concretizes as an active object.

Finally, there is an interesting similitude as both call for *global localization*: the need to determine the location of an entity, potentially worldwide. Computational mobility, changing the location of an activity, requires a strategy for localizing an active object (or routing requests to it). First-class futures (passing futures between activities), and delegation, requires a strategy for routing future values to the appropriate locations. Implementation techniques are indeed rather similar; forwarding or centralizing strategies can be used in both cases.

	Nature	Reference	Communication passing	Localization need due to	Localization strategy
Active object	Object: stateful, mutable	Global	Reference semantics	Mobility	Forwarding Server TTL-TTU
Future	Method result: single assignment immutable	Global	Reference + Copy semantics	First-class futures Delegation	Eager: forward / message Mixed Lazy
Object	Stateful, mutable	Local	Copy	None	None

Table 22.1. Duality active objects (stateful) and futures (immutable)

Table 22.1 illustrates the duality between active objects and futures. One can compare these to the characteristics of standard, non-active, objects. Of course standard objects are mutable stateful entities. Due to the deep copy semantics, they are local to an activity, and never require any localization strategy.

22.5 Perspectives

ASP determinism is partially based on taking *interfering requests* into account. Two requests are interfering if:

- they are sent by two different active objects on the same target method, or
- they are sent by two different active objects on two different methods both appearing in the same serve primitive(s).

Non-interfering requests can have their order safely exchanged in the request queue, and they will still be served in an invariant order. Other requests are interfering, they can be served by the same service primitive, and their order cannot be freely exchanged in the request queue.

However, even if they are interfering, some requests might not be *conflicting requests*. By not conflicting, we mean that they could still be freely exchanged in the request queue. In practice, some methods are commutative with respect to some others, and could be served in an inverted order. In some cases, an entire activity might be stateless, or might feature an internal state which is immutable. Let us just mention for example a Web Service container that can be fully stateless: the order in which such an activity serves requests can be significantly relaxed. In short, interfering requests proceed from concurrency and service strategy, while conflicting requests take into account the functional behavior of the methods.

We envision that the commutative nature of a selected number of methods (potentially all in a stateless active object) can be integrated in the DON property. It is only needed to change the definition of the potential services $(\mathcal{M}_{\alpha_P})$ in the DON definition (Definition 9.1, page 122). For instance, the sets made entirely of fully functional methods will completely disappear from $\mathcal{M}_{\alpha_P}$, since such methods can be served at any time without consequences. Of course, this will reduce the number of conflicting requests, and more ASP program to be identified as determinate. Just taking into account commutativity locally into $\mathcal{M}_{\alpha_P}$ would permit one to grasp a crucial aspect of parallel programs, the commutativity of some operations, while preserving all the remaining properties. It would be a powerful extension of ASP determinism.

Let us now focus on the static identification of deterministic programs.

Confluence and determinism currently rely on dynamic properties. Some approximations of these properties have been shown in this book, like *SDON terms* (Sect. 9.2, page 124) or *programs communicating over trees* (Sect. 9.3, page 126), but no static verifier for deterministic programs or terms has been implemented or specified.

In order to find a static approximation of DON, the set of active objects and their topology should be approximated statically. Classical abstract interpretation or static analysis techniques [60, 61, 140] can be used. However, a simpler methodology like balloon types [13] could also be useful and very effective. For example, in [19], following the ideas of Sagiv et al. [140] for *form analysis*, the topology of an object graph is statically inferred in order to parallelize programs.

Balloon types [13], related to *ownership types* or *ownership analysis* [57, 56, 40], express a way of restricting the object topology by typing techniques. The balloon types topology is a sub-case of the topology that is sufficient for the confluence of ASP programs, and it is rather simple to verify (typing). Indeed, if we applied a balloon types methodology for parallelizing or distributing a given program, it would create an object topology where references between activities form a tree, and these references only link active objects. In ASP, passive objects can reference active ones. Thus the topology of objects ensured by balloon types is too restrictive.

It would also be very valuable to specify a type system for $\mathcal{M}_{\alpha P}$, either for static service verification, or for inferring the potential services. Indeed, such a type system would also be useful to identify SDON programs.

As another important perspective, a study of migration and reconfiguration of components, and a formalization of the concept of components presented in this book, would make ASP an appropriate basis for a calculus of distributed components.

Concerning the implementation aspect, distributed object systems such as ProActive could be equipped with new future update strategies (e.g., on-demand). This would allow us to analyze the impact and efficiency of each strategy within real applications, potentially leading to the design of adaptive strategies.

Moreover, following the demonstration that asynchronous one-to-all FIFO ordering preserves all ASP properties (Sect. 18.4, page 232), a relaxed communications semantics can be implemented. It would allow us to avoid rendezvous, just using for each active object a single FIFO outgoing queue for all requests and activity creation. Such a strategy should hide communication latency in an even more significant manner, opening the way to very large-scale distributed objects. In the end, it should pave the way toward effective computing on the Grid.

Epilogue

As usual, writing down what you thought you had understood is a process for further clarifying some ideas, but also the source of new questions and new perspectives. This final chapter puts together several important aspects of this book which, we believe, bring in a promising disclosure: semantically sound adaptivity.

More specifically, we explore further and draw new perspectives from a first clue mentioned above in Chap 22: ASP rendezvous-based properties are kept with asynchronous one-to-all FIFO communications. Combined with the capacity to control pipelining and boundless future-update strategies, it will reveal the adaptive nature of ASP systems.

ASP formal semantics and properties have been set in the framework of a rendezvous. It means that buffering occurs at the target side, in the form of a *pending queue*. However, chap. 18, *Losing Rendezvous*, has demonstrated that another buffering queue can be placed in such a distributed object system: one that stores outgoing requests together with activity creations. Let us call that second buffering structure the *departing queue*.

Adding such a departing queue maintains all ASP properties as long as the structure is truly FIFO. In practice it means that a separate thread can be used to send requests in parallel to the active object thread. If a given request cannot be successfully sent to a target activity, the departing queue thread cannot move on to deal with the next request to be delivered. Of course, making provision systematically for such an extra queue and a thread per active object in the system globally reinforces the overall asynchrony. Furthermore, the potential for such a departing queue is rather high.

First, it makes it possible to turn the default ASP *eager* strategy into a potentially more *lazy* strategy; request evaluations do not even have to be asked for systematically, along the lines of functional lazy evaluations. Second, the *batched future* is another well-known strategy [34] that can be captured with departing queues. For instance, one can postpone sending calls to a given target until a request is to be sent to a different destination – systematically grouping all consecutive requests going to the same target. Third, the management of a *disconnected mode*, where the system has to manage temporarily unreachable activities, is another application of the departing queue. Upon the failure of a request sending, the departing queue can silently keep trying at various paces until success. Respecting the FIFO ordering in such a situation will guarantee that temporary disconnections won't have any semantic consequences. Finally, we can even imagine parameterized strategies. For instance, a *Time To Send* (TTS) parameter can control how often we should flush the departing queue.

The second crucial clue of this epilogue, besides ASP rendezvous combined with FIFO one-to-all, is given by Chap. 19, *Controlling Pipelining*.

ASP activities are naturally eager to send requests and to keep on going, with the potential risk of flooding some target activities (e.g., in configurations not featuring application loop-back like in the *push* version of the sieve of Eratosthenes, Figure 5.5). However, coming from the thirty-year-old theory of Process Networks, analyzed and applied to ASP at chapter 19, it was shown that *demand-driven evaluation* strategies are possible, the extreme being a pure-demand driven one where an activity is activated only when another one is blocked in need for a request the former can produce. Intermediate strategies provide controlled pipelining. For instance, within a given activity the number of pending requests from a given source can be limited. This requires that we send control messages back to the source – very much alike in a Transfer Control Protocol (TCP), ensuring a dynamically adapted pipelining. Such strategies can be easily parameterized, with one or several values controlling the size of pending queues, and overall the pipelining. Such parameters can have global, system-wide values, or local setting controlled by local resource availability — an activity on a large server clearly featuring more buffering capacity than one on a thin client. Still, both can control the amount of pipelining they accept, and interact one with another in a sound manner.

The third and last clue of this epilogue lies in the capacity to take advantage of various *future update* strategies.

As explained in Chap. 17, based on the properties that future updates can occur at any time without consequence on the execution, many strategies are possible. Updating the value of futures can occur lazily on demand, upon the use of a future, or eagerly, propagating a future value as soon as it has been computed. Between those two extremes, various mixed strategies can be designed. Again, parameterized strategies are perfectly possible, for instance limiting the size of the future value list. Once parameterized, such a strategy can also be configured, potentially dynamically.

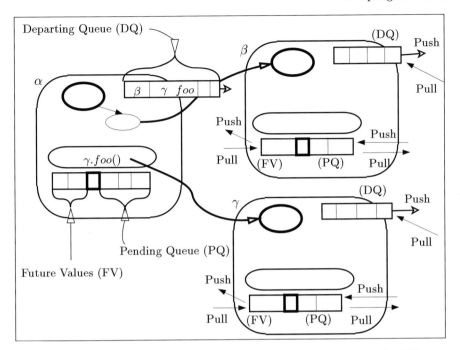

Fig. 23.1. Potential queues, buffering, pipelining, and strategies in ASP

To summarize, Fig. 23.1 illustrates all the buffering and the dynamics that can finally occur in an ASP system. Besides the pending queues (PQ) and the future values (FV) that were present in previous illustrations, the important adjunct is a departing queue (DQ) per activity. In practice the DQs can be equipped with a single thread in charge of sending the outgoing requests and active object creations in a FIFO manner. The PQs can be limited in size, using a transfer control protocol. Lazy pull management of the PQs is also possible, up to an explicit on-need-only activation of an activity upon a downstream blocking service.

As explained above, DQs and PQs can be managed according to various strategies. An important parameter to characterize and to classify those dynamic strategies is the maximum sizes of the DQs and PQs.

Figure 23.2 provides a structured view in a 2D space. The horizontal axis increases the PQ size, while the vertical axis increases the DQ size. The bottom left corner, with DQ=PQ=0, corresponds to an on-demand sequential-like execution. Going up to the top left corner, still PQ=0 but DQ=∞, captures a lazy parallel calculus where requests are directly fetched from the DQs to be executed, for instance in a lazy parallel evaluation. The bottom right corner, with DQ=0 but PQ potentially infinite, characterizes the ASP calculus as formally defined by the reduction rules on Fig. 6.2 (page 92). Going up to the top right corner, DQ=PQ=∞, we reach unlimited parallelism and unlimited

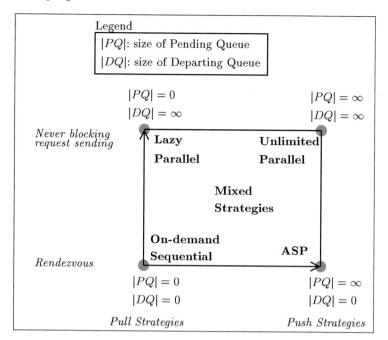

Fig. 23.2. Classification of strategies for sending requests

pipelining with a FIFO departing queue as illustrated in Fig. 23.1. Overall, the left vertical axis captures all *pull* strategies where requests are fetched from activities. The right vertical axis captures all *push* strategies where a request can always be pushed where it has to be executed. The bottom horizontal maintains a rendezvous between caller and callee, while the top horizontal ensures that an activity sending a request is never blocked. Of course, the inner rectangle symbolizes the existence of many mixed variations, e.g. with DQ and PQ bounded in size.

Figure 23.3 captures future update strategies. They can be classified according to two dimensions:

- the size needed to store and maintain at each activity the already computed future values (FV),
- the length of the update path (UP).

The *Update Path* is the maximum number of activities a future value traverses in order for a future update to take place. The activity where the future value has been computed and the activity where the value is to be sent are not counted; i.e., the direct update with a single communication between the two accounts for UP=0.

Again the left vertical axis captures *lazy* strategies, with FV=∞, while the right vertical axis captures *eager* strategies, with FV=0.

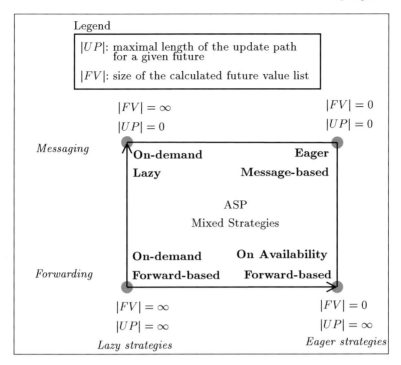

Fig. 23.3. Classification of strategies for future update

The bottom left corner, FV=∞ and UP=∞, represents the singular point of an on-demand forward-based future update. This strategy might seem useless, as being on-demand one can always directly ask the activity where the future is to be computed for the value. However, in some special cases it might be necessary to follow the forward path, e.g., in the case of limited connectivity or for security reasons. The right bottom corner, FV=0 and UP=∞, captures the eager on-availability forward-based future update. Future values follow the path of the original future forwarding, as soon as the future value is available. This strategy offers quite a good balance between eagerness and extra messages. This is indeed the main principle used in the ProActive future update implementation.

On-demand lazy updates are depicted with FV=∞ and UP=0, top left corner. In that case, the update is always direct upon a message initiated by the activity waiting-by-necessity. However, without any specific distributed garbage collection of futures, the future values have to be kept forever. Finally, the top right corner, FV=0 and UP=0, captures an interesting strategy: the eager message-based update. In that case, at the expense of potentially useless messages and updates, futures can be updated as soon as possible and directly; note that such a strategy can also be achieved with a broadcast-to-all of future values. Besides a needless archiving of future values, this strategy is also characterized by reducing as much as possible the latency.

At this point let us remind ourselves that all those strategies, parameterized or not, locally or globally set, statically or dynamically managed, still enjoy the confluence and DON properties. Overall, this versatility should ease the way to a most wanted quality of modern distributed systems: being adaptive.

Appendices

A

Equivalence Modulo Future Updates

This appendix formalizes the equivalence modulo future updates briefly defined in Sect. 8.2 page 111. First, Sects. A.1 and A.2 present some prerequisites concerning equivalence between ASP configurations that do not take into account future updates. Then Sect. A.3 defines equivalence modulo future updates, and Sects. A.4, A.5, and A.6 present the properties of this equivalence relation. Section A.7 gives another definition of the equivalence modulo future updates, Sect. A.8 states that such an equivalence relation is decidable, and finally, Sect. A.9 gives examples of equivalent configurations.

Recall that activities are chosen deterministically.

Both appendices will not consider the particular cases of the REQUEST and the REPLY rule when $\alpha = \beta$; indeed, proofs of cases associated with these rules can be deduced directly from the more general REQUEST and REPLY rules.

A.1 Renaming

Let us introduce a set Θ of renaming of futures from configuration P to configuration Q (Θ is an alpha conversion of futures):

$$\Theta ::= \{\!\{ f_i^{\beta \to \alpha} \leftarrow f_i'^{\beta \to \alpha}, \ldots \}\!\};$$

Remember: we consider that activities' identifiers are chosen deterministically and thus renaming of activities' identifiers is irrelevant.

A.2 Reordering Requests ($R_1 \equiv_R R_2$)

The equivalence relation must be defined modulo the reordering of some requests. Indeed two requests can be exchanged if they concern different methods which cannot interfere; that is to say, if there is no service concerning both method labels.

Two request queues are equivalent if all their restrictions on requests that can interfere in the same $Serve(M)$ are equivalent. In other words, for every set M of labels belonging to a $Serve(M)$ primitive of α the list of requests that can be captured by $Serve(M)$ is equivalent in both configurations (α_P and α_Q). Moreover, in this book, we only compare terms coming from the same initial configuration P_0; as $\mathcal{M}_{\alpha_{P_0}}$ is a static approximation, the potential services of two compared configurations are the same.

$$\frac{\{M \in \mathcal{M}_{\alpha_{P_0}} | m_1 \in M\} \cap \{M \in \mathcal{M}_{\alpha_{P_0}} | m_2 \in M\} = \emptyset}{R_1 :: [m_1; \iota_1; f_1] :: [m_2; \iota_2; f_2] :: R_2 \equiv_R R_1 :: [m_2; \iota_2; f_2] :: [m_1; \iota_1; f_1] :: R_2}$$

$$R \equiv_R R$$

$$\frac{R \equiv_R R_1 \quad R_1 \equiv_R R'}{R \equiv_R R'}$$

Table A.1. Reordering requests

R_1 is a correct reordering of the request queue R_2 if and only if $R_1 \equiv_R R_2$ where $\equiv_R$ is defined in Table A.1. The first rule expresses the fact that two requests can be exchanged if they do not interfere. The other two rules are reflexivity and transitivity rules.

A.3 Future Updates

The equivalence modulo future updates consists in considering the reference to calculated futures like the local reference to a deep copy of the value of the future. In other words, future references can be followed as if they were local references to a deep copy. Thus, when two future references concern the same future, they are not considered as aliases.

Figure A.1 illustrates a simple update of future value. The two configurations are equivalent.

A.3.1 Following References and Sub-terms

Let us formalize the idea that "future references can be followed as if they were local references." In the following, the relation $\overset{\alpha}{\mapsto}_L$ expressing paths inside an activity is defined first. Then $\overset{\alpha*}{\mapsto}_L$ expresses paths that can possibly follow future references.

Table A.2 describes the rules that define $a \overset{\alpha}{\mapsto}_x b$. Note that there is no b such that $AO(\beta) \overset{\alpha}{\mapsto}_x b$ or $fut(f^{\gamma \to \beta}) \overset{\alpha}{\mapsto}_x b$.

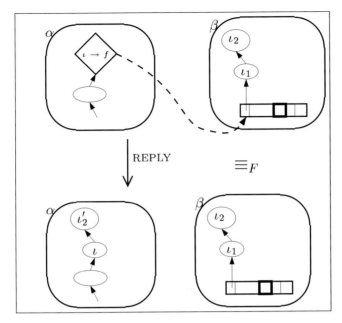

Fig. A.1. Simple example of future equivalence

Table A.2 is divided into three parts. The first part defines the paths inside ASP objects and terms defined by ASP syntax. Equivalence on methods ensures both text equality for a non-evaluated method and equivalence of locations inside the method body when they appear. Bounded variables are renamed inside the rule that enters a method body in order to avoid considering alpha conversion of formal parameters at a higher level.

The second set of rules defines the paths starting from an activity. Starting with an activity identifier, a path begins with an access to the current term a, active object location ι, futures values F, current future f, or pending requests. Equivalence of pending requests is defined using the reordering equivalence $\equiv_R$ of Table A.1.[1]

The last set of rules defines paths inside lists of requests and future values.

We do not follow paths inside stores, and thus terms are identified modulo garbage collection inside each activity. However, the following of paths inside the store could also be added.

Definition A.1 ($a \overset{\alpha}{\mapsto}_L b$)
$a \overset{\alpha}{\mapsto}_L b$ means that b is reached from a by following, inside the activity α, the path defined by L. Such paths are defined inductively from the definition of Table A.2 as follows:

$$a \overset{\alpha}{\mapsto}_\emptyset a$$
$$a \overset{\alpha}{\mapsto}_{L.x} b \text{ if } a \overset{\alpha}{\mapsto}_L a' \wedge a' \overset{\alpha}{\mapsto}_x b$$

---

[1] However, a more complex definition using only paths seems possible.

$$\iota \overset{\alpha}{\mapsto}_{ref} \sigma_\alpha(\iota) \qquad\qquad [l_i = b_i; m_j = \varsigma(x_j, y_j)a_j]_{j\in 1..m}^{i\in 1..n} \overset{\alpha}{\mapsto}_{l_i} b_i$$

$$[l_i = b_i; m_j = \varsigma(x_j, y_j)a_j]_{j\in 1..m}^{i\in 1..n} \overset{\alpha}{\mapsto}_{m_j(s',x')} a_j\{\!\{x_j \leftarrow s', y_j \leftarrow x'\}\!\}$$

$$a.l_i \overset{\alpha}{\mapsto}_{field(l_i)} a \qquad a.l_i := b \overset{\alpha}{\mapsto}_{Update1(l_i)} a \qquad a.l_i := b \overset{\alpha}{\mapsto}_{Update2(l_i)} b$$

$$a.l_i(b) \overset{\alpha}{\mapsto}_{Invoke1(l_i)} a \qquad a.l_i(b) \overset{\alpha}{\mapsto}_{Invoke2(l_i)} b \qquad clone(a) \overset{\alpha}{\mapsto}_{clone} a$$

$$Active(a, m_j) \overset{\alpha}{\mapsto}_{Active(m_j)} a \qquad\qquad Serve(M) \overset{\alpha}{\mapsto}_{Serve(M)} \emptyset$$

$$a \Uparrow f, b \overset{\alpha}{\mapsto}_{\Uparrow curr} a \qquad a \Uparrow f, b \overset{\alpha}{\mapsto}_{\Uparrow f} a \qquad a \Uparrow f, b \overset{\alpha}{\mapsto}_{\Uparrow cont} b$$

$$\alpha_p \overset{\alpha}{\mapsto}_{ct} a_\alpha \qquad \alpha_p \overset{\alpha}{\mapsto}_{ao} \iota_\alpha \qquad \alpha_p \overset{\alpha}{\mapsto}_{cf} \iota_\alpha \qquad \alpha_p \overset{\alpha}{\mapsto}_{fv} F_\alpha$$

$$\frac{R_\alpha \equiv_R R'}{\alpha_p \overset{\alpha}{\mapsto}_{rq} R'}$$

$$[m; \iota; f] :: R \overset{\alpha}{\mapsto}_{reqs\_meth} m \qquad\qquad [m; \iota; f] :: R \overset{\alpha}{\mapsto}_{reqs\_arg} \iota$$

$$[m; \iota; f] :: R \overset{\alpha}{\mapsto}_{reqs\_fut} f \qquad\qquad [m; \iota; f] :: R \overset{\alpha}{\mapsto}_{reqs\_cdr} R$$

$$\{f_i^{\gamma \to \alpha} \mapsto \iota\} :: F \overset{\alpha}{\mapsto}_{futs\_id} f_i^{\gamma \to \alpha} \qquad\qquad \{f_i^{\gamma \to \alpha} \mapsto \iota\} :: F \overset{\alpha}{\mapsto}_{futs\_val} \iota$$

$$\{f_i^{\gamma \to \alpha} \mapsto \iota\} :: F \overset{\alpha}{\mapsto}_{futs\_cdr} F$$

Table A.2. Path definition

Extending the preceding definition, $\overset{\alpha}{\mapsto}_{L_1.L_2}$ denotes the concatenation $\overset{\alpha}{\mapsto}_{L_1}\overset{\alpha}{\mapsto}_{L_2}$. More generally the following notations are equivalent:

$$a \overset{\alpha}{\mapsto}_{L_1.L_2} b \Leftrightarrow a \overset{\alpha}{\mapsto}_{L_1}\overset{\alpha}{\mapsto}_{L_2} b$$
$$\Leftrightarrow \exists c, a \overset{\alpha}{\mapsto}_{L_1} c \overset{\alpha}{\mapsto}_{L_2} b$$
$$\Leftrightarrow \exists c, a \overset{\alpha}{\mapsto}_{L_1} c \wedge c \overset{\alpha}{\mapsto}_{L_2} b$$

Let $\overset{\alpha*}{\mapsto}_L$ be the preceding relation where one can follow futures if necessary and thus cover other activities than α:

Definition A.2 ($a \overset{\alpha*}{\mapsto}_L b$)

$$a \overset{\alpha*}{\mapsto}_{L_0...L_n} b \Leftrightarrow \begin{cases} (n = 0 \wedge a \overset{\alpha}{\mapsto}_{L_0} b) \ \vee \\ \exists \iota_i, f_i, \beta_i, \gamma_i^{i \le n} \begin{cases} a \overset{\alpha}{\mapsto}_{L_0} fut(f_1^{\gamma_1 \to \beta_1}) \wedge F_{\beta_1}(f_1^{\gamma_1 \to \beta_1}) = \iota_1 \wedge \\ \sigma_{\beta_1}(\iota_1) \overset{\beta_1}{\mapsto}_{L_1} fut(f_2^{\gamma_2 \to \beta_2}) \wedge F_{\beta_2}(f_2^{\gamma_2 \to \beta_2}) = \iota_2 \\ \wedge \ldots \wedge \\ \sigma_{\beta_n}(\iota_n) \overset{\beta_n}{\mapsto}_{L_n} b \end{cases} \end{cases}$$

This definition first follows a path inside an activity α, then follows a future reference from α to β_1, and continues the path in β_1 etc. Note that when one follows a future reference, two local (ref) and one future references are in fact considered as identical to a single local reference. In other words, the following of local and future references from $fut(f_i^{\gamma_i \to \beta_1})$ in α to $\sigma_{\beta_1}(\iota_1)$ in β_1 is not taken into account in the path L.

For example, in Fig. A.1 the three arrows of the first configurations that are around the future reference (around the dashed arrow) are considered as equivalent with a single arrow on the second configuration.

Note that trivially:

Lemma A.3 ($\overset{\alpha}{\mapsto}_L$ and $\overset{\alpha*}{\mapsto}_L$)

$$a \overset{\alpha}{\mapsto}_L b \Rightarrow a \overset{\alpha*}{\mapsto}_L b$$

Furthermore, the following of paths is (generally) unique. Following a path from a given term leads to the same expression except if the destination of the path is a future reference in one of the two configuration:

Lemma A.4 (Uniqueness of path destination)

$$a \overset{\alpha*}{\mapsto}_L b \wedge a \overset{\alpha*}{\mapsto}_L b' \Rightarrow b = b'$$
$$\vee \exists f_n, \iota_n, \beta_n, \gamma, \delta \begin{cases} (\sigma_{\beta_n}(\iota_n) = fut(f_n^{\gamma \to \delta}) \vee F_\delta(f_n^{\gamma \to \delta}) = \iota_n) \\ \wedge (b = \iota_n \vee b' = \iota_n) \end{cases}$$

The particular case (when $b \neq b'$) occurs when the destination of the path is a future reference. Thus, the path does not necessarily follow this reference. For example, if $b = \iota_n$ in β_n where $\sigma_{\beta_n} = fut(f_n^{\gamma \to \delta})$ then one can have $b' = \iota_f$ where ι_f is the location of future $fut(f_n^{\gamma \to \delta})$ in β. A more precise formulation of the preceding lemma would be:

$$a \overset{\alpha*}{\mapsto}_L b \wedge a \overset{\alpha*}{\mapsto}_L b' \Rightarrow b = b' \vee \exists \iota_n, \iota'_n, \begin{cases} (\sigma_{\beta_n}(\iota_n) = fut(f_n^{\gamma \to \delta}) \wedge F_\delta(f_n^{\gamma \to \delta}) = \iota'_n) \\ (b = \iota_n \wedge b' = \iota'_n) \vee (b = \iota'_n \wedge b' = \iota_n) \end{cases}$$

A.3.2 Equivalence Definition

Below is a formal definition of equivalence modulo future updates based on the paths' definitions of the preceding section. The first condition (1) expresses the equivalence both inside an activity and by following futures and the last two conditions (2, 3) express the correctness of aliasing (alias must be the same in both configurations). These two last conditions will be named *alias conditions* in the following. Note that in the alias conditions the existence of a' and a'' such that $\alpha_P \overset{\alpha*}{\mapsto}_L a'$ and $\alpha_P \overset{\alpha*}{\mapsto}_{L'} a''$ is already ensured by the first condition. Consequently, the alias conditions ensure that $a' = a''$ and a' and a'' are "correctly" aliased.

Definition A.5 (Equivalence modulo future updates: $P \equiv_F Q$)

$$P \equiv_F Q \Leftrightarrow \forall \alpha \ s.t. \ \alpha \in P \vee \alpha \in R, \forall L \left(\exists a, \ \alpha_P \overset{\alpha*}{\mapsto}_L a \Leftrightarrow \exists a', \ \alpha_R \overset{\alpha*}{\mapsto}_L a' \right) (1)$$

$$\wedge \ \forall L, L', a \left(\alpha_P \overset{\alpha}{\mapsto}_L a \wedge \alpha_P \overset{\alpha}{\mapsto}_{L'} a \Rightarrow \exists c, L_0, L'_0, a', L_1, L'_1, \gamma \right.$$

$$\left. \begin{cases} L = L_0.L_1 \wedge L' = L'_0.L'_1 \wedge L_1 \neq \emptyset \\ \alpha_R \overset{\alpha*}{\mapsto}_{L_0} c \overset{\gamma}{\mapsto}_{L_1} a' \\ \wedge \alpha_R \overset{\alpha*}{\mapsto}_{L'_0} c \overset{\gamma}{\mapsto}_{L'_1} a' \end{cases} \right) (2)$$

$$\wedge \ \forall L, L' a \left(\alpha_R \overset{\alpha}{\mapsto}_L a \wedge \alpha_R \overset{\alpha}{\mapsto}_{L'} a \Rightarrow \exists c, L_0, L'_0, a', L_1, L'_1, \gamma \right.$$

$$\left. \begin{cases} L = L_0.L_1 \wedge L' = L'_0.L'_1 \wedge L_1 \neq \emptyset \\ \alpha_P \overset{\alpha*}{\mapsto}_{L_0} c \wedge \alpha_P \overset{\alpha*}{\mapsto}_{L'_0} c \\ c \overset{\gamma}{\mapsto}_{L_1} a' \wedge c \overset{\gamma}{\mapsto}_{L'_1} a' \end{cases} \right) (3)$$

where $R = Q\Theta$ and Θ is a renaming of future identifiers like those defined in Sect. A.1.

The alias conditions can be expressed in the following way: "if two paths lead to a common term (e.g., the same location) then in the equivalent configuration these paths also lead to a common term." On the left of the implication, the paths are local to an activity. Actually two references to a future leads to the same future value, and are aliased; while the two updated futures will be two different deep copies of the future value which is both logical and sound. Consequently, ensuring correctness of aliases is sufficient on local paths.

The paths on the right of the implication can follow the future references but the *last* alias must be local to an activity. This condition ensures that the last pair of paths (L_1 and L'_1) will still be aliased when the future values is updated. If some aliases appear before the last one (if $L_0 \neq L'_0$), then alias conditions also have to be verified with L_0 and L'_0: $\alpha_R \overset{\gamma}{\mapsto}_{L_0} c \wedge \alpha_R \overset{\gamma}{\mapsto}_{L'_0} c$ must correspond to aliased objects in α_P.

This definition formalizes the shorter explanations given in Sect. 8.2 page 111. And the informal points ensuring the equivalence in the examples of this section (Sect.8.2.1, page 114) can now be considered as hints in order to prove that both terms of Fig. 8.3 verify the equivalence definition concerning both the main condition and the alias conditions of the definition of equivalence (Definition A.5, conditions (2, 3)).

The roles of the different paths in the alias conditions are also illustrated in Fig. A.2. One can verify that the alias of paths L and L' in the bottom configuration is simulated by two aliases in the first one. Note that the last alias is local to an activity.

Note also that the above equivalence does not take garbage collectable sub-terms into account. But this will have no effect on the subsequent reductions

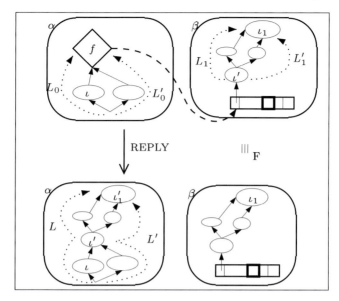

Fig. A.2. The principle of the alias conditions

and as explained before, one could make this equivalence more precise and make the definition of paths in Table A.2 sensitive to garbage collection.

Property A.6 (Equivalence relation)
$\equiv_F$ *is an equivalence relation.*

In the following equivalence of sub-terms will be needed. In fact *sub-terms are equivalent if they are part of equivalent expressions.*

Definition A.7 (Equivalence of sub-terms)

$$a \equiv_F a' \Leftrightarrow \exists L,\, a \in \alpha_P \wedge a' \in \alpha_Q \wedge P \equiv_F Q \wedge \left(\alpha_P \overset{\alpha*}{\mapsto}_L a, \Leftrightarrow \alpha_Q \overset{\alpha*}{\mapsto}_L a' \right)$$

This definition means that equivalent sub-terms will be implicitly related to the configurations to which they belong. Consequently, writing $a \equiv_F a'$ will suppose that there are two configurations P and Q such that $P \equiv_F Q$.

The definition of equivalence modulo future updates on configurations has the following consequences on the sub-terms:

Lemma A.8 (Sub-term equivalence)

$$a \equiv_F a' \Rightarrow \forall L \left(\exists b, a \overset{\alpha*}{\mapsto}_{L'} b \Leftrightarrow \exists b', a' \overset{\alpha*}{\mapsto}_{L'} b' \right)$$

$$\wedge \; \forall L, L', b, \; a \overset{\alpha}{\mapsto}_L b \wedge a \overset{\alpha}{\mapsto}_{L'} b \Rightarrow \exists c, L_0, L'_0, b', L_1, L'_1, \gamma$$
$$\begin{cases} L = L_0.L_1 \wedge L' = L'_0.L'_1 \wedge L_1 \neq \emptyset \\ a' \overset{\alpha*}{\mapsto}_{L_0} c \overset{\gamma}{\mapsto}_{L_1} b' \\ a' \overset{\alpha*}{\mapsto}_{L'_0} c \overset{\gamma}{\mapsto}_{L'_1} b' \end{cases}$$

$$\wedge \; \forall L, L', b, \; a' \overset{\alpha}{\mapsto}_L b \wedge a' \overset{\alpha}{\mapsto}_{L'} b \Rightarrow \exists c, L_0, b', L_1, L'_1, \gamma$$
$$\begin{cases} L = L_0.L_1 \wedge L' = L'_0.L'_1 \wedge L_1 \neq \emptyset \\ a \overset{\alpha*}{\mapsto}_{L_0} c \overset{\gamma}{\mapsto}_{L_1} b' \\ a \overset{\alpha*}{\mapsto}_{L'_0} c \overset{\gamma}{\mapsto}_{L'_1} b' \end{cases}$$

A.4 Properties of $\equiv_F$

The following property is a direct consequence of Tables A.1, A.2, and Definition A.5:

Property A.9 (Equivalence and compatibility)

$$P \equiv_F Q \Rightarrow P \bowtie Q$$

Consider now the case where a new entry is added to the store of two equivalent terms and is referenced from the same place in both terms. Adding equivalent sub-terms at the same place in two equivalent configurations produces equivalent configurations:

Lemma A.10 ($\equiv_F$ and store update)

$$\begin{cases} P \equiv_F Q \quad \wedge \quad a \equiv_F a' \\ \iota \in dom(\sigma_{\alpha P}) \wedge \iota' \in dom(\sigma_{\alpha Q}) \quad \wedge \quad \iota \equiv_F \iota' \\ P' = P \; except \; \sigma_{\alpha P'} = \{\iota \to a\} + \sigma_{\alpha P} \\ Q' = Q \; except \; \sigma_{\alpha Q'} = \{\iota' \to a'\} + \sigma_{\alpha Q} \\ \vdash P' \text{ OK} \wedge \; \vdash Q' \text{ OK} \end{cases} \Rightarrow P' \equiv_F Q'$$

The condition "$\vdash P'$ OK $\wedge \; \vdash Q'$ OK" is useful to ensure that local or generalized references inside a and a' are already defined in P and Q. In the following proofs, a and a' will always be sub-terms of P and Q respectively and thus this condition will always be verified.

Furthermore, $\iota \equiv_F \iota'$ is a necessary condition because ι and ι' are already in P and Q and thus must be reached by the same paths.

An equivalent version consists in replacing the condition $\iota \in dom(\sigma_{\alpha P}) \wedge \iota' \in dom(\sigma_{\alpha Q}) \wedge \iota \equiv_F \iota'$ by:

$$\exists L, \alpha_P \overset{\alpha}{\mapsto}_L \iota \wedge \alpha_Q \overset{\alpha}{\mapsto}_L \iota$$

The fact that this formulation is equivalent to the one of Lemma A.10 is a direct consequence of the definition of sub-term equivalence. Note that the path L leading to ι is not necessarily unique.

Proof (Lemma A.10): We will use the existence of the path L introduced above. The objective of this proof is to verify:

$$\begin{cases} P \equiv_F Q \\ a \equiv_F a' \quad \wedge \quad \exists L, \alpha_P \overset{\alpha}{\mapsto}_L \iota \wedge \alpha_Q \overset{\alpha}{\mapsto}_L \iota \\ P' = P \text{ except } \sigma_{\alpha_{P'}} = \{\iota \to a\} + \sigma_{\alpha_P} \\ Q' = Q \text{ except } \sigma_{\alpha_{Q'}} = \{\iota' \to a'\} + \sigma_{\alpha_Q} \\ \vdash P' \text{ OK } \wedge \ \vdash Q' \text{ OK} \end{cases} \Rightarrow P' \equiv_F Q''$$

Let Θ be the future renaming that has to be applied to Q to prove $P \equiv_F Q$. Let $R' = Q'\Theta$.

Let us first focus on the first condition of the equivalence definition (Definition A.5, condition (1)). That to say is, suppose:

$$\beta_{P'} \overset{\beta*}{\mapsto}_{L'} b$$

Let us make a recurrence on the number n of times $\overset{\beta*}{\mapsto}_{L'}$ passes by the location ι of the activity α.

- If $n = 0$, the fact that $P \equiv_F Q$ is sufficient to conclude.
- If $n = 1$ and $\alpha = \beta$ and ι is reached locally from $\alpha_{P'}$:

$$\alpha_{P'} \overset{\alpha}{\mapsto}_L \iota \overset{\alpha*}{\mapsto}_{L''} b$$

Then one has $\alpha_{R'} \overset{\alpha}{\mapsto}_L \iota'$ by hypothesis, and $\iota' \overset{\alpha*}{\mapsto}_{L''} b'$ by definition of $a \equiv_F a'$ (Lemma A.8). This proves, in the case where $n = 1$ and $\alpha = \beta$ and $\alpha_{P'} \overset{\alpha}{\mapsto}_L \iota \overset{\alpha*}{\mapsto}_{L''} b$:

$$\exists a, \alpha_{P'} \overset{\alpha*}{\mapsto}_{L'} a \Rightarrow \exists a', \alpha_{R'} \overset{\alpha*}{\mapsto}_{L'} a'$$

- Else:

$$\beta_{P'} \overset{\beta*}{\mapsto}_{L_0} fut(f^{\gamma \to \alpha}) \wedge \sigma_\alpha(F_\alpha(f^{\gamma \to \alpha})) \overset{\alpha}{\mapsto}_L \iota \overset{\alpha*}{\mapsto}_{L''} b$$

This last case uses the recurrence hypothesis (implication in the case $n-1$) and/or the same arguments as those in upper case with more complex notation and will not be detailed. Finally, one obtains:

$$\forall L_0 \, \forall \beta \, \exists a, \beta_{P'} \overset{\beta*}{\mapsto}_{L_0} a \Rightarrow \exists a', \beta_{R'} \overset{\beta*}{\mapsto}_{L_0} a'$$

The opposite implication stated in the first condition for equivalence is similar (symmetric).

For alias conditions (Definition A.5, conditions (2, 3)), suppose:

$$\exists L_0, L_0', d \;\; \alpha_{P'} \overset{\alpha}{\mapsto}_{L_0} b \wedge \alpha_{P'} \overset{\alpha}{\mapsto}_{L_0'} b \tag{4}$$

The most complicated case is when there are several L_i such that (of course, L is one of the L_i):

$$\alpha_{P'} \overset{\alpha}{\mapsto}_{L_i} \iota \wedge \alpha_{P'} \overset{\alpha}{\mapsto}_{L_{i'}} \iota \tag{5}$$

In the following, we will first verify the alias condition with L_i and $L_{i'}$ and focus on the terms inside a and a'.

By hypothesis, as $P \equiv_F Q$, one has:

$$\exists L_1, L_1', L_2, L_2' \begin{cases} L_i = L_1.L_2 \wedge L_{i'} = L_1'.L_2' \\ \alpha_{R'} \overset{\alpha*}{\mapsto}_{L_1} c \overset{\beta}{\mapsto}_{L_2} \iota'' \\ \alpha_{R'} \overset{\alpha*}{\mapsto}_{L_1'} c \overset{\beta}{\mapsto}_{L_2'} \iota'' \end{cases} \tag{6}$$

Moreover, as L is one of the L_i and $\alpha_{R'} \overset{\alpha}{\mapsto}_{L} \iota'$ (path local to α) the preceding assertion is simplified to ($\iota'' = \iota'$ and $L_1.L_2$ is inside α):

$$\alpha_{R'} \overset{\alpha}{\mapsto}_{L_i} \iota' \wedge \alpha_{R'} \overset{\alpha}{\mapsto}_{L_{i'}} \iota'$$

This ensures the alias condition for the path reaching ι and ι' (comparing (4) and (5) $L_0 = L_i$ and $L_0' = L_{i'}$).

For terms inside a and a', the most general case is when there are $L_i, L_{i'}, L', L'', b$ such that ($L_0 = L_i.L'$ and $L_0' = L_{i'}.L''$):

$$\alpha_{P'} \overset{\alpha}{\mapsto}_{L_i} \iota \overset{\alpha}{\mapsto}_{L'} b \wedge \alpha_{P'} \overset{\alpha}{\mapsto}_{L_{i'}} \iota \overset{\alpha}{\mapsto}_{L''} b$$

Lemma A.8 ensures that in R':

$$\exists c, L_3, L_3', b', L_4, L_4', \gamma \begin{cases} L' = L_3.L_4 \wedge L'' = L_3'.L_4' \wedge L_3 \neq \emptyset \\ \iota' \overset{\alpha*}{\mapsto}_{L_3} c \overset{\gamma}{\mapsto}_{L_4} b' \\ \iota' \overset{\alpha*}{\mapsto}_{L_3'} c \overset{\gamma}{\mapsto}_{L_4'} b' \end{cases} \tag{7}$$

From (6) and (7) one obtains ($L_5 = L_i.L_3$ and $L_5' = L_{i'}.L_3'$):

$$\exists L_5, L_5', L_4, L_4' \begin{cases} L_0 = L_5.L_4 \wedge L_0' = L_5'.L_4' \\ \alpha_{R'} \overset{\alpha*}{\mapsto}_{L_5} c \overset{\beta}{\mapsto}_{L_4} b' \\ \alpha_{R'} \overset{\alpha*}{\mapsto}_{L_5'} c \overset{\beta}{\mapsto}_{L_4'} b' \end{cases} \tag{8}$$

Thus we verify the alias condition (2) for terms inside a and a'.

Finally, other cases for the verification of the alias conditions are by application of the same hypothesis and lemmas. $\qquad\square$

In the following proofs, the arguments related to renaming will not always be detailed. That is to say, we will generally suppose that, when $P \equiv_F Q$, P

and Q use the same futures names (or more precisely, renaming of futures has already been applied). Proofs will focus on parts of proof related to updates of futures. In the same way, terms are identified modulo renaming of locations. For example, when a fresh location has to be taken, one can choose the location that makes the proof simple and concise (e.g., the one that has been chosen in another reduction). This is always possible modulo alpha conversion of the different terms involved.

Lemma A.11 ($\equiv_F$ and substitution)

$$\iota \equiv_F \iota' \Rightarrow a\{\!\{x \leftarrow \iota\}\!\} \equiv_F a\{\!\{x \leftarrow \iota'\}\!\}$$

The proof is straightforward. This lemma will be useful for the cases of the following proofs concerning method invocation. It proves the soundness of $\equiv_F$ with respect to the substitution applied in the INVOKE rule.

Recall that (Definition 6.1):

$$Copy\&Merge(\sigma, \iota \ ; \ \sigma', \iota') \triangleq Merge(\iota', \sigma', \, copy(\iota, \sigma)\{\!\{\iota \leftarrow \iota'\}\!\})$$

The following definition of deep copy is adapted to the proofs on equivalence relations:

Lemma A.12 (A characterization of deep copy)

$$a \in copy(\iota, \sigma_\beta) \Leftrightarrow \exists L, \ \iota \overset{\beta}{\mapsto}_L a$$

Of course, such a definition only describes the domain of the deep copy; the following requirement is still necessary to specify that the codomain of the copied store is identical to the original one:

$$\iota' \in dom(copy(\iota, \sigma)) \Rightarrow copy(\iota, \sigma)(\iota') = \sigma(\iota')$$

The following lemma is a consequence of the preceding properties:

Lemma A.13 (Copy and merge)
If $P' = P$ except $\sigma_{\alpha_{P'}} = Copy\&Merge(\sigma_{\beta_P}, \iota_0 \ ; \ \sigma_{\alpha_P}, \iota)$ then

$$\iota_0 \overset{\beta_P}{\mapsto}_L a \Leftrightarrow \iota \overset{\alpha_{P'}}{\mapsto}_L a'$$

and

$$\iota_0 \overset{\beta_{P}*}{\mapsto}_L a \Leftrightarrow \iota \overset{\alpha_{P'}*}{\mapsto}_L a'$$

Lemma A.13 states that the part of the store that is deeply copied verifies Lemma A.12 and thus paths starting from the destination of the deep copy in $\alpha_{P'}$ are the same as paths starting from the source location in β_P.

The following property states that adding equivalent deep copies to equivalent configurations produces equivalent configurations.

Lemma A.14 ($\equiv_F$ and store merge)

$$\begin{cases} P \equiv_F Q \ \wedge \ \iota \in \alpha_P \ \wedge \ \iota' \in \alpha_Q \wedge \iota_0 \in \beta_P \ \wedge \ \iota'_0 \in \beta_Q \\ a \equiv_F a' \quad \wedge \quad \iota \equiv_F \iota' \quad \wedge \quad \iota_0 \equiv_F \iota'_0 \\ P' = P \ except \ \sigma_{\alpha_{P'}} = Copy\&Merge(\sigma_{\beta_P}, \iota_0 \ ; \ \sigma_{\alpha_P}, \iota) \\ Q' = Q \ except \ \sigma_{\alpha_{Q'}} = Copy\&Merge(\sigma_{\beta_Q}, \iota'_0 \ ; \ \sigma_{\alpha_Q}, \iota') \end{cases} \Rightarrow P' \equiv_F Q'$$

Proof: There is θ_0 such that:

$$Copy\&Merge(\sigma_{\beta_P}, \iota_0 \ ; \ \sigma_{\alpha_P}, \iota) = Merge(\iota, \sigma_{\alpha_P}, copy(\iota_0, \sigma_{\beta_P})\{\!\{\iota_0 \leftarrow \iota\}\!\})$$
$$= copy(\iota_0, \sigma_{\beta_P})\theta_0 + \sigma_{\alpha_P}$$

From Lemma A.12, one has:

$$a \in copy(\iota_0, \sigma_{\beta_P}) \Leftrightarrow \exists L, \ \iota_0 \overset{\beta_P}{\mapsto}_L a$$

Thus, using Lemma A.13, for all $a \in copy(\iota_0, \sigma_{\beta_P})$:

$$\iota_0 \overset{\beta_P}{\mapsto}_L a \Leftrightarrow \iota \overset{\alpha_{P'}}{\mapsto}_L a\theta_0 \tag{9}$$

This property also holds for configuration Q.

Informally, if a location is in the merged sub-store of $\alpha_{P'}$ then it comes from the sub-store $copy(\iota_0, \sigma_{\beta_P})$ of P and it is equivalent to a location inside $copy(\iota'_0, \sigma_{\beta_Q})$ or in a future referenced by $copy(\iota'_0, \sigma_{\beta_Q})$ which corresponds to a location in the merged sub-store of $\alpha_{Q'}$ or in a future value referenced by this sub-store, because $\iota_0 \equiv_F \iota'_0$. More formally:

$$\iota \overset{\alpha_{P'}}{\mapsto}_L a\theta_0 \Rightarrow \iota_0 \overset{\beta_P}{\mapsto}_L a \qquad \text{from (9)}$$
$$\Rightarrow \exists a', \ \iota'_0 \overset{\beta_{Q}*}{\mapsto}_L a' \quad \text{because } \iota_0 \equiv_F \iota'_0$$
$$\Rightarrow \exists a', \ \iota' \overset{\alpha_{Q'}*}{\mapsto}_L a'\theta'_0 \quad \text{Lemma A.13}$$

Symmetrically:

$$\iota' \overset{\alpha_{Q'}}{\mapsto}_L a'\theta'_0 \Rightarrow \exists a, \ \iota \overset{\alpha_{P'}*}{\mapsto}_L a\theta_0$$

Thus:

$$\left(\iota \overset{\alpha_{P'}}{\mapsto}_L a \Leftrightarrow \iota' \overset{\alpha_{Q'}}{\mapsto}_L a' \right)$$

Then, let L_0 be a path leading to ι in $\alpha_{P'}$; it also leads to ι' in $\alpha_{Q'}$ because $\iota \equiv_F \iota'$ and consequently:

$$\left(\alpha_{P'} \overset{\alpha_{P'}*}{\mapsto}_{L_0.L} a \Leftrightarrow \alpha_{Q'} \overset{\alpha_{Q'}*}{\mapsto}_{L_0.L} a' \right)$$

The general case follows similar reasoning (with a recurrence on the number of times we pass by location ι) and finally we obtain (1):

$$\forall \beta, \beta_{P'} \overset{\beta_{P'}*}{\mapsto}_L a \Leftrightarrow \beta_{Q'} \overset{\beta_{Q'}*}{\mapsto}_L a$$

The proof of alias conditions (2, 3) is similar too. It is based on the following:

$$\begin{cases} \iota \overset{\alpha_{P'}}{\mapsto}_L b\theta_0 \\ \iota \overset{\alpha_{P'}}{\mapsto}_{L'} b\theta_0 \end{cases} \Rightarrow \begin{cases} \iota_0 \overset{\beta_P}{\mapsto}_L b \\ \iota_0 \overset{\beta_P}{\mapsto}_{L'} b \end{cases} \qquad \text{from (9)}$$

$$\Rightarrow \exists c, L_0, L_0', L_1 \neq \emptyset, L_1' \begin{cases} L = L_0.L_1 \\ L' = L_0'.L_1' \\ \iota_0' \overset{\beta_Q*}{\mapsto}_{L_0} c \overset{\gamma_Q}{\mapsto}_{L_1} b \\ \iota_0' \overset{\beta_Q*}{\mapsto}_{L_0'} c \overset{\gamma_Q}{\mapsto}_{L_1'} b \end{cases} \qquad \text{because } \iota_0 \equiv_F \iota_0'$$

$$\Rightarrow \exists c, L_0, L_0', L_1 \neq \emptyset, L_1' \begin{cases} L = L_0.L_1 \\ L' = L_0'.L_1' \\ \iota_0' \overset{\alpha_{Q'}*}{\mapsto}_{L_0} c \overset{\delta_{Q'}}{\mapsto}_{L_1} b \\ \iota_0' \overset{\alpha_{Q'}*}{\mapsto}_{L_0'} c \overset{\delta_{Q'}}{\mapsto}_{L_1'} b \end{cases} \qquad \text{Lemma A.13}$$

where δ is voluntarily not specified in order to avoid a long case study. Finally P' and Q' are equivalent. $\qquad \square$

A.5 Sufficient Conditions for Equivalence

In the following, let T be any parallel reduction rule so that T ranges over {LOCAL, NEWACT, REQUEST, SERVE, ENDSERVICE, REPLY}. $\overset{T}{\longrightarrow}$ denotes the application of a parallel rule named T (cf. Table 6.2).

The following properties relate the formal definition of $\equiv_F$ to the intuitive one saying that two configurations are equivalent modulo future updates if they differ only by the update of some calculated futures, that is the application of some REPLY rules.

As explained informally in Sect. 8.2, two configurations differing only by some future updates are equivalent:

Property A.15 (REPLY and $\equiv_F$)

$$P \xrightarrow{\text{REPLY}} P' \Rightarrow P \equiv_F P'$$

Proof: One only has to prove that the updated store is equivalent to the old one. The other activities and other parts of the updated activity are unchanged.

REPLY:

$$\frac{\sigma_\alpha(\iota) = fut(f_i^{\gamma\to\beta}) \quad F_\beta(f_i^{\gamma\to\beta}) = \iota_f \quad \sigma'_\alpha = Copy\&Merge(\sigma_\beta, \iota_f \; ; \; \sigma_\alpha, \iota)}{\begin{array}{c} P = \alpha[a_\alpha; \sigma_\alpha; \iota_\alpha; F_\alpha; R_\alpha; f_\alpha]\|\beta[a_\beta; \sigma_\beta; \iota_\beta; F_\beta; R_\beta; f_\beta]\|Q \longrightarrow \\ \alpha[a_\alpha; \sigma'_\alpha; \iota_\alpha; F_\alpha; R_\alpha; f_\alpha]\|\beta[a_\beta; \sigma_\beta; \iota_\beta; F_\beta; R_\beta; f_\beta]\|Q = P' \end{array}}$$

There are two renamings θ and θ_0 such that:

$$\begin{aligned}
\sigma'_\alpha &= Merge(\iota, \sigma_\alpha, copy(\iota_f, \sigma_\beta)\{\iota_f \leftarrow \iota\}) \\
&= copy(\iota_f, \sigma_\beta)\{\iota_f \leftarrow \iota\}\theta + \sigma_\alpha \\
&= copy(\iota_f, \sigma_\beta)\theta_0 + \sigma_\alpha
\end{aligned}$$

Let ι' be in the updated part of the store of α in the configuration P': $\iota \overset{\alpha_{P'}}{\mapsto}_L \iota'$. Then $\iota' = \iota_0\theta_0$ where $\iota_0 \in copy(\iota_f, \sigma_\beta)$ and (Lemma A.13):

$$\iota_f \overset{\beta_P}{\mapsto}_L \iota_0 \Leftrightarrow \iota \overset{\alpha_{P'}}{\mapsto}_L \iota'$$

Let L_0 be such that $\alpha_P \overset{\alpha}{\mapsto}_{L_0} \iota$. If there is no such L_0 then ι can be garbage collected and the equivalence relation is trivially verified for ι. Thus, when the path passes one time by location ι, it is of the form $L_0.L$ (with L_0 and L defined above):

$$\left(\alpha_P \overset{\alpha_P}{\mapsto}_{L_0} \iota \wedge \sigma_\alpha(\iota) = fut(f_i^{\gamma\to\beta}) \wedge F_\beta(f_i^{\gamma\to\beta}) = \iota_f \wedge \iota_f \overset{\beta_P}{\mapsto}_L \iota_0\right) \quad (10)$$

$$\Leftrightarrow \left(\alpha_{P'} \overset{\alpha_{P'}}{\mapsto}_{L_0} \iota \wedge \iota \overset{\alpha_{P'}}{\mapsto}_L \iota_0\right) \quad (11)$$

$$\Leftrightarrow \left(\alpha_{P'} \overset{\alpha}{\mapsto}_{L_0.L} \iota'\right)$$

Note that $(11) \Rightarrow (10)$ is ensured by the premiss of the REPLY rule: $\sigma_\alpha(\iota) = fut(f_i^{\gamma\to\beta})$ and $F_\beta(f_i^{\gamma\to\beta}) = \iota_f$.

The more general assertion:

$$\forall \gamma_P, L, \quad \gamma_P \overset{\gamma_P*}{\mapsto}_L a \Leftrightarrow \gamma_{P'} \overset{\gamma_{P'}*}{\mapsto}_L a$$

is obtained by recurrence on the number of times the path L passes by ι.

For the alias conditions, let us focus on condition (3): every alias in P' must exist in P.

First suppose that one of the two aliased path belongs to the updated future (the other cases are trivial): $\alpha_{P'} \overset{\alpha}{\mapsto}_{L_0.L} \iota_0$ and $\alpha_{P'} \overset{\alpha}{\mapsto}_{L'} \iota_0$ then $L' = L_1.L'' \wedge \alpha_P \overset{\alpha}{\mapsto}_{L_1} \iota$ by definition of the $Merge$ operator (the only common location between original and merged store is ι) and thus, because the deep copy creates a part of store similar to the original one (Lemma A.13):

$$\alpha_P \overset{\alpha}{\mapsto}_{L_0} \iota \wedge \sigma_\alpha(\iota) = fut(f_i^{\gamma\to\beta}) \wedge F_\beta(f_i^{\gamma\to\beta}) = \iota_f \wedge \begin{cases} \iota_f \overset{\beta}{\mapsto}_L \iota_0 \\ \iota_f \overset{\beta}{\mapsto}_{L''} \iota_0 \end{cases}$$

This proves the alias condition (3). Other cases necessary to prove the equivalence are similar. □

More precisely, we have the following sufficient condition for equivalence modulo future updates:

Property A.16 (Sufficient condition for equivalence)

$$\begin{cases} P_1 \xrightarrow{\text{REPLY}} P' \\ P_2 \xrightarrow{\text{REPLY}} P' \end{cases} \Rightarrow P_1 \equiv_F P_2$$

$$\begin{cases} P \xrightarrow{\text{REPLY}} P_1 \\ P \xrightarrow{\text{REPLY}} P_2 \end{cases} \Rightarrow P_1 \equiv_F P_2$$

These assertions are easily proved by transitivity of $\equiv_F$ (Property A.6).

Note that this condition is not a necessary condition for equivalence modulo future updates as it does not deal with mutual references between futures (see the example of Fig. 8.5 page 117).

A.6 Equivalence Modulo Future Updates and Reduction

The objective here is to prove that if a reduction can be made on a configuration then the same one can be made on an equivalent configuration. This is a very important property as it somewhat proves the correctness of $\equiv_F$ with respect to reduction. The proof is decomposed in two parts. First, one may need to apply several REPLY rules to be able to perform the same reduction on the two terms. Indeed one of the configurations can be stuck by a wait-by-necessity for the value of a future in order to perform the reduction: by definition of equivalence modulo future updates, some futures may be updated in a configuration and calculated but not updated in an equivalent configuration. The second part of the proof consists in verifying that the application of the same reduction rule on equivalent terms leads to equivalent terms. Note that there is a similarity with the properties of bisimulation: two equivalent configurations can perform the same reduction and become equivalent configurations, REPLY being a non-observable transition.

Property A.17 ($\equiv_F$ and reduction(1))

$$P \equiv_F P' \wedge P \xrightarrow{T} Q \Rightarrow \begin{cases} \text{if } T = \text{REPLY } then \ Q \equiv_F P' \\ else \ \exists Q', \ P' \xrightarrow{\text{REPLY*}} \xrightarrow{T} Q' \wedge Q' \equiv_F Q \end{cases}$$

This property leads us to define the new reduction $\Longrightarrow$:

Let $\Longrightarrow$ be the reduction $\longrightarrow$ preceded by some applications of the REPLY rule if the rule of $\longrightarrow$ is not REPLY and any (possibly 0) number of applications of the REPLY if the rule is REPLY. More formally:

Definition A.18 (Parallel reduction modulo future updates)

$$\stackrel{T}{\Longrightarrow} \quad = \quad \begin{array}{l} \xrightarrow{\text{REPLY}*} \stackrel{T}{\longrightarrow} \quad \textit{if } T \neq \text{REPLY} \\ \xrightarrow{\text{REPLY}*} \quad\quad\quad \textit{if } T = \text{REPLY} \end{array}$$

Note that if the applied rule is REPLY, $\stackrel{T}{\Longrightarrow}$ may do nothing. That is nec-essary, for example, to simulate the update of a future on an (equivalent) configuration where this future has already been updated.

Using this new reduction, Property A.17 can be rewritten in the following manner:

Property A.19 ($\equiv_F$ and reduction(2))

$$P \equiv_F P' \wedge P \stackrel{T}{\longrightarrow} Q \Rightarrow \exists Q', P' \stackrel{T}{\Longrightarrow} Q' \wedge Q' \equiv_F Q$$

Properties A.17 and A.19 are equivalent. The following proof is valid for both.

Proof (of Properties A.17 and A.19): First note that from a given source configuration a reduction is uniquely specified by the name of the applied rule and the names of the different activities concerned, except in the case of the REPLY rule where the future identifier is also necessary.

If one cannot apply the same reduction as $P \longrightarrow Q$ (same rule on the same activities) on P', then $\xrightarrow{\text{REPLY}}$ is applied enough times ($P' \xrightarrow{\text{REPLY}*} P''$) to be able to apply this reduction: P' may be performing a wait-by-necessity on the value of some *calculated* futures. The principle is that for each awaited future reference, since P can perform the reduction, the future has already been calculated in P, and $P \equiv_F P'$ implies that the future has also been calculated in P'. Thus P' only needs to update it.

More precisely, it is straightforward to check that if two configurations are equivalent, the same reduction can be applied on the two configurations except if one of them is stuck. Stuck configurations can occur in two situations:

- In the case of a forbidden access to an object (e.g., field access on an active object or non-existing field or method) by the definition of equivalence, the reduction on the two equivalent terms should lead to the same error. This is impossible because P can be reduced.
- In the case of an access to a future (wait-by-necessity): if in an activity of P' one has $a_{\alpha_{P'}} = \ldots \iota' \ldots$ and $\sigma_{\alpha_{P'}}(\iota') = fut(f_i^{\gamma \to \beta})$ and the operation performed on ι' is strict then in P, $a_{\alpha_P} = \ldots \iota \ldots$ and $\sigma_{\alpha_P}(\iota)$ is not a future. The future equivalence ensures that $f_i^{\gamma \to \beta} \in F_{\beta_{P'}}$.
  Then it is possible to update $f_i^{\gamma \to \beta}$ in P': $P' \xrightarrow{\text{REPLY}} P'_1$. If in P_1 $\sigma_{\alpha_{P'_1}}(\iota') = fut(f_j^{\gamma \to \beta})$ then, another time, we update the future f_j. Af-ter a finite number of updates, we obtain P'' such that $P' \xrightarrow{\text{REPLY}*} P''$ and

$\sigma_{\alpha_{P''}}(\iota')$ is not a future reference. Indeed, if the number of updates was infinite, then neither P' nor P could be reduced, which would contradict the hypothesis.

Then $P' \xrightarrow{\text{REPLY*}} P''$ where $P'' \equiv_F P$ (Property A.15) and in P'' $\sigma_{\alpha_{P''}}(\iota')$ is not a future reference. Then the same reduction can be applied on P'' and P. Actually the REPLY rule needs to be applied:

- 0 times if the object to be accessed is not a future,
- 1 time if it is actually a future whose value is not a future,
- n times if it is a future whose future value is $n-1$ times itself a future reference.

Note that only the objects accessed directly by the reduction T may have to be updated.

Now, one has to verify that if $P'' \equiv_F P$ and the same reduction rule is applied on P and P'' on equivalent activity(ies) one obtains equivalent configurations:

$$\begin{cases} P \xrightarrow{T} Q \\ P'' \xrightarrow{T} Q' \Rightarrow Q' \equiv_F Q \\ P'' \equiv_F P \end{cases}$$

where both applications of the rule T are the same (same application points and same activities concerned).

The proof consists in a (long) case study detailed below. The different cases depend on the reduction applied and the rules applied to prove the equivalence. In the following the proofs will focus only on the cases where one of the locations involved in the reduction points to a future in P and is an object in P'' (updated future). Other cases (several futures or no future) can be trivially obtained. Of course, we will use the fact that if two terms are equivalent, they have the same form (in fact, such arguments are detailed only for the FIELD local rule). In the following, no details about the renaming of futures and locations are given: one could easily prove a first step toward the whole proof concerning only renaming:

$$\begin{cases} P \xrightarrow{T} Q \\ P'' \xrightarrow{T} Q' \Rightarrow Q' \equiv Q \\ P'' \equiv P \end{cases}$$

LOCAL One should consider cases depending on the local rule applied:

STOREALLOC Consequence of Lemma A.10.

FIELD

FIELD:

$$\sigma(\iota) = [l_i = \iota_i; m_j = \varsigma(x_j, y_j)a_j]_{j\in 1..m}^{i\in 1..n} \qquad k \in 1..n$$

$$(\mathcal{R}[\iota.l_k], \sigma) \rightarrow_S (\mathcal{R}[\iota_{k1}], \sigma)$$

Because of the equivalence between current terms of P and P', one has:

$$a_P = \iota.l_k \equiv_F \iota_2.l_k = a_{P''}$$

then $\iota \equiv_F \iota_2$ and $\iota_{k1} \equiv_F \iota_{k2}$ (where ι_{k2} is the location of field l_k in P'') because $\iota \overset{\alpha_P}{\mapsto}_{l_k} \iota_{k1}$ and $\iota_2 \overset{\alpha_{P''}}{\mapsto}_{l_k} \iota_{k2}$. Thus $P'' \equiv_F Q$.

The following cases will often use arguments similar to this one which will not be detailed.

INVOKE Straightforward: note that the two method bodies must be equivalent and the two arguments too. The final equivalence comes from Lemma A.11.

UPDATE Direct from Lemma A.10 and the equivalence of the involved terms.

CLONE Cloning of futures is forbidden by ASP semantics. Other cases are trivial.

This case justifies the fact that cloning a future is considered as a strict operation: the future update consists in a deep copy of the value whereas the *clone* operator performs a shallow clone. Thus performing a CLONE and then a REPLY reduction creates two deep copies of the future value. On the contrary performing a REPLY before a CLONE reduction creates only one deep copy with two shallow copies of the first object of the future value. Consequently, for the coherence of the calculus, cloning is considered as a strict operation (cloning a future is blocking and generates a wait-by-necessity). Of course such blocking states can create deadlocks.

NEWACT

NEWACT:
$$\gamma \text{ fresh activity} \quad \iota' \notin dom(\sigma) \quad \sigma' = \{\iota' \mapsto AO(\gamma)\} :: \sigma$$
$$\sigma_\gamma = copy(\iota'', \sigma) \quad Service = (\text{if } m_j = \emptyset \text{ then } FifoService \text{ else } \iota''.m_j())$$

$$\alpha[\mathcal{R}[Active(\iota'', m_j)]; \sigma; \iota; F; R; f] \parallel P \longrightarrow$$
$$\alpha[\mathcal{R}[\iota']; \sigma'; \iota; F; R; f] \parallel \gamma[Service; \sigma_\gamma; \iota''; \emptyset; \emptyset; \emptyset] \parallel P$$

The only interesting case is the presence of futures in the newly created activity. In this case, Lemma A.14 is sufficient to conclude. Indeed in NEWACT, $\sigma_\gamma = copy(\iota'', \sigma_\alpha)$ could be written $\sigma_\gamma = Copy\&Merge(\sigma_\alpha, \iota'' ; \emptyset, \iota'')$.

REQUEST

REQUEST:

$$\frac{\sigma_\alpha(\iota) = AO(\beta) \quad \iota'' \notin dom(\sigma_\beta) \quad f_i^{\alpha \to \beta} \ new\ future \quad \iota_f \notin dom(\sigma_\alpha)}{\sigma_\beta' = Copy\&Merge(\sigma_\alpha, \iota'\ ;\ \sigma_\beta, \iota'') \quad \sigma_\alpha' = \{\iota_f \mapsto fut(f_i^{\alpha \to \beta})\} :: \sigma_\alpha}$$

$$\alpha[\mathcal{R}[\iota.m_j(\iota')]; \sigma_\alpha; \iota_\alpha; F_\alpha; R_\alpha; f_\alpha] \parallel \beta[a_\beta; \sigma_\beta; \iota_\beta; F_\beta; R_\beta; f_\beta] \parallel P \longrightarrow$$
$$\alpha[\mathcal{R}[\iota_f]; \sigma_\alpha'; \iota_\alpha; F_\alpha; R_\alpha; f_\alpha] \parallel \beta[a_\beta; \sigma_\beta'; \iota_\beta; F_\beta; R_\beta :: [m_j; \iota''; f_i^{\alpha \to \beta}]; f_\beta] \parallel P$$

Modulo renaming, one can choose the same name for the created future in P and Q, and the same location for the copy of the argument. Lemma A.14 can be applied to manage futures that can be present in the deep copy of the requests parameters.

The rest of the proof is straightforward. For example, the equivalence of requests $([m_j; \iota; f_i^{\alpha \to \beta}] \equiv_F [m_j'; \iota; f_i^{\alpha \to \beta}])$ is ensured by the fact that we take the same location, the same future name, and moreover $m_j = m_j'$ because $a_{\alpha_P} \equiv_F a_{\alpha_{P'}}$.

SERVE This is one of the most important case of the proof. Informally, the equivalence between the two request lists implies that the served requests are equivalent, which is sufficient to conclude.

The fact that the equivalence definition is defined modulo a reordering of requests is essential here; more precisely:

$$P'' \equiv_F P \Rightarrow \forall M \in \mathcal{M}_{\alpha_P}, \ R_{\alpha_P}\big|_M \equiv_F R_{\alpha_{P''}}\big|_M$$

Thus the first request of $R_{\alpha_P}\big|_M$ will be equivalent modulo future updates in both configurations. Consequently, SERVE will serve equivalent requests.

ENDSERVICE The equivalence between future lists is straightforward. The proof is based on the application of Lemma A.14.

REPLY In this case $P' \equiv_F Q$ and $P' \Longrightarrow P'$. Thus $Q = P' = P''$ is sufficient. Note that without any consequence on the property, in the case of the REPLY rule, we may be unable to directly apply the same rule on the two equivalent terms for three reasons:

• several future updates may be needed to have the reference on which the concerned future must be updated (several future updates are needed to apply the same rule), or
• the future has already been updated in the equivalent term (this REPLY rule can no longer be applied), or
• there was a cycle of future references and the order of futures updated was different (in Fig. 8.5 we can have references either only to future f_1 or to future f_2).

Note that most of this proof has been simplified by the Lemma A.14. □

The following property is a direct consequence of Property A.19.

Corollary A.20 ($\equiv_F$ and reduction)

$$P \equiv_F P' \wedge P \xrightarrow{T} Q \Rightarrow \exists Q', \ P' \xrightarrow{T} Q' \wedge Q' \equiv_F Q$$

Proof: If $T = \text{REPLY}$ then the proof is straightforward. Else $P \overset{T}{\Longrightarrow} Q$ can be decomposed in $P \xrightarrow{\text{REPLY*}} P_1 \xrightarrow{T} Q$. The conclusion comes from the application of the preceding property to P_1 ($P_1 \equiv_F P'$ because of the transitivity of $\equiv_F$). □

A.7 Another Formulation

Let us formalize another definition of equivalence between terms based on renaming. This definition is indeed equivalent to the preceding one.

Let us extend the renaming of futures defined in Sect. A.1 with a renaming on locations inside an activity θ_{α_i} and between two activities $\theta_{\alpha_i \to \alpha'_j, \iota'}$. θ_{fut} is the renaming of futures defined in Sect. A.1; it is a bijection from $FL(\alpha_P)$ to $FL(\alpha_Q)$:

$$\Theta ::= (\theta_{fut}, \theta_\alpha^{\alpha \in P}, \ldots, \theta_{\alpha \to \beta, \iota}^{\alpha \in P, \beta \in Q}, \ldots)$$
$$\theta_{fut} ::= \{.f_i^{\beta_P \to \alpha_P} \leftarrow f_i'^{\beta_Q \to \alpha_Q}, \ldots\};$$

for $\alpha \in P \wedge \alpha \in Q$,
$$\theta_\alpha ::= \{\iota_1 \leftarrow \iota'_1 \ldots\} \text{ where } \iota_1 \in dom(\sigma_{\alpha_P}), \iota'_1 \in dom(\sigma_{\alpha_Q})$$

for $\alpha_P \in P, \beta_Q \in Q, \iota \in dom(\sigma_{\alpha_P}), \iota' \in dom(\sigma_{\beta_Q})$,
$$\theta_{\alpha_P \to \beta_Q, \iota'} ::= \{\iota_1 \leftarrow \iota'_1, \ldots\} \text{ where } \iota_1 \in dom(\sigma_{\alpha_P}), \iota', \iota'_1 \in dom(\sigma_{\beta_Q})$$

$$\theta_{\alpha_P \leftarrow \beta_Q, \iota} ::= \{\iota_1 \leftarrow \iota'_1, \ldots\} \text{ where } \iota, \iota_1 \in dom(\sigma_{\alpha_P}), \iota'_1 \in dom(\sigma_{\beta_Q})$$

The last two renamings of locations allow us to express future updates: in the two last lines ι and ι' represent the location of an updated future. Suppose that, inside β, ι contains a future reference to $f_i^{\gamma \to \alpha}$ in P but this future has been updated in the corresponding location ι' of Q. To prove that the future value of $f_i^{\gamma \to \alpha}$ in the activity α of P and the updated future (indirectly) referenced by ι' in the activity β of Q are equivalent, one must provide a renaming $\theta_{\alpha \to \beta, \iota'}$.

Moreover, each renaming must be bijective and a given location cannot be the destination of several renamings:

- for each $\beta \in Q$ the sets $codom(\theta_\beta)$, $(codom(\theta_{\alpha \to \beta, \iota'}))_{\alpha \in P, \iota \in dom(\sigma_\beta)}$ are disjuncts;
- for each $\alpha \in P$ the sets $dom(\theta_\alpha)$, $(dom(\theta_{\alpha \leftarrow \beta, \iota}))_{\beta \in Q, \iota \in dom(\sigma_\alpha)}$ are disjuncts.

Finally, the equivalence modulo future updates can also be formalized as follows:

Definition A.21 (Equivalence modulo future updates (2))
To prove $P \equiv_F Q$, one must provide

$$\Theta = (\theta_{fut}, \theta_\alpha^{\alpha \in P}, \ldots, \theta_{\alpha \to \beta, \iota}^{\alpha \in P, \beta \in Q}, \ldots)$$

such that the rules of Table A.3 are coinductively verified (for all activities α of P and Q).

$$fut(f) \equiv_x fut(f\theta_{fut}) \qquad AO(\alpha) \equiv_x AO(\alpha) \qquad \emptyset \equiv_x \emptyset$$

$$\frac{\sigma_{\alpha P}(\iota) \equiv_\alpha \sigma_{\alpha Q}(\iota\theta_\alpha)}{\iota \equiv_\alpha \iota\theta_\alpha}$$

$$\frac{\sigma_{\alpha P}(\iota_1) \equiv_{\alpha \leftarrow \beta, \iota_0} \sigma_{\beta Q}(\iota_1 \theta_{\alpha \leftarrow \beta, \iota})}{\iota \equiv_{\alpha \leftarrow \beta, \iota_0} \iota\theta_{\alpha \leftarrow \beta, \iota}}$$

$$\frac{b \text{ is in the location } \iota \text{ of the activity } \gamma \text{ of } P}{F_{\beta Q}(f_i^{\alpha \to \beta}) = \iota' \quad \iota \equiv_{\gamma \leftarrow \beta, \iota} \iota'}$$
$$\frac{}{b \equiv_x fut(f_i^{\alpha \to \beta})}$$

$$\frac{\sigma_{\alpha P}(\iota) \equiv_{\alpha \to \beta, \iota_0'} \sigma_{\beta Q}(\iota\theta_{\alpha \to \beta, \iota_0'})}{\iota \equiv_{\alpha \to \beta, \iota_0'} \iota\theta_{\alpha \to \beta, \iota_0'}}$$

$$\frac{a \text{ is in the location } \iota' \text{ of the activity } \gamma \text{ of } Q}{F_{\beta P}(f_i^{\alpha \to \beta}) = \iota \quad \iota \equiv_{\beta \to \gamma, \iota'} \iota'}$$
$$\frac{}{fut(f_i^{\alpha \to \beta}) \equiv_x a}$$

$$\frac{\iota \equiv_\alpha \iota' \quad R_{\alpha P} \equiv_\alpha R_{\alpha Q}}{[m_j, \iota, f] :: R_{\alpha P} \equiv_\alpha [m_j, \iota', f\theta_{fut}] :: R_{\alpha Q}}$$

$$\frac{\iota \equiv_\alpha \iota' \quad F \equiv_\alpha F'}{\{f_i^{\gamma \to \alpha P} \mapsto \iota\} :: F \equiv_\alpha \{f_i^{\gamma \to \alpha Q} \theta_{fut} \mapsto \iota'\} :: F'}$$

$$\frac{a_{\alpha P} \equiv_\alpha a_{\alpha Q} \quad \iota_{\alpha P} \equiv_\alpha \iota_{\alpha Q} \quad F_{\alpha P} \equiv_\alpha F_{\alpha Q}}{\forall M \in \mathcal{M}_{\alpha P}, R_{\alpha P}\big|_M \equiv_F R_{\alpha Q}\big|_M \quad f_{\alpha Q} = f_{\alpha P}\theta_{fut}}$$
$$\frac{}{\alpha[a_{\alpha P}; \sigma_{\alpha P}; \iota_{\alpha P}; F_{\alpha P}; R_{\alpha P}; f_{\alpha P}] \equiv_\alpha \alpha[a_{\alpha Q}; \sigma_{\alpha Q}; \iota_{\alpha Q}; F_{\alpha Q}; R_{\alpha Q}; f_{\alpha Q}]}$$

$$\frac{\exists \Theta = (\theta_{fut}, \theta_{\alpha_1}, \ldots) \quad \alpha \in P \Leftrightarrow \alpha \in Q}{\forall \alpha \in P, \alpha[a_{\alpha P}; \sigma_{\alpha P}; \iota_{\alpha P}; F_{\alpha P}; R_{\alpha P}; f_{\alpha P}] \equiv_\alpha \alpha[a_{\alpha Q}; \sigma_{\alpha Q}; \iota_{\alpha Q}; F_{\alpha Q}; R_{\alpha Q}; f_{\alpha Q}]}$$
$$\frac{}{P \equiv_F Q}$$

Table A.3. Equivalence rules

In Table A.3, x replaces α or $\alpha \to \beta, \iota'$ or $\alpha \leftarrow \beta, \iota$. All the trivial induction rules corresponding to operators in the syntax are not given explicitly in this table.

$\equiv_\alpha$ denotes the equivalence between (sub-)terms that appears in α in both configurations. $\equiv_{\alpha \to \beta, \iota'}$ denotes the equivalence between terms contained in a future calculated in the activity α of P and its updated value in the location ι' of the activity β of Q. $\equiv_x$ denotes any equivalence relation (either inside an activity when $x = \alpha$ or between activities when x is of the form $\alpha \leftarrow \beta', \iota$ or $\alpha \to \beta', \iota'$).

The existence of $\theta_{\alpha \to \beta, \iota'}$ means that the future calculated in the activity α of P has been updated in the location ι' of the activity β of Q. The renaming $\theta_{\alpha \to \beta, \iota'}$ must be applied to locations of the activity α of the configuration P in order to obtain locations (corresponding to a deep copied future value) in the activity β of the configuration Q.

Symmetrically, $\theta_{\alpha \leftarrow \beta, \iota}$ is useful when a future in the activity β of Q has been updated in the activity α of P, at the location ι.

This definition is coinductive because one may need to use the fact that $\iota \equiv_F \iota'$ to prove that $\iota \equiv_F \iota'$ as references between objects may produce cycles. Figure A.4 shows the example of a configuration where such a kind of definition is necessary.

Property A.22 (Equivalence of the two equivalence definitions)
The two definitions of the equivalence modulo future updates presented in this appendix are equivalent.

A.8 Decidability of $\equiv_F$

Property A.23 (Decidability)
$\equiv_F$ *is decidable.*

Proof: Let us focus on the first definition of the equivalence modulo future updates. Verifying the equivalence consists in first applying a renaming Θ on the futures. The set of such renamings is finite and could be enumerated and applied, and equivalence could be verified for each of them (even if it is probably not the best way to proceed in practice).

Then one has to follow arrows starting from each activity of the first configuration and verify that every arrow can also be followed in the second configuration, following future values if necessary (and the same thing starting from the second one). Of course, as soon as a cycle is found, the verification can be stopped. In the worst case, starting from every activity, one follows paths that lead to all locations in this activity and all locations in all the future values. The set of locations being finite, this verification is finite even if the set of paths is infinite.

The alias conditions can be verified by checking that for each location such that two sub-terms of its activity points to it, take the two shortest paths using these two references[2] and verify that these paths are also aliases in the other configuration. This must be performed for all pairs of aliases of all activities (which are finite as soon as loop are considered only once).   □

A.9 Examples

A list of examples of equivalent terms is given below. The verification of the first definition of equivalence modulo future updates consists in simply following the arrows on the diagrams in order to verify conditions (1), (2), and (3). The figures are considered as proofs hints.

In order to illustrate the second definition of the equivalence relation, some details on the renaming that has to be used are given.

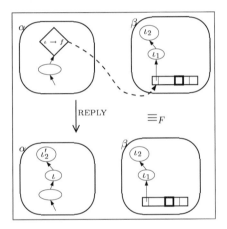

Fig. A.3. Simple example of future equivalence

In the case of Fig. A.3, a simple future value is updated. Thus, one must take:

$$\theta_{\beta \to \alpha, \iota} = \big\{ \iota_1 \leftarrow \iota, \iota_2 \leftarrow \iota_2' \big\}$$

Figure A.4 illustrates a case of cyclic proof. Note that this may only happen when there is a cycle of local references (locations).

Figure A.5 illustrates the case where there is a cycle of future references. The proof of equivalence is based on the renamings:

---

[2] Thus, we avoid having more than one cycle in each path, and we only have a cycle when the aliasing is due to a cycle of references.

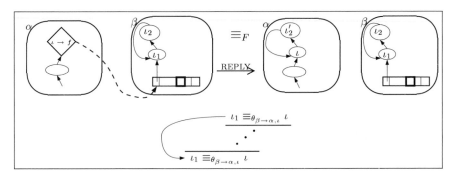

Fig. A.4. Example of a "cyclic" proof

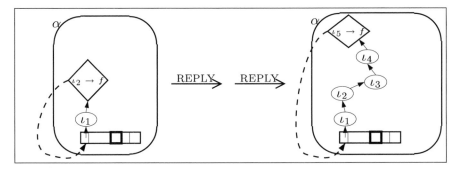

Fig. A.5. Equivalence in the case of a cycle of futures

$$\theta_{\alpha \to \alpha, \iota_2} = \{\!\{ \iota_1 \leftarrow \iota_2, \iota_2 \leftarrow \iota_3 \}\!\}$$
$$\theta_{\alpha \to \alpha, \iota_3} = \{\!\{ \iota_1 \leftarrow \iota_3, \iota_2 \leftarrow \iota_4 \}\!\}$$
$$\theta_{\alpha \to \alpha, \iota_4} = \{\!\{ \iota_1 \leftarrow \iota_4, \iota_2 \leftarrow \iota_5 \}\!\}$$

Figure A.6 illustrates the importance of the bijectivity properties and of the alias conditions. Indeed, the alias condition (3) is verified neither between Q and Q' nor between Q_0 and Q'. Concerning the second definition, in Q' every renaming is bijective but, to prove equivalence, one would need to have $\theta_{\beta \to \alpha, \iota} = \{\!\{ \iota_1 \leftarrow \iota, \iota_2 \leftarrow \iota_2' \}\!\}$ and $\theta_{\beta \to \alpha, \iota'} = \{\!\{ \iota_1 \leftarrow \iota', \iota_2 \leftarrow \iota_2' \}\!\}$ which would contradict the fact that $codom(\theta_{\beta \to \alpha, \iota})$ and $codom(\theta_{\beta \to \alpha, \iota'})$ are disjuncts.

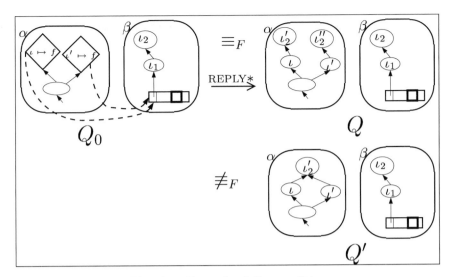

Fig. A.6. Example of alias condition

B

Confluence Proofs

This appendix proves the confluence theorem of Sect. 8 (Theorem 8.10). After some notation and preliminary lemmas, we focus on a simpler local confluence property and finally Sect. B.5 generalizes this local confluence in order to prove Theorem 8.10.

B.1 Context

Let $\xrightarrow{\neg\text{REPLY}}$ consist in applying any reduction except the REPLY rule. Two configurations are said to be confluent if they can be reduced to equivalent configurations (Definition 8.9 page 118):

$$P_1 \curlyvee P_2 \Leftrightarrow \exists R_1, R_2, \begin{cases} P_1 \xrightarrow{*} R_1 \\ P_2 \xrightarrow{*} R_2 \\ R_1 \equiv_F R_2 \end{cases}$$

Let P_0 be an initial configuration. The goal of this appendix is to prove the following confluence property (which is also Theorem 8.10 of page 118):

Property B.1 (Confluence)

$$\begin{cases} P_0 \xrightarrow{*} Q \\ P_0 \xrightarrow{*} Q' \Longrightarrow Q \curlyvee Q' \\ Q \bowtie Q' \end{cases}$$

Let us consider two configurations Q and Q' obtained from the same initial one: $P_0 \xrightarrow{*} Q$, $P_0 \xrightarrow{*} Q'$. Let us suppose that the two configurations are compatible; $Q \bowtie Q'$, that is to say their RSLs have a least upper bound.

Let $\mathcal{Q}(Q, Q')$ represent the set of configurations obtained from P_0 and having requests sender lists smaller than the ones of Q or Q':

$$\mathcal{Q}(Q,Q') = \{R|P_0 \xrightarrow{*} R \wedge \forall M \in \mathcal{M}_{\alpha_{P_0}}, \forall \alpha \in R,$$
$$RSL(\alpha_R)\big|_M \trianglelefteq RSL(\alpha_Q)\big|_M \vee RSL(\alpha_R)\big|_M \trianglelefteq RSL(\alpha_{Q'})\big|_M\}$$
$$= \{R|P_0 \xrightarrow{*} R \wedge \forall \alpha \in R, RSL(\alpha_R)\big|_M \trianglelefteq \left(RSL(\alpha_Q)\big|_M \sqcup RSL(\alpha_{Q'})\big|_M\right)\}$$

The well definition of least upper bounds is a consequence of the compatibility between Q and Q'. Note that $Q, Q' \in \mathcal{Q}$; and also for all intermediate configuration between P and Q (P' such that $P \xrightarrow{*} P' \xrightarrow{*} Q$), one has $P' \in \mathcal{Q}$.

The principle of the proof is that in order to reduce terms Q and Q' to a common one, the terms derived from them will be constrained to stay inside $\mathcal{Q}$. Then completing the missing reductions from Q and Q' will lead to a common term (thus proving confluence).

B.2 Lemmas

The following lemma is a direct consequence of the definition of the set $\mathcal{Q}(Q,Q')$:

Lemma B.2 ($\mathcal{Q}$ and compatiblity)

$$\forall R, R' \in \mathcal{Q}(Q,Q'), R \bowtie R'$$

The following lemma gives simple consequences (on appending and merging of stores) of the fact that two stores are disjunct.

Lemma B.3 (Independent stores)

$$dom(\sigma_1) \cap dom(\sigma_2) = \emptyset \Rightarrow \begin{cases} \sigma_1 :: \sigma_2 = \sigma_2 + \sigma_1 \\ \sigma_1 :: \sigma_2 = \sigma_2 :: \sigma_1 \\ \sigma_1 + \sigma_2 = \sigma_2 + \sigma_1 \\ \sigma_1 + (\sigma_2 :: \sigma) = \sigma_2 :: (\sigma_1 + \sigma) \end{cases}$$

Lemma B.4 (Extensibility of local reduction)

$$(a,\sigma) \rightarrow_S (a',\sigma') \Rightarrow (a, \sigma_0 :: \sigma) \rightarrow_S (a'', \sigma_0 :: \sigma'') \text{ where } (a'',\sigma'') \equiv_F (a',\sigma')$$

Proof: This lemma is trivially proved by checking it on each sequential reduction rule. □

Note that we consider configurations where all the futures and the active objects of σ, σ_0, and σ' are well defined (it is necessary for $\equiv_F$ to be well defined). That is to say, all stores and expressions are parts of a well-formed parallel configuration (this will always be the case when we use this lemma).

Lemma B.5 (copy and locations)

$$dom(copy(\iota,\sigma)) \subseteq dom(\sigma)$$

Proof: Direct consequence of the definition of the deep copy. $\square$

Lemma B.6 (Multiple copies)

$$\iota \in dom(copy(\iota',\sigma')) \;\Rightarrow\; (copy(\iota,\sigma) + copy(\iota',\sigma') = copy(\iota',copy(\iota,\sigma) + \sigma'))$$

Proof: This proof will only focus on verifying the domain of the deep copy. The content of the store follows the same arguments but needs some properties on the update (+) of two stores that are not presented in this book.

Let us consider $\iota_0 \in copy(\iota,\sigma) + copy(\iota',\sigma')$. The following property is trivially verified:

$$\sigma \subseteq \sigma' \Rightarrow dom(copy(\iota,\sigma)) \subseteq dom(copy(\iota,\sigma')) \tag{12}$$

Thus if $\iota_0 \in copy(\iota',\sigma')$ then $\iota_0 \in copy(\iota',copy(\iota,\sigma) + \sigma')$.

Else $\iota_0 \in copy(\iota,\sigma)$ and we prove $\iota_0 \in copy(\iota',copy(\iota,\sigma)+\sigma')$ by recurrence on the length of the path necessary to reach ι_0. This length is the number of times the second rule defining the domain of the deep copy (Table 6.1 page 90) must be applied to infer that $\iota_0 \in copy(\iota,\sigma)$.

- either $\iota_0 = \iota$ so that $\iota_0 \in dom(copy(\iota',\sigma'))$ by hypothesis and $\iota_0 \in dom(copy(\iota',copy(\iota,\sigma) + \sigma'))$ because of (12);
- else $\iota_1 \in dom(copy(\iota,\sigma)) \wedge \iota_0 \in locs(\sigma(\iota_1))$ and by the recurrence hypothesis $\iota_1 \in dom(copy(\iota',copy(\iota,\sigma) + \sigma'))$:

$$\sigma(\iota_1) = (copy(\iota,\sigma) + \sigma')(\iota_1) \qquad \text{because } \iota_1 \in dom(copy(\iota,\sigma))$$

Then $\iota_0 \in locs\,((copy(\iota,\sigma) + \sigma')(\iota_1)) = locs(\sigma(\iota_1))$. Finally, the second rule defining the domain of the deep copy applied to $copy(\iota',copy(\iota,\sigma)+\sigma')$ ensures that:

$$\left\{\begin{array}{l} \iota_1 \in copy(\iota',copy(\iota,\sigma) + \sigma') \\ \iota_0 \in locs\,((copy(\iota,\sigma) + \sigma')(\iota_1)) \end{array}\right. \Rightarrow \iota_0 \in dom(copy(\iota',copy(\iota,\sigma) + \sigma'))$$

which is the recurrence hypothesis for ι_0.

We proved that:

$$copy(\iota,\sigma) + copy(\iota',\sigma') \subseteq copy(\iota',copy(\iota,\sigma) + \sigma')$$

The other inclusion (which is more natural) is a little easier to prove but still necessitates a recurrence proof. $\square$

Lemma B.7 (Copy and store update)

$$\sigma' + Copy\&Merge(\sigma_1,\iota \;;\; \sigma_2,\iota') \equiv_F Copy\&Merge(\sigma_1,\iota \;;\; \sigma' + \sigma_2,\iota')$$
$$if \; \left\{\begin{array}{l} dom(\sigma') \cap dom(Copy\&Merge(\sigma_1,\iota \;;\; \sigma_2,\iota')) \subseteq dom(\sigma_2) \\ \iota' \notin dom(\sigma') \end{array}\right.$$

This lemma is a direct consequence of the definition of the *Merge* operator: on the right side of the equality, the only location that can belong to both the initial and the merged store is ι' (Property 6.2). Thus if $\iota' \notin dom(\sigma')$ the two stores σ' and $Copy\&Merge(\sigma_1, \iota \; ; \; \sigma_2, \iota')$ define disjunct locations (but their codomain can be interleaved). Moreover, σ' and the merged store (taken from σ_1) are disjuncts by hypothesis; thus the presence of the store σ' has no influence on $Copy\&Merge(\sigma_1, \iota \; ; \; \sigma_2, \iota')$: σ' can be seen as an independent part of σ_2.

In fact we can choose conveniently created locations and only have to verify $\iota' \notin dom(\sigma')$. That is due to the fact that configurations can be identified modulo renaming of locations:

Corollary B.8 (Copy and store update) *If $\iota' \notin dom(\sigma')$ then there is a way of choosing locations allocated by $Copy\&Merge(\sigma_1, \iota \; ; \; \sigma_2, \iota')$ such that:*

$$\sigma' + Copy\&Merge(\sigma_1, \iota \; ; \; \sigma_2, \iota') \equiv_F Copy\&Merge(\sigma_1, \iota \; ; \; \sigma' + \sigma_2, \iota')$$

B.3 Local Confluence

This section presents and proves what we call *local confluence*: that is, a classical confluence property starting from a given term and performing two concurrent reductions; it is necessary to establish the confluence properties of Chap. 8. This property is strongly based on the definition of compatibility between configurations ($\bowtie$) because of use of the set $\mathcal{Q}$.

Property B.9 (Diamond property)
Let P be a configuration obtained from P_0: $P_0 \xrightarrow{\ *\ } P$:

$$\begin{cases} P \xrightarrow{T_1} P_1 \\ P \xrightarrow{T_2} P_2 \\ P, P_1, P_2 \in \mathcal{Q}(Q, Q') \end{cases} \implies P_1 \equiv_F P_2 \vee \exists P_1', P_2', \begin{cases} P_1 \xrightarrow{T_2} P_1' \\ P_2 \xrightarrow{T_1} P_2' \\ P_1' \equiv_F P_2' \\ P_1', P_2' \in \mathcal{Q}(Q, Q') \end{cases}$$

Proof: This proof is a (long) case study on the conflict (concurrency) between rules. Cases where one of the applied rules is REPLY will not be detailed. These cases can be verified but are not useful for the proof of the Property B.12. Indeed, for the REPLY rule we only need to use Property A.17. However, conflicts between REPLY and other rules are detailed (under other hypotheses) in [86].

This analysis is only interesting when there is a real conflict between two rules. That is to say, at least a component of one activity can be read or modified by two rules. This definition of conflict between rules follows the definition of concurrency (Definition 1.2). The following cases are labeled with the two rules in conflict.

Recall that we can suppose that one can choose any location or future name when one needs a fresh one. The fact that activities are chosen deterministically avoids the problem of renaming activities and ensures that the name of an activity will be the same for two applications of the same NEWACT rule.

In the following, if the conflicting rules are different, the activities (α, β) will be indexed by the corresponding rule (e.g., α_{REQUEST} is the activity α of the REQUEST rule: the source activity of the request). If the rules are the same, the activities will be indexed by 1 and 2.

The proof can be divided into four parts. Except for concurrent request sending part, the fact that $P_1', P_2' \in \mathcal{Q}(Q, Q')$ is straightforward as the RSL of P_1' and P_2' are either the ones of P_1 or the ones of P_2.

B.3.1 Local vs. Parallel Reduction

LOCAL/LOCAL

Obvious consequence of the determinism of local reduction.

LOCAL/NEWACT

No conflict: $\alpha_{\text{LOCAL}} = \alpha_{\text{NEWACT}}$ impossible because $\mathcal{R}[Active(\iota, m)]$ cannot be reduced locally.

LOCAL/REQUEST

$\alpha_{\text{LOCAL}} = \alpha_{\text{REQUEST}}$ impossible (this would correspond to a method call which would be both local and distant).

$\alpha_{\text{LOCAL}} = \beta_{\text{REQUEST}}$; let $\alpha = \alpha_{\text{REQUEST}}$ and $\beta = \alpha_{\text{LOCAL}} = \beta_{\text{REQUEST}}$.

LOCAL:

$$\frac{(a_\beta, \sigma_\beta) \rightarrow_S (a_{\beta 1}, \sigma_{\beta 1})}{\beta[a_\beta; \sigma_\beta; \iota_\beta; F_\beta; R_\beta; f_\beta] \| Q \longrightarrow \beta[a_{\beta 1}; \sigma_{\beta 1}; \iota_\beta; F_\beta; R_\beta; f_\beta] \| Q = P_1}$$

REQUEST:

$$\frac{\sigma_\alpha(\iota) = AO(\beta) \quad \iota'' \notin dom(\sigma_\beta) \quad f_i^{\alpha \rightarrow \beta} \text{ new future} \quad \iota_f \notin dom(\sigma_\alpha)}{\sigma_{\beta 2} = Copy\&Merge(\sigma_\alpha, \iota' \; ; \; \sigma_\beta, \iota'') \quad \sigma_{\alpha 2} = \{\iota_f \mapsto fut(f_i^{\alpha \rightarrow \beta})\} :: \sigma_\alpha}$$

$$\frac{}{\alpha[\mathcal{R}[\iota.m_j(\iota')]; \sigma_\alpha; \iota_\alpha; F_\alpha; R_\alpha; f_\alpha] \| \beta[a_\beta; \sigma_\beta; \iota_\beta; F_\beta; R_\beta; f_\beta] \| Q \longrightarrow}$$
$$\alpha[\mathcal{R}[\iota_f]; \sigma_{\alpha 2}; \iota_\alpha; F_\alpha; R_\alpha; f_\alpha] \| \beta[a_\beta; \sigma_{\beta 2}; \iota_\beta; F_\beta; R_\beta :: [m_j; \iota''; f_i^{\alpha \rightarrow \beta}]; f_\beta] \| Q = P_2$$

Let us first perform the local reduction on P_2. One can suppose (up to renaming) that the locations added to σ_β by the two rules are disjuncts. The deep copy of the argument of the request is added in an independent store; thus $\sigma_{\beta 2} = \sigma :: \sigma_\beta$. Thus Lemma B.4 allows us to perform the local reduction on the extended store:

$$(a_\beta, \sigma_\beta) \to_S (a_{\beta 1}, \sigma_{\beta 1}) \Rightarrow (a_\beta, \sigma :: \sigma_\beta) \to_S (a'_{\beta 2}, \sigma :: \sigma'_{\beta 2})$$

where $(a'_{\beta 2}, \sigma'_{\beta 2}) \equiv (a_{\beta 1}, \sigma_{\beta 1})$ and $(a'_{\beta 2}, \sigma :: \sigma'_{\beta 2}) \equiv (a_{\beta 1}, \sigma :: \sigma_{\beta 1})$. Finally:

$$P_2 = \alpha[\mathcal{R}[\iota_f]; \sigma_{\alpha 2}; \iota_\alpha; F_\alpha; R_\alpha; f_\alpha] \| \beta[a_\beta; \sigma_{\beta 2}; \iota_\beta; F_\beta; R_{\beta 2}; f_\beta] \| Q$$
$$\longrightarrow \alpha[\mathcal{R}[\iota_f]; \sigma_{\alpha 2}; \iota_\alpha; F_\alpha; R_\alpha; f_\alpha] \| \beta[a'_{\beta 2}; \sigma'_{\beta 2} :: \sigma; \iota_\beta; F_\beta; R_{\beta 2}; f_\beta] \| Q = P'_2$$

Now we will focus on the application of the request rule to P_1 and consider that $\sigma_{\beta 1}$ is obtained by some updates on σ_β (indeed every action of a local rule on the store can be written as a store update):

$$\sigma_{\beta 1} = \sigma_0 + \sigma_\beta$$

Corollary B.8 is used for adding the request to the store obtained by local reduction. One can apply the request rule to P_1. Let $\sigma'_{\beta 1}$ be the new store:

$$\sigma'_{\beta 1} = Copy\&Merge(\sigma_\alpha, \iota' \; ; \; \sigma_{\beta 1}, \iota'') \equiv_F \sigma_0 + Copy\&Merge(\sigma_\alpha, \iota' \; ; \; \sigma_\beta, \iota'')$$
$$= \sigma_0 + \sigma_{\beta 2} \qquad (13)$$

and obtain a configuration equivalent to P'_2 by Lemma B.3. More precisely:

$$(a'_{\beta 2}; \sigma :: \sigma'_{\beta 2}) \equiv_F (a_{\beta 1}, \sigma :: \sigma_{\beta 1})$$
$$\equiv_F (a_{\beta 1}, \sigma :: (\sigma_0 + \sigma_\beta))$$
$$\equiv_F (a_{\beta 1}, \sigma_0 + (\sigma :: \sigma_\beta))$$
$$\equiv_F (a_{\beta 1}, \sigma'_{\beta 1}) \qquad \text{by (13)}$$

LOCAL/ENDSERVICE

No conflict because a location ι cannot be reduced.

LOCAL/SERVE

No conflict.

B.3.2 Creating an Activity

NEWACT/NEWACT

No conflict.

NEWACT/REQUEST

One only has to prove that (if $\alpha_{\text{NEWACT}} = \beta_{\text{REQUEST}}$) creating a new activity does not interfere with receiving a request. This is similar to the case LOCAL/REQUEST.

NEWACT/ENDSERVICE

No conflict.

NEWACT/SERVE

No conflict.

B.3.3 Localized Operations (SERVE, ENDSERVICE)

● SERVE:

SERVE/SERVE

No conflict

SERVE/REQUEST

The only conflicting case occurs when $\alpha_{\text{SERVE}} = \beta_{\text{REQUEST}}$. Informally, if one can perform a $serve(M)$ on P then there is a request matching the labels of M in the request queue; so adding a new request to the request queue will not change the served one because SERVE takes the *first* request matching M. Figure B.1 illustrates this case (we consider that this figure is sufficiently explicit to avoid us giving the technical details of the proof), we suppose in this figure that $m_j \in M$.

Note that the fact that the first request is taken is essential to ensure confluence. A more complicated service primitive (like serving the last request that arrived) would require further studies and would probably not verify confluence properties. But a service of the form $serve(\alpha)$ serving the *first request coming from the activity* α does not produce any difficulty here (see Sect. B.4).

● ENDSERVICE:

ENDSERVICE/ENDSERVICE

No conflict.

REQUEST/ENDSERVICE

There can only be a conflict when $\alpha_{\text{ENDSERVICE}} = \beta_{\text{REQUEST}} = \beta$. The principle of the proof concerning this case is shown in Fig. B.2.

REQUEST:

$$\frac{\sigma_\alpha(\iota) = AO(\beta) \quad \iota'' \notin dom(\sigma_\beta) \quad f_i^{\alpha \to \beta} \text{ new future} \quad \iota_f \notin dom(\sigma_\alpha)}{\sigma_{\beta 1} = Copy\&Merge(\sigma_\alpha, \iota' \; ; \; \sigma_\beta, \iota'') = \sigma + \sigma_\beta \quad \sigma_{\alpha 1} = \{\iota_f \mapsto fut(f_i^{\alpha \to \beta})\} :: \sigma_\alpha}$$

$$\begin{array}{l} \alpha[\mathcal{R}[\iota.m_j(\iota')]; \sigma_\alpha; \iota_\alpha; F_\alpha; R_\alpha; f_\alpha] \| \beta[a_\beta; \sigma_\beta; \iota_\beta; F_\beta; R_\beta; f_\beta] \| Q \\ \longrightarrow \alpha[\mathcal{R}[\iota_f]; \sigma_{\alpha 1}; \iota_\alpha; F_\alpha; R_\alpha; f_\alpha] \| \beta[a_\beta; \sigma_{\beta 1}; \iota_\beta; F_\beta; R_\beta :: [m_j; \iota''; f_i^{\alpha \to \beta}]; f_\beta] \| Q = P_1' \end{array}$$

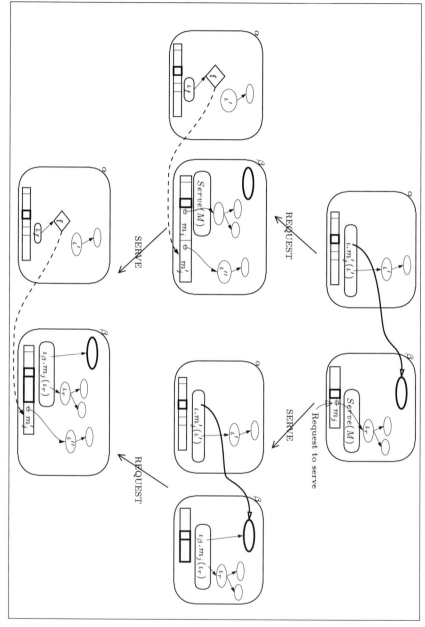

Fig. B.1. SERVE/REQUEST

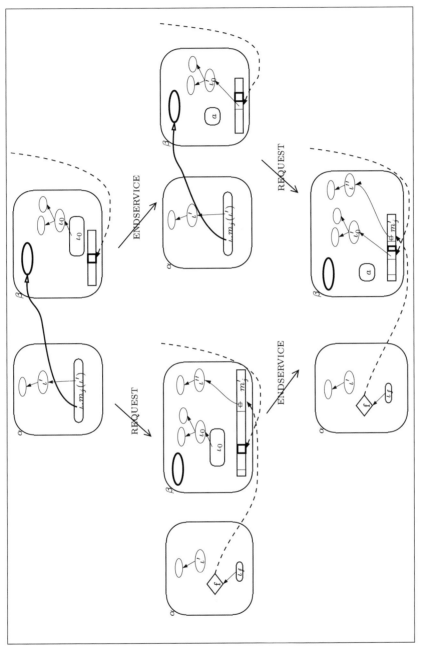

Fig. B.2. ENDSERVICE/REQUEST

ENDSERVICE:

$$\frac{\iota'_0 \notin dom(\sigma_\beta) \quad F'_\beta = F_\beta :: \{f_\beta \mapsto \iota'\}}{\sigma_{\beta 2} = Copy\&Merge(\sigma_\beta, \iota_0 \; ; \; \sigma_\beta, \iota'_0) = \sigma' + \sigma_\beta}$$

$$\overline{\beta[\iota_0 \Uparrow f_i^{\delta \to \beta}, a; \sigma_\beta; \iota_\beta; F_\beta; R_\beta; f_\beta]\|\|P \longrightarrow \beta[a; \sigma_{\beta 2}; \iota_\beta; F'_\beta; R_\beta; f_i^{\delta \to \beta}]\|\|P = P'_2}$$

The conflict only concerns the store. But the merges that are performed on the store are independent ($\iota'' \notin dom(\sigma_\beta)$); and we can suppose that these two operations create disjuncts sets of locations. Then one can perform the missing rule on each configuration: P'_1 and P'_2. A configuration with the following stores is obtained (modulo renaming, the same stores updates as in the first two rules can be performed):

$$\sigma'_{\beta 2} \equiv_F \sigma + \sigma_{\beta 2} \qquad \text{and} \qquad \sigma' + \sigma_{\beta 1} \equiv_F \sigma'_{\beta 1}$$

The proof is not completely detailed here but the crucial point of the proof consists in the following equality:

$$\begin{aligned}
\sigma'_{\beta 2} &\equiv_F \sigma + \sigma_{\beta 2} \\
&= \sigma + \sigma' + \sigma_\beta \\
&= \sigma' + \sigma + \sigma_\beta \quad \text{Lemma B.3} \\
&= \sigma' + \sigma_{\beta 1} \\
&\equiv_F \sigma'_{\beta 1}
\end{aligned}$$

ENDSERVICE/SERVE

No conflict.

B.3.4 Concurrent Request Sending: REQUEST/REQUEST

$\alpha_1 = \beta_2$ or $\beta_1 = \alpha_2$ Same kind of argument as in the case LOCAL/REQUEST with $\alpha_{\text{LOCAL}} = \beta_{\text{REQUEST}}$.

$\alpha_1 = \alpha_2$ No conflict.

$\beta_1 = \beta_2$ As $P_1, P_2 \in Q$, if $\beta_1 = \beta_2$, then (RSL compatibility) either the two requests come from the same activity, $\alpha_1 = \alpha_2$, and there is no conflict or the two requests m_1 and m_2 cannot interfere: $\nexists M \in \mathcal{M}_{\alpha_{P_0}}$ such that $\{m_1, m_2\} \subseteq M$. In that second case, adding requests in any order leads to equivalent configurations due to the equivalence rule for pending requests. Let P'_1 be the configuration obtained from P_1 by sending the missing request from α_2; and P'_2 the configuration obtained from P_2 by sending the missing request from α_1. The crucial point is to show that the RSL are compatible, let $m_1 \in M_1$ and $m_2 \in M_2$ (M_1 and M_2 are not unique but belong to disjoint sets):

$$RSL(\alpha_{P'_1})\big|_{M_1} = RSL(\alpha_{P_1})\big|_{M_1} = RSL(\alpha_{P'_2})\big|_{M_1} \trianglelefteq RSL(\alpha_Q)\big|_{M_1} \sqcup RSL(\alpha_{Q'})\big|_{M_1}$$

$$RSL(\alpha_{P_1'})\big|_{M_2} = RSL(\alpha_{P_2})\big|_{M_2} = RSL(\alpha_{P_2'})\big|_{M_2} \lhd RSL(\alpha_Q)\big|_{M_2} \sqcup RSL(\alpha_{Q'})\big|_{M_2}$$

And finally, $P_1', P_2' \in \mathcal{Q}(Q, Q')$, and RSLs are compatible.

The proof of $P_1' \equiv_F P_2'$ applies the same arguments to pending requests instead of RSLs. $\square$

Note that the preceding proof widely uses (indirectly) the following facts:

- the isolation of those parts of the store containing the request arguments and the future values (Property 7.3),
- the RSL and configurations compatibility through the set $\mathcal{Q}$ (Definitions 8.3 and 8.4), and of course
- the definition and properties of the equivalence modulo future updates (Sect. 8.2 and Appendix A).

B.4 Calculus with service based on activity name: $Serve(\alpha)$

This section shows the consequences of replacing the service primitive determined by the method label ($Serve(M)$) by a service primitive determined by the source activity of requests ($Serve(\alpha)$).

In this case, requests can be safely exchanged as soon as they do not come from the same activity. As a consequence, no compatibility relation is necessary. The equivalence modulo future updates on requests queues uses the restriction of the request queue to those requests having a given source activity. That is to say the first rule of Table A.1 is replaced by the following:

$$\frac{\alpha \neq \beta}{\begin{array}{l} R_1 :: [m_1; \iota_1; fut(f_i^{\alpha \to \gamma})] :: [m_2; \iota_2; fut(f_j^{\beta \to \gamma})] :: R_2 \\ \equiv_R R_1 :: [m_2; \iota_2; fut(f_j^{\beta \to \gamma})] :: [m_1; \iota_1; fut(f_i^{\alpha \to \gamma})] :: R_2 \end{array}}$$

Note that this new equivalence relation also verifies:

$$P \equiv_F P' \wedge P \xrightarrow{\text{SERVE}} Q \Rightarrow \exists Q',\ P' \xrightarrow{\text{SERVE}} Q' \wedge Q' \equiv_F Q$$

because for any $Serve(\beta)$ performed by α, the equivalence modulo future updates ensure that the first request from β is the same (modulo the application of some REPLY rules) in P and P'.

Then, there can be a conflict in the concurrent request sending for $\beta_1 = \beta_2 \wedge \alpha_1 \neq \alpha_2$. But this conflict has no consequence because once the missing request sending is performed, we trivially obtain equivalent configurations. The request queues are of the form:

$$R_1' = R :: r1 :: r2 \qquad\qquad R_2' = R :: r2 :: r1$$

with r_1 and r_2 coming from different activities, which is sufficient for the equivalence of request queues defined above.

To sum up, confluence comes from the facts that

- Two requests coming from the same activity cannot overtake each other and this is sufficient to ensure equivalence modulo future updates.
- Even with such an imprecise equivalence relation, the request served by a $Serve(\alpha)$ primitive is the same for two equivalent terms.

B.5 Extension

This section extends the local diamond property presented earlier to obtain a general diamond property which will allow us to conclude on the confluence of ASP calculus.

Lemma B.10 ($\equiv_F$ and $\mathcal{Q}(Q, Q')$)
If P is in Q and P is equivalent modulo future updates to P' then P' is in Q:

$$P \equiv_F P' \wedge P \in \mathcal{Q}(Q, Q') \wedge P_0 \stackrel{*}{\longrightarrow} P' \Rightarrow P' \in \mathcal{Q}(Q, Q')$$

Proof: Direct consequence of equivalence definition:
$\forall M \in \mathcal{M}_{\alpha_{P_0}}, R_P\big|_M \equiv_F R_{P'}\big|_M.$ □

Lemma B.11 (REPLY vs. other reduction)

$$P \stackrel{\neg REPLY}{\longrightarrow} R \wedge P \stackrel{REPLY}{\longrightarrow} P' \Rightarrow P' \stackrel{\neg REPLY}{\longrightarrow} R' \wedge R' \equiv_F R$$

Proof: This lemma could be considered as strongly linked to the Property A.19, but Property A.19 would ensure that there is an R' such that $P' \stackrel{REPLY*}{\longrightarrow} \stackrel{\neg REPLY}{\longrightarrow} R'$ which is not sufficient to conclude.

In this particular case, it is easy to verify that if a rule (different from REPLY) can be applied on P then it can be applied on P' and the second part of the proof of Property A.19 is sufficient to conclude for Lemma B.11. □

Then, global confluence is a consequence of local confluence. The following property is a generalized local confluence:

Property B.12 (Diamond property with $\equiv_F$)

$$\begin{cases} P_1 \stackrel{T_1}{\Longrightarrow} Q_1 \\ P_2 \stackrel{T_2}{\Longrightarrow} Q_2 \\ Q_1, Q_2 \in \mathcal{Q}(Q, Q') \\ P_1 \equiv_F P_2 \end{cases} \Longrightarrow Q_1 \equiv_F Q_2 \vee \exists R_1, R_2, \begin{cases} Q_1 \stackrel{T_2}{\Longrightarrow} R_1 \\ Q_2 \stackrel{T_1}{\Longrightarrow} R_2 \\ R_1 \equiv_F R_2 \\ R_1, R_2 \in \mathcal{Q}(Q, Q') \end{cases}$$

Proof: Figure B.3 illustrates the proof detailed in the following.

If one of the $\Longrightarrow$ on the left of the implication consists only in some REPLY rules then one can conclude immediately by Corollary A.19.

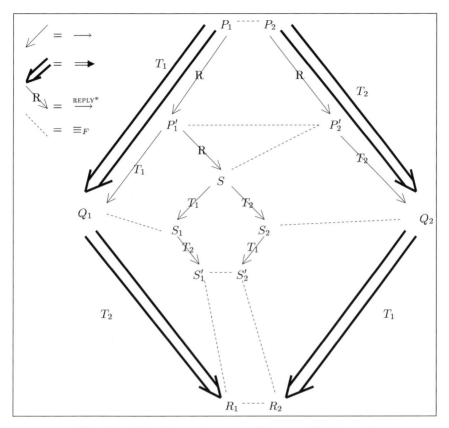

Fig. B.3. The diamond property (Property B.12) proof

Else, both T_1 and T_2 are reduction rules different from REPLY and can be decomposed: there is P_1' such that:

$$P_1 \xrightarrow{\text{REPLY*}} P_1' \xrightarrow{T_1} Q_1$$

Note that one could have $P_1 = P_1'$. In the same way, there is P_2' such that:

$$P_2 \xrightarrow{\text{REPLY*}} P_2' \xrightarrow{T_2} Q_2$$

By Property A.6, $\equiv_F$ is transitive and then $P_1' \equiv_F P_2'$. By Corollary A.20:

$$\exists S_2, \ P_1' \overset{T_2}{\Longrightarrow} S_2 \wedge S_2 \equiv_F Q_2$$

Thus there is a configuration S such that:

$$P_1' \xrightarrow{\text{REPLY*}} S \wedge S \xrightarrow{T_2} S_2 \wedge S_2 \equiv_F Q_2$$

Moreover, by Lemma B.11:

$$
\begin{cases} P_1' \xrightarrow{\text{REPLY*}} S \\ P_1' \xrightarrow{T_1} Q_1 \end{cases} \Rightarrow \begin{cases} S \xrightarrow{T_1} S_1 \\ S_1 \equiv_F Q_1 \end{cases}
$$

Then, using diamond Property B.9 (Lemma B.10 ensures $S_1, S_2 \in \mathcal{Q}$):

$$
\begin{cases} S \xrightarrow{T_1} S_1 \\ S \xrightarrow{T_2} S_2 \\ S_1, S_2 \in \mathcal{Q} \end{cases} \Longrightarrow S_1 \equiv_F S_2 \vee \exists R_1, R_2, \begin{cases} S_1 \xrightarrow{T_2} S_1' \\ S_2 \xrightarrow{T_1} S_2' \\ S_1' \equiv_F S_2' \\ S_1', S_2' \in \mathcal{Q} \end{cases}
$$

Finally, using Property A.19:

$$
S_1 \xrightarrow{T_2} S_1' \wedge S_1 \equiv_F Q_1 \Rightarrow Q_1 \xRightarrow{T_2} R_1 \wedge S_1' \equiv_F R_1
$$

$$
S_2 \xrightarrow{T_1} S_2' \wedge S_2 \equiv_F Q_2 \Rightarrow Q_2 \xRightarrow{T_1} R_2 \wedge S_2' \equiv_F R_2
$$

Note that $R_1 \equiv_F R_2$ and $R_1, R_2 \in \mathcal{Q}$ are trivially obtained and finally:

$$
\begin{cases} Q_1 \Longrightarrow R_1 & \wedge & Q_2 \Longrightarrow R_2 \\ R_1 \equiv_F R_2 & \wedge & R_1, R_2 \in \mathcal{Q} \end{cases}
$$

$\square$

Proving confluence from Property B.12 is a classical result sometimes known as "local confluence $\Rightarrow$ confluence" and will not be detailed here. Note that this proof also relies on the fact that all intermediate configurations between P_0 and Q, and between P_0 and Q' in Property B.1 belong to $\mathcal{Q}$.

References

1. Martín Abadi and Luca Cardelli. An imperative object calculus. In P. D. Mosses, M. Nielsen, and M. I. Schwartzbach, editors, *TAPSOFT '95: Theory and Practice of Software Development*, volume 915 of LNCS, pages 471–485. Springer-Verlag, Berlin, Heidelberg, 1995.
2. Martín Abadi and Luca Cardelli. An imperative object calculus: Basic typing and soundness. In *SIPL '95 – Proceedings of the Second ACM SIGPLAN Workshop on State in Programming Languages*. Technical Report UIUCDCS-R-95-1900, Department of Computer Science, University of Illinois at Urbana–Champaign, 1995.
3. Martín Abadi and Luca Cardelli. *A Theory of Objects*. Springer-Verlag, New York, 1996.
4. A Theory of Objects web page. Available at `http://www.luca.demon.co.uk/TheoryOfObjects.html`, and related courses at `http://www.luca.demon.co.uk/TheoryOfObjects/RelatedCourses.html`.
5. Anurag Acharya, M. Ranganathan, and Joel Saltz. Sumatra: A language for resource-aware mobile programs. In J. Vitek and C. Tschudin, editors, *Mobile Object Systems: Towards the Programmable Internet*, volume 1222, pages 111–130. Springer-Verlag, Berlin, Heidelberg, 1997.
6. ACM SIGACT-SIGPLAN. *Conference Record of the 22nd ACM SIGACT-SIGPLAN Symposium on Principles of Programming Languages (POPL'95)*, San Francisco, January 22–25, 1995. ACM Press, New York.
7. ACM SIGACT-SIGPLAN. *Conference Record of the 23rd ACM SIGACT-SIGPLAN Symposium on Principles of Programming Languages (POPL'96)*, St. Petersburg, Florida, January 21–24, 1996. ACM Press.
8. Actor foundry. Available at `http://osl.cs.uiuc.edu/foundry/`.
9. Gul Agha. An overview of actor languages. *ACM SIGPLAN Notices*, 21(10):58–67, 1986.
10. Gul Agha, Ian A. Mason, Scott F. Smith, and Carolyn L. Talcott. Towards a theory of actor computation (extended abstract). In W. R. Cleaveland, editor, *CONCUR'92: Proceedings of the Third International Conference on Concurrency Theory*, pages 565–579. Springer-Verlag, Berlin, Heidelberg, 1992.
11. Gul Agha, Ian A. Mason, Scott F. Smith, and Carolyn L. Talcott. A foundation for actor computation. *Journal of Functional Programming*, 7(1):1–72, 1997.

12. Gul Agha and Prasanna Thati. An algebraic theory of actors and its application to a simple object-based language. In *Essays in Memory of Ole-Johan Dahl*, volume 2635, pages 26–57, 2004.

13. Paulo Sergio Almeida. Balloon types: Controlling sharing of state in data types. In Mehmet Akşit and Satoshi Matsuoka, editors, *ECOOP'97 – Object-Oriented Programming 11th European Conference, Jyvskyl, Finland*, volume 1241, pages 32–59. Springer-Verlag, New York, 1997.

14. Pierre America. Issues in the design of a parallel object-oriented language. *Formal Aspects of Computing*, 1(4):366–411, 1989.

15. Pierre America. Formal techniques for parallel object-oriented languages. In Jos C. M. Baeten and Jan Friso Groote, editors, *CONCUR'91, 2nd International Conference on Concurrency Theory, Amsterdam, The Netherlands, August 26–29, 1991, Proceedings*, volume 527 of LNCS, pages 1–17. Springer-Verlag, Berlin, Heidelberg, 1991.

16. Gregory R. Andrews. *Concurrent programming: principles and practice*. Benjamin-Cummings Publishing Co., Inc., 1991.

17. Arvind, Rishiyur S. Nikhil, and Keshav K. Pingali. I-structures: Data structures for parallel computing. *ACM Transactions on Programming Langanguages and Systems*, 11(4):598–632, 1989.

18. Isabelle Attali, Denis Caromel, and Arnaud Contes. Hierarchical and declarative security for grid applications. In *International Conference on High Performance Computing, HIPC, Hyderabad, India, December 17–20*, LNCS, pages 363–372, Springer-Verlag, Berlin, Heidelberg, 2003.

19. Isabelle Attali, Denis Caromel, and Romain Guider. A step toward automatic distribution of Java programs. In S. F. Smith and C. L. Talcott, editors, *4th IFIP International Conference on Formal Methods for Open Object-Based Distributed Systems*, pages 141–161. Kluwer Academic Publishers, Dordrecht, 2000.

20. Isabelle Attali, Denis Caromel, and Fabrice Huet. Procédé de localisation d'objets mobiles communicants au sein d'un réseau de communications, par transmission d'identifiants de localisation par des répéteurs et mise à jour de serveur, 2003. Patent. Brevet déposé le 23 juillet 2003, No FR 03 08990, copropriété INRIA-Université de Nice – Sophia Antipolis, à l'INPI.

21. Laurent Baduel, Françoise Baude, and Denis Caromel. Efficient, flexible, and typed group communications in Java. In *Joint ACM Java Grande – ISCOPE 2002 Conference*, pages 28–36, Seattle, 2002. ACM Press, New York.

22. Henk P. Barendregt. *The Lambda Calculus, Its Syntax and Semantics*, volume 103 of *Studies in Logics and the Foundations of Mathematics*. North-Holland, Amsterdam, 1981.

23. Françoise Baude, Denis Caromel, Christian Delbé, and Ludovic Henrio. A fault tolerance protocol for ASP calculus: Design and proof. Research Report, INRIA Sophia-Antipolis, June 2004. RR-5246.

24. Françoise Baude, Denis Caromel, Fabrice Huet, and Julien Vayssiere. Communicating mobile active objects in Java. In *Proceedings of HPCN Europe 2000*, volume 1823 of LNCS, pages 633–643. Springer-Verlag, Berlin, Heidelberg, May 2000.

25. Françoise Baude, Denis Caromel, Lionel Mestre, Fabrice Huet, and Julien Vayssière. Interactive and descriptor-based deployment of object-oriented grid applications. In *Proceedings of the 11th IEEE International Symposium on*

High Performance Distributed Computing, pages 93–102, Edinburgh, Scotland, July 2002. IEEE Computer Society.

26. Françoise Baude, Denis Caromel, and Matthieu Morel. From distributed objects to hierarchical grid components. In *International Symposium on Distributed Objects and Applications (DOA), Catania, Sicily, Italy, 3–7 November*, LNCS. Springer Verlag, Berlin, Heidelberg, 2003.

27. Joachim Baumann, Fritz Hohl, and Kurt Rothermel. Mole – concepts of a mobile agent system. Technical Report TR-1997-15, 1997.

28. Nick Benton, Luca Cardelli, and Cédric Fournet. Modern concurrency abstractions for C#. In *Proceedings of the 16th European Conference on Object-Oriented Programming*, pages 415–440. Springer-Verlag, Berlin, Heidelberg, 2002.

29. Gérard Berry. Real time programming: Special purpose or general purpose languages. In G. X. Ritter, editor, *Information Processing 89*. Elsevier Science, Amsterdam, 1989.

30. Gérard Berry and Georges Gonthier. The Esterel synchronous programming language: Design, semantics, implementation. *Science of Computer Programming*, 19(2):87–152, 1992.

31. Philippe Bidinger and Jean-Bernard Stefani. The kell calculus: operational semantics and type system. In *Proceedings 6th IFIP International Conference on Formal Methods for Open Object-based Distributed Systems (FMOODS 03)*, Paris, France, November 2003.

32. Andrew Birrell, Greg Nelson, Susan Owicki, and Edward Wobber. Network objects. *Software – Practice and Experience*, 25(S4):87–130, 1995.

33. R. Blumofe, C. Joerg, B. Kuszmaul, C. Leiserson, K. Randall, and Y. Zhou. Cilk: An efficient multithreaded runtime system. In *Proceedings of the 5th Symposium on Principles and Practice of Parallel Programming*, 1995.

34. Phillip Bogle and Barbara Liskov. Reducing cross-domain call overhead using batched futures. In *Proceedings of OOPSLA '94*, pages 341–359. ACM Press, New York, 1994.

35. Gérard Boudol. Asynchrony and the π-calculus (note). Rapport de Recherche 1702, INRIA Sophia-Antipolis, May 1992.

36. Gérard Boudol. The recursive record semantics of objects revisited. In *Proceedings of the 10th European Symposium on Programming Languages and Systems*, pages 269–283. Springer-Verlag, Berlin, Heidelberg, 2001.

37. Rabéa Boulifa and Eric Madelaine. Proof of behaviour properties for proactive programs. Technical Report RR-4460, INRIA, France, 2002. Available at ftp://ftp-sop.inria.fr/pub/rapports/RR-4460.ps.gz.

38. Rabéa Boulifa and Eric Madelaine. Model generation for distributed Java programs. In N. Guelfi, E. Astesiano, and G. Reggio, editors, *Workshop on scientiFic engIneering of Distributed Java applIcations*, volume 2652 of LNCS, Luxembourg, november 2003. Springer-Verlag, Berlin, Heidelberg.

39. Jonathan Bowen's web page on Concurrent Systems. London South Bank University, Centre for Applied Formal Methods. Available at `http://www.jpbowen.com/`, and `http://vl.fmnet.info/concurrent/`.

40. Chandrasekhar Boyapati, Robert Lee, and Martin Rinard. Ownership types for safe programming: Preventing data races and deadlocks. In *Object-Oriented Programming, Systems, Languages, and Applications (OOPSLA)*, November 2002.

41. Sébastien Briais and Uwe Nestmann. Mobile objects "must" move safely. In *Formal Methods for Open Object-Based Distributed Systems IV – Proceedings of FMOODS'2002, University of Twente, the Netherlands.* Kluwer Academic Publishers, 2002.

42. Kim B. Bruce, Angela Schuett, and Robert van Gent. PolyTOIL: A type-safe polymorphic object-oriented language. In Walter G. Olthoff, editor, *Proceedings of ECOOP'95*, volume 952 of LNCS, pages 27–51. Springer-Verlag, Berlin, Heidelberg", 1995.

43. Roberto Bruni, Losé Meseguer, and Ugo Montanari. Symmetric monoidal and cartesian double categories as a semantic framework for tile logic. *Mathematical Structures in Computer Science*, 12(1):53–90, 2002.

44. A. P. W. Bhm, David C. Cann, R. R. Oldehoeft, and John T. Feo. SISAL reference manual language version 2.0. CS 91-118, Colorado State University, Fort Collins, Colorado, 1991.

45. Luca Cardelli. A language with distributed scope. In *Conference Record of the 22nd ACM SIGACT-SIGPLAN Symposium on Principles of Programming Languages (POPL'95)* [6], pages 286–297.

46. Luca Cardelli and Andrew D. Gordon. Types for mobile ambients. In *Proceedings of POPL'99*, pages 79–92. ACM Press, New York, 1999.

47. Luca Cardelli and Andrew D. Gordon. Mobile ambients. *Theoretical Computer Science*, 240(1):177–213, 2000. An extended abstract appeared in *Proceedings of FoSSaCS '98*, pages 140–155.

48. Denis Caromel. Programming abstractions for concurrent programming. In *Technology of Object-Oriented Languages and Systems, TOOLS Pacific'90*, pages 245–253, 1990.

49. Denis Caromel. Toward a method of object-oriented concurrent programming. *Communications of the ACM*, 36(9):90–102, September 1993.

50. Denis Caromel, Christian Delb, Ludovic Henrio, and Romain Quilici. Patent "Dispositif et procédé asynchrones et automatiques de transmission de résultats entre objets communicants", November 2003. 11/26/2003, No FR 03 138 76.

51. Denis Caromel, Ludovic Henrio, and Bernard Serpette. Asynchronous sequential processes. Research Report, INRIA Sophia-Antipolis, 2003. RR-4753.

52. Denis Caromel, Ludovic Henrio, and Bernard Paul Serpette. Asynchronous and deterministic objects. In *Proceedings of the 31st ACM SIGACT-SIGPLAN symposium on Principles of programming languages*, pages 123–134. ACM Press, 2004.

53. Denis Caromel, Wilfried Klauser, and Julien Vayssière. Towards seamless computing and metacomputing in Java. *Concurrency: Practice and Experience*, 10(11–13):1043–1061, 1998. ProActive available at **http://www.inria.fr/oasis/proactive**.

54. Franck Cassez and Olivier Roux. Compilation of the Electre reactive language into finite transition systems. *Theoretical Computer Science*, 146(1–2):109–143, july 1995.

55. B. Charron-Bost, F. Mattern, and G. Tel. Synchronous, asynchronous, and causally ordered communications. *Distributed Computing*, 9:173–191, September 1996.

56. David G. Clarke, James Noble, and John Potter. Simple ownership types for object containment. In *Proceedings of the 15th European Conference on Object-Oriented Programming*, pages 53–76. Springer-Verlag, Berlin, Heidelberg, 2001.

57. David G. Clarke, John M. Potter, and James Noble. Ownership types for flexible alias protection. In *Proceedings of the 13th ACM SIGPLAN conference on Object-Oriented Programming, Systems, Languages, and Applications*, pages 48–64. ACM Press, New York, 1998.

58. Aramira Corporation. Jumping beans, 1999. http://www.jumpingbeans.com/.

59. Pasqua D'Ambra, Marco Danelutto, Daniela di Serafino, and Marco Lapegna. Advanced environments for parallel and distributed applications: a view of current status. *Parallel Comput.*, 28(12):1637–1662, 2002.

60. Alain Deutsch. Interprocedural may-alias analysis for pointers: Beyond *k*-limiting. In *PLDI'94 Conference on Programming Language Design and Implementation*, pages 230–241, Orlando, Florida, June 1994. *ACM SIGPLAN Notices, 29(6)*.

61. Alain Deutsch. Semantic models and abstract interpretation techniques for inductive data structures and pointers. In *Proceedings of the ACM SIGPLAN Symposium on Partial Evaluation and Semantics-Based Program Manipulation*, pages 226–229, La Jolla, California, June 21–23, 1995.

62. E language. Available at http://www.erights.org/.

63. Patrick Thomas Eugster and Sebastien Baehni. Abstracting remote object interaction in a peer-2-peer environment. In *Proceedings of the 2002 joint ACM-ISCOPE Conference on Java Grande*, pages 46–55. ACM Press, New York, 2002.

64. GianLuigi Ferrari and Ugo Montanari. Tiles for concurrent and located calculi. In C. Palamidessi and J. Parrow, editors, *Electronic Notes in Theoretical Computer Science*, volume 7. Elsevier, Amsterdam, 2000.

65. Fabrice Le Fessant. Detecting distributed cycles of garbage in large-scale systems. In *Conference on Principles of Distributed Computing(PODC)*, Rhode Island, August 2001.

66. Cormac Flanagan and Matthias Felleisen. The semantics of future and its use in program optimization. In *Conference Record of the 22nd ACM SIGACT-SIGPLAN Symposium on Principles of Programming Languages (POPL'95)* [6], pages 209–220.

67. Cédric Fournet, Michele Boreale, and Cosimo Laneve. Bisimulations in the join calculus. In *Proceedings of the IFIP Working Conference on Programming Concepts, Methods and Calculi (PROCOMET)*, June 1998.

68. Cédric Fournet and Georges Gonthier. The reflexive CHAM and the join-calculus. In *Conference Record of the 23rd ACM SIGACT-SIGPLAN Symposium on Principles of Programming Languages (POPL'96)* [7], pages 372–385.

69. Cédric Fournet and Georges Gonthier. A hierarchy of equivalences for asynchronous calculi. In Larsen et al. [107], pages 844–855.

70. Cédric Fournet, Georges Gonthier, Jean-Jacques Levy, Luc Maranget, and Didier Remy. A calculus of mobile agents. In U. Montanari and V. Sassone, editors, *Proceedings of the 7th International Conference on Concurrency Theory (CONCUR)*, volume 1119 of LNCS, pages 406–421. Springer-Verlag, Berlin, Heidelberg, August 1996.

71. R. J. Fowler. The complexity of using forwarding addresses for decentralized object finding. In *Proceedings of PODC'86*, pages 108–120. ACM Press, New York, August 1986.

72. Hubert Garavel, Frédéric Lang, and Radu Mateescu. An overview of CADP 2001. Technical Report RT-254, INRIA, France, 2001. Also in: European

Association for Software Science and Technology (EASST) Newsletter, e 4: 13–24, August 2002.

73. Philippa Gardner's web page and courses. Department of Computing, Imperial College. Available at `http://www.doc.ic.ac.uk/~pg/`, and `http://www.doc.ic.ac.uk/~pg/Concurrency/course.html`.

74. Narain Gehani and William D. Roome. *The concurrent C programming language*. Silicon Press, Summit, New Jersey, 1989.

75. Narain H. Gehani and Thomas A. Cargill. Concurrent programming in the Ada language: The polling bias. *Software – Practice and Experience*, 14(5):413–427, May 1984.

76. Seth C. Goldstein, Klaus E. Schauser, and David E. Culler. Enabling primitives for compiling parallel languages. In *Third Workshop on Languages, Compilers, and Run-Time Systems for Scalable Computers*, May 1995.

77. Seth C. Goldstein, Klaus E. Schauser, and David E. Culler. Lazy threads: Implementing a fast parallel call. *Journal of Parallel and Distributed Computing*, 37(1):5–20, 1996.

78. Andrew D. Gordon and Paul D. Hankin. A concurrent object calculus: Reduction and typing. In *Proceedings HLCL'98*, volume 16. Elsevier ENTCS, amsterdam, 1998.

79. Andrew D. Gordon, Paul D. Hankin, and Sren B. Lassen. Compilation and equivalence of imperative objects. Research Series RS-97-19, BRICS, Department of Computer Science, University of Aarhus, July 1997. Appears also as Technical Report 429, University of Cambridge Computer Laboratory, June 1997.

80. Andrew D. Gordon, Paul D. Hankin, and Sren B. Lassen. Compilation and equivalence of imperative objects. *FSTTCS: Foundations of Software Technology and Theoretical Computer Science*, 17:74–87, 1997.

81. Andrew D. Gordon and Gareth D. Rees. Bisimilarity for a first-order calculus of objects with subtyping. In *Conference Record of the 23rd ACM SIGACT-SIGPLAN Symposium on Principles of Programming Languages (POPL'96)* [7], pages 386–395.

82. James Gosling, Bill Joy, Guy Steele, and Gilad Bracha. *The Java Language Specification Second Edition*. Addison-Wesley Longman, Boston, MA, Boston, Massachusets, 2000. Also available at: `http://java.sun.com/docs/books/jls/second\_edition/html/j.title.doc.htm%1`.

83. Robert H. Halstead, Jr. Multilisp: A language for concurrent symbolic computation. *ACM Transactions on Programming Languages and Systems (TOPLAS)*, 7(4):501–538, 1985.

84. Kevin Hammond. Parallel functional programming: An introduction (invited paper). In H. Hong, editor, *First International Symposium on Parallel Symbolic Computation (PASCO'94), Linz, Austria*, pages 181–193. World Scientific Publishing, Singapore, 1994.

85. Mark Hapner, Rahul Sharma, Rich Burridge, Joseph Fialli, and Kim Haase. *Java Message Service API tutorial and reference: Messaging for the J2EE platform*. Addison-Wesley Longman, Boston, Massachusets, 2002.

86. Ludovic Henrio. *Asynchronous Object Calculus: Confluence and Determinacy*. PhD thesis, Université de Nice – Sophia-Antipolis – UFR Sciences, November 2003. `http://www.inria.fr/oasis/Ludovic.Henrio/these/`.

87. C. A. R. Hoare. Monitors: An operating system structuring concept. *Communications of the ACM*, 17(10):549–577, October 1974.

88. C. A. R. Hoare. Communicating sequential processes. *Communications of the ACM*, 21(8):666–677, August 1978.

89. C. A. R. Hoare. *Communicating sequential processes*. Prentice Hall, Englewood Cliffs, New Jersey, 1985.

90. Kohei Honda and Mario Tokoro. An object calculus for asynchronous communication. In *ECOOP '91: Proceedings of the European Conference on Object-Oriented Programming*, LNCS, pages 133–147. Springer-Verlag, Berlin, Heidelberg, 1991.

91. Jean D. Ichbiah. Preliminary Ada reference manual. *SIGPLAN Notices*, 14(6a):1–145, 1979.

92. ISO. Information Processing Systems – Open Systems Interconnection – LOTOS – A Formal Description Technique based on the Temporal Ordering of Observational Behaviour. ISO/IEC 8807, International Organisation for Standardization, Geneva, Switzerland, 1989.

93. Alan Jeffrey. A distributed object calculus. In *ACM SIGPLAN Workshop Foundations of Object Oriented Languages*, 2000.

94. Cliff Jones. A pi-calculus semantics for an object-based design notation. In Eike Best, editor, *Proceedings of CONCUR'93*, volume 715 of LNCS, pages 158–172. Springer-Verlag, Berlin, Heidelberg, 1993.

95. Cliff B. Jones. An object-based design method for concurrent programs. Technical report, University of Manchester, 1992. UMCS-92-12-1.

96. Cliff B. Jones. Process-algebraic foundations for an object-based design notation. Technical report, University of Manchester, 1993. UMCS-93-10-1.

97. Cliff B. Jones and Steve J. Hodges. Non-interference properties of a concurrent object-based language: Proofs based on an operational semantics. In Burkhard Freitag, Cliff B. Jones, Christian Lengauer, and Hans-Jrg Schek, editors, *Object-Orientation with Parallelism and Persistence*, chapter 1, pages 1–22. Kluwer Academic Publishers, Dordrecht, 1996.

98. Eric Jul, Henry Levy, Norman Hutchinson, and Andrew Black. Fine-grained mobility in the Emerald system. *ACM Transactions on Computer Systems*, 6(1):109–133, February 1988.

99. Gilles Kahn. The semantics of a simple language for parallel programming. In J. L. Rosenfeld, editor, *Information Processing '74: Proceedings of the IFIP Congress*, pages 471–475. North-Holland, New York, 1974.

100. Gilles Kahn and David MacQueen. Coroutines and networks of parallel processes. In B. Gilchrist, editor, *Information Processing'77: Proc. IFIP Congress*, pages 993–998. North-Holland, Amsterdam, 1977.

101. Owen Kaser, Shaunak Pawagi, C. R. Ramakrishnan, I. V. Ramakrishnan, and R. C. Sekar. Fast parallel implementation of lazy languages – the EQUALS experience. In *LFP'92: Proceedings of the 1992 ACM conference on LISP and functional programming*, pages 335–344. ACM Press, New York, 1992.

102. Morry Katz and Daniel Weise. Continuing into the future: On the interaction of futures and first-class continuations. In *Proceedings of the 1990 ACM Conference on LISP and Functional Programming*, pages 176–184. ACM Press, New York, 1990.

103. WooYoung Kim and Gul Agha. Efficient support of location transparency in concurrent object-oriented programming languages. In *Proceedings of the 1995 ACM/IEEE conference on Supercomputing (CDROM)*, page 39. ACM Press, 1995.

104. Naoki Kobayashi, Benjamin C. Pierce, and David N. Turner. Linearity and the pi-calculus. In *Proceedings of POPL '96*, pages 358–371. ACM, January 1996.

105. Naoki Kobayashi and Akinori Yonezawa. Type-theoretic foundations for concurrent object-oriented programing. In *Proceedings of the Ninth Annual Conference on Object-Oriented Programming Systems, Languages, and Applications*, pages 31–45. ACM Press, New York, 1994.

106. Bernard Lang, Christian Queinnec, and José Piquer. Garbage collecting the world. In *Conference Record of the Nineteenth Annual ACM Symposium on Principles of Programming Languages, ACM SIGPLAN Notices*, pages 39–50, January 1992.

107. Kim G. Larsen, Sven Skyum, and Glynn Winskel, editors. *25th Colloquium on Automata, Languages and Programming (ICALP) (Aalborg, Denmark)*, volume 1443 of LNCS. Springer-Verlag, Berlin, Heidelberg, July 1998.

108. Douglas Lea and Doug Lea. *Concurrent Programming in Java: Design Principles and Patterns*. Addison-Wesley Longman, Boston, Massachusets, 1996.

109. Barbara Liskov, Alan Snyder, Russell Atkinson, and Craig Schaffert. Abstraction mechanisms in CLU. *Communications of the ACM*, 20(8):564–576, August 1977.

110. Xinxin Liu and David Walker. Confluence of processes and systems of objects. In Peter D. Mosses, Mogens Nielsen, and Michael I. Schwarzbach, editors, *TAPSOFT '95: Theory and Practice of Software Development, 6th International Joint Conference CAAP/FASE*, volume 915 of LNCS, pages 217–231. Springer-Verlag, Berlin, Heidelberg, 1995.

111. Xinxin Liu and David Walker. Partial confluence of processes and systems of objects. *Theoretical Computer Science*, 206(1–2):127–162, 1998.

112. Olivier Maffes and Axel Poigné. Synchronous automata for reactive, real-time or embedded systems. Technical Report 967, Arbeitspapiere der GMD, Germany, 1996. Available at http://ais.gmd.de/EES/papers/SAforRRES/SAforRRES.html.

113. Friedemann Mattern and Stefan Fünfrocken. A non-blocking lightweight implementation of causal order message delivery. In K. P. Birman, F. Mattern, and A. Schiper, editors, *Theory and Practice in Distributed Systems*, volume 938 of LNCS, pages 197–213. Springer-Verlag, Berlin, Heidelberg, 1995.

114. Massimo Merro, Josva Kleist, and Uwe Nestmann. Mobile objects as mobile processes. *Information and Computation*, 177(2):195–241, 2002.

115. Massimo Merro and Davide Sangiorgi. On asynchrony in name-passing calculi. In Larsen et al. [107], pages 856–867.

116. Bertrand Meyer. *Object-oriented software construction (2nd edition)*. Prentice-Hall, Englewood Cliffs, New Jersey, 1997.

117. Robin Milner. *Communication and Concurrency*. International Series in Computer Science. Prentice-Hall, Englewood Cliffs, New Jersey, 1989. SU Fisher Research 511/24.

118. Robin Milner. The polyadic π-calculus: A tutorial. In Friedrich L. Bauer, Wilfried Brauer, and Helmut Schwichtenberg, editors, *Logic and Algebra of Specification*, volume 94 of Series F. NATO ASI, Springer-Verlag, Berlin, Heidelberg, 1993. Available as Technical Report ECS-LFCS-91-180, University of Edinburgh, October 1991.

119. Robin Milner. *Communicating and Mobile Systems: the π-Calculus*. Cambridge University Press, May 1999.

120. Robin Milner, Joachim Parrow, and David Walker. A calculus of mobile processes, part I/II. *Journal of Information and Computation*, 100:1–77, September 1992.

121. D. S. Milojičić, W. LaForge, and D. Chauhan. Mobile Objects and Agents (MOA). In *Proceedings of USENIX COOTS '98, Santa Fe, New Mexico*, April 1998.

122. Uwe Nestmann, Hans Huttel, Josva Kleist, and Massimo Merro. Aliasing models for object migration. In *European Conference on Parallel Processing*, pages 1353–1368, 1999.

123. Uwe Nestmann, Hans Hüttel, Josva Kleist, and Massimo Merro. Aliasing models for mobile objects. *Information and Computation*, 175(1):3–33, 2002.

124. Uwe Nestmann and Martin Steffen. Typing confluence. In Stefania Gnesi and Diego Latella, editors, *Proceedings of FMICS'97*, pages 77–101. Consiglio Nazionale Ricerche di Pisa, 1997. Also available as report ERCIM-10/97-R052, European Research Consortium for Informatics and Mathematics, 1997.

125. Uwe Nestmann's web page on Calculi for Mobile Processes. Ecole Polytechnique Fédérale de Lausanne (EPFL). Available at http://lamp.epfl.ch/~uwe/, and http://lamp.epfl.ch/mobility/.

126. Bradford Nichols, Bick Buttlar, and Jackie Proulx Farrell. *Pthreads Programming*. O'Reilly & Associates, Inc., 981 Chestnut Street, Newton, MA 02164, USA, 1996.

127. Martin Odersky. Functional nets. In Gert Smolka, editor, *Proceedings of ESOP 2000*, volume 1782 of LNCS, pages 1–25. Springer-Verlag, Berlin, Heidelberg, 2000.

128. Olaf Owe, Stein Krogdahl, and Tom Lyche, editors. *From Object-Orientation to Formal Methods, Essays in Memory of Ole-Johan Dahl*, volume 2635 of LNCS. Springer, 2004.

129. Thomas Parks and David Roberts. Distributed Process Networks in Java. In *Proceedings of the International Parallel and Distributed Processing Symposium (IPDPS2003)*, Nice, France, April 2003.

130. Benjamin C. Pierce. Programming in the pi-calculus: A tutorial introduction to PICT (PICT version 4.1), 1998.

131. Benjamin C. Pierce and David N. Turner. Concurrent objects in a process calculus. In Takayasu Ito and Akinori Yonezawa, editors, *Proceedings of Theory and Practice of Parallel Programming (TPPP'94)*, Sendai, Japan, LNCS, pages 187–215. Springer-Verlag, Berlin, Heidelberg, 1995.

132. Benjamin C. Pierce and David N. Turner. PICT: A programming language based on the pi-calculus. In Gordon Plotkin, Colin Stirling, and Mads Tofte, editors, *Proof, Language and Interaction: Essays in Honour of Robin Milner*, Foundations of Computing. MIT Press, Cambridge, Massachusets, May 2000.

133. *POSIX. System Application Program Interface (API) [C Language]*. Information technology – Portable Operating System Interface (POSIX). IEEE Computer Society, 345 E. 47th St, New York, NY 10017, USA, 1996. ISO/IEC 9945-1:1996.

134. ProActive API and environment. Available at http://www.inria.fr/oasis/proactive (under LGPL).

135. Christian Queinnec and Kathleen Callaway. *Lisp in small pieces*. Cambridge University Press, 1996, reprint 2003.

136. John H. Reppy. CML: A higher concurrent language. In *Proceedings of the Conference on Programming Language Design and Implementation*, pages 293–305. ACM Press, New York, 1991.

137. Rémi Revire, Florence Zaral, and Thierry Gautier. Efficient and easy parallel implementation of large numerical simulations. In Jack Dongarra, Domenico Laforenza, and Salvatore Orlando, editors, *Recent Advances in Parallel Virtual Machine and Message Passing Interface*, volume 2840 of LNCS, pages 663–666. Springer-Verlag, Berlin, Heidelberg, October 2003.

138. Jean-Louis Roch. Ordonnancement de programmes parallèles sur grappes : théorie versus pratique. In *Actes du Congrès International ALA 2001, Universit Mohamm V*, pages 131–144, Rabat, Maroc, 28–31 May 2001.

139. Mooly Sagiv, Thomas Reps, and Susan Horwitz. Precise interprocedural dataflow analysis with applications to constant propagation. *Lecture Notes in Computer Science*, 915:651–??, 1995.

140. Mooly Sagiv, Thomas Reps, and Susan Horwitz. Precise interprocedural dataflow analysis with applications to constant propagation. *Theoretical Computer Science*, 167(1–2):131–170, 1996.

141. Davide Sangiorgi. *Expressing Mobility in Process Algebras: First-Order and Higher-Order Paradigms*. PhD thesis, LFCS, University of Edinburgh, 1993. CST-99-93 (also published as ECS-LFCS-93-266).

142. Davide Sangiorgi. The typed π-calculus at work: A proof of Jones's parallelisation theorem on concurrent objects. *Theory and Practice of Object-Oriented Systems*, 5(1), 1999. An early version was included in the *Informal Proceedings of FOOL 4*, January 1997.

143. Davide Sangiorgi. Asynchronous process calculi: The first-order and higher-order paradigms (tutorial). *Theoretical Computer Science*, 253(2):311–350, February 2001.

144. Davide Sangiorgi and David Walker. *The π-calculus: a Theory of Mobile Processes*. Cambridge University Press, 2001.

145. Alan Schmitt and Jean-Bernard Stefani. The M-calculus: A higher-order distributed process calculus. In *Proceedings of the 30th ACM SIGACT-SIGPLAN symposium on Principles of Programming Languages (POPL)*, pages 50–61. ACM Press, New York, 2003.

146. Marc Shapiro, Peter Dickman, and David Plainfoss. SSP chains: Robust, distributed references supporting acyclic garbage collection. Rapport de Recherche 1799, INRIA, Rocquencourt, November 1992.

147. S. Skedzielewski and J. Glauert. *IF1 An Intermediate Form for Applicative Languages*. Lawrence Livermore National Laboratory, Livermore, California, USA, 1985.

148. David B. Skillicorn and Domenico Talia. *Programming languages for parallel processing*. IEEE Computer Society Press, 1995.

149. David B. Skillicorn and Domenico Talia. Models and languages for parallel computation. *ACM Comput. Surv.*, 30(2):123–169, 1998.

150. Brian Cantwell Smith. Reflection and semantics in Lisp. In *Conference Record of the Eleventh Annual ACM Symposium on Principles of Programming Languages*, pages 23–35, Salt Lake City, Utah, January 15–18, 1984. ACM Press, New York.

151. Guy L. Steele, Jr. Making asynchronzous parallelism safe for the world. In *POPL'90. Proceedings of the Seventeenth Annual ACM Symposium on Prin-*

ciples of Programming Languages, January 17–19, 1990, San Francisco, CA, pages 218–231. ACM Press, New York, 1990.

152. Jean Bernard Stefani. A calculus of higher-order distributed components. Technical report, INRIA Rhones Alpes, 2003. RR-4692.

153. Chris Steketee, Weiping Zhu, and Philip Moseley. Implementation of process migration in amoeba. In *International Conference on Distributed Computing Systems*, pages 194–201, 1994.

154. Chantal Taconet and Guy Bernard. A localization service for large scale distributed systems based on microkernel technology. In *Proceedings of ROSE'94*, 1994.

155. Andrew S. Tanenbaum and Maarten van Steen. *Distributed Systems: Principles and Paradigms*. Prentice-Hall, Englewood Cliffs, New Jersey, 2002.

156. Éric Tanter, Jacques Noyé, Denis Caromel, and Pierre Cointe. Partial behavioral reflection: Spatial and temporal selection of reification. In Ron Crocker and Guy L. Steele, Jr., editors, *Proceedings of the 18th ACM SIGPLAN conference on Object-oriented Programing, Systems, Languages, and Applications (OOPSLA 2003)*, pages 27–46, Anaheim, California, October 2003. ACM Press, New York.

157. P. H. J. van Eijk, C. A. Vissers, and M. Diaz, editors. *The Formal Description Technique LOTOS – Results of the ESPRIT/SEDOS Project*. North-Holland, Amsterdam, 1989.

158. Takuo Watanabe and Akinori Yonezawa. Reflection in an object-oriented concurrent language. In *Conference Proceedings on Object-oriented Programming Systems, Languages and Applications*, pages 306–315. ACM Press, New York, 1988.

159. Daren L. Webb, Andrew L. Wendelborn, and Julien Vayssière. A study of computational reconfiguration in a Process Network. In *Proceedings of the 7th Workshop on Integrated Data Environments Australia (IDEA '7)*, February 2000.

160. Peter Wegner. Concepts and paradigms of object-oriented programming. *SIGPLAN OOPS Mess.*, 1(1):7–87, 1990. Expansion of OOPSLA'89 Keynote Talk, October 4.

161. Akinori Yonezawa, Jean-Pierre Briot, and Etsuya Shibayama. Object-oriented concurrent programming in ABCL/1. In *Proceedings OOPSLA'86*, pages 258–268, November 1986. Published as *ACM SIGPLAN Notices*, 21.

162. Akinori Yonezawa, Etsuya Shibayama, Toshihiro Takada, and Yasuaki Honda. Modelling and programming in an object-oriented concurrent language ABCL/1. In A. Yonezawa and M. Tokoro, editors, *Object-Oriented Concurrent Programming*, pages 55–89. MIT Press, Cambridge, Massachusets, 1987.

163. Silvano Dal Zilio. Mobile processes: A commented bibliography. In *Modeling and Verification of Parallel Processes, 4th Summer School, MOVEP 2000, Nantes, France, June 19–23, 2000*. Springer-Verlag, Berlin, Heidelberg, 2001.

Notation

Concepts

| Cycle of futures | set of future identifiers $\{fut(f_i^{\gamma_i \to \beta_n})\}$ such that $\beta_0 \dots \beta_n$ verify: | 116 |

$$\begin{cases} \forall i,\, 0 < i \le n,\, fut(f_{i-1}^{\gamma_{i-1} \to \beta_{i-1}}) \in \\ \qquad\qquad copy(F_{\beta_i}(fut(f_i^{\gamma_i \to \beta_i})), \sigma_{\beta_i}) \\ fut(f_n^{\gamma_n \to \beta_n}) \in copy(F_{\beta_0}(fut(f_0^{\gamma_0 \to \beta_0})), \sigma_{\beta_0}) \end{cases}$$

Core Syntax: ASP Source Terms

$[l_i = b_i;$ $m_j = \varsigma(x_j, y_j)a_j]_{j \in 1..m}^{i \in 1..n}$	Object definition	64
$a.l_i$	Field access	64
$a.l_i := b$	Field update	64
$a.m_j(b)$	Method call	64
$clone(a)$	Superficial copy	64
$Active(a, m_j)$	Object activation	71
$Serve(M)$	Request service	71
M	list of method labels	71

Encoding of Classical Primitives

$let\ x = a\ in\ b$	$[; m = \varsigma(z, x)b].m(a)$	64
$a; b$	$[; m = \varsigma(z, z')b].m(a)$	64
$\lambda x.b$	$[arg = [], val = \varsigma(x)b\{\!\{x \leftarrow x.arg\}\!\}]$	64
$(b\ a)$	$(clone(b).arg := a).val()$	64
$Repeat(a)$	$[; repeat = \varsigma(x)a; x.repeat()].repeat()$	89
$FifoService$	$Repeat(Serve(\mathcal{M}))$	89
$Repeat\ a\ Until\ b$	$[; rep = \varsigma(x)a;\ if\ (not(b))\ then\ x.rep()].rep()$	89

ASP Intermediate Terms and Semantic Structures

(a, σ)	Sequential configuration	66
α, β	Activities: $\alpha[a_\alpha; \sigma_\alpha; \iota_\alpha; F_\alpha; R_\alpha; f_\alpha]$	69
	[current term, store, active object, future values, pending requests, current future]	87
ι	Locations	64
$locs(a)$	Set of locations occurring in a	65
P, Q	Parallel configuration	88
$\alpha \in P$	Activity α belongs to the configuration P	98
$a \Uparrow f, b$	a with continuation b	71
	f is the future associated with the continuation	
$AO(\alpha)$	Generalized reference to the activity α	73
$f_i^{\alpha \to \beta}$	Future identifier	87
$fut(f_i^{\alpha \to \beta})$	Future reference	88

$r = [m_j; \iota; f_i^{\alpha \to \beta}]$	Request: asynchronous remote method call	69
$R_\alpha = \{[m_j; \iota; f_i^{\alpha \to \beta}]\}$	Pending requests: a queue of requests	88
$R :: r$	Adds a request r at the end of the pending requests R	88
$r :: R$	Takes the first request r at the beginning of the pending requests	88
$F :: \{f_i \mapsto \iota\}$	Adds a new future association to the future values	88

General Notation

$\{a_i\}$	List	66
$\{a \mapsto b\}$	Association/finite mapping	66
$\theta ::= \{\!\{b \leftarrow c\}\!\}$	Substitution	65
$\overset{*}{\to}$	Transitive closure of any reduction $\to$	103
$\oplus$	Disjoint union	105
$L\vert_M$	Restriction of (RSL) list L to labels belonging to M	108
L_n	n^{th} element of the list L	108
$\sqcup$	Least upper bound	110
$\exists^1$	There is at most one	122

Stores

σ	Store: finite map from locations to objects (reduced or generalized reference) $\sigma ::= \{\iota_i \mapsto o_i\}$	66
$dom(\sigma)$	set of locations defined by σ	66
$\sigma :: \sigma'$	Append of disjoint stores	66
$\sigma + \sigma'$	Updates the values defined in σ' by those defined in σ: $(\sigma + \sigma')(\iota) = \begin{cases} \sigma(\iota) & \text{if } \iota \in dom(\sigma) \\ \sigma'(\iota) & \text{otherwise} \end{cases}$	66
$Merge(\iota, \sigma, \sigma')$	Store merge: merges σ and σ' independently except for ι which is taken from σ': $Merge(\iota, \sigma, \sigma') = \sigma'\theta + \sigma$ where $\theta = \{\!\{\iota' \leftarrow \iota'' \mid \iota' \in dom(\sigma') \cap dom(\sigma)\backslash\{\iota\}, \iota'' \text{ fresh}\}\!\}$	90
$copy(\iota, \sigma)$	Deep copy of $\sigma(\iota)$	89
$Copy\&Merge(\sigma, \iota \,; \sigma', \iota')$	Appends in $\sigma'(\iota')$ a deep copy of $\sigma(\iota)$ $= Merge(\iota', \sigma', copy(\iota, \sigma)\{\!\{\iota \leftarrow \iota'\}\!\})$	91

Semantics

Equivalences

Properties

$\vdash P \text{ OK}$	Well-formed configuration	99
$RSL(\alpha) \bowtie RSL(\beta)$	RSL compatibility	110
$P \bowtie Q$	Configuration compatibility	110
$P_1 \curlyvee P_2$	Configuration confluence:	118
	$\exists R_1, R_2, P_1 \xrightarrow{*} R_1 \wedge P_2 \xrightarrow{*} R_2 \wedge R_1 \equiv_F R_2$	
$\mathcal{G}(P_0)$	Approximated call graph	125
	α can send a request foo to β implies	
	$(\dot{\alpha}, \dot{\beta}, foo) \in \mathcal{G}(P_0)$	
Request flow graph	$\alpha \rightarrow_R \beta$ if α has sent a request to β	126
$DON(P)$	Deterministic Object Network	122
$SDON(P)$	Static Deterministic Object Network	125
$TDON(P)$	Tree Deterministic Object Network	126

Syntax of ASP Calculus

Source terms

$$a, b \in L ::= x \qquad \text{variable}$$

$$\mid [l_i = b_i; m_j = \varsigma(x_j, y_j)a_j]_{j \in 1..m}^{i \in 1..n} \quad \text{object definition}$$

$$\mid a.l_i \qquad \text{field access}$$

$$\mid a.l_i := b \qquad \text{field update}$$

$$\mid a.m_j(b) \qquad \text{method call}$$

$$\mid clone(a) \qquad \text{superficial copy}$$

$$\mid Active(a, m_j) \qquad \text{activates object:}$$

deep copy + activity creation

m_j is the activity method

or $\emptyset$ for FIFO service

$$\mid Serve(M) \qquad \text{Serves a request among}$$

a set of method labels

where M is a set of method labels used to specify which request has to be served.

$$M = m_1, \ldots, m_k$$

Intermediate Terms

Terms

$$
\begin{aligned}
a, b \in L' ::= \ & x && \text{variable} \\
\mid\ & [l_i = b_i; m_j = \varsigma(x_j, y_j)a_j]_{j\in 1..m}^{i\in 1..n} && \text{object definition} \\
\mid\ & a.l_i && \text{field access} \\
\mid\ & a.l_i := b && \text{field update} \\
\mid\ & a.m_j(b) && \text{method call} \\
\mid\ & clone(a) && \text{superficial copy} \\
\mid\ & Active(a, m_j) && \text{object activation} \\
\mid\ & Serve(M) && \text{service primitive} \\
\mid\ & \iota && \text{location} \\
\mid\ & a \Uparrow f, b && \text{a with continuation b}
\end{aligned}
$$

Configurations

$$
P, Q ::= \alpha[a; \sigma; \iota; F; R; f] \parallel \beta[\ldots] \parallel \ldots
$$

Requests

$$
R ::= \{[m_j; \iota; f_i^{\alpha \to \beta}]\}
$$

Future Values

$$
F ::= \{f_i^{\gamma \to \alpha} \mapsto \iota\}
$$

Store

$$
\sigma ::= \{\iota_i \mapsto o_i\}
$$

$$
\begin{aligned}
o ::= \ & [l_i = \iota_i; m_j = \varsigma(x_j, y_j)a_j]_{j\in 1..m}^{i\in 1..n} && \text{reduced object} \\
\mid\ & AO(\alpha) && \text{active object reference} \\
\mid\ & fut(f_i^{\alpha \to \beta}) && \text{future reference}
\end{aligned}
$$

Operational Semantics

STOREALLOC:
$$\frac{\iota \notin dom(\sigma)}{(\mathcal{R}[o], \sigma) \rightarrow_S (\mathcal{R}[\iota], \{\iota \mapsto o\} :: \sigma)}$$

FIELD:
$$\frac{\sigma(\iota) = [l_i = \iota_i; m_j = \varsigma(x_j, y_j)a_j]_{j \in 1..m}^{i \in 1..n} \quad k \in 1..n}{(\mathcal{R}[\iota.l_k], \sigma) \rightarrow_S (\mathcal{R}[\iota_k], \sigma)}$$

INVOKE:
$$\frac{\sigma(\iota) = [l_i = \iota_i; m_j = \varsigma(x_j, y_j)a_j]_{j \in 1..m}^{i \in 1..n} \quad k \in 1..m}{(\mathcal{R}[\iota.m_k(\iota')], \sigma) \rightarrow_S (\mathcal{R}[a_k\{\!\{x_k \leftarrow \iota, y_k \leftarrow \iota'\}\!\}], \sigma)}$$

UPDATE:
$$\frac{\begin{array}{c} \sigma(\iota) = [l_i = \iota_i; m_j = \varsigma(x_j, y_j)a_j]_{j \in 1..m}^{i \in 1..n} \quad k \in 1..n \\ o' = [l_i = \iota_i; l_k = \iota'; l_{k'} = \iota_{k'}; m_j = \varsigma(x_j, y_j)a_j]_{j \in 1..m}^{i \in 1..k-1,\, k' \in k+1...n} \end{array}}{(\mathcal{R}[\iota.l_k := \iota'], \sigma) \rightarrow_S (\mathcal{R}[\iota], \{\iota \rightarrow o'\} + \sigma)}$$

CLONE:
$$\frac{\iota' \notin dom(\sigma)}{(\mathcal{R}[clone(\iota)], \sigma) \rightarrow_S (\mathcal{R}[\iota'], \{\iota' \mapsto \sigma(\iota)\} :: \sigma)}$$

Table 1. Sequential reduction

$$\iota \in dom(copy(\iota, \sigma))$$

$$\iota' \in dom(copy(\iota, \sigma)) \Rightarrow locs(\sigma(\iota')) \subseteq dom(copy(\iota, \sigma))$$

$$\iota' \in dom(copy(\iota, \sigma)) \Rightarrow copy(\iota, \sigma)(\iota') = \sigma(\iota')$$

Table 2. Deep copy

LOCAL:

$$\frac{(a, \sigma) \rightarrow_S (a', \sigma') \quad \rightarrow_S \text{ does not clone a future}}{\alpha[a; \sigma; \iota; F; R; f] \parallel P \longrightarrow \alpha[a'; \sigma'; \iota; F; R; f] \parallel P}$$

NEWACT:

$$\frac{\begin{array}{c}\gamma \text{ fresh activity} \quad \iota' \notin dom(\sigma) \quad \sigma' = \{\iota' \mapsto AO(\gamma)\} :: \sigma \\ \sigma_\gamma = copy(\iota'', \sigma) \quad Service = (\text{if } m_j = \emptyset \text{ then } FifoService \text{ else } \iota''.m_j())\end{array}}{\begin{array}{c}\alpha[\mathcal{R}[Active(\iota'', m_j)]; \sigma; \iota; F; R; f] \parallel P \longrightarrow \\ \alpha[\mathcal{R}[\iota']; \sigma'; \iota; F; R; f] \parallel \gamma[Service; \sigma_\gamma; \iota''; \emptyset; \emptyset; \emptyset] \parallel P\end{array}}$$

REQUEST:

$$\frac{\begin{array}{c}\sigma_\alpha(\iota) = AO(\beta) \quad \iota'' \notin dom(\sigma_\beta) \quad f_i^{\alpha \to \beta} \text{ new future} \quad \iota_f \notin dom(\sigma_\alpha) \\ \sigma'_\beta = Copy\&Merge(\sigma_\alpha, \iota' ; \sigma_\beta, \iota'') \quad \sigma'_\alpha = \{\iota_f \mapsto fut(f_i^{\alpha \to \beta})\} :: \sigma_\alpha\end{array}}{\begin{array}{c}\alpha[\mathcal{R}[\iota.m_j(\iota')]; \sigma_\alpha; \iota_\alpha; F_\alpha; R_\alpha; f_\alpha] \parallel \beta[a_\beta; \sigma_\beta; \iota_\beta; F_\beta; R_\beta; f_\beta] \parallel P \longrightarrow \\ \alpha[\mathcal{R}[\iota_f]; \sigma'_\alpha; \iota_\alpha; F_\alpha; R_\alpha; f_\alpha] \parallel \beta[a_\beta; \sigma'_\beta; \iota_\beta; F_\beta; R_\beta :: [m_j; \iota''; f_i^{\alpha \to \beta}]; f_\beta] \parallel P\end{array}}$$

SERVE:

$$\frac{R = R' :: [m_j; \iota_r; f'] :: R'' \quad m_j \in M \quad \forall m \in M, m \notin R'}{\begin{array}{c}\alpha[\mathcal{R}[Serve(M)]; \sigma; \iota; F; R; f] \parallel P \longrightarrow \\ \alpha[\iota.m_j(\iota_r) \Uparrow f, \mathcal{R}[[]]; \sigma; \iota; F; R' :: R''; f'] \parallel P\end{array}}$$

ENDSERVICE:

$$\frac{\iota' \notin dom(\sigma) \quad F' = F :: \{f \mapsto \iota'\} \quad \sigma' = Copy\&Merge(\sigma, \iota ; \sigma, \iota')}{\alpha[\iota \Uparrow (f', a); \sigma; \iota; F; R; f] \parallel P \longrightarrow \alpha[a; \sigma'; \iota; F'; R; f'] \parallel P}$$

REPLY:

$$\frac{\sigma_\alpha(\iota) = fut(f_i^{\gamma \to \beta}) \quad F_\beta(f_i^{\gamma \to \beta}) = \iota_f \quad \sigma'_\alpha = Copy\&Merge(\sigma_\beta, \iota_f ; \sigma_\alpha, \iota)}{\begin{array}{c}\alpha[a_\alpha; \sigma_\alpha; \iota_\alpha; F_\alpha; R_\alpha; f_\alpha] \parallel \beta[a_\beta; \sigma_\beta; \iota_\beta; F_\beta; R_\beta; f_\beta] \parallel P \longrightarrow \\ \alpha[a_\alpha; \sigma'_\alpha; \iota_\alpha; F_\alpha; R_\alpha; f_\alpha] \parallel \beta[a_\beta; \sigma_\beta; \iota_\beta; F_\beta; R_\beta; f_\beta] \parallel P\end{array}}$$

Table 3. Parallel reduction (used or modified values are non-gray)

Overview of Properties

The objective of Fig. 2 is to show the dependencies between properties and definitions given in this book. This diagram is very informal and should help the reader to understand the main dependencies between ASP properties and definitions.

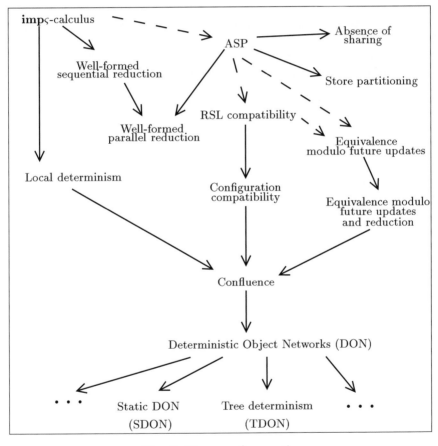

Fig. 2. Diagram of properties

The top left part of Fig. 2 shows properties and definitions related to imperative ς-calculus and which are *local* to an activity.

The *absence of sharing* and *store partitioning* properties are somewhat independent, even if in fact they have important consequences on all the other properties of ASP. These properties are used indirectly for proving all the other ones; for example, without store partitioning, a future value could be altered after the end of the corresponding service which would contradict with the properties of the equivalence modulo future updates.

Most of the properties shown in this book are related to *confluence* and its consequences. The principles of the confluence theorem can be summarized by: *concurrency can only originate from the application of two interfering* REQUEST *rules on the same destination activity*; for example, the order of updates of futures never has any influence on the reduction of a term. Moreover, an ASP execution is only characterized by the order of the request senders inside each activity.

The bottom part (last line) of the diagram shows the approximation of Deterministic Object Networks (DON) that can be performed. This book focused on two approximations: the static DON (SDON), and the deterministic behavior of programs communicating over a tree (TDON).

Overview of ASP Extensions

man dvips We present here most of the features that have been added to ASP in Part IV. We provide a brief summary, based on the syntax, and most of the reduction rules associated with these features. When several and somehow equivalent reduction rules exist for the same feature, we choose one of them.

Three Confluent Features:

1. Delegation

Delegates to another activity the responsibility to reply to the current request (confluent).

Syntax

$$delegate(a)$$

Reduction Rules

Parallel DELEGATE:

$$\sigma_\alpha(\iota) = AO(\beta) \quad \iota'' \notin dom(\sigma_\beta)$$
$$\sigma'_\beta = Copy\&Merge(\sigma_\alpha, \iota' \ ; \ \sigma_\beta, \iota'') \quad f_\emptyset \text{ new future}$$

$$\frac{}{\alpha[\mathcal{R}[delegate(\iota.m_j(\iota'))]; \sigma_\alpha; \iota_\alpha; F_\alpha; R_\alpha; f_i^{\gamma \to \alpha}] \parallel \beta[a_\beta; \sigma_\beta; \iota_\beta; F_\beta; R_\beta; f_\beta] \parallel P \longrightarrow}$$
$$\alpha[\mathcal{R}[[]]; \sigma_\alpha; \iota_\alpha; F_\alpha; R_\alpha; f_\emptyset] \parallel \beta[a_\beta; \sigma'_\beta; \iota_\beta; F_\beta; R_\beta :: [m_j; \iota''; f_i^{\gamma \to \alpha}]; f_\beta] \parallel P$$

Sequential DELEGATE:

$$\sigma_\alpha(\iota) = [l_i = \iota_i; m_j = \varsigma(x_j, y_j)a_j]_{j \in 1..m}^{i \in 1..n} \quad k \in 1..m$$

$$\frac{}{\alpha[\mathcal{R}[delegate(\iota.m_j(\iota'))]; \sigma_\alpha; \iota_\alpha; F_\alpha; R_\alpha; f_\alpha] \parallel P \longrightarrow}$$
$$\alpha[\mathcal{R}[a_k \{\!\{x_k \leftarrow \iota, y_k \leftarrow \iota'\}\!\}]; \sigma_\alpha; \iota_\alpha; F_\alpha; R_\alpha; f_\alpha] \parallel P$$

Generalized REPLY:

$$\frac{\sigma_\alpha(\iota) = fut(f_i^{\gamma \to \delta}) \quad F_\beta(f_i^{\gamma \to \delta}) = \iota_f \quad \sigma'_\alpha = Copy\&Merge(\sigma_\beta, \iota_f \; ; \; \sigma_\alpha, \iota)}{\alpha[a_\alpha; \sigma_\alpha; \iota_\alpha; F_\alpha; R_\alpha; f_\alpha] \parallel \beta[a_\beta; \sigma_\beta; \iota_\beta; F_\beta; R_\beta; f_\beta] \parallel P \longrightarrow \atop \alpha[a_\alpha; \sigma'_\alpha; \iota_\alpha; F_\alpha; R_\alpha; f_\alpha] \parallel \beta[a_\beta; \sigma_\beta; \iota_\beta; F_\beta; R_\beta; f_\beta] \parallel P}$$

2. Explicit Wait

Waits for a future update (confluent).

Syntax

$$waitFor(a)$$

Encoding

$$[\![l_i = b_i; m_j = \varsigma(x_j, y_j)a_j]_{j \in 1..m}^{i \in 1..n}]\!] \triangleq [wait = [\,], l_i = b_i; m_j = \varsigma(x_j, y_j)a_j]_{j \in 1..m}^{i \in 1..n}$$

$$[\![waitFor(a)]\!] \triangleq a.wait$$

3. Method Update

Changes the code associated to a method (confluent).

Syntax

$$x.foo \Leftarrow b$$

Five Non-confluent Features:

1. Testing Future Reception

Returns "true" if a future is awaited, and "false" if it has already been updated.

Syntax

$$awaited(a)$$

Reduction Rules

WAITT:

$$\frac{\sigma(\iota) = fut(f_i^{\alpha \rightarrow \beta})}{(\mathcal{R}[awaited(\iota)], \sigma) \rightarrow_S (\mathcal{R}[true], \sigma)}$$

WAITF:

$$\frac{\sigma(\iota) \neq fut(f_i^{\alpha \rightarrow \beta})}{(\mathcal{R}[awaited(\iota)], \sigma) \rightarrow_S (\mathcal{R}[false], \sigma)}$$

2. Non-blocking Service

Serves a request if it is in the request queue, else continues the execution.

Syntax

$$ServeWithoutBlocking(M)$$

Reduction Rules

SERVEWBSERVE:

$$\frac{R = R' :: [m_j; \iota_r; f'] :: R'' \quad m_j \in M \quad \forall m \in M, m \notin R'}{\begin{array}{c} \alpha[\mathcal{R}[ServeWithoutBlocking(M)]; \sigma; \iota; F; R; f] \parallel P \longrightarrow \\ \alpha[\iota.m_j(\iota_r) \Uparrow f, \mathcal{R}[[]]; \sigma; \iota; F; R' :: R''; f'] \parallel P \end{array}}$$

SERVEWBCONTINUE:

$$\frac{\forall m \in M, m \notin R}{\alpha[\mathcal{R}[ServeWithoutBlocking(M)]; \sigma; \iota; F; R; f] \parallel P \longrightarrow \alpha[\mathcal{R}[[]]; \sigma; \iota; F; R; f] \parallel P}$$

3. Testing Request Reception

Returns "true" if a corresponding request is in the request queue.

Syntax

$$inQueue(M)$$

Reduction Rules

INQUEUET:

$$\frac{\exists m \in M,\, m \in R}{\alpha[\mathcal{R}[inQueue(M)]; \sigma; \iota; F; R; f] \parallel P \longrightarrow \alpha[\mathcal{R}[true]; \sigma; \iota; F; R; f] \parallel P}$$

INQUEUEF:

$$\frac{\forall m \in M,\, m \notin R}{\alpha[\mathcal{R}[inQueue(M)]; \sigma; \iota; F; R; f] \parallel P \longrightarrow \alpha[\mathcal{R}[false]; \sigma; \iota; F; R; f] \parallel P}$$

4. Join Pattern Example

The term below encodes a join pattern cell: the cell reacts to the simultaneous presence of two messages, either s and set, or s and get. s is used to store the internal state of the cell.

Encoding a Join Pattern Cell

$$
\begin{aligned}
Cell \triangleq Active&([s_v = [], \; set_v = []; \\
&set = \varsigma(this, v)this.set_v := v \\
&s = \varsigma(this, v)this.s_v := v \\
&get = \varsigma(this)[] \\
&srv = \varsigma(this)Repeat(if \; inQueue(s) \wedge inQueue(set) \; then \\
&\qquad\qquad\qquad\qquad\qquad this.setcell() \\
&\qquad\qquad\quad if \; inQueue(s) \wedge inQueue(get) \; then \\
&\qquad\qquad\qquad\qquad\qquad this.getcell()), \\
&setcell() = \varsigma(this)(Serve(set); Serve(s); thisActivity.s(set_v)), \\
&getcell() = \varsigma(this)(Serve(get); Serve(s); thisActivity.s(s_v); s_v)
\end{aligned}
$$

Example of usage

$$Cell.s([]); Cell.set([x = 2]); Cell.get()$$

5. Extended Join Services

$$Join((m_{11}, m_{12}, \ldots, m_{1n_1}), (m_{21}, \ldots, m_{2n_2}), \ldots (m_{k1}, \ldots, m_{kn_k}))$$

$$
\begin{aligned}
Join((m_1, m_2), (m_1, m_3)) \triangleq{}& let\ served = false\ in \\
& Repeat \\
& \quad if\ (inQueue(m_1) \wedge inQueue(m_2))\ then \\
& \qquad (Serve(m_1);\ Serve(m_2);\ served := true) \\
& \quad else\ if\ (inQueue(m_1) \wedge inQueue(m_3))\ then \\
& \qquad (Serve(m_1);\ Serve(m_3);\ served := true) \\
& Until(served = true)
\end{aligned}
$$

Migration

Simulates the migration: makes the current activity forward the requests to a newly created activity.

Syntax

$$thisActivity.Migrate()$$

Encoding

$$Migrate \triangleq \varsigma(this)\,let\ newao = Active(this, sevice)\ in$$
$$(CreateForwarders(newao); FifoService)$$

$$CreateForwarders(newao) \triangleq \forall m_j,\ m_j \Leftarrow \varsigma(x, y)newao.m_j(y)$$

Groups

Entity containing several objects that can be accessed as a single one.

Passive Groups

Syntax

$$Group(a_k^{k \in 1..l})$$

Reduction Rules

$$\mathcal{R} ::= \dots |\ Group(\iota_k, \mathcal{R}, b_{k'})^{k \in 1..m-1, k' \in m+1..l}$$

Store group:

$$\frac{\iota \notin dom(\sigma)}{(Group(\iota_k)^{k \in 1..l}, \sigma) \rightarrow_G (\iota, \{\iota \mapsto Gr(\iota_k)^{k \in 1..l}\} :: \sigma)}$$

Field access:

$$\frac{\sigma(\iota) = Gr(\iota_k)^{k \in 1..l}}{(\mathcal{R}[\iota.l_i], \sigma) \rightarrow_G (Group(\iota_k.l_i)^{k \in 1..l}, \sigma)}$$

Field update:

$$\frac{\sigma(\iota) = Gr(\iota_k)^{k \in 1..l}}{(\mathcal{R}[\iota.l_i := \iota'], \sigma) \rightarrow_G (Group(\iota_k.l_i := \iota')^{k \in 1..l}, \sigma)}$$

Invoke method:

$$\frac{\sigma(\iota) = Gr(\iota_k)^{k \in 1..l}}{(\mathcal{R}[\iota.m_j(\iota')], \sigma) \rightarrow_G (Group(\iota_k.m_j(\iota'))^{k \in 1..l}, \sigma)}$$

Active Groups

Syntax

$$ActiveGroup(a_1, \ldots, a_n, m)$$

Encoding

$$ActiveGroup(a_1, \ldots, a_n, m) \triangleq Group(Active(a_1, m), \ldots, Active(a_n, m))$$

Components

Primitive Component

A *primitive component* is defined from an activity α, a set of *server interfaces* (SI, a subset of the served methods), and a set of *client interfaces* (CI, references to other activities contained in fields):

$$SI_i \subseteq \bigcup_{M \in \mathcal{M}_{\alpha P_0}} M$$

$$PC ::= C_n < a, srv, \{SI_i\}^{i \in 1..k}, \{CI_j\}^{j \in 1..l} >$$

Composite Component

A composite component is a set of components (either primitive (PC) or composite (CC)) exporting some server interfaces (some SI_i), some client interfaces (some CI_j), and connecting some client and server interfaces (defining a partial binding (CI_i, SI_j)). Such a component is given a name C_n. CC is a composite component and C either a primitive or a composite one:

$$CC ::= C_n \ll \; C_1, \ldots, C_m; \{(C_{i_p}.CI_{j_p}, C_{i'_p}.SI_{j'_p})\}^{p \in 1..k};$$
$$\{C_{i_q}.CI_{j_q} \to CI_q\}^{q \in 1..l}; \{C_{i_r}.SI_{j_r} \to SI_r\}^{r \in 1..l'} \gg$$

$$C ::= PC|CC$$

where each C_i is the name of one included component C_i ($i \in 1..m$), supposed to be pairwise distinct; each exported SI is only bound once to an included component, and each internal client interface $(C_i.CI_j)$ appears at most one time:

$$\forall p, p' \in 1..k, \forall q, q' \in 1..l, \forall r, r' \in 1..l' \begin{cases} p \neq p' \Rightarrow C_{i_p}.CI_{j_p} \neq C_{i_{p'}}.CI_{j_{p'}} \\ q \neq q' \Rightarrow C_{i_q}.CI_{j_q} \neq C_{i_{q'}}.CI_{j_{q'}} \\ C_{i_p}.CI_{j_p} \neq C_{i_q}.CI_{j_q} \\ r \neq r' \Rightarrow SI_r \neq SI_{r'} \end{cases}$$

Deterministic Primitive Component (DPC)

A DPC is a primitive component defined from an activity α, such that server interfaces SI are disjoint subsets of the served method of the active object of α such that every $M \in \mathcal{M}_{\alpha P_0}$ is included in a single SI_i:

$$\begin{cases} \forall i, k, i \neq k \Rightarrow SI_i \cap SI_k = \emptyset \\ \forall M \in \mathcal{M}_{\alpha P_0}, \forall M_1 \subseteq M, \forall M_2 \subseteq M \; (M_1 \subseteq SI_i \wedge M_2 \subseteq SI_j) \Rightarrow i = j \end{cases}$$

Deterministic Composite Component (DCC)

A DCC is

- either a DPC,
- or a composite component connecting some DCCs such that the binding between server and client interfaces is one to one. More precisely the following constraints must be added to the ones of Definition 14.2:

$$
\begin{cases}
\text{Each } C_i \text{ is a DCC} \\
\\
\forall p, p' \in 1..k, \forall q, q' \in 1..l, \forall r, r' \in 1..l' \begin{cases}
p \neq p' \Rightarrow C_{i'_p}.SI_{j'_p} \neq C_{i'_{p'}}.SI_{j'_{p'}} \\
r \neq r' \Rightarrow C_{i_r}.SI_{j_r} \neq C_{i_{r'}}.SI_{j_{r'}} \\
C_{i'_p}.SI_{j'_p} \neq C_{i_r}.SI_{j_r} \\
q \neq q' \Rightarrow CI_q \neq CI_{q'}
\end{cases}
\end{cases}
$$

Index